WONDERLAND
A V E N U E

THE DOORS
The Illustrated History

NO ONE HERE GETS OUT ALIVE
(*with Jerry Hopkins*)

WONDERLAND
AVENUE

TALES OF GLAMOUR AND EXCESS

· · · · · · · · · · · ·

DANNY SUGERMAN

WILLIAM MORROW AND COMPANY, INC.   NEW YORK

/

Library of Congress Cataloging-in-Publication Data

Sugerman, Daniel.
    Wonderland Avenue : tales of glamour and excess / Danny Sugerman.
      p.   cm.
    ISBN 0-688-04656-8
    1. Sugerman, Daniel.   2. Narcotic addicts—California—Biography.
  I. Title.
  HV5805.S4A3   1989
  362.2'93—dc19
  [B]   88-26011
                                                                                  CIP

Printed in the United States of America

First Edition

1   2   3   4   5   6   7   8   9   10

BOOK DESIGN BY JAYE ZIMET

THIS BOOK IS DEDICATED

w/love to the memory of my father

w/love and gratitude to my brother Joey

and w/a very special heartfelt thanks to
Ray Manzarek & Stephen Abrams

ACKNOWLEDGMENTS

• • • • • • • • • •

IN addition to those to whom this book is dedicated I would like to thank: Rosemary Carroll for her loyalty and dedication, professional as well as personal; John Brockman and Katinka Matson for believing and doing; Floyd Peluce and Connie Medford for their faith and aid; Gene Kirkwood and Oliver Stone for their encouragement and support; Jim Landis and Jane Meara for their patience and commitment; John Densmore and Robby Krieger for their music, friendship and trust . . . without all of whom this book would not have been possible.

I also credit, thank, and gratefully acknowledge the following friends, associates, and heroes: Jim Carroll, Todd Gray, Hal Ashby, Melissa Gilbert, John Branca, Jim Osterberg, Dr. Ed Kantor, Fiona Flanagan, Stiv Bator, Jello Biafra, Michael McClure, Allen Ginsberg, Anne Barhydt/Smith, Patty Wicker, Marsha Gleeman, John Randall, Dr. Murray Zucker, Dr. Harvey Karkus, Studio 12 & Tom Kenney, Marilyn Saltzman, Carrie Hamilton, Buddy Arnold & Carol Fields, Cassandra, James Grauerholz, Bill Burroughs, Harvey Kubernik, Dorothy Manzarek, Pablo Apollo Manzarek, Julia Densmore/Negron, Lynn Krieger, Bill Siddons, Patti Smith, Alice Cooper, Shep Gordon, Alan Lanier, Joe Kanter, Jim & Shelly Ladd, Cameron Crowe, Alex Lopez, Jr., Alexandra Taylor/Abrams (Ali), Marty Fox, Jerry Swartz, Ray Parat, Fred Nigro and Michael Karlin, Robin White, Alan Douglas, Benjamin Edmonds, Susan Hill, Mary Hall-Mayer, Charles M. Young, Krista Errickson, Paul Rothchild, Bruce Botnick, Bob Krasnow, Hale Milgrim, Eric Rudolph, Jim Stein, Kate Franklin, Toby Mamis, Michael Talbot, Nigel Harrison, Robyn Riggs, Harriet Vidal, Elmer Valentine, Mario, and David Goldman. They have all given my mission encouragement and support in one form or another at one time or another and to each and all of them I am thankful.

I must also give credit and thanks to the Doors fans everywhere, who have been so loyal in the past and who continue to give me so much support and inspiration, and among whose ranks I proudly count myself.

C O N T E N T S

CONTENTS

PROLOGUE

• • • • • • • • • • • •

Welcome to my nightmare
I think you're gonna like it . . .
—ALICE COOPER

I already knew I was sick. I'd felt lousy for weeks. No doubt the result of living the good life nonstop and too well, or not well enough, it was getting hard to tell the difference. Too much alcohol to celebrate and too much cocaine to go up and stay up, followed by handfuls of downers to come down (or fall down as was often the case), the whole crazy while zigzagging through the canyons of the Hollywood Hills in the Cobra at suicide speeds in no condition to drive. A thousand nightclub booths and backstage passes blurred with too many parties, too little sleep, and too much fucking (around) all combined to pretty much exhaust me. Plus, lately I'd begun shooting up absurd quantities of drugs, anything to dissolve the pain, anything water-soluble, injectible, and intoxicating. Too much of too much too often. Nothing was not permitted. The summary phrase best describing this style of living probably being "life in the fast lane." . . . What a fucking joke. Everyone knows there are no lanes in a destruction derby.

Besides heroin, I wasn't even sure what other drugs I might be addicted to. I never knew whether I was sick from too many drugs or not enough of the right ones. Every time I shot up, I threw up. I couldn't eat anything without puking, and as a result, lost about thirty pounds in as many days. To complicate matters further, I was rapidly turning a curious tint of a bad yellow. The good life was obviously taking its toll. But I couldn't be absolutely sure how much that toll was, or how sick I'd gotten, or even exactly what the problem was. As far as I knew, it could have been anything, from the flu to dry rot of the soul.

Then the doctor I'd been seeing, and lately avoiding, gave me the call.

"So, Doc," I asked him, "what's the final verdict?"

"Danny, you cannot continue injecting heroin."

"That's okay," I said. "I was planning to kick junk anyway."

"Listen, this is very serious. It's important you understand what

I'm saying to you. When you inject drugs, it allows toxins to flow into your liver unfiltered."

"Yeah? So?" Thinking, unfiltered, that's the whole point of shooting up.

"Your liver cannot tolerate it anymore. And we've got another problem. One of the test results reveals an infection on your primary heart valve. Your heart is in very bad condition."

"So," I said, "I'll kick it—what's the problem?"

The doctor sighed. "You can't just kick it. You're too weak. You've got hepatitis at an advanced stage, and on top of that you're malnourished. Your body wouldn't be able to withstand the withdrawal symptoms. You'd never live through cold turkey. The problem is you'll die if you continue injecting drugs and you'll die if you suddenly stop. Unless you check into a hospital and get yourself medical attention immediately, I give you less than a week to live."

"Jesus," I said, "sorry I asked."

I knew I had developed a bit of a problem, but somehow I hadn't realized just how serious it had gotten. No more denial. I'd taken it to the limit of whatever path I was on, and now it was impossible to continue and there was no U-turn or easy way out in sight. But still, the thought dominating my mind was not how bad off I was but rather what *kind* of hepatitis did I have.

I was rooting for Type A, infectious hepatitis, because then I could petition my family for help and tell them I'd got it from falling into bed with the wrong girl. However, if it were Type B, serum hepatitis, that could mean only one thing: blood, as in needles, and if that were the case, I would have to tell my family the truth about the rest of my condition, and that was an event I was determined to put off as long as possible—preferably forever.

I thanked the doctor for the information, hung up the telephone, and considered my options. Death was *one*, and telling my family the truth was *two*, and doing massive amounts of drugs for a few more days and then telling my family was *three*. Less than a week until I died—that could mean I still had as many as six days before I really had to choose between options one and two. Less than a week could also be a couple of days, or a couple of hours, or a couple of minutes. So it was down to death or the truth.

I decided to call my older brother, also a doctor and currently in residency at the Los Angeles County Hospital. I knew telling him would be tantamount to telling my father in that I knew he would immediately turn around and advise my father about what was going on, but I hoped Joey would go a little easier on me. I braced myself and dialed his office number.

"Hello, Joey? This is your little brother."

"Where the hell have you been for the past year?"

"Has it been that long?" I tried to sound casual. No need to get hysterical and alarm anyone. He remained silent and waited for an answer. "Well, you know, I've been busy, going to a lot of parties, doing a lot of drugs. . . ." I tried to laugh. And then my whole game just fell apart.

"I'm strung out and I have hepatitis. I got this thing on my heart. This doctor at UCLA Hospital just told me I have less than a week to live."

Silence.

"I don't know what to do," I whispered into the phone, all pretense gone.

"Where are you?" he asked.

"Wonderland Avenue. You know the house."

"Stay where you are," he told me. "I'm coming right over."

"Okay," I answered even though I wasn't at all sure it was. There were several more moments of silence on the line before he spoke again.

"Danny," he said.

"What?"

"You really blew it this time."

"I know," I answered.

And I did know. Or at least a part of me did. I had gotten into plenty of trouble before, but gradually some semblance of a realization was dawning on me that this time it was different, this time I'd taken it too far. Still, other voices hammered away, telling me I could kick the thing myself if I were careful; the doctor didn't know what he was talking about; I shouldn't have gone and told my brother, now my father was going to kill me if I didn't die first, and given a choice, I'd rather die by my hand than his; I didn't need my brother or anyone else either. What I needed was a good long vacation, in Bora-Bora, say, someplace where there weren't any drugs.

But I had told him, and he was already on his way over. As I waited for him to arrive, I paced the floor in the downstairs office, alternately agreeing with the voices and fighting them. Then I remembered I still had some dope left, not a lot, but maybe enough to calm myself down a bit.

I fixed the last of my smack and took the last couple of Quaaludes.

What was I supposed to do? Throw them away? *No way.* I never went for that down-the-toilet-I'm-through-never-again! demonstrative routine. Strictly wasteful histrionics. Not that I ever had anything against histrionics, or waste per se, but throwing away the last of your dope after paying perfectly good money for it was simply too counterproductive to consider. Besides, another voice reasoned, this would certainly have to be the last time. Unfortunately the drugs succeeded only in making me even more confused and incoherent. I sat down on the couch, head in hands, and tried as hard as I could to avoid thinking about the future.

I'm not too sure what happened next. I remember my brother's arriving and giving me an injection of liquid Valium to allay a display of pyrotechnics on my part that bordered on the psychotic as I wondered aloud what in the fuck I was doing. One administration of the tranquilizer didn't do the job. I kept babbling. He gave me another, commenting on my body's resistance. And another. Just before I finally went under, I heard him get on the phone.

"Hi, Dad. It's about Danny. Are you sitting down?"

Then I passed out.

I vaguely recall later being loaded into the passenger seat of his car. On the way out I grabbed a carton of Kools and Bob Dylan's latest album, *Blood on the Tracks.*

The next thing I remember clearly was waking up in a hospital. I was surrounded by equipment, and there were tubes running into and out of each arm with blood coursing through them. As I gradually came to, my first instinct was to rip them out, to disentangle myself from the strange amalgam of man and machine I had become; but then I looked up, and there before me I saw two impressively large black male nurses, dressed in whites, standing on either side at the foot of my bed.

"Who are you supposed to be?" I asked.

"Your father hired us to make sure you stay put," the one on the left told me.

"You're not going to give us any trouble, are you?" the other one asked.

If I could have, maybe I would have. As it was, I had enough trouble raising my head. Before I could give them an answer, a rather small, balding, gnomish, pipe-smoking man strolled into the room. He introduced himself as Dr. Pullman.

"How are you?" he asked.

"I'm fucking *dying*, Jack; how do you think I am?" was what I wanted to say, but then decided a question that stupid didn't even merit an answer.

Instead I asked, "*Where* am I?"

"In a hospital," he returned informatively.

This doctor guy was a real bundle of observational powers. Then, for the first time, I looked around and saw the room was unusually nice. It had carpeting, a mirror over a bureau, a desk, a closet. In fact, besides the bed, it was quite unlike any other hospital room I had ever seen.

"What hospital? Where?" I asked, trying to get my bearings.

"The Brentwood."

"There's no hospital in Brentwood," I said, growing more confused.

And then it dawned on me. "You mean, the *mental* hospital!" I gasped. "What the hell am I doing in a mental hospital?"

"Your family brought you."

"*Why?*"

"Because this is the only hospital in the state that can cater to both your physical and mental problems."

"But I don't have any mental problems," I argued. "I have a drug problem."

He almost chuckled. "You think somebody who sticks needles into his body and injects himself every day with one of the strongest poisons in the world until he's on the verge of death doesn't have a serious mental problem?"

Put like that, it was rather difficult to argue. "Well, anyway," I said, "as soon as I'm straight, I'm leaving."

"We'll see about that," he said, leaning over and giving me a shot that sent me spinning off to sleep.

The next day, I woke up screaming. I was sicker than I'd ever been, drenched with sweat, and it felt as if someone had jammed a knife into my stomach and were wrenching it around. I lifted up the blanket and looked down at my stomach and saw it actually rippling as the muscles knotted and writhed beneath my skin. The nurses, still in attendance, seemed unconcerned, taking the matter far more placidly than I thought warranted. I felt gas churning around violently inside me, and I farted, except it wasn't gas.

"Do something!" I cried.

The nurses still looked undecided about whether to restrain me, aid me, or go get some help. I decided to help them make up their minds.

"Go get somebody, you *stupid fucks!*" I screamed.

But by that time somebody was already on the way. A woman who appeared to be the head nurse came in and, seeing my condition, started to summon the appropriate medical personnel. As she tried to poke a thermometer in my mouth, I became overwhelmed with nausea and vomited. When I finished puking, I pulled myself up while a doctor and several other nurses worked around me, trying to administer various pills and injections.

And as I lay there, engulfed in shit and sweat and vomit, trying to catch my breath, watching my stomach as it continued to ripple and writhe, a nurse leaned over and, wiping my steaming forehead with a damp cloth, asked, "What in God's name did you do to yourself?"

"Good question," I groaned.

It was a damn good question. I thought I'd done everything right, followed my best instincts, stayed true to myself whenever possible, taken every appropriate step in achieving my version of the American Dream. I was twenty-one years old. I had a gorgeous house in Laurel Canyon, a beautiful girlfriend, all the money, drugs, fast cars, and hot shit a young man could want. I was young and successful in the business of my choice. I had it made. I had it all. And look where it got me—locked inside a Looney Toon, in a bedful of puke with two Green Bay Packers for my very own personal security guards. Now everything I once had was gone, and all I had left was a five-hundred-dollar-a-day drug habit and maybe, if I didn't die in this insane asylum first, just *maybe*, my life.

BOOK · I

YOUTH

CHAPTER ONE

· · · · · · · · · · · ·

Go, and beat your crazy head against the sky
Try, and see beyond the houses and your eyes
It's okay to shoot the moon.
                    —THE LOVIN' SPOONFUL

I guess at one time, very early in life, I was well behaved, and as the saying goes, slept like a baby, undisturbed by and undisturbing to the rest of the world. But if this is so, I don't remember it. And besides, even if I did, you don't want to know about that sort of polite, civilized crap any more than I want to write about it. What you want to hear about is the trouble, which is much more fun (and certainly more interesting) than being good, any day.

I learned this one lesson well and early, from the time I could speak, or walk, whichever came first, but whenever it was, it was too soon for nearly all parties concerned. Mom swears I was up and walking first, by about nine months old, but it probably just seemed like that to her since she spent the most time with me. Dad insists I learned to talk first, and haven't shut up since, but I think it just seems like that to him, too, since it always seemed to me he was overly sensitive in that particular area. We all tend to exaggerate personal tragedies.

I do know it wasn't long after I turned three that my mother's friends all got together and sent her a letter requesting her to refrain from bringing me along if she planned to drop by their homes; otherwise she was no longer welcome. On previous visits I had insisted on emptying onto the floor the contents of any drawer within my reach, often carrying off whatever my child's arms could hold to the bathroom, where I would try to make the evidence do a water ballet and disappear by flushing it down the toilet. Usually I succeeded only in jamming the plumbing. Tennis and Ping-Pong balls I found particularly satisfying. On one occasion I filled a hot bathtub with about twenty packets of strawberry Jell-O.

"No offense intended," they wrote Mom. "Just please leave the kid at home when you visit us."

By the time I was five years old, I had the distinction of being the first preschooler to be eighty-sixed from Gelsons, the local Beverly Hills grocery store infamous for its upper-class clientele and even higher prices. After stumbling upon the hose used to freshen the vegetables and testing its range and strength on passing customers, when the store manager approached to seize me, I turned it on and sprayed him. Unfortunately the fire-hydrant-like gusher I expected failed to materialize and all that emerged was a rather fine spray.

I wanted to test the effectiveness of both bans but my Mom figured everything would be easier if we just stayed close to home for a while.

Home was Beverly Hills. My dad had money. He doesn't like me saying how much. A lot. How he made it was anyone's guess. I never knew for sure *what* my old man did. The one time I asked him, straight out, he said he made *belts*. I wasn't sure if he was being humble or joking. My dad made belts like God made people. Very controversially and maybe not at all.

You don't grow up in Beverly Hills without being aware that you are where everyone else would like to be. You learn from an early age to let other people think it's as good as they want to believe it is. You act like you've got it, pretend you know it (but remember to be humble), and pretend you appreciate it (but don't be ungrateful). You know you're lucky to have it, even if you don't feel lucky, if for no reason other than you've been told it enough times. *It*, of course, being money. But, how're you supposed to feel privileged when you've never known anything different? It was normal for me and I liked it just fine. I liked the huge backyard and big house, the four-car garage and the Olympic-size pool. I liked lots of color TVs and having whatever I wanted. It was a great way to live and I would have recognized that even if Raquel Welch and Fred Astaire hadn't been our neighbors. You just can't expect gratitude from a little kid. It's too abstract. *More*, a kid can conceive of. *Less* goes against his nature. It did mine, at least.

It was weird, though, having frequent busloads of tourists continually stopping in front of our house. The only defense is to grow the hedges as high as possible or else shield your house with fences and gates. Ours was far enough back from the street that Dad didn't think it made a difference in terms of privacy. And in terms of security, he wasn't about to be intimidated. We had a German shepherd named Champ (Dad named all his shepherds Champ; that way, he never forgot their name) and Dad had a gun he kept in his nightstand, and as far as he was concerned, anybody who wanted to break in was welcome to go ahead and try. What we did have in our front yard was a gigantic gnarled old sycamore tree stretching out over the street, which I used to climb up into and watch the tourist buses from, occasionally letting fall the odd rock or stone on the less lucky who had come to gawk at our houses and jam our otherwise clear and tranquil streets with their noisy lumbering presence.

Mom took me to a doctor to see what was wrong with me or if anything could be done about my constant activity and insatiable supply of wants. He prescribed tranquilizers. Now, instead of being talkative and always darting about from place to place, I was groggy and clumsily staggering from here to there. I started sleeping fifteen hours at a stretch, which I guess was peaceful enough, but Mom didn't want a kid in a coma, she just wanted a little peace and quiet. Apparently, when I was awake, it wasn't much better, and I spent a good deal of time staring off into space with a vacant, glazed look in my eyes. After a few weeks she took me off the pills, and I rebounded to my previous state of frenzy.

Not long after the grocery store ban curiosity got hold of me again, and I developed a preoccupation with turtles and frogs. As a special treat my mother had taken me to the pond at UCLA's Botanical Gardens, where I spent hours poking around, catching anything that moved: polliwogs; frogs; turtles. Glad to see me occupied and happy, she agreed to allow me to bring a few specimens home.

It didn't take much time for nature to take its course, and with a few return trips to the pond, I had quite an impressive collection. No doubt thinking it was an infinitely wise manipulative decision on her part, Mom suggested I might be able to sell some of the overflow of turtles and frogs that were threatening to take over my bedroom. She packed me and a few buckets of amphibians into the car and drove us all over to a local pet shop that belonged to an old friend of an old friend of hers. I struck a deal with the owner whereby not only could I trade what I had for an equivalent worth of other animals, but in exchange for cleaning cages, I could take home animals on loan and continue to add to my collection for free.

By the age of six all this activity had resulted in my amassing a rather sizable assortment of turtles, frogs, snakes, and lizards. Not only did I have numerous tanks in my room, but my collection had expanded out to the backyard, which was scattered with laundry tubs full of turtles, garbage cans teeming with polliwogs, and about a dozen buckets of frogs.

One day I moved operations to the front yard, where I dug a moat around the sycamore tree and stocked it with my brother's prize Siamese fighting fish along with a few newly arrived snapping turtles.

Within an hour the moat was dry, the fish were dead, the turtles were gone, and the front lawn was a mess. When my brother, Joey, found out, he tried to exterminate me by sticking me headfirst into a mummy bag, tying the top drawstring around my ankles, and tickling my feet until I passed out and then stashing me in a closet. When I came to, I retaliated by letting all my mealworms go in his bed. To get back at me for doing that, he transferred what worms he could round up into our parents' bed, knowing they'd come after me—not him.

Needless to say, these were not thrilling events for Mom and Dad. At the time the yelling started, I was up the tree, with one of my snakes and a pocketful of stones, waiting for an unsuspecting tourist bus. Suddenly I heard a crash and turned in time to see the kitchen blender come sailing through a window. The screaming rang out after it, loud and clear.

"God damn that kid!" I heard my father yell. "Where the hell is he? I'll kill him, I'll break him in half!" He meant me, I was sure.

"Leave him alone," I heard my mother say. "He's only a child."

"A child couldn't do this," my father roared, appearing at the back door and kicking a trash can full of polliwogs. "A child couldn't do all of that!" he said, gesturing at the backyard full of turtles. "A goddamn college professor would have trouble doing all of that. This isn't a house anymore. It's a goddamn zoo. I'm telling ya, Harriet. You must have been sleeping with someone else because that kid is no blood of mine. *Please*, tell me he's not! I'll *pay* you to tell me I'm not his father." He was actually trying to bribe her.

My mother didn't go for it. "He's your son, Arnold. *I* haven't been sleeping with anyone else."

In spite of the fact that I was barely six years old at the time, I couldn't help noticing the curious stress she put on the word "I." I knew it referred to something incomprehensible and grown-up, although I wasn't quite sure of what. I noticed it sure shut Dad up quick.

I was hurt, if not surprised, by my father's anger. I knew he loved me, but still, it was easy to be afraid of him. He was a large and imposing man, both in stature and in spirit. He had a great sense of humor, but he had an equally terrible temper. When he laughed, the room lit up. But when he yelled, the storm rolled in. Sometimes he yelled so loud and what he said scared me so much I wished he'd just haul off and slug me instead.

He tracked me down in the tree and told me to come down.

"Only if you promise not to yell anymore," I called down to him.

"Get down here before I knock you down," he yelled back. On second thought I decided I preferred a yelling.

On the ground he warned me I'd better "get the menagerie the hell out of the house" or else he was "going to take matters" into his own hands.

I knew "matters" meant animals. What I failed to realize until much later was that "house" also meant yard. I got rid of all the indoor reptile-filled aquariums, except for one, a secret rosy boa constrictor I'd been keeping in my closet. All the rest of the indoor pets I either returned to the pet shop owner or gave away. In my sincere and well-intentioned effort to please my father, I even gave up a good number of frogs and turtles just for good measure.

No sooner had the animal issue abated than there was my concerted effort to trap the tooth fairy. One night before I went to bed, I turned out the light, then soundlessly and carefully wove an entire ball of fishing line around the bedroom, in and around the lamps, bedposts, doorknobs, behind the dresser, under the bookcase, and so on. Over fifty yards of Bounty Fishers finest line were made up into some crazy spider-web quilt all over my bedroom from waist to ceiling. Carefully placing myself in bed, I laid my molar under my pillow and waited for sleep. I was rudely awakened by the sound of furniture crashing and a lot of yelling. I shot up in bed, careful not to get caught in the line and, remembering the trap I'd set, joyously thought I had actually succeeded in catching the tooth fairy. This was followed promptly by another, more dismal thought—it didn't sound like a tooth fairy—right down to mortal terror . . . and an overwhelming sense of regret. I reached over and flicked on the night-light and saw my dad flailing around the room, caught in the web, pulling and cursing as the furniture jerked and fell this way and that.

My mother rushed in wearing her bathrobe and placed her hand carefully on the overhead light switch near the door, throwing an annoying glare into my tired eyes. It must have been quite a sight for her, her youngest primly tucked into bed, a good, safe two feet under a zigzagging mesh of fishing line, and her dear husband virtually bound and gagged, stuck in the middle of the room, snagged between a chair and the desk, five-dollar bill firmly wedged in the palm of one wrapped hand.

So much for belief in the tooth fairy.

Taking no further chances of ambush, both my parents individually apprised their Jewish son of the nonexistence of one Santa Claus the coming holiday, before open season was declared on St. Nick, too.

Then came the fall of 1962 and one of the wettest L.A. winters in more than a decade. Rain had been coming down nonstop. Los Angeles has never been able to handle wet weather well. The rain continued coming down after it had begun sloshing up over the drainpipes, over the curbs, and up onto the lawns. All the water eventually overflowed the remaining turtle cans still in the backyard, and the whole neighborhood became an expanded version of my collection. A painted turtle was run over by a car up the street. Frogs and toads were hopping around everywhere. One of our neighbors found a family of turtles living in his lawn mower grass catcher. Tree frogs and bullfrogs were found blocks away for weeks to come. Steve McQueen's malamute had cornered a snapping turtle and was barking his face off.

It was so cold we were forced to use the house heater, a real rarity in L.A. The only snake I had kept, the one in the closet, was a seven-foot-long boa constrictor named Mr. Big. Now, human beings, of course, are warm-blooded, so the cold was not unendurable to any of my family members. And all that water was amphibian euphoria for the turtles and frogs. But Mr. Big, normally used to the tropical weather in the rain forests of South America, was miserable. He was moving lethargically around in his prison for days, vainly, pathetically searching for a way out. One day I went to feed him his monthly rat ration, and he was gone. Mom called me to run an errand with her, and I temporarily abandoned the search.

The last thing I wanted to do was inform my parents there was a seven-foot boa constrictor loose in our house; they had been intimidated enough by a few measly turtles. Several days later I noticed a strange smell filtering through the house. I wasn't the only one to pick up on it. Everybody thought the house was beginning to stink. Mom had the maid throw away everything in the refrigerator. The house was cleaned and scrubbed, carpets were shampooed, but the odor remained.

To escape the stink, Dad took the family out for a Sunday drive. While driving the family down the freeway, Dad suddenly let out a shriek, which was kind of surprising because Dad wasn't really the sort inclined to shriek. He drove the car up on the shoulder of the highway, screeched to a halt, jumped out of the car, and started dancing on the side of the road, shaking his foot as if he had a hot match in his shoe. Then I saw the rat that had been intended for Mr.

Big, and that I'd lost a few days ago come bounding out of Dad's pants cuff up into the air, and land a few yards away. As I scampered out of the car to retrieve it, Dad got back in the car, not feeling too proud about the whole public display he'd just given (and even less thrilled with its provocation), and drove away, leaving me stranded. But Mom kept whacking him about the head and shoulder to stop the car, which he did, as I ran up to it and climbed in the back seat with my sister, Nan, and Joe.

The smell continued to waft through the house for days more while numerous searches by family members and professionals turned up nothing until the stench reached a sort of noxious crescendo and my father finally traced it to the heater in the hallway.

We all stood in curious anticipation around Dad as he opened the grille to the heater. He removed the front panel, and inside, we saw what looked like a coiled burnt hose. My father gingerly touched the object. It fell apart, sending a little plume of black dust into the air as it crumbled to the floor. As I stared at the litter of charred remains, recognition dawned upon me. Instinctively searching for his tropical rain forest, Mr. Big had made his way up into the heater and, unable to back himself out, had baked himself to a cinder.

My father turned to me and glared.

"I'm afraid to ask," he said.

Not as afraid as I was to answer.

"I suppose you know nothing about this mess?" he said, trying to keep his cool, but not doing very well at it, then very intensely: "I suppose you had *nothing* at all to do with this?"

I was too terrified to respond.

"*I don't believe it,*" he yelled. He was really working himself up.

"Goddamm it, Harriet," he said to Mom, "that does it. First we got turtles all over the backyard and frogs climbing up the bathroom walls then we got polliwogs in the sink and rats in the car. . . . I'm afraid to get in bed at night. And now this! I need a break. I need a vacation from being a father. *I can't take it anymore.* I can't take that kid anymore. . . ."

He glowered at me for a couple of seconds and finally, too angry to address me directly, stomped out of the house.

My brother and sister were properly speechless and didn't know whether to comfort me, follow Dad, or help Mom as she began to clean up the mess.

It wasn't long after that my parents separated for good. For the past two years Dad had been getting written up in the gossip columns for seeing this actress at that restaurant, and for as long as she could,

Mom ignored it. When it happened this time around, she packed his bags and left them outside the front door. To her surprise, he took them and never came back home.

I felt it was my responsibility to do something about it. It was my fault he'd left home, and it was my job to get him back. Every day I called him to ask when he was coming home, and because someplace in his mind he, too, wished everything could be put back together the way it was and because he didn't have the heart to tell a seven-year-old kid it was all over, he promised me, "Soon, soon, someday soon, I'll be home." I believed him, and I waited. Maybe he couldn't admit it was over any more than I could. At first he promised he'd be home by summer. Then it was Thanksgiving. Then it was Christmas. Every time I asked, he pushed back the date. Every time I waited. I actually prayed for the first time in my life. I didn't go to my knees or anything desperate like that. It was nothing fancy, just "Dear God, please make Dad come home. I'm sorry if I was bad." Mom sat in her rocking chair, staring out the window, watching for Dad to come home, while I jumped from tree to tree, as a lookout for his car, in a state of constant anticipation. Always one to make things easier, I responded to the pressure by becoming more uncontrollable than ever. Mom was in no mood for my tricks and promptly took me back to the doctor, who put me back on tranquilizers while she licked her wounds.

When the divorce was about to go through, it was explained to me that Dad had just married too young and it wasn't because he didn't love us that he had left. We kids had nothing to do with his decision to leave and everything to do with his decision to stay near and be available for us. But none of that mattered. I still blamed myself. I hadn't been able to get him back. I'd let everyone down. I was a royal fuck-up. Boy, did I feel lousy.

My brother and sister continued in senior and junior high school respectively. Mom took me off the pills and returned to her rocking chair by the window while I went back to jumping from tree to tree. An uncomfortable silence filled the large house. At least when Dad had been home, it seemed we were a family despite those occasional protestations otherwise. We loved each other. We fought, but we also laughed a lot and always made up. Those days were gone for good.

In all fairness to Mom, raising three kids on her own couldn't have been very easy or an endeavor she would relish doing by herself for very long. Finding a willing suitor or potential husband in her position wasn't an enviable task. Three kids and a thirty-five-year-old housewife aren't a real deal for a healthy, successful, moral single man considering his options. Throw yours truly into the proposal, and it isn't exactly what you could call an invitation to everlasting peace and tranquillity.

I don't know if Mom doubted she could do it alone or got bored, or horny, or what, but one day she simply interrupted her brooding and announced, "Enough." The next week she began dating. Mom decided we kids, myself in particular, needed a daily masculine presence to discipline us. So it wasn't for her she did what she was about to do; it was for us. Her being a good mother depended on bringing us home a father so we could be a family again.

I couldn't have been more than seven and a half years old when Mom called all of us together to inform us she had invited home a man she hoped would ask her to marry him.

It's a very big deal. She's making a big dinner for this guy Clarence. Excitement is in the air as we all pitch in to help. Then he arrives. He's brought his three daughters, and one of them is younger than I am! One of the others is about my sister's age and one closer to my brother. The youngest one's name is Cindy, and we hit it off straight away. She has brown bangs down to her eyebrows, precious lips, a cherub's face, and a high ponytail, which I couldn't resist yanking. Just like a train whistle—each time you pulled, a loud screech sounded. We run outside to play and I show her my favorite spot in the tree and how to get to it. She's surprisingly adept as a climber. Then we're called for dinner. But dinner isn't totally ready yet. Cindy and I resume chasing each other around the house, through the den, into the living room, onto the patio, into the kitchen, up the tree, down the tree . . . until we're called for dinner again.

We march into the kitchen, but dinner still isn't ready. It's not on the table yet, and in our house we never sit down until the food is on the table. So I just keep chasing Cindy around, through the kitchen, into the living room, and back through the kitchen, between Mom's new boyfriend, who she hopes will ask her to marry him, and my mom, around and around. Mom says, "Dinnertime, last call!" but the food still isn't on the table so this time I ignore the call and I just keep doing what I'm doing until it is, and I'm about ready to put my feet into high gear and catch up with Cindy's tempting ponytail bobbing away when suddenly this huge guy's hand grabs me by my left arm, practically yanking it out of the socket, and whips me right

33

off my feet. Slamming me down on his knee, he begins smacking me, spanking my heretofore unslapped virgin ass. *Spanking me!* In my own house!

Freeze this frame. It's important. Everyone is watching. This big guy is telling me, "You come when your mother says come! Do you understand, young man?" Before I can answer, he whacks me again. I look desperately to my mother for help. She stands to the side with her arms folded; my brother and sister stand helplessly by her side; his kids watch smugly. He's still spanking me. Why didn't Mom do something? Why isn't she *helping* me? This guy's hitting me! This stranger! In *our* house. How could she let him get away with it? I was her son, her own flesh and blood, and who was he? I hated her at that moment. I looked at her watching him hitting me, and I wanted her to die. Then, just as quickly, I realized I couldn't wish that. Then I'd really be alone. I turned the evil eye inward, instead, ashamed.

I thought of my father. He'd stop this guy; he wouldn't let him get away with it; he'd barge through that door any second and simply chop this guy's fat head off his fat neck. But that didn't happen. This strange man just kept spanking away on me. And no one raised a finger to help me.

I don't know if my mom thought this was the sort of discipline I needed or if she was just afraid of being unmarried. Convinced that he'd be a good father and husband, she went ahead and married the jerk. She must already have said yes in her mind, assured herself she could make it work, but a blind man could've seen from the start it was bad. Too bad she hadn't filled him in on her cohabitational expectations. What she didn't know was he didn't want to be a father any more than I wanted him to be one; he wanted a woman to slave for his kids. And he got it, a combination wife, nursemaid, mother, cook, and nanny. We all were his slaves.

I had been tossed out of the family unit of which I had felt an integral part and condemned to an isolated existence. Now I was in the way. Even if I had been asked back, I couldn't have returned. I had seen myself already as apart and unwanted, and I believed it. Clarence could go ahead and persecute my body, my spirit, but he couldn't touch my otherness. He only strengthened it with every opportunity for defiance he gave me. This behavior has a name and its name is pride. I removed myself to avoid hurt, to not care, and to survive. I didn't place myself above or below, only separate and against.

Clarence decided Beverly Hills was no place to bring up three wholesome midwestern girls. The truth was he and his daughters didn't fit in. It was obvious. He never would have felt comfortable in Beverly Hills anyway. Our house was put up for sale.

"Go ahead, move," I told my mother. "I'm staying." I refused to budge. Alas, my mother knew me too well.

I had always hated the idea of putting animals in cages. I much preferred having them in an environment resembling their natural habitat as much as possible. One image I was particularly attracted to was having a couple of large iguanas in a large tropical pen with several banana trees. Iguanas love bananas, and their long toenails are custom-built for climbing. Mom told me the new house actually had real banana trees, several of them, in fact, a real cluster in the front yard. I didn't believe her.

"It's true," she soothingly assured me. "If it's not, you don't have to stay." I reluctantly agreed to check out the premises, visions of me and Iguana sharing a ripe banana in the shade of a grove. Thus was I bamboozled into giving up the fort.

It was a cheap trick. Made all the worse and more underhanded when Clarence stepped into the negotiations and forbade me to bring any of my pets, beginning with the amphibians I had and ending with the reptiles I had planned to get. Although I protested mightily, it was all to no avail.

And so it came to pass at the age of eight I found myself uprooted and torn away from everything I had known and loved, taken from a posh and beautiful, comfortable home in the greatest neighborhood in the whole country, and moved to Westchester, California, near the airport. Just another city you drive through on your way to someplace else . . . A land of beanfields and the Hughes Aircraft Tool Company, with a bevy of blue-collar yokels and overalled farmers as our neighbors. Clarence fitted right in with the rest of the hicks. Any hopes I might have still secretly harbored of my parents' getting back together were now dashed for good. I left all my friends behind, and to make matters still worse, I was the only Jewish kid in my school. The other kids had never seen a bagel, and lox was the most exotic thing they'd ever seen anybody put in their mouth, and they let me know as much. To add further to my feelings of isolation and aloneness, my brother Joe and I were relegated to living in a small guesthouse that was quite some distance from the actual house.

In the unhappy days to follow, the colors of Clarence's flag became increasingly clear. His chosen profession was as a prosecuting attorney and he never let us forget it, practicing at home, on all of Mom's kids, but it seemed his favorite mark was me. Of course, I wasn't exactly passive in this sick game either.

He figured one problem out of many was the question of my loyalty. As long as I persisted in defending my father's memory, there were bound to be problems. Therefore, his first concentrated attack focused on breaking up that stronghold.

One night not long after the move Mom and Clarence said they wanted to have a talk with me. My reaction was typical. "What did I do now?" But I had done nothing wrong. There was something they wanted very much for me to consider. "What's that?" I wanted to know. They wanted me to start calling Clarence Dad. At first I thought they were kidding and actually started to laugh. But Clarence's face turned mean, and Mom looked flustered. They weren't kidding at all. They were dead serious.

"No way," I said, backing out of the room. "I already have a father," I said. "No way."

From that incident on, life became an unending avalanche of rules, verbal assaults, commands, accusations, and insults.

I wasn't allowed to use ketchup unless Clarence or one of his kids asked for it first. If I did manage to sneak some onto my food and was found out, I'd be fed a tomato and a bowl of sugar for the next three days.

There was no end to the harassment. Our clothing was criticized; our table manners were corrected; our speech was torn apart and put back together. One of Clarence's favorite tactics was to overload me with household chores. He refused to use a grass catcher when he mowed the lawns in front and back and forced me to rake up all the dead grass by hand. I was required to clean the pool not once but twice a day. One of his most ruthless mandates involved an ancient and massive rubber tree that grew in our backyard. Every day it dropped a never-ending onslaught of leaves onto the lawn, and it was my duty to see none of these ever remained on the ground for more than a few seconds. If there was so much as one leaf lying on the grass when he gazed out the window, off he'd go into one of his harangues. In the fall this game really got to be hellish. If Clarence ever saw me doing something so disrespectful as sitting down and relaxing, he would find something for me to do, anything from washing out the trash cans to picking up his ugly dalmatian's shit. The only time I could let down my guard was when he was away at work, but even then there was always the possibility of a surprise ambush.

* * *

"Isn't it about time you got your hair cut, young man?" Clarence asked me one night at the dinner I remember as the Spanish Inquisition of my childhood.

I had turned ten years old, the Beatles had been out for a while, and hair length was becoming an increasingly controversial topic.

"I guess so," I responded. I knew I was asking for it because one of his most steadfast rules was that children weren't allowed to say no to an adult; you weren't ever supposed to say anything to a grown-up but yes, preferably with a sir or ma'am tagged on the end. I don't know why he even bothered asking anybody anything. He was never in quest of information. He was in quest of yes. I was becoming quite adept at giving every conceivable answer other than yes or no.

"What kind of answer is that?" he demanded.

"It's not a no," I pointed out.

"Answer me! Don't you think it's about time you got a haircut? You look like a pansy."

"I like the way I look."

"That's not what I asked. You answer me now, goddammit!" he thundered, hitting his fist on the table. All the silverware jumped a neat two inches off the tabletop.

"I don't know," I replied.

"You don't know what?" Clarence said, frustrated.

"I don't know if it's time to get a haircut. I don't keep a schedule of my haircuts. I don't know when I got the last one. I don't know when it'll be time to get the next one. It depends. It varies."

"What do you mean, it varies?"

"Month to month. It grows faster in the summer. It varies—"

"Cut the crap. You get a haircut every two weeks. Do you understand?"

"I don't have any money."

"Then you get that deadbeat bum of an old man to give you the money. It's the least he can do."

"He's not going to pay for something he doesn't agree with," I returned.

A vein began to bulge out and throb in Clarence's forehead. Little beads of sweat were popping up above his lips, too.

"Did you hear that, Harriet?" he yelled at Mom.

She had to hear it. We all heard it, and she was sitting at the same table as the rest of us, and Clarence was shouting at the top of his lungs. My mother told him as much.

"You're yelling, honey. You don't need to shout; I can hear you, honey."

I hated it when she called him that.

"I'M NOT SHOUTING. GODDAMMIT, DOESN'T ANYBODY AROUND HERE UNDERSTAND ENGLISH? I WILL NOT BE DISOBEYED OR TALKED BACK TO AT MY DINNER TABLE." He was really carrying on quite loudly. Then to me he said, "You get that haircut tomorrow, and not a day later, do you understand me?" He reached across my stepsister Cindy and shook my arm. "You are not to come to dinner, you are not to come into this home, without that hair cut short, or else there will be hell to pay around here."

That's when my brother spoke up. He had been pretty sick for quite a while with mononucleosis, so his voice was rather weak, but Clarence heard him just fine.

Joey said, "I don't think it's any of your business whether he gets a haircut."

Clarence began frothing about the mouth. "Who pulled your horn?" he yelled at him.

"No one had to," Joe said. "He's my brother, and I'm telling you it's none of your business."

"Oh," he said, with his voice dripping with sarcasm, "and whose business is it?"

Joe stood his ground. "It's his business," he said, pointing at me. "It's my mother's and my father's business, but it's certainly none of yours."

Clarence hauled off and walloped my brother on the side of the head, knocked him out of his chair, and then he lunged forward and was all over Joey like a big grizzly bear.

Even his kids cringed with shame.

"Cut it out!" my mother screamed.

"I will not cut it out!" Clarence yelled back. "I will not tolerate backtalk in my house. Your kids are animals, and I will not let them run wild—"

"I'd hardly call vagueness about a haircut and telling the truth running wild." My mother defended us.

"NOW HEAR THIS"—Clarence boomed as if addressing a courtyard of soldiers—"I WILL NOT LEAVE ANYBODY ALONE, AND I WILL NOT MIND MY OWN BUSINESS. THIS IS MY HOUSE, AND I WILL RUN IT THE WAY I WANT!" Argument presumably ended, Clarence sat back down and continued to eat his dinner.

My mother just shook her head. "These children's house and my house paid for this house, and don't you ever forget it."

Clarence raised his eyes in disgust. "You're pathetic," he said.

The next day Joey left and went to live with my father. The persecution continued unabated. One day I playfully pushed Cindy into the pool, and Clarence came running up behind me and kicked me into the outside wall of my bedroom, nearly breaking my back but really only damaging my pride a little bit more.

Finally, not knowing what else to do, I told my father about Clarence's brutality, and furious, my father called Mom and told her to get the hell out, immediately, if not sooner. But my father should have known Mom was nothing if not loyal. Dad told her if Clarence ever so much as laid another finger on any of his kids again, he'd come over and split his head open with a baseball bat. The news appeared to have no immediately obvious effect on Clarence.

A few days following the threat, however, Clarence received a visit from the FBI. The agents wanted to know if he knew what my father did for a living. Did Clarence know I had a godfather who was allegedly the head of the crime syndicate west of the Rockies? They were referring to my uncle Vinnie, Dad's oldest and best friend. They assumed Clarence might be mixed up with the Mafia, La Cosa Nostra to be precise. He wasn't, of course, but he figured out my father very possibly could be and remembered my father's threat and apparently took it seriously because from that day forward he never again hit any of us. His verbal assaults and nonphysical punishments, unfortunately, intensified. He took away my bicycle and grounded me for "finking" on him.

He forbade me to have any curtains in the guesthouse so he could be in the main house with his binoculars and have a clear view of anything I might be doing. He also installed an intercom so that he could bellow at me or eavesdrop whenever he had the urge. Later I discovered he'd even installed a wiretap on my private telephone line that my dad paid for.

To escape, I began watching hours of television. It wasn't long before there was a rule regarding that, too. An hour per week was the new limit. But I had just discovered something I couldn't get enough of. Wrestling, live from the Olympic Auditorium. When I got home from school, and Clarence was at work, I would plunk myself down in front of the television and dive into the color, excitement, and flash of televised wrestling.

To my surprise, no one seemed to object to my interest in wrestling, not as much as to my zoological pursuits, and so, thus unbridled,

I entered into my new interest with a vengeance. I buried myself in wrestling, collecting, memorizing, and soon imitating. To display my growing obsession, in my room I erected two six-by-ten whitewashed bulletin boards over the windows that faced the Hughes airfields and tacked up my newly acquired collection of posters and pictures.

I spent hours practicing wrestling holds. Cindy, Clarence's youngest daughter, was my primary sparring partner, and as a testimony to her unsullied character, she learned how not to cry (lest Clarence try one of his holds on me). I continued watching Channel 5 in the afternoons, and afterward I'd run outside and practice what I'd just seen. I was getting pretty good; I'd even mastered the Destroyer's deadly figure-four leg lock and I knew how the Frenchman Edward Carponteaux reversed it. After weeks of practice I finally perfected the Mummy's Deathwrap. Soon I felt confident enough to try out an actual wrestling match.

I got my chance when Scott Hooper came up to me one day during Nutrition and insisted wrestling was a fake, a sham. Well, it might be, I conceded, so what? But he didn't stop. "No," he said, "I mean all of it, everything, it's all phony." I offered to fight him. He could fight however he wanted, no holds or punches barred, and I'd use only "phony" wrestling holds. He immediately accepted. We set up the fight to start behind the Lutheran church for three-thirty. The word went out through the school, and at fight time a rather sizable crowd attended.

I pulled my Destroyer's mask out of my jacket pocket and slipped it over my head and entered the circle of kids. Scott immediately made a fist and hit me in the face. I recovered and ran toward him, jumped up in the air, and caught his neck between my legs in a flying head scissors. We both went down. Scrambling on the ground, I got him in a headlock and rolled him over. Somehow he escaped and began kicking me. I grabbed his left leg, brought him down face first, put my legs between his, pulled his ankles together and across, wrapped the back of my shins against them, and I had him in the unbreakable Deathwrap. He couldn't get out. But he kept trying. In an effort to still him, I leaned back. But he wriggled again, and I lost my balance, and with his feet stuck under my shins, just like that, it happened. I heard the scream first. Then I heard the grisly crack. The crowd dropped their jaws and then turned heel and split. There was a moment of silence, and then everyone fanned out in different directions and kept going. I ran to get myself lost, quick.

When I got home later that afternoon, I still had no idea whether the school had learned of the fight and had called home or not. Uncertainly I walked around, trying to discover some vague clue to the fate awaiting me. I found Clarence in the den, leisurely wadding up paper and feeding it into a fire he was building.

"Hi, Clarence," I said. I waited for him to tell me to pick up the leaves, or clean the pool, or something.

"Hello!" he said, smiling, almost happy. Something was definitely up. Then it struck me as strange that he was building a fire on a not particularly chilly day. I looked closer at one of the pieces of colored paper he was throwing into the fire and to my sudden horror saw that it was one of my wrestling posters.

"What do you think you're doing?" I demanded.

"What does it look like I'm doing?" he said, practically singing the words. "You've seen your last wrestling match in this house."

I looked at him and then at the fire, back to him, and into the fire again. It was roaring, fed by all of my wrestling memorabilia, program souvenir booklets, posters, fan club information, autographed pictures, everything.

"You can't do that!" I cried. "Those aren't yours!"

"I don't care," he snapped, laughing.

I stormed out of the den and into the kitchen, where my mother stood making dinner. "Do you see what that fuck husband of yours is doing now?" I demanded, beginning to sniffle.

Clarence was right behind me. "Watch your mouth, young man, or I'll really give you something to cry about."

"Oh, Clarence, be nice to him. He doesn't deserve that."

"He's a criminal, a juvenile delinquent. Look at him . . . he's disgraceful."

I looked at her. "How could you let him do this? What did I do?"

Now it was my mother's turn to get angry. "You know perfectly well what you've done. . . . You put Scotty Hooper in the hospital with two broken kneecaps! I should think you would show a little remorse."

"But he started it! He picked the fight. . . ."

She didn't want to hear about it. "We'll talk about it later." She dismissed me. "Go to your room and hope his family has good health insurance."

When I walked into my bedroom, the impact of what was happening hit me full force. Both my bulletin boards were completely bare. I hadn't meant to hurt Scott. But everybody was so aghast at the incident even my father refused to take me to any more wrestling matches. I wasn't allowed *any* television. Maybe they were right. I felt like a real insensitive shit for putting Scott out of commission.

But I also knew it wasn't totally my fault. Nevertheless, once again something that really mattered to me had been snatched away. All that was left was an aching emptiness. I swore that whatever caught my attention next, whatever my next discovery, whatever my next thing proved to be, I would never allow anyone to take it away. It was a conscious decision. I promised myself "never again." Now all I had to do was to find something.

It was at least six months before I was again allowed to watch anything on television, and the moment I resumed, I saw it. Our pathetic excuse for a family had gathered to watch Red Skelton, the comedian who dressed as a clown and imitated two birds flying south for the winter, ordinarily pretty innocuous stuff. But on this particular night, to compete with Ed Sullivan, who had introduced the Beatles to America, Red Skelton was bringing on another English band, the Rolling Stones. And let me tell you, when they came on camera and sang, this boy sat up. The singer vibrated and danced like a motor; he was big lips and all confidence, sass, and arrogance. Decidedly unhealthy in appearance, they all were skinny and long-haired, wore skintight pants, sleeveless sweatshirts, and Italian boots. They weren't much on melody, all din and mad noise, big beats, smashed and crunched and hammered home like a welcome stampede. Words were lost, but you heard enough. It was the sound of my own heartbeat, as if heard for the very first time. "Hey-hey-you-you, get off of my cloud," they sang. Clarence tried to turn it off. Physically I blocked him. "Don't even think about it," I snarled. I don't know if it was Dad's threat or he heard enough of Scott Hooper's kneecaps in my voice; but he backed off. "Oh, for chrissakes," he mumbled. I turned my attention back to the screen.

It was all bounce and power. I didn't listen to the music. I held on and rode it, chaotic, beautiful, anarchic. It was hyperactive teenage heaven. When it was over, I felt as if someone had lifted me up and set me aside to share a cosmic secret. I giggled under my breath. Happy days are here again—I'd found it. I walked out of the den without a word.

He wouldn't ever want to take the credit for it; in fact, he'd be absolutely loath to admit it, but it was my father who was responsible for my first in-person rock and roll experience, the one that really shook things up forever. At around the age of eight I started playing baseball. I'd always had an interest in sports, and although wrestling was hands down my favorite, baseball was my old standby. It was the one sport I was ideally suited for. I was too short for basketball, too light for football, bored by tennis, and I hated volleyball. But I was well coordinated, lithe, and quick—perfect for baseball.

My father was, for once, delighted. He'd been a semiprofessional ballplayer when he was young, before he had been drafted. When my older brother tried out for Little League, he hadn't fared too well. To ensure I was accepted, my father offered to sponsor a team. When it turned out I had a natural knack for the game and was one of the first players chosen during the tryouts, he was so thrilled he signed up to sponsor a second team. Needless to say, this gave me no small amount of prestige in the league.

In the fall of 1966 I was twelve years old, and the umpire who handled most of the games was a young college student named Evan Parker umping Little League for some extra pocket money. He drove a VW micro bus, which qualified him to haul equipment for his neighbor's rock band. Evan had longish hair and a mustache and occasionally gave me a cigarette, which I smoked amid the amplifiers and drums in his van. By contemporary standards he was hip. By Westchester standards he was almost radical.

At the end of one game early in the season Evan and I had an argument on the field. He'd called me out on a third strike, and I thought it was rather high and outside, a ball, not a strike. He called me out anyway. But I insisted it was a ball until he ordered me back to the dugout.

I refused. "What bullshit!" I screamed, and tossed the bat back to the dugout ahead of me.

This just angered Evan more. "Throwing the bat! Out of the game!" he yelled, and jerked his thumb for me to retire to the dugout permanently.

"You call that throwing the bat? That was *rolling* the bat!" I challenged indignantly. I retrieved the bat and hurled it with all my might in his direction. "*That's* throwing the bat!" I yelled. "You're fucking blind. Calling a ball a strike and then saying—" Before I could finish, I stopped short. I had thrown the bat not only in his direction but smack into his shin.

"Outta the game! Offa the field! You're benched!" he cried, hopping up and down, holding the side of his leg. Then Coach Rhodes ran over to him and tried to calm him down. He whispered something in his ear. Evan turned and glared at me. Then he nodded his head. I knew Coach Rhodes was just getting to the facts of Little League

Life and Finance: that my father paid his salary and most of the other expenses. Maybe that pitch was high and outside after all. Maybe I was off the hook and back in the game.

After the game Evan started in my direction. I started to run. "Wait a second," he called, "I'm not going to hurt you." I slowed down, stopped, and waited for him. He limped over and took me by the shoulder.

"You think you're pretty hip, don't you?" he asked. I didn't know what to say, so I kept my mouth shut. "I don't care if your old man sponsors the whole goddamn city," he said, "what you did out there today just is not cool. You're a good little ballplayer, but you're blowing it with these stunts you insist on pulling."

I accepted the words solemnly, impressed an adult was utilizing reason rather than rage to deal with me, talking with me and not at me. I apologized profusely.

After that incident our relationship became close. He saw me hit about ten home runs that year and was vaguely impressed. I sensed this and, enjoying the reflection of myself in his eyes, began spending time with him after other team games. It wasn't long before we even started to joke about the bat-throwing incident like a couple of old war buddies. I'd get up to bat and Evan would joke, "Hey, make sure you get a hit, willya, Sugerman. I can't take another strikeout." Of course, his ability to discern what were balls and what were strikes when I was at bat had also improved.

The crux of our relationship and the turning point of my relationship with the world at large came when my team, the Stars, were up against the other team my father sponsored, the Pirates. The two teams were tied for first place. We'd each won twelve games and lost two, once to each other. Now we were set to play against each other for the play-off game of the season. The winner would go on to the city play-off games. Because of this, and because the Pirates had a wunderkind pitcher named Robby Fisher, it appeared that all of Westchester had turned out for the game; the bleachers were packed.

Naturally Evan was the umpire. For the first three innings neither team scored. Then our pitcher walked two, and there was a single. He managed a strikeout; but then there was a pop-up, and one run scored. The Pirates moved ahead. The score was 1–0. Then a Pirate hit a double, and they moved ahead 3–0. The Pirates continued to hold the Stars scoreless until the Stars came up to bat in the bottom of the ninth. The score was still 3–0. We finally managed to fill the bases with our players, but in the process we also racked up two outs. The crowd was going bananas, screaming for its favorite team. The championship was within either team's grasp. If the Stars could get a rally and score enough runs, they'd be the winners. However, if the Pirates could get just one more batter out, they'd be the league champions.

That's when it was my turn at bat. The crowd was going nuts. Scared because I'd already struck out twice in this game, the coach was screaming at me. "Don't swing at anything you don't like," he yelled. "Make him pitch to you."

The first pitch I cut a hard, smooth swing and missed by a solid foot. My teammates kept up the chatter: "You can do it," or, "Wait for your ball," and, "You'll get the next one." The next pitch came in low and outside. I let it go. One ball, one strike.

"Attaboy, don't swing at anything that isn't good," I heard the coach yelling. The next pitch arrived, and I took a ferocious cut at a low-and-outside ball, fouling it long and left. The coach was frantic now. Two strikes. "Don't try to kill it. Just hit it; all we need is a hit."

"All we need is a fucking miracle," I said under my breath.

Evan called out, "One ball, two strikes."

I fouled one more pitch that would have been another perfect strike. Then I took a low-and-inside ball. I fouled another bad pitch and took another ball. Full count. Three balls and two strikes. The Pirates were yelling, encouraging their pitcher by putting me down: "C'mon, he can't hit, no hitter. . . ." My team was cheering me on by putting down the pitcher: "He can't pitch, easy pitcher, no problem. . . ." Everybody was chattering. The coach was hollering; everybody was yelling so loud I couldn't hear him. I stepped out of the batter's box and called time-out. Now only Coach Rhodes was yelling at me, really yelling loud, and everybody could hear him. Frankly it was embarrassing. "Don't swing for the fence," he's hollering. "Don't try to be a hero! Just touch the ball, just meet it, just a base hit, that's all we need, a little rally, don't show off, come on now, let's go"— he clapped his hands—"just get on base." He looked as if he were about to have a hemorrhage right there in front of the dugout. He was really worried.

I turned around and looked at Evan. He smiled.

That's when I uttered the eleven and a half words that would permanently alter the course of my life and put me on a collision course with my destiny:

"What a dork," I told Evan. "I'm gonna hit a home run."

Evan just laughed. "Tell you what: You hit a home run, and I'll take you to see the Doors tonight."

I'd been pestering him to take me to see the band whose equipment he'd been lugging around all season. I assumed that they were the Doors. Either that or we were going to be spending the night at a hardware store.

"Right over the scoreboard," I told him.

Time-in was called. I waited for Fisher to throw me the best pitch he had. He wound up and let fly. I leaned back on my right foot and stepped into the pitch with my left, leaning into the swing with all my power. I knew the second I felt the baseball crack the wood. . . . The ball careened beautifully off the bat in a long, slowly rising arc and it kept going. The announcer's words came into my ears as I rounded first base, "It's going, it's going . . . it's gone!" The announcer was my brother, Joey, in the cage behind home plate. The crowd erupted. I looked up in time to see the ball sail over the scoreboard. I took a high skip into the air, hitting second base, and continued rounding the bases.

Robby Fisher looked pissed off.

Evan Parker just shook his head.

Joey couldn't believe it. He kept yelling into the mike, "He called it, he called the shot!"

Coach Rhodes looked like he was loosing one in his pants he was so happy.

Grand-slam home run.

Hot shit.

CHAPTER TWO

· · · · · · · · · · ·

**It's my mind and I'll think how I want
It's my life and I'll do what I want.
—THE ANIMALS**

MY mother was doing her hysteri-cal-concerned-Jewish-mother bit, galloping around the kitchen from phone to stove to refrigerator and back, the whole while bombarding me with questions I had very few answers for. She had to know who I was going with and everything about him. Whom were we going to see? No one had heard of the Doors. Where were we going? Why was I going? Twelve-year-olds don't go to concerts. All her mothering fears had come to fruition. She had to be certain Evan was a real, decent person taking me to a real concert, not some child molester taking me to a drug orgy. She didn't trust him because he had a mustache, and what grown man invites a little kid to a rock concert? She didn't trust his motives. That he umpired Little League games only indicated he really liked little kids and not necessarily in a healthy manner either.

None of this mattered. I was going. "I can take care of myself," I insisted, and to my surprise, she believed me.

"Okay." She relented. "But promise me, absolutely promise me you will be home no later than midnight." Of course, I promised, even though I had never been to a concert before and I had no idea how long concerts were. For this one, I had no idea the lead singer's idea of a fashionable entrance was to arrive onstage two hours after the scheduled start time.

After Evan and I arrived at Cal State Los Angeles, where the concert was being held in the gym, we unloaded the equipment he carried in his VW van. When most of it was set up onstage inside, I scrambled back inside the van to pull the microphone cables out from under the dashboard. Looking up, I was shocked to see the dark outline of a figure through the windshield. I scurried back out of the van, and the same dark, long-haired figure blocked my exit.

"What the fuck do you think you're doing?" he demanded.

"I'm helping Evan," I stammered. "This is his van."

"Yeah? How do I know you're not stealing this stuff?"

I looked around frantically for Evan. He was nowhere in sight.

"I'm not! I'm helping."

"I should call the cops."

I was really spooked. I spilled the whole story out to this guy. "I came here with Evan. He told me if I hit a home run, he'd take me to see this band tonight, and here I am."

"Oh, so you're the kid who whacked Parker with the baseball bat?"

How did this guy know that? I was about to ask him when Evan appeared.

"I was just about to call the cops on this kid I caught stealing our equipment, Evan. What do you think we should do with him?"

"I think we should hang him by his ankles with these microphone cables and beat the shit out of him," Evan said.

Now I didn't know whether to laugh, or run.

"That's not a bad idea," the guy said. Evan winked. I breathed easier.

At that moment a pretty red-haired girl came up and put her arm around the guy with the long hair. "Hello, honey," she said kissing him on the cheek.

He slipped his arm around her waist. "Well, I guess I'll let you go this time, but watch it in the future," he said to me. Then they walked away.

"That was Jim Morrison," Evan told me. "You two oughta really get along. He's crazier than you are."

A group called the Sunshine Company opened the show, followed by the Nitty Gritty Dirt Band. The audience was polite to the first band but had become rude and impatient by the time the second was wrapping up its set. Then there was a long, long break.

The four members of the Doors were in the locker room, underground and beneath the gym, which was serving as the dressing room. They were completely unaware of the tension mounting upstairs back in the hall. The Dirt Band had left the stage early, about ten forty-five. The Doors were to go on at eleven-fifteen. It was already eleven-thirty, the audience was growing increasingly intolerant, and it was becoming obvious I wasn't going to make it home by midnight. The stage was finally readied for the Doors at eleven forty-five. Sixteen black Jordan amplifiers were erected into four individual towers looking like Greek columns, one stack of four on each side of the drum riser. In front of the stage was a lone, slightly bent, chrome microphone stand. Just to its immediate left was a red and black Vox organ with a silver, metal-flake bass keyboard by Fender riding piggyback on the organ's left shoulder.

At midnight the prerecorded music from the PA was turned off, the audience tensed. But no Doors. I was standing between Evan and another man whom Evan introduced to me as the Doors' manager, Bill Siddons. "Listen, how'd you like to do me a favor?" Bill asked.

"Sure."

"Go downstairs and tell those guys it's show time."

I dashed down the stairs and into the dressing room, my enthusiasm barely contained, and repeated the message. I was met with darkness and silence. I had to peer into the room to make them out.

I heard a deep voice: "Tell Bill we know." I stood there and waited for more, but when no more came, I decided I'd done the job I was asked to do and ran back upstairs. I relayed the message to Bill.

"Go tell them I said *now*!" I ran back down the stairs.

"Bill said now!" Silence.

Another voice answered this time.

"All right." More silence. No movement. I waited awhile. What were they waiting for? Nobody talked.

I left, ran back upstairs, and told Bill they said "all right."

"Tell them the contract reads eleven-fifteen, and we're already over an hour late."

I didn't want to tell them that. Walking into that dressing room was like entering the river Styx. But I didn't want to disobey. I went back downstairs, my legs getting tired by now, and told them what Bill said.

"Tell Bill we'll be right up," the baritone answered. I climbed back upstairs.

"Tell them the audience is going apeshit," Bill told me.

I hobbled down the stairs and delivered the message.

"Let 'em, it's good for them."

This time I tried to run back up the stairs with the reply, but I confess I walked two or three of them.

I told Bill. "Why don't you go talk to them? I don't think they're listening to me," I said.

"Don't take it personally," he told me. "Those guys don't listen to anybody." He gave me a new message. "Tell them if we don't go on now, this second, we're gonna be in default, got that?" I nodded, afraid to speak for fear of forgetting the message. I trotted back downstairs and fed the information into the darkness. Silence.

"Tell him we don't give a fuck about the money." I didn't want to tell anybody that.

"Tell him we're on our way," another voice said. What were they doing in there anyway? I wondered. I was beginning to have strange feelings about these guys.

Back upstairs, I gave Bill the latest news. "Go watch for them at the top of the stairs, and when you see them, come tell me, okay?" The crowd was stomping and clapping and hollering for the Doors. I waited a good ten minutes at the top of the stairs. It was almost one o'clock. I had a long time ago given up getting home before two. Then I saw three musicians coming up the stairs: a tall blond, well-dressed man who looked nice and wore rimless glasses; a frizzy-haired, slightly dazed-looking guy who looked as if he were wearing a carpet over his shoulder and who carried a burgundy Gibson guitar; and a colorful, almost pixie-looking guy with lousy skin. Where was the fourth guy, Morrison? Hadn't he heard me? Oh, shit. I'd assumed he was in the dressing room.

I ran and told Bill they were coming. Three of them at least. He said something into his headphone mike, and the houselights dimmed. The audience hushed and inhaled. The place smelled of pot. I'd smelled it once or twice before, but not like this. A spotlight came on. "Ladies and gentlemen"—Bill Siddons's voice boomed throughout the gym —"please welcome the Doors!" Wild applause. Then the spotlight went out, and you saw nothing but some buttons of red light beaming. The music started in total darkness. It sounded as if a carnival were beginning. That was my first thought. Had the fourth guy made it? That was my next thought. Where was he? Was he coming? Had he heard me? Oh, shit. Was I in trouble with these guys already? I hoped not. I'd just met them!

Nothing in my life prepared me for the arrival of Jim Morrison.

I had gotten my seat, up front, and sat cross-legged with dozens of other members of the audience, pressed tightly together. They sat alert, as if awaiting a lecture, not a concert. They knew something I didn't. I tried to be cool. I made some room for myself and tried to fit in.

Should I go back and get him? That was my last thought, and I might as well have left it in another world. Then it happened.

I heard a scream, long, pained, thick, and husky, loud enough and strong enough to wake me up. In his black leather, with his long brown hair and angelic features, the singer was a phantom, staggering across the stage, about to fall but somehow keeping his balance, bellowing his lungs out. The rest of the band looked unconcerned. The keyboardist's eyes were closed, his head slowly winding from side to side in time with the music. The drummer was raising his hands and drumsticks in the air and bringing them down with an exaggerated motion. The guitarist stood stone still.

The lead singer was still yelling, but slower now, in time with the music, hard grunts and groans.

He stopped, as if regaining awareness, and looked right in our faces, held our stares as the music began to build. He dropped back, then leaped forward, throwing his face at ours, his eyes agog, ter-rorized, tearing at the microphone, hands a blur, on the verge of insanity, and he screamed again, the sound of a thousand curtains torn. The audience, already on the edges of the seats, was bolted and locked into the Doors' current. Jim crumpled onto the stage in a lifeless heap, the music pounding. I thought he was dead, electrocuted, maybe shot.

He rose from the ground slowly and did a beautiful leap straight up, as if jettisoned. He landed easily but staggered a bit as he ap-proached the microphone. He touched it easily, slowly, and blinked, opened his mouth to sing, but thought of something else and closed his mouth. (Had he forgotten the words?) The music continued, re-peating itself, waiting for him to enter. The audience was frozen in expectation and attention. The singer just rode it all, letting the music build and build, blind to stares. Then, just when it felt as if the room would blow its roof off, he slipped the words in, closing his eyes as he sang:

> When the music's over,
> When the music's over, yeah
> When the music's over, turn out the lights
> The music is your special friend,
> Dance on fire as it intends
> Music is your only friend . . .
>   until the end. . . .

It was the end. It was the end of the world as I had known it. Nothing would ever again be the same for me again.

It was 3:30 A.M. by the time we finished loading the equipment back in Evan's van. I felt different—lighter, freer. We were sitting on the curb in the parking lot, talking about it, having a smoke when a police car pulled up in front of us with its lights shining in our faces. Evan and Bill got real nervous real fast. A cop got out of each door. One was a policeman; the other, a campus security cop. The official cop said, "Danny Sugerman?"

"Yes, Officer?" My father had taught me always to be polite to cops.

"Your mother is looking for you," the other one finished.

I had completely forgotten.

When I was dropped off at home, Clarence and my mother were both up, waiting for me. I was still walking on air.

"What are you stoned on?" Clarence asked.

"Nothing," I said truthfully.

"Look at him, he's potted."

"Where have you been?" my mother asked.

"At the concert."

"What have you been doing all night? You were supposed to be home by midnight." Before I could answer: "You're grounded, young man, and you're forbidden ever to see that creep again who took you tonight."

I didn't even bother arguing. They couldn't stop me. Their threats were hollow; their questions, meaningless. They couldn't touch me anymore. No one could.

I couldn't talk about anything else for days afterward. Nothing had ever affected me so much. I had to know, Where else did this happen? Did other people react the same way? Were all the bands around this great? Who was this guy Jim? How crazy was he? He seemed ultimately sane. He was the sanest, best thing that ever happened to me. I hadn't gone expecting anything other than a good time. It was as if I had been asleep for twelve years and suddenly slapped awake. I didn't know exactly what had happened, but that something had happened I was certain. I had no frame of reference for it. My mind raced for days to make sense of it, to categorize it, to place it somewhere I could reach for it when I needed it.

I had to have some answers. My mission in life became to find out as much as possible about this new world. That meant, first thing, seeing Jim again. I was not aware of simply wanting his approval. Oh, sure, I wanted him to like me, but it was so much more. The way a man dying of thirst heads toward water, I started toward Morrison. I was certain he would not reject me. I might have been twelve years old and he twenty-two, him famous, me a nobody, but I didn't think of that. I had to get close to that band. The attraction was blinding. Here was a man not afraid of being out of control and in doing so seemed to possess the greatest strength of all. I wanted some of that strength for myself. I needed it. My survival seemed to depend on it.

* * *

One night during dinner Clarence cleared his throat and said, "Harriet has an announcement to make."

Mom looked up and smiled. "I'm pregnant. I'm going to have a baby." A strange silence followed, broken by my older sister, Nan, going totally apeshit, it turned out, on principles of general sensitivity alone—i.e., the thought of Mom and Clarence's having screwed was too much for her. After a twelve-hour crying jag Nan packed her bags and left to move in with my father. Two down, one to go.

That left me alone with Clarence. Oh, sure, Mom was there, but what could she do? She did the only thing she could (besides leave him, which I gave up hoping for): She refereed. But it didn't make any difference. In his eyes I always lost and I couldn't help thinking that since she chose to stay with him, she must feel the same about me somewhere in her heart. I wasn't about to stop fighting. The odds had just clicked one more up against me.

In keeping with the Christmas spirit, Clarence invoked a new law that stated that since I received presents from two families and an abundance of gifts from my father, and his kids had neither a rich father who lavished them with gifts nor a second household from which to receive presents, it was only fair I share my booty with his children. Like, if I got four gifts from Dad, I had to let his girls choose one apiece. If I refused, then I could not bring them into *his* household at all. His kids, in addition, were forbidden to share any of their Christmas gifts with me. It just succeeded in turning his kids against him even more.

I kept the ruse away from Dad's ears for the same reason I kept quiet about almost everything else that went on with Clarence and Mom that conspired to make life a daily war zone for me. I didn't want Dad to go over there and knock Clarence's brains all over the wall and end up in jail. It frustrated him to hear about the cruel shit that was pulled on me and then not be able to do anything about it. It got his ulcers going but good.

As long as I'd been going to school, I'd been getting into trouble. Nothing truly hideous, I simply wasn't disciplined enough to learn what the teachers wanted to teach me. I was capable of learning; I just wasn't interested. As usual, I couldn't sit still or stay in my seat. When I was interested, then I had a hundred questions, but I couldn't keep it together long enough to raise my hand to get called on to ask them, so I usually just blurted them out. Or anything else that was on my mind, too, for that matter. At first it was mostly a disciplinary problem. Although no one had actually used the word "hyperactive" yet to describe my condition, they were getting ready to. The word meant physical, verbal, and insistent. Uncontrollable. Unable to discipline oneself. Impulsive. Not malicious—disruptive, not destructive. "Hyperactive acting out" was the diagnosis in practically no time.

But that was all before I saw the Doors in concert, after which something inside me opened up to the greater possibilities before me as a teenager, and I found myself thinking about more creative, intelligent trouble. Simply witnessing Morrison in concert opened me up to my own potential. Before we had even spoken, I fancied myself in his tradition. And I still knew nothing about him.

Robby Fisher (the pitcher from the Pirates) had become one of my best friends. He'd been working in the school administration office for class credit and one afternoon stumbled on the school's plumbing blueprints in the back of a file cabinet. His dad was an engineer, so he was really into stuff like that. Meanwhile, another friend of mine who'd gotten me started on cigarettes, Mark Ladd (whom everyone called Bad Ladd for obvious reasons), had scored a whole shoebox full of M-80 firecrackers. They're not really firecrackers—they're actually miniature sticks of dynamite—but we didn't know that. We just thought they were unusually large firecrackers.

Robby came to school one day with a shit-eating grin on his face. Something was up. Then he told me. He'd stolen the blueprints to the school's entire plumbing system. "Yeah? So what?"

"Well, doesn't Ladd have some M-eighties?"

"Yeah? So?"

"And aren't the fuses waterproof?"

Then I started grinning, too.

When we told Ladd, he caught on immediately. Somehow, we decided, we were going to introduce the M-80s to the school's plumbing system and see how they interacted.

Turns out when Robby had taken the blueprints home, he'd really studied them. He had determined the most vulnerable juncture, the weakest joint in the school's entire plumbing apparatus. Robby commenced to lead us to the lavatory in the H-Building, which is where the biology classes were held.

We opened the shoebox of firecrackers and attached ten M-80s together, combining all their fuses into one short, fat one. Then we extended three other fuses together so there would be a good delayed reaction and give us time to get our faces out of the way, and we hooked the long one to the short one. That was my particular responsibility, to time the fuse. We lit it, dropped the chunk of dynamite into the center of three toilets, and ran like cats outside the head into the hallway, where we very anxiously anticipated the explosion.

We didn't figure anyone might decide to use the bathroom at that time. That hadn't been part of our plan. It was the one thing that could go wrong we hadn't considered. We knew it the second we saw Gregory Saddolwright heading toward us. He was enormous—the school tub. Everyone called him Satellite because he was so big and fat and round. Satellite was already a bit leery of us. One lunch hour in the cafeteria we'd been screwing around and Ladd threw a fork at me. When I ducked, it hit Satellite in the forehead and stuck there until he pulled it out. So he wasn't real thrilled to see the three of us together again. But it didn't stop him from entering either.

At just the moment we're plugging our ears and falling against the lockers in giggles, here comes Satellite, bouncing into the bathroom to take a dump. No one ever actually used those doorless toilets to evacuate their bowels. But apparently he really had to go, and he picked what he thought was a quiet time during class so he could have some privacy. He'd even brought a paperback with him, so we knew he wasn't going to be just pissing. And we wait: There still hasn't been any explosion. We wait another minute. It's been about three minutes now. I want Robby to go in and check the fuse. He wants me to go in and check the fuse. "It was *your* responsibility," he points out. Ladd suggests all three of us go. We agree it's a good idea, and we all go back in together.

The first thing that hits us back inside is the stench. This is mixed with another smell—gunpowder. Definitely an unpleasant combination. The fuse has obviously burned somewhat. Right there in front of us, spreading over the toilet seat like a lump of melting Jell-O with short, fat, little legs, is Satellite with his pants down around his ankles. At least he's not in the middle stall, I think, relieved. He's alarmed, however, to see the three of us together, during class and in the head. And we aren't even smoking, so what the hell are we doing there? You can just about see the look of puzzlement and disapproval on his face. He all but scratches his head and frowns. Ladd decides to go over and check the fuse. We can actually see the smoke rising out of the center toilet. Satellite can't see anything because of the walls in between the shitters. But he definitely senses something is up. Then smoke begins billowing out of both toilets. The fuse has apparently really sunk down into the pipes. But it isn't coming out of the far toilet he's sitting on because he so completely and fatly covers the toilet bowl, there's no room for the smoke to escape.

Satellite is looking confused and worried and a bit embarrassed. Ladd is sticking his face in the center john, trying to find out what's happening with our package, debating on whether or not he's going to put his hand down there. Robby is having a stare-down with Satellite, and I'm gagging, trying not to puke. Ladd comes over to me and says, "Jesus Christ, what did you use? A fucking piece of rope for that fuse?" Satellite picks up on this remark and his eyebrows rise and he lets out a long, rambling fart, which causes Ladd to say, "That's disgusting, Satellite, you ought to be shot." Then it happened.

It sounded as if a goddamn bomb got shot through the walls with a cannon. The entire place rumbled and shook. The windows blew right out. The entire toilet we dropped the M-80s in shattered. Water was streaming out, jetting to the ceiling. Satellite at that point went into a total state of panic and confusion. He didn't know what to do, whether to pull up his pants, wipe his ass, or run. Nothing at all happened to him or the toilet he was on. He'd created such a vacuum between his fat ass and the water bowl that the toilet just sort of gulped and expanded. Then we watched it belch and crack. Satellite, however, now sounded like he might be hurt. He started screaming his head off, which sounds something like the indignant baying of a wounded moose. It turns out an exploding geyser of water has just careened right up his susceptible asshole and suddenly he's off like a cork. We tried to catch him as he ran out, pants around his ankles, underwear aflutter, pocketbook clutched to bosom. We couldn't stop him, though. He dashed right past us. He was too big and fast and we were too slow and weak with laughter. Robby stumbled out to give pursuit and try to catch him to prevent him from finking on us, which is where we collectively assumed he was headed. Then we all decided we'd better haul ass and split ourselves.

But I couldn't move. My system couldn't decide whether to puke or laugh. I was having serious trouble breathing. My sides were aching. Every time I'd try to inhale, I'd smell this wretched smell and I'd choke all over again. I was just gagging away and making this sort of high-pitched retching sound on the in breath, followed by a series of ugly hacks. And the sewage was rising, floating all over the place, and just the thought of giving Satellite a fifteen-gallon enema would put me right back into convulsions all over again.

And then Ladd says, "Didja see that? It came out his nose!" He's howling, "He had water coming outta his nose!" and he makes his fingers in the V sign, taps the space under his nostrils, and pulls them down and this just sets me off on another episode of hysterics.

Meanwhile, somebody had pulled a fire alarm, mistakenly thinking where there was smoke there must be fire. Ladd managed to drag me out of the bathroom and into the hallway, where he dropped me. Then he fled, roaring with laughter, rolling against the lockers all the way down the flooded hall, while all I could do was helplessly watch him make good his escape. I couldn't even stand up I was so caught up in this horrible mixture of choking and laughing and trying not to puke. Students had been pouring out of the classrooms, when out of nowhere Satellite returned, fully dressed now and pissed off to the max, and started kicking my already sore and aching sides and yelling, "I don't think it's funny, I don't think it's funny," over and over again and I'm lying there in the middle of the floor gulping for air, trying not to die of a seizure.

That's how they found me, Mr. Tanner, the boys' VP, and a PE coach, awash in piss water, having a spaz attack, getting assaulted by the school blimp.

They dragged me up to Mr. Tanner's office in the Administration Building, and there they calmed me down with their paddles. Mr. Tanner used his prize weapon of assault, which was a mean two-and-one-half-foot-long piece of aluminum wrapped with black electrical tape, attached to a foot-long handle. The paddle was so long it actually wrapped around my ass and almost slapped my balls when it landed. The coach used a wet tennis shoe as his standard weapon of choice. And then they took turns spanking me.

I learned we'd succeeded in blowing out the plumbing for not only the whole school but the whole southern end of Westchester as well. Members of the Department of Water and Power were considering a lawsuit against the school, naming me as the culprit of the crime. The school, meanwhile, was rapidly checking its insurance coverage.

Like a good, loyal, decent friend, I took the entire rap for Robby and Ladd. The people who were supposedly authorities on the subject thought the behavior I'd exhibited was the most irresponsible, despicable, thoughtless, vile, and mean they'd ever encountered outside a juvenile criminal institution of incarceration, and they seemed stuck for a while between making an example of me and trying to help me. Then they decided. They ended up doing the former at the cost of the latter. They expelled me. On the spot.

Which was fine with me. I'd learned from Evan that the Doors were getting ready for their next album and he was opening offices in West Hollywood and needed some help moving. Did I want to help him? Theoretically I was grounded. But realistically an army couldn't have kept me away from the track that led directly to the Doors. I figured the school would get around to calling home soon enough. They always did. My ass and my sides would continue to hurt for days.

The whole incident must have been pretty traumatic for Satellite, too, because for the rest of my professional high school life, whenever he saw me coming, he'd take off waddling at top speed in the opposite direction.

Helping Evan was just about as much fun as bombing the bathroom, without any of its punishing aftereffects. I really liked Evan. He trusted me with responsibility and seemed intuitively to know how to direct my energy. When I learned I couldn't overwhelm or intimidate him, I rewarded him with a job well done. We both were grateful for the arrangement.

I started out helping him unload the car and move into the office. I ended up answering his newly installed phones and taking messages. I began discovering what agents were, who they were, what they did. Evan had become a concert promoter, and the first band he was presenting was the Doors.

At that time the band was in rehearsal. The Doors had just moved into an old building in West Hollywood, also on Santa Monica Boulevard, just down the street from Evan's new office.

Just knowing the Doors were rehearsing nearby, I started pestering Evan. Where? One block or one mile? How nearby? Rehearsing what? Did the singer move in rehearsal the way he had in concert? Was there going to be another concert? Did he ever watch them practice?

"Well," Evan said, "I have some contracts that need to be delivered to Bill right now. I was going to call a messenger, but how'd you like to run them over, get them signed, and bring them back to me? Maybe you'll be able to catch them working. Maybe then you'll leave me the fuck alone." He was only half joking. He gave me the address and a piece of advice. "Don't get in their way."

I didn't walk to the office where the Doors were. I ran like someone had shot the starting gun in the thousand-yard dash. Downstairs at the address there was music being played. It was the Doors!

Curtains were drawn. I dared not go in. Yet at the moment there was nothing I ever wanted to do more in my life than walk in and watch them. For the time being I had to content myself with simply knowing where they were and being able to hear them play. I felt like I had the only map to a buried treasure. I went up the stairs to where their business was conducted.

I dropped off the contracts and was told to wait while they were brought to the guys. Off the coffee table I picked up a copy of the Doors' biography printed by their record company, Elektra. Jim Morrison said: "I am interested in anything about revolt, disorder, chaos, especially activity which appears to have no meaning." *Goddamn*, I thought, *I know how to do that!* "I've always been attracted to ideas that were about revolt against authority. It seems to me to be the road to freedom. When you make your peace with authority, you become authority." I read that line no less than ten times. It made perfect sense to me. I knew exactly what he was talking about. I implicitly had his approval, and I knew it. They were his words, but they were my thoughts: his concept, my demolished toilet.

I read the rest of his biography. He was twenty-two years old. His favorite color was black. He was a Sagittarius, but he didn't believe in astrology. His parents were dead. Dead? That's what it said.

The other members of the group were Ray Manzarek; he was the handsome, gentle blond man I'd talked with backstage for two seconds when telling them to come onstage. The frizzy-haired guitarist was Robby Krieger. Evan lived next door to him and was best friends with his twin brother. John Densmore was the pixielike drummer.

They had one album out. A single called "Break On Through" was getting a lot of airplay on KRLA in Los Angeles. I made a mental note to listen to KRLA from now on. There was a copy of the album. A whole box of albums was on the floor right next to the couch. "Is it all right if I have one of these?" I asked the secretary. She told me I'd have to ask Bill.

Just then Bill came back upstairs with the signed contracts for me to take back to Evan. The thought of simply stealing the whole box and running appealed to me, but I vetoed it as impractical. They'd notice, and I'd never be welcomed back. Instead, I asked. He said sure, I could have an album, and he asked if I wanted a biography of the band and a few photos as well. "Are you kidding?" I asked him. "I'll take everything you've got!"

"How about just one of everything I've got?" Bill smiled. That would do fine.

He made me a pile of the LP, the single, three pictures, a few articles, the bio, and a poster. I was profuse in my thanks. I began to run toward the door. "Hey!" he shouted.

"Yeah, what?"

"Aren't you forgetting something?" he asked me.

"What?"

"These!" he said, waving the papers I'd brought over for signature.

"Oh, those. Yeah." I grabbed them and put them neatly atop my bundle and rushed down the stairs.

I almost ran headfirst into Jim Morrison, who was heading up the stairs. "How come every time I see you, you're running off with something that belongs to me?" I just looked at him, thinking he was nuts and probably dangerous, too. He felt dangerous. He was still in his black leather pants but with a blue pea coat, collar up. His hair was the longest I'd ever seen. And as much as I was embarrassed to admit it, he was beautiful. His eyes were like green marbles, alive and flaming. He looked like a crazy angel. I was nervous.

But I'd be damned if I let him know it. "I don't know," I said. "How come every time I'm running off with something that belongs to you, you're standing right in front of me blocking my way?"

He cocked his head. I thought he was going to haul off and slug me. Instead, he smiled. "Do you always answer a question with a question?" he asked me. "You must know that's not polite. You look like a well-bred young man to me."

"Bill gave this stuff to me." I finally answered his original question. "And these papers are for Evan."

"He's put you to work again, huh?"

I nodded.

"Make sure he pays you," Jim said, heading up the stairs.

I ran back to Evan's office as fast as I could without dropping the bundle. "What did you do, steal that stuff?" Evan asked me as I walked in the door.

"How come everybody asks me that? Actually I was thinking of it."

"You must have seen Morrison again."

"Yeah, I did. He said you should pay me. That guy's weird."

"He has that effect on everybody." Evan laughed.

"But I like him. I never met anybody like him before."

"You're shaking, you know that?" Evan asked me.

I hadn't noticed. I was so excited and scared I really was actually shaking.

"Do you smoke? Here, want a hit of this?" He offered me a

joint. I'd smoked grass only once before, with Ladd, and hadn't really felt it. I took a few hits inhaling deeply and holding it. This time I felt it.

It was getting late, time to get home. The La Cienega No. 2 bus took me almost all the way to Westchester. I walked the additional two miles home. It had been dark for over an hour. The family was just sitting down to dinner. There was no plate set for me. And I was famished.

"What am I supposed to eat off of? The floor?"

"That's too good for you," Clarence said. "If you expect to live in this house, then by God, you'll obey the rules of this house."

"What rules?" I asked. There were so many, and they varied day to day.

"Whatever I say is a rule!" he yelled at me.

"Okay, what rule did I break this time?" I gave in.

"Are you really that stupid? Because you better not be talking back to me."

"I don't know. Maybe . . ."

He looked at me like I was out of my head. Which I was. I was ripped. "You're supposed to be grounded."

"For what?" I asked. I couldn't exactly remember. I wasn't so sure he remembered either.

He gave me his you-really-are-stupid gape and said, "You've just been expelled from school!" The school had obviously called.

"Oh," I said. "That. Wait a minute, you can't ground me for that! You can't punish me for getting punished." It was a mistake. It only made him get specific.

"I can do anything I want. You're being punished, young man, for staying out until three in the morning. And let me remind you, while we're on the subject, you're forbidden to see that creep who was responsible for you that night."

Hoping to change the topic, my mother, as if on cue, said, "Where have you been all day, honey?"

Now I tried to change the topic. "So how long am I grounded for?"

Mom tried again to break up the conversation. "What did you do today, Danny?"

I looked at her, afraid to speak. Clarence yelled, "Answer your mother!"

"I was working," I half lied.

Her eyes brightened, and she looked at Clarence as if to say, "So there." Her motherly pride got itself up, and she wanted to hear more. There was no stopping her. "Where were you working?"

"It's not important," I mumbled.

"Oh, don't be so modest," she insisted, "tell me." Everyone was listening in, the whole family.

I couldn't avoid the question any longer. I decided I'd give her a clue to back off. "Up in Hollywood." But that one word was too much. I should have used something more subtle like "the other side of town" or "just some office."

"Who do you know in Hollywood?" she asked, still not catching on.

I just shrugged and decided to let the shit hit the proverbial fan. I said one word: "Evan." You coulda knocked her over wid a fedder.

Clarence all but grinned with sick delight, caught himself, and gave me his worst grimace. "The umpire. You just don't learn, do you? From now on, you're grounded!"

I had to laugh. "I'm already grounded!"

"You're grounded again. Until further notice, get in your room," he growled, "without any privileges! Now, git!"

It was so absurd I couldn't believe it. "Privileges! What privileges? I've never had any! What are you gonna take away? The privilege of picking up a thousand leaves a day?" Before he could answer, I turned and left the kitchen. As I rounded the pool, I spit a good looger in it and went into my bedroom, avoided looking at the blank white walls, put on the Doors' first album full blast, put on the headphones, and lay down: "You know the day divides the night/night divides the day/try to run/try to hide/break on through to the other side. . . ."

The next morning I woke up with the headphones still on, the end of the record skipping, and fully dressed. I put on a clean blue T-shirt, traded my tennis shoes for my cowboy boots, and pulled on a denim jacket. I peeked out the window to make sure Clarence wasn't around, scooted out the front door of my bedroom, rounded the side of the room, and jumped the fence of our backyard, which abutted the Hughes airfield property. I ran down the side of the hill, almost losing momentum, and arrived at the intersection of Sepulveda and Centinela less than a minute later. I stuck out my thumb and headed north. I had only two bucks, and I needed that for cigarettes.

The Doors' office was just up the street from where I was dropped off. I knew it was early, and no one would be there; but I didn't know where else to go, so I decided to check the front door just in case. It was unlocked. Someone must have forgotten to lock it the day before. I didn't think anyone would mind if I waited inside. Once inside, I locked the door. Very properly I sat on the waiting-room couch and read the latest issue of *Rolling Stone.*

The door from Siddons's office squeaked open. A naked girl, a brunette, took a step out, took one look at me, said hello, and returned to the room, closing the door partway behind her.

"There's a kid out there," I heard her say.

It was Jim Morrison's voice that answered. "Kid? There's no kid up here. . . . Wait a second. . . ."

Jim emerged, scratching his gravelly chin. "What are you doing here? How'd you break in?"

"I didn't break in." I defended myself. "The door was open. I thought someone might've forgot to lock it. I locked it behind me."

"Yeah, good for you. What time is it anyway? What are you doing here so early?"

"It's about eight o'clock. What are *you* doing here so early?"

He waited almost a full minute before answering me. "I work here," he finally said. "What's your excuse?"

"I'm grounded," I told him. "And I just like up here better than down there."

"What's down there?" He laughed.

"Westchester, by the airport, near the beach. Farmland."

"Is that where you're from?" he asked me.

"I'm from Beverly Hills. That's where I was born, at least. I was bullshitted into moving to Westchester."

"Who bullshitted you?" he said, still standing.

I was getting a little nervous, but I was delighted we were speaking to each other. "My mother. She told me the new house had real banana trees with actual bananas."

"And does it?" he said.

"It does, but you get sick if you eat them. I've lived there since I was seven and not one goddamn banana has ever ripened. Bananas can't ripen in this climate. Anyway, that wasn't even the point. The whole deal was to get an iguana. Iguanas love bananas."

"Iguanas, huh?" He laughed, a far-off incipient lizard king grin taking shape. "You know, I keep bumping into you, but I don't really know anything about you. Tell me why you're grounded. Wanna beer?"

"Sure," I told him. He disappeared into the room and brought out two large Colt 45's and handed me one. We drank.

"I got grounded for seeing you."

"Oh, I see. So it's my fault."

"It is." I laughed. "If you'd have gone onstage on time, I wouldn't have gotten home at three A.M., and none of this ever would have happened."

"Usually, when one is grounded, it means, at least when I was a kid, it meant you're not allowed to leave your bedroom."

"It still means that, I guess. But I mean, *fuck them*."

"But what about school? How old are you? What, thirteen, fourteen? When I was your age—"

"Technically," I said, "I'm expelled. For two weeks. First I was grounded for getting home late after Evan took me to that concert. Then I blew up the bathroom in the H-Building biology wing. Then I got expelled. Then I got grounded again for getting expelled."

"They can't do that!" Jim laughed. "That's double jeopardy!"

"What's that?"

"It means trying the same person twice for the same crime. It's supposed to be illegal."

"He's a lawyer, too."

"Who's a lawyer?"

"My mother's husband."

"Your father?"

"No, God forbid. He's only a stepfather."

"Well, if he's an attorney, he should know better."

"I didn't say he had any honor. Anyway, last night I got grounded again. They don't want me coming up here. They don't like Evan much; they don't even know him. I mean, I've had more fun up here than I've had in my whole life, and they're behaving like I'm blowing up banks or something real sick, for godsakes. So when I woke up this morning, I just couldn't take the idea of hanging around down there all day when I could be up here. Fuck what they say."

"You've run away from home then?" he asked me.

"It's not official," I said. "I'll call my mom later on so she doesn't worry. She's pretty cool. It's my stepfather who's a thorough shitheel. A real classic fuckhead marine mentality."

"Yeah, I know what you mean. So when was the last time you ate? You must be hungry."

I held up the can of beer, indicating it was okay alone. But he insisted. "I mean," he said, "if your mother is going to trust you here, at least you've got to eat."

"I don't have any money," I told him.

"Don't worry about it." He laughed. "None of my friends have any money."

I didn't care if I never went home again. In fact, for the first time in years I felt as if I was home.

He took the girl and me to Duke's Coffee Shop for breakfast. He ordered a Spanish omelet, garlic bread, black coffee, and tomato juice. I had an order of scrambled eggs, an English muffin, and black coffee and orange juice and asked the waitress to buy me a pack of Marlboros. She ignored me. "They don't do that here," Jim said. "You'll have to get up and get them yourself." When I got back to the table, Jim and the girl were talking about her: where she came from, where she was going. Then there was a long silence, and we all ate. Jim looked up with the slightest trace of a smile on his face and very, very softly asked me, "And who are you supposed to be?"

I'd never given much thought to it, but hard as I could, I tried to say the right thing. "Well," I carefully began, "my sister is going to be a judge someday, and my brother is going to go to medical school." I'd read Jim and Ray had gone to college, UCLA film school, and therefore concluded an education was important to him.

"That's not what I asked," he said.

I was becoming uncomfortable. I really wanted to say the right thing.

"What do you want to do when you grow up? You know, a professional life in the democratic society?" he asked.

"My father wants me to be a baseball player and then a lawyer. All ballplayers have short careers and should plan to have some follow-up career, but then, it's hard to get through law school when you're pursuing a career in sports. And my mother thinks I should go to—"

He didn't let me finish. "That's still not what I asked. What do *you* want to do?"

Christ, Jim, I'm fucking thirteen years old. Gimme a break. I don't know what I'm gonna be doing for lunch, let alone fifty years from now. To myself I said that.

To him I shrugged and told the truth. "I don't know what the fuck I want to do."

"That's good." He sounded pleased. "It sounded for a minute there like you had the rest of your life nailed down. That would have been a drag. How do you get along with your teachers? I'm assuming you don't get along with your parents too well."

Inside Duke's Coffee Shop on a warm Tuesday morning in February 1967, I told Jim Morrison the story of my life, concentrating on the last year. I couldn't seem to stay out of trouble, I told him. Everything I liked always got me into trouble. Somewhere, sometime, someone always stepped in and said, "You can't do that anymore." People did it with animals. They did it with wrestling. I paused. "And now they're trying to do it with rock and roll." It was really making me sad. "*And* they're trying to get me to see this doctor about some pills to slow me down. I don't know what to do."

He seemed concerned. "You know, I think there must be an unwritten rule somewhere that says, 'Don't let your kids become who they are.' Break the spirit, that's what they aim to do. In the South, where I come from, they admit it. Break the spirit, and it allows their god to enter, their rules to take root." He paused. "What kind of pills?"

I told him what I knew. I'd been diagnosed as hyperactive; I'd been getting into a lot of trouble at school. The school said my parents had to do something. In fact, the school and my mother were getting together this very day to talk about what to do with me. A doctor had proposed something called Ritalin, which is actually an upper but which for some reason acts as a calming agent on hyperactive kids. These kids are born with an abundance of the sleep hormone, and to counteract the constant feeling of sleepiness, they develop a subconscious defense mechanism which keeps them alert and awake. This defense manifests itself in extreme activity, an inability to sit still or shut up, to compensate for the sleepiness. The Ritalin slows down the flow of the sleep-inducing agent and eliminates the need for defensive behavior.

Morrison listened and got furious. "What bullshit! Now, you listen to me. Don't let them do it. Just because you don't fit into their system and their expectations, they try to break you and bend you to fit. It's bullshit. Don't let them control you. You've just been blessed with a lot of energy. Don't let them kill it with their fucking pills. You just be yourself. God," he said to his girl, "can you believe this?"

"But," I stammered, "what if you don't know who you're supposed to be?" I had intended on impressing Morrison, and here I went making a thorough fool of myself.

He didn't give a fuck. "No kid your age knows what it's all about. You'll find out, you can do it," he encouraged me. "Just don't limit yourself. That's how you find out. You experience everything there is, and you find out how to relate to the world, and in doing that, you begin to define yourself. But don't let them change you. Insist on the freedom to try everything at least once. Don't limit yourself. You think you can do that?"

"I've been doing it my whole life!" I exclaimed.

"Well then, good, don't stop now."

It's too late to stop now, I thought.

* * *

I really didn't want to go home after rehearsal. I'd finally seen the Doors rehearse! It was fucking great. I played pinball with Ray Manzarek on the machine downstairs, and all day long I listened to them work and play. I never had more fun, felt more secure or special in my entire life. I didn't want to go home and ruin it.

Jim said I could crash on the couch in the office if I wanted to. I wanted to.

He told me to wait until everybody left and then come back. He gave me five dollars to get dinner. After dinner at Duke's I had a great night drinking beer out of the refrigerator, reading contracts out of the file cabinet, careful to return them where I'd gotten them. I cleaned up the bathroom and the hallway, listened to records, and finally fell asleep, reading the latest copy of *Billboard*, on the couch.

When I awoke, it was drizzling and just getting light outside. I lit a cigarette, found one of Jim's jackets in the closet, put it on, and locked up the office on my way out. I hung out at Duke's and drank coffee until ten o'clock before going back to the office. Bill was just walking up to the door.

"You're right on time. My secretary can't make it in today. How'd you like to answer the telephones for me?"

"Yeah!"

"Okay, let's get to work."

And so my education in the business of rock and roll began, answering the Doors' manager's telephone. The first call rang as we were walking in. Bill picked it up. He handed it to me. I thought he must want me to handle the first call.

"Doors' office," I said.

"Oh, Danny, I've been worried sick about you."

"Hello, Mom."

"Have you eaten? What are you doing about food?" *Typical Jewish mother*, I thought. *Not how are you or even where did you sleep? Only did my stomach have anything in it?*

"I'm fine, Mom, really. I've actually gained weight, I bet." I told her about Duke's. "You'd love it, Mom. It's practically home-cooked food. It's like a kitchen for musicians around here. The portions are huge—"

She wasn't listening. "You've got to come home. I'm coming to get you."

"You can't! Don't. Not now."

"You're testing me."

69

"I'm not testing you!" I laughed. "I just don't want to leave. I'm having fun. Listen, you know where I am." We had an unwritten understanding. I could do pretty much whatever I wanted as long as she knew where I was. "You can pick me up at five o'clock. I promised Bill I'd work for him today since his secretary ain't coming in." I gave her directions to the office. "Not before five, Mom."

Typically she was there an hour early, waiting in the parking lot, nursing her new baby, embarrassing the soul out of me. There I sat, diligently working, as my very own mother waited for me not twenty feet away. I only prayed none of the Doors came by. Luckily they didn't.

"When we get home, we have to talk, Danny. We've got to figure something out. We'll all talk nicely and work something out, something we all can live with." Oh, shit, she must have been to the school.

Clarence was waiting in the den. There was a fire. I took it as a bad omen. "If you were my son—"

"Which I'm not." I cut him off.

He frowned at the interruption. "Which you're not, thank God, I'd put you over my knee and beat the living skin off you."

"You'd love to, though, wouldn't you?" I wasn't going to be intimidated.

He just smiled. "Try me."

He reached for his belt.

"Oh, hush up, both of you," my mom interrupted. "We have a proposal for you. The school says something has to be done. They will let you back in, under the condition, and it's very important you understand this, we come to an agreement."

I waited. "You are on probation at school," she continued. "They're making a special exception in your case because they believe you have potential. You've got to understand, if you get in any more trouble, you're going to be sent to a military school." She eyed me carefully to make sure I was listening. "Or you can go see the doctor now and start this medication we're all certain will make life easier for you." I stiffened.

It was time for something desperate. Time to make my move.

"Okay. I'm on probation. If I screw up again, I'll go see the doctor." It was a stall. But it might work. It had to. Military school was unthinkable. A dozen Clarences five times a day, twenty-four hours a day. What's more, short hair, and I'd probably have to carry a gun. Worse, no Doors. I wasn't delighted with the option of being forced to take any pills either.

I decided to put off both for as long as possible. The stall worked. I was off the hook. For how long I had no idea.

CHAPTER THREE

. . . .

**Natural child/terrible child
Not your mother's or your father's child
You're our child/
Screamin' wild . . .
Wild Child . . .**

—THE DOORS

WITH a rapidly developing ability to attract good luck, I made it through school and into summer vacation. Military school and Ritalin still hung over my head, but for the time being I'd escaped them. Nevertheless, when school began in the fall, they were the threats, as I called them, or the alternatives, as my parents called them. Now another issue awaited me. Without school as a diversionary tactic, someone had to come up with another option quickly. Otherwise, they were certain (and not incorrect) I would be spending all my time up in Hollywood under the dubious influence of the Doors.

Everyone had a notion about what to do with the "problem." Mom and Clarence voted for summer school, basically more of the same lousy thing I'd just gotten out from under. Thankfully the school didn't want to take me. "Give us a break," it asked my mother. "You take him, it's your turn," or words to that effect. That stumped that side of the family, and it was beginning to look like freedom for me.

The Doors were going to be in and out of town a lot, and Evan was keeping busy promoting concerts at the Shrine Exposition Hall, L.A.'s Fillmore. He'd offered me a summer job, which included free tickets and passes in exchange for putting posters and flyers around town for the concerts he'd booked. Among the groups scheduled to appear were the Doors.

Also, I'd been picked for the all-star team, as shortstop and leadoff batter. This was the only non rock 'n' roll activity I approached with any enthusiasm whatsoever. I thought it was going to be a cool summer all right, what with the concerts, the all-star games, and watching the Doors.

My father had some ideas of his own. His definition of the problem was simple. He blamed rock 'n' roll: we wild boys and girls obeying no authority and bearing no responsibility, playing havoc with America in a mindless quest for the good time we wrongly believed was owed to us by the world. My father was no fool. He knew what was going on. The rub was I didn't believe him.

"That goddamn music gets you all excited, and then you can't calm down enough to behave yourself like a rational human being. Then you go to that Doors place, and I know there's dope there, I wasn't born yesterday."

"No, there's not!" I argued. "Honest, there's no dope there," and I tried to convince him it was not only a safe environment but a healthy one. "You should see all the stuff I'm learning about the rock business," I said. He didn't want to listen. He didn't want to understand. I was certain if he could just meet them and see for himself, he'd feel different. For the time being I gave up trying to convince him, and I decided to let it ride.

But he wasn't going to let anything ride. He thought he not only had the problem pegged but also thought he had the solution.

Up at his house on Father's Day I answered the doorbell to find a handsome, blue-eyed, white- and wavy-haired gentleman who introduced himself as Manny. He looked familiar, but I couldn't place where I'd seen that face before. "Hey, Dad, there's some guy here with a buncha film stuff," I yelled to my father, who was in the room at the other end of the house, watching a ball game. He yelled back to me to let the man inside. "Okay," I hollered back to him, "he's inside." When my father didn't come out to the living room to meet him, it puzzled me at first, but then I began to realize it wasn't my father this man was interested in.

"That's okay, we can start without him," Manny told me as he began to set up the equipment.

"Do I know you?" I asked him, still trying to place the face.

"Not that I know of," he replied.

My father finally came in; with his hairy body and boxer shorts and skinny legs, he still managed to make a formidable impression.

He walked over to Manny, introduced himself, and they shook hands. Suddenly I remembered where I'd seen that face before. "Hey, Dad," I said, "doesn't he look just like Timothy Leary?"

"See what I mean," my father said to Manny. "The kid's thirteen years old, and his whole universe revolves around that rock and roll crap." I had a bit of an instinct to run—the old fight-or-flight impulse. But I resisted, curious about the film equipment and what this Manny was going to show with it.

"What we have," Manny explained, "is a summer camp in the High Sierras. It's right on Huntington Lake." He turned out the lights and let the projector roll as he talked over the pictures. "Each camper has his own horse to ride and take care of," he said as footage of snowcapped peaks panned down to kids riding horses joyfully through a grassy meadow. "There's also water-skiing," Manny continued. Cut to pictures of kids my age being pulled along by an awesome speedboat. "We actually have an island in the middle of the lake where you stay during your skiing instructions." Cut to a log cabin and campers and a cool-looking counselor serving hotcakes. "We specialize in sports and outdoor activities.

"Well, Danny, what do you think?" Manny asked me. "How'd you like to join us this summer for two months?"

"It looks great. I'm sure it's a wonderful place and those pictures are real and not staged. But I can't make it this summer," I told him, which wasn't what Dad wanted to hear.

"You don't know what you're talking about!" Dad yelled at me. "This is the best camp in the country. It's the best thing for a kid your age that money can buy. It's the best, most exclusive camp there is. It's got the best, smartest kids in the world going up there, and you're going to be one of them. Hell, I'd like to spend two months up there this summer."

"Well, Dad, you should go in my place 'cause I can't go anywhere this summer." That wasn't the right thing to say either.

"Oh, yeah, what else do you got that's better? If you think I'm going to stand by while you run wild in Hollywood every day with people twice your age, who do nothing but use you, you're crazy. This is just the thing you need. Outdoors with other kids your own age, activities to channel all that goddamn energy of yours. It'll be great for you." He was really working himself up. "You should be thankful I have the money to send you to this camp." He turned to Manny and said, "Sign him up. He'll be there."

Manny left, and Dad turned his attention back to me. "I've already put down a deposit of five hundred dollars to hold you a place there, and it's nonrefundable. The decision has been made, Danny. You're as good as gone. You have no choice."

I panicked. "But I'll miss the all-star game, Dad. You don't want me to miss the all-star game." I tried to appeal to his paternal instincts. He loved baseball. It was the one thing I did well that he was really proud of. "We could go to the state championships. It's a great team—"

"Then they'll just have to make it there without you because camp starts in two weeks and you'll be in the High Sierras having the time of your life by then."

"And what if I don't go?"

"Then you're gonna be the first teenager in orbit."

I decided to try another tactic. Dad had played baseball. He'd understand team commitment. "But the team needs me! I'm the only shortshop they got!"

"You're nuts. Get outta here. The team will survive. I don't want to talk about it anymore—my ulcer's killing me. You're going, and that's that, if I have to drag you down to the train station personally and hire somebody to sit on you the whole ride there."

For the same reasons my father wanted me gone, I wanted to stay right where I was. It was the first glint of the summer of 1967, goddamnit; things were jumping into high gear and I sure didn't want to be hijacked up to some gold-plated adolescent wimp colony five hundreds miles away from where the nearest action was, tied to a redwood tree, or skipping up a hill playing John Muir or Daniel Boone or whatever it was they were going to expect from me up there.

Unless once there I took off from Redwood City and headed west across the state of San Francisco and Haight/Ashbury, I was gonna miss out on all the fun.

Besides driving me to the train, Dad gave the train conductor fifty bucks to make sure I didn't get off before Fresno, which was where the camp bus picked me up to take me to Huntington Lake. I was incapable of doing anything about it, too. Boy, was I depressed. I was so sad I didn't know I was getting mad until a good six hours later, by which time it was definitely too late to do anything, making me even angrier. By the time the train pulled into Fresno, I was one upset youngster.

"This had *better* be good," I told the camp representative there to meet us.

He was all jolly and happy. "Oh, you'll absolutely love it." During the ride into camp he kept trying to open my head up and get me to talk, only I wasn't biting.

All I kept saying was: "This had *better* be good."

He got sick of being Mr. Nice Guy and said back, "Yeah? And what if it isn't? What are *you* gonna do about it?"

For the first time that day I brightened up. "The possibilities," I assured him, "are endless."

To tell you the absolute truth, camp wasn't that bad. It wasn't where I wanted to be, but for a while I managed to forget that fact and get on with the business at hand. The camp population was a veritable who's who of celebrity kids. Don Knotts's kid was there; so was Debbie Reynolds and Eddie Fisher's kid. Gregory Peck had sent his son, and Ken Venturi, the golf pro, had signed his kid up, too. And there were some congressmen's kids and all sorts of child actors. The kid who did the voice for Linus on *Charlie Brown* became a good buddy. One of Dad's best friends, Steve Crane (who owned the Luau, my favorite restaurant, and had been married to Lana Turner), had sent his son Steve Crane Jr. there. All these kids were very civilized and very well behaved. Borderline pussies, if you really want to know. Nobody smoked. Nobody drank. Archery, which I hated, was a favorite sport. Whines went up when the ski boat went too fast, and protests rang out when I'd kick a horse into a gallop and all the others in line would kick up and follow.

Other than that, we were a great bunch of kids in a great camp. We knew how to act privileged. It was the old unspoken agreement: Aren't we lucky? Well, I still didn't feel lucky. I felt more trapped than lucky.

One night around the campfire someone brought out a transistor radio and turned it on to the local pop station. A familiar sound came to my ears. It was the Doors! My adrenaline started pumping. I ordered the kid to turn it up and everyone else to shut the fuck up. We caught only the end of the song. The DJ came on and said, "That was by a new group out of L.A. called the Doors with a song called 'Light My Fire,' this week the number one song in the country." I couldn't believe my ears. I was trembling with excitement. Number one. The Doors. "I know them," I told anyone who cared to listen and quite a few who didn't. It's kind of hard to impress someone whose father or mother impresses everyone else. I was impressed, though. Excited, too—much too excited to fall asleep.

One of the major camp taboos was to take out a boat without permission. Going across the lake to the civilized area was strictly verboten. But I had already learned the lesson that it's much easier to apologize than it is to get permission, as I reminded myself as I crawled out of the sleeping bag, out of our cabin, and down to the lake. My idea was to go to Lakeshore City, across the lake about two miles, and call Evan or Bill from there. None of the powerboats had any keys in them, so I had to take one of the canoes. The idea of paddling for two hours didn't really appeal to me, and to complicate matters, it was beginning to rain. It was difficult to make the lights out across the lake, but I figured if I just aimed the canoe straight across, I'd hit it, no problem.

Midway across Huntington Lake on this cold, overcast night, the drizzle kicked up into a full-blown storm. The lake started getting rough, and for every ten feet I traveled, I was thrown back five, and the water from the lake and the water coming from the sky were getting wilder and wilder. It took me about four hours to make it over to the café with the phone booth at Lakeshore. And by the time I arrived, my shoulders were killing me and the rain was coming down in blankets and sheets. I was cold, wet, but undaunted and went straight to the phone booth and called Evan collect at home. He wasn't in. I tried Bill at home. He wasn't home either. Then I loaded in about six dollars in quarters and dialed the office; the service answered, and I left a message to say I called, and "Congratulations on 'Light My Fire' being number one, and I'll see you guys as soon as possible." Because of the storm, I didn't even try to go back across the lake and instead went inside the all-night café to stay warm and drink hot chocolate until the weather cleared up. At dawn I climbed back in the canoe and began the water crawl back to the campgrounds. This trip it took me only two hours or so, and it was 8:30 A.M. when I arrived back at camp.

Nobody was at the cabin. *Must be at the mess hall*, I thought, but nobody was there either. Strange. Where was everybody? It took me a half hour to locate over a hundred campers and twenty-five staff people. Everybody was gathered at the amphitheater grounds. They were holding church services. Of course, it was Sunday. Being Jewish, I felt like a sort of spy. Very reverently I tiptoed closer to the ceremony and hid behind a tree; careful not to interrupt Manny's solemn concentration, I listened in. They were praying! Manny had his foot up on a rock and his head bowed, hands clasped, eyes closed. They all had their heads bowed, eyes closed, and hands clasped, sitting on the log pews as Manny led them in a prayer. His wife, Edith, was sobbing quietly into a handkerchief. Something bad had happened. I listened in.

"Our Father in heaven, we pray to thee, let our fellow camper be found and safe. Please, Lord, help us to find him safe from harm."

Obviously someone was out looking for me and just as obviously hadn't found me and therefore concluded I might be dead, maybe not, probably so, or close.

What a stupid misunderstanding. I strode down the dirt aisle to the front row and bowed my head in prayer, hoping maybe Manny'd see me and feel better. He finally finished the prayer, asking God to watch over the other campers and thanking Him for the bountiful life we all had and asking Him one more time for me to be found safe from harm. He opened his eyes, and I waved to him. Hi, Manny, don't worry anymore.

But he wasn't pleased to see me at all. I'd never seen anyone go from so solemn to so pissed in my life. What was he so mad at? Had he looked at things differently, he might have seen it as an instant miracle.

"Where the hell have you been?" he yelled. The amphitheater was silent. "We've been going crazy looking for you all night and all morning long. We thought you were dead!" Now I was really embarrassed. He had obviously jumped to a stupid conclusion and acted on it in front of the whole world to see. Then here I came and showed up, and he felt like a real asshole, so he was taking it out on me. I understood perfectly, and I let him rant and rave until he was done. "I'm sorry," I said. "I didn't mean to worry anybody."

He dragged me into his office and called my father, who was furious now, too. One moment everyone is crying about your being possibly dead, and the next moment everyone is pissed with you for being alive. It is a very uncomfortable and unwanted feeling.

Manny wanted to know where I'd been, I told him to Lakeshore, and that was enough for him. He wanted to know what I had done there, and I told him I had some hot chocolate and called some friends, waited for the storm to pass, then came back, and here I was. "You coulda gotten killed!" he yelled at me.

"Well, obviously that isn't the case," I pointed out to him.

He looked at me like I was certifiably nuts. "You are an idiot, Danny Sugerman."

I looked him in the eye and said, "I've heard that one before."

My father wasn't going for the story. "Who the hell were you calling at three o'clock in the morning?"

"Friends," I said.

He still wasn't buying it. "What friends? What was so goddamn important you had to take a goddamn canoe two miles across a lake in a storm and call Los Angeles, six hundred miles away, before the crack of dawn?!"

"You don't want to know the answer to that question, Dad. You really don't want to know."

"I'm sure you're right! I'm sure I don't, but you're going to tell me anyway."

"You don't, I promise, you don't."

"*Goddamn it, Danny,*" he screamed at me from Beverly Hills. "*Answer me!*"

I took a deep breath and told him. "Dad?" I asked. "Dad, say something." Which was stupid. I didn't want to hear what he was going to say either.

"Don't start that bullshit with me again," he hissed. "I don't want to hear about it. Forget about it, Danny. Drop it. You're up there to get away from that crap." I promised him I would. I told him no one was home when I called anyway.

He was semiplacated. Now everyone had to decide what the punishment was going to be. I knew this period of suspense all too well. I suggested a couple of possible alternatives. We could forget the whole thing. . . . it won't happen again . . . paddling for six hours in a storm-thrown lake was punishment enough . . . send me to the cabin for the day, I'm tired anyway. The staff took a vote, and it seemed it was example time for me again. "We're sending you home." I looked at them like they were nuts. That wasn't punishment. That was what I wanted. So they wouldn't get suspicious, I figured I better play along.

"Are you positive you want to do that?" I asked them, secretly hoping they did. They said they were sure, and I didn't push the matter any further.

They packed me off with a refund check for my father, and the same counselor who picked me up drove me back to the train station. My father would be waiting for me in L.A., and he wasn't going to be happy to see me. I turned on the car radio to take my thoughts off my imminent dismemberment.

Dad was waiting at the same train station he'd dropped me off at only three weeks earlier. We drove home in silence. After the hourlong drive we pulled up to his house. My father yanked the bags out of the Rolls and carried them inside, where he retired to his bedroom and turned on the television.

I hadn't ever thought too much about the presence of God, but what happened next certainly got me to wondering that maybe there was something to this God and fate stuff after all. The moment I walked into Dad's bedroom, Ed Sullivan had just finished introducing the Doors "performing their number one hit single, 'Light My Fire.' " Dad aimed the remote control at the song. "Don't turn, don't turn, please don't turn it, Dad, watch it, who knows? You might like it."

Jim was so hot you could see him steaming, a real live wire, writhing and twisting, ready to explode. Damp curls of long hair fell about his face with its broad jaw and old eyes. Dirty white shirt cuffs poked out from a tight black leather jacket. He jumped and moaned and groaned and sang "Light My Fire" with a gigantic hard-on straining inside his black leather pants; he leaned into the camera, eyes clamped shut, pleading, intense. I was, of course, delighted. It was unexpected and thoroughly enjoyed. I actually felt what might be called blessed for the first time in my life and with my very own father there to witness this miracle. I turned to him expectantly after the song finished. He gave me his I'm-trying-to-remain-calm look, and I knew I was in for trouble.

"So that's your new buddy, huh? Great. My youngest son's hero is a sex pervert. Listen, do me a favor, stay away from that guy, willya?"

I was understandably disappointed in my father's failure to appreciate the Doors, his inability to share my pleasure. I wanted everybody to partake as freely of the Doors' tree as I did. But I wasn't so stupid as to show my disappointment. Instead, I said, "Sure, Dad, it's over, forget it." I mean, after all, how was he going to find out any different?

Fifteen minutes later the Doors were back performing "People Are Strange." We'd been watching the ball game, but it was a commercial break, so we really caught this one by luck. Maybe this time he'd see the light. My faith was getting stronger by the minute. I hadn't heard the song before. It must have been the new single they had talked about releasing in front of their second LP, *Strange Days*, which they'd finished recording just a few months before. Where "Light My Fire" was intense and celebratory, "People Are Strange" was somber and eerie. Jim kept his eyes closed nearly the whole time, refusing to confront the world, but his presence was no less strong, his threat no less real. The sullen emotion in his voice, as I heard it in front of my father, made me realize it would never work: My father would never accept Jim. I couldn't put my finger on it, but where my father prided himself on being in control, Jim prided himself on his ability to be out of control. Where my father believed in family, materialism, security, and self-respect, Jim was hedonistic, a self-proclaimed sybarite and proud of it. My father disliked hedonists immensely and was not ashamed of it. He was establishment in capital letters. Jim was an anarchist and was proud of it. Yet, even with all this going against it, I still hoped my dad could learn to like the Doors or at least could understand and accept my attraction to them. It would mean he understood and accepted me. His refusal to do so, in my eyes, was tragic. By rejecting Jim, he was also rejecting me.

I also hoped Jim would like my father. It was important to me that Jim see and accept that I was my father's son and therefore shared his strength and power. Someday, I prayed to my newfound faith, the two would meet and we all would laugh together.

"People Are Strange" ended. Dad clicked off the television with the remote control, and glared at me.

"Listen, Danny, I'm not asking you, I'm telling you: Stay away from that guy. I don't want you to see any of them anymore. I've got some experience in this world that you haven't got. You listen to me. I'll turn your kneecaps into Frisbees if I find out you're hanging around with them."

This was obviously not the reaction I had been hoping for, but I bit my lip, threw a curse at God for His lousy sense of timing, and I told my father that night in his bedroom I would not see Jim Morrison and the Doors anymore.

But I think we both knew better.

I hadn't been back in school a month and already my behavioral shit was hitting the disciplinary fan. As with all new semesters, I began this one with hopes high, resolving to behave, do my homework, get to class on time, and stay there for the full period.

Actually the teachers themselves (if they hadn't had me in their class before) started off with expectations equally high. Years before they had my brother, then my sister exercise their impeccable scholarly expertise, achieving top grades and hovering in the upper stratosphere of learning and comprehension.

"Well, you're certainly not stupid," they observed. It could get really tough on occasion when they'd decide they'd be the one to bring to fruition all this "potential." Unfortunately they never did; worse still, their failure to do so meant my failure in their classes.

Whenever members of a teaching staff tell any kid he's not "living up to his potential," what they're really saying is they haven't been able to make him do what they want, that *they're* failing with him, not the other way around. That way it puts the burden on the kid's shoulders, not theirs. It's quite a sleazy, if not genuinely mean, move to pull.

I tried not to resent Nan's or Joe's achievements in school. Still, I didn't appreciate it that my sister had recently been accepted into UCLA or that my brother was planning on medical school. The events conspired with everything else to make both my present and my future more difficult. I took both their efforts as a personal affront.

I was still making the trek to Hollywood whenever possible, doing my level best to keep up appearances at home and school. That meant covering my absences in school and getting home in time for dinner. Before long the teachers began to notice my repeated absences, and despite my strongest efforts, my cover-up began to unravel. It was too much pressure anyway—keeping it away from the family and school. Not just parents and teachers either but the kids, too. They didn't believe I even knew the Doors, and that was getting to be a real drag, a constant source of embarrassment I was powerless to change. It's no fun when everyone thinks you're a liar, especially when you're just a teenager, which I was beginning to regard as something akin to a prolonged case of temporary insanity.

"Hey, Sugerman! Where were ya yesterday? Seein' *the Doors* again?" someone would shout, and everyone would rudely laugh and giggle and maybe flip the finger at me. And that was just the guys.

The girls weren't what I'd call generous in their appraisal either. "Tell Morrison I said hi!" One day Lisa Millward said in front of practically everybody, "Why don't you get me Jim Morrison's home phone number? Then we'll believe you." I tried to explain to them that Jim didn't have a home phone number, that he was staying in a hotel, but no one was listening. Everybody was too busy laughing at me.

Some days I'd start off toward school, and just the thought of what lay ahead would nauseate me so much I'd have to turn around at the gate and hitch to the Doors' office instead.

The teachers started demanding excuses. For a while I covered myself with a rather ingenious combination of lies and forgeries. In the past two weeks I'd been able to get away only once. It occurred to me I was going to have to start coming up with some better excuses. I hadn't even bothered checking in at homeroom this particular day. Tomorrow I'd either have to face the consequence or not bother showing up, and that would just postpone the inevitable.

I was sitting on the steps outside the rehearsal room, leading up to the Doors' office, trying to figure out what I was going to do. Jim Morrison stepped out of the room and asked me if I'd mind getting us both a beer. I jumped up and dashed upstairs, knocked on Bill's door, got the "come in" I was waiting for, and grabbed two big Coors out of the refrigerator. "One's for Jim," I told Bill, not wanting him to think I was stealing beer or taking advantage of his hospitality or anything along those lines.

Jim had come upstairs and was shuffling through a magazine when I handed him his beer.

"Is it just my imagination," he asked me, "or have you been coming around here less? It's been so quiet lately."

"Fucking school is worse than prison," I said, popping open the beer.

"You mean, you *do* go to school?"

"Oh, yeah, sure, I go. I just don't always stay."

83

"You mean, they just let you walk out?"

"Well, no. Not exactly." I explained to him how, to get out of class, I'd been having a lot of close family members dying. He looked at me oddly, but he understood what I was talking about.

"Which means there must be a lot of funerals you're required to attend."

"That's right. So there have been an unusual amount of deaths in the family lately. The problem is I think they're getting hip to that ruse. I've used it at least once on each teacher. Besides that, I'm running out of relatives to knock off."

"Ya think they're getting suspicious, huh?"

"Yeah, I think so, but see, I'm not sure *they're* sure. I think maybe they also feel kind of sorry for me, so they don't really push the issue. I usually have a sixth sense about this sort of thing, and I don't think I can take it any further without getting busted."

Jim stared at his beer as if making up his mind about something. "You want to know what I used to tell my teachers?" he finally asked me.

"Yeah, I could use some new ideas."

"This is a good one. You should use it. It used to work for me. I used to tell 'em I had to go in for surgery."

"Surgery? You mean *your* surgery?" I'd told one of my teachers I had to visit my grandfather in the hospital before he was operated on, to set the stage for his imminent funeral, but this was something completely different here.

Jim was laughing as he remembered. "Yeah, man, I'd tell them I had a tumor in my brain, the left hemisphere, in the region of the medulla oblongata. Nonmalignant, of course. I didn't want to make it sound too farfetched."

I looked at him with something akin to awe. "And they believed you?" I asked.

"Sure. They did until one of them got wise and called my mother to inquire how the operation went."

We both laughed. "I'll try it!" I said.

"Go ahead. But you still have to pass your classes. You have to take care of your assignments. I fucked around *a lot*, but I always got good grades, I always read the books. Just because the teachers can't teach and class is a drag doesn't mean you don't need an education. I love history, and literature, too, man; there's some incredible stuff there, fascinating. There're some good books for you to read, and you shouldn't be prejudiced against them just because some teacher said you gotta read them. Read them anyway."

When I bumped into Jim again a few days later, he asked me, "So, how'd it go?"

"Perfect," I told him.

"What did you tell them?"

"Shoulder. Something about X rays."

"Yeah, and it worked?"

"I'm here, ain't I?"

The next time I saw him, a few weeks later, the Doors had just returned from a series of gigs and were getting ready to go out again. Jim stuck his head out of the rehearsal room and, seeing me, asked, "How's it going? What did you use this time?"

"Testes," I said.

"*Testes?*" He guffawed.

"Yeah. Cancer of the testes."

"And they *believed* you?"

"I got two weeks off to recuperate!"

"No shit? See, I told you it'd work."

It was becoming obvious I couldn't keep coming up with these far-fetched excuses much longer. After two weeks off for the cancer pitch, I returned for a few days but couldn't take it any longer and just began staying away, hanging out either at Evan's office, smoking pot and drinking beer, or at the beach, getting high. Then to my dismay I began getting bored and actually started missing school. I wasn't looking forward to my readmission; they weren't going to let me just waltz back into school without any absence slip, no excuse, nothing. Then I was hit with an enlightenment. *What the fuck can they do to me anyway?* They couldn't *make* me go to military school. They couldn't *make* me take a pill. I decided to call their bluff. Besides, I really wanted to get through the ninth grade. My mother and father naturally expected me to as well. Even Morrison said only bums drop out.

It was for such marvelous reasons I returned.

"It's nice to see you back with us, Mr. Sugerman," the kind lady in the attendance office said. "Now where is your excuse so we can issue you an absence slip and readmit you?" I told her I had no excuse. "I see here you were gone for two weeks, for which you were qualified." She looked up and inquired, "You're all right now, then?"

"Yes, fine, thanks."

"However, that excuses you for only two weeks. It indicates

here"—she moved her finger down the page—"you are unexcused for, why, practically a week and a half!"

"Time sure flies when you're having fun," I mumbled.

"I guess it must," she said. "Well, I can't resolve this for you, I'm afraid. I simply can't readmit you without a reason." I had a million reasons, but I didn't think she was about to buy any of them. "I'm sorry, Mr. Sugerman, but I'm going to have to ask you to wait and speak with your counselor."

Mr. Kortick, who was my English teacher, one of the few classes I did well in, was also my ninth-grade counselor.

"I've been expecting you." He welcomed me. His face was in a file. He looked up smiling. "So, how was the surgery?"

"Fine. Fine."

"No complications?" He grinned.

"No. None," I told him, "everything went fine."

"All right. That takes care of the first two weeks. Let's hear your excuse for this last week and a half."

"I don't have one."

"I don't believe it."

"It's true. I just didn't want to come to school."

"Nobody wants to come to school at your age. But they still do. It's expected of them. It's their responsibility."

"I know that now. I really do, sir. I realize that. That's why I'm back."

He let out a long breath and asked me if I was back to stay.

"Yes, sir, I am."

"I hope so. I'm going to let you back in this time. I'll cover for you. You try taking a vacation like this in the middle of the semester again, and it's out of my hands, and God help you with Mr. Tanner. I shouldn't be doing this at all. Next time I won't, and you'll be on your own."

"Well, I appreciate it, Mr. Kortick, I really do."

"I hope so. You know, I should lecture you, but somehow I doubt if it would do any good. Jesus, is school really so boring for you that you can't find anything about it you like?"

"Yes, sir. But I'll find something, I promise, I will. I'll try, Mr. Kortick. Honest I will."

I did try. I really did. I stayed in class and away from the Doors' office. I read the assignments and did the homework, and I hated every single second of it. "You have a horrible attitude problem," the teachers told me and they were right. But I was staying there. I was doing it, and I was absolutely miserable. The pain has to come out somewhere, doesn't it? Sure, it does. It came out right there, in the classroom. I insulted the kids. I ridiculed the teachers. I started coming to class stoned on pot, refusing to speak at all. It was as if I were punishing them for making me be there. Then an interesting phenomenon began happening. The teachers began *inviting* me to leave. "I won't report you," one said. I was sure it was a trick. "You're free to go anytime. The sooner, the better." It might have been a trick, I concluded, but at least I had witnesses.

I wasn't into my new routine for more than a month when my math teacher sent me up to Tanner's office for simply showing up one day. I tried to reason with her.

"He'll expel me. You don't understand!" I told her.

"Good," she said, writing out the warrant and thrusting it at me.

"What have I done wrong?"

"Ha, what have you done right is more like it."

"But you can't!" I almost yelled at her.

"Don't you raise your voice at me, young man. I can and I will."

"Ah, go fuck yourself, you old twat," I told her when I realized there was no reasoning with her.

She snatched back the warrant and added, "Cussing in class."

I marched myself up to Tanner's office. To my surprise and relief, he let me off. Being in an expansive mood, he told me as much. "I'm in too good a mood today to let you ruin it, Sugerman. Go to lunch and then to your next class, and don't let me see you up here again."

The very next day the history teacher had two students personally escort me to Mr. Tanner's door for telling the class KKK stood for KoKaine Karma.

"Sugerman, you wear me out."

It was in actuality a tactic I hadn't thought of yet, and I wasn't too sure if I was glad it was working.

"I know the trouble you're in better than you do, and I want you to know I'm on your side. Listen, you're a smart kid. Surely you appreciate the position you're putting me in. Lookit, I know you took the rap for your friends on that little explosives experiment—that goes to show you're a good kid."

"You mean I'm a stupid kid."

"No. That's not what I mean. You're loyal, if nothing else. I don't know what your problem is, but I know stupidity isn't it. As much as I hate to admit it, we're very close to where we were last year. You've got one more chance to straighten out. What you do with it is up to you. You're back on probation. So much as one more violation and you're gone. Do we understand each other?" I assured him we did, hoping to get off with a lecture.

"Now you know what we have to do," he said as if reading my mind. He walked over to his closet and took out his ass whacker. I walked over to his desk and leaned over, holding the corners. "Your toes," he said. I was stiff and couldn't reach down that far, but he helped me by placing his large man's hand on my young boy's back, folding me in half. Holding my back down with one hand, he pulled his paddle back with the other and spanked me red-hot for what felt like a solid ten minutes. He was out of breath when he finally finished. I wanted to kick his nuts up through his hairy noseholes.

At home, it wasn't going much better. Clarence caught me red-handed as I attempted to perfect Morrison's leap and fall during "The End," blaring full bore from the stereo. As Jim sang, "Father, 'yes, son,' I want to kill you; Mother, I want to . . . Aarrgghhh" and then screamed out "Fuck you" and tumbled to the stage, I was practicing the same before my full-length dressing mirror. Clarence had been standing just outside the door, peeking inside, chuckling to himself, no doubt, as I confirmed his certainty I was a human of inferior quality and questionable sanity as I solemnly intoned the "Killer awoke before dawn, he put his boots on" segment. The scene apparently ceased to be funny when his ears picked up the "Father" gambit, and even less so when Jim finished his Oedipal drama, so by the time I finished my leap and landed on my side on the floor, groaning into the imaginary microphone, and Clarence crashed in, he was not in what I would call an entertained mood.

His entrance caught me totally off guard. Surprised and embarrassed, I lay there, pretending nothing was out of the ordinary. I just happened to be lying on the floor. Clarence stood directly above me and, after shutting off the stereo, started yelling.

"You're a goddamn freak!" He shook his head. "Look at you. You belong in a circus. You parade your goddamn freak show right here under my roof, and I won't have it. Have you *no* shame? From now on I want you to stay away from everybody in this house. You're not fit to associate with them. You're sick, boy." Then he turned to leave, growling, "You're sick, and I don't want you infecting this household. Now I mean it—you stay away from my kids!"

It didn't take too long before word of my little dramatic recitation had made it through the rest of the family. The image of a Junior High school student singing about killing Dad and shtuppin' Mom didn't go down real well with anyone, least of all the father and mother.

"You're really beginning to worry me, Danny," Mom told me the next morning. "Please don't spend any more time with the Doors for a while." I looked at her in disbelief. Mom, too.

"But it's only a song!"

"That song," she told me, "has your stepfather and me very upset."

"Oh, for chrissakes," I said, "I'm sorry." She suggested it might be a good idea if I went to see a psychiatrist.

"For what?" I asked.

"Isn't there anything on your mind you might want to talk to somebody about?" she asked.

"No, nothing. I'm fine, Mom, really. Don't worry."

Back in school I found myself becoming increasingly frustrated with this inability to conform. It did sound easy. I looked around me: Other kids were able to do it simply enough. "You're not trying," they said when the awful truth was I didn't know how. To their surprise, I agreed.

My history and math teachers had stopped bothering to report my absences. I didn't even have to show up to their classes. What about the others? They'd probably gone ahead and reported me as "absent without excuse." But even that could be dealt with. Report cards were coming out, and I not only had to show up but had to suffer the humiliation of taking my card around, getting it graded and signed.

Then I had to bring the bad news home for a parent's perusal. My mother looked at the double row of *U*'s in the cooperation and work habits columns; the double-digit numbers in the "Absent" and "Tardy" columns; the two fails, three *D*'s, and one *A* (in phys ed). The comments were almost worse than the grades.

"What if I refuse to sign this?" Mom asked me.

"I don't know. The authorities come and take me away?"

"Don't joke," she said.

"C'mon, Mom, this isn't that serious. It's not like I've totally flunked ninth grade, ya know."

"This *is* serious," she said very sadly. "I don't think you know how serious this is."

"Well, it's not the end of the world, is it?" I asked her, trying to lighten up what was becoming a rather gloomy afternoon.

"You know, maybe I am too permissive with you. I'm afraid if I try to lay down the law, then you won't even bother checking in with me. I'll never know where you are or what you're doing. Maybe I overdid it." She checked to make sure I wasn't judging her. "Giving you too much slack," she added.

"No, Mom, you didn't. You did okay. I'm fine. Honest."

But reassurance wasn't enough. "Lookit, Danny, I know it hasn't been a picnic around here," she said in what amounted to the grandest understatement between us in my whole life spent communicating with her. "I always felt like you were entitled to get out of the house. I not only permit you to get away with it but enable you. Maybe I'd better stop. Maybe I shouldn't have allowed you to go out to that concert in the first place. Maybe things would be different now."

"No, Mom, please don't say that. That was the best thing that ever happened to me. Don't ever blame yourself for that. I don't care about all the trouble breaking out. The music makes the trouble bearable; it makes life endurable. You did the right thing. I'd have gone anyway, you know that."

She nodded. "Get me a pen" was all she said, and she signed the tragedy.

It was cold and overcast while I waited for the bell to ring signaling the end of phys ed. A bunch of us were standing on the asphalt behind the painted yellow line we weren't supposed to step over. I was wearing the sheepskin-lined leather jacket of Morrison's that I'd borrowed from the office. I couldn't take it home because I knew I'd be tempted to tell someone where it came from. Naturally in school I'd been unable to keep from mouthing off about whom the jacket really belonged to.

All the guys from PE class were standing around when this one dickhead who was always hassling me about knowing the Doors decided it would be a good time to hassle me some more. A lot of guys had been stepping over the forbidden yellow line, testing the teacher's aide whose job it was to keep us behind the line. The aide was trying to talk them into stopping it when this guy I was talking about pushed me out over the line, hoping I'd get caught. I gave him a good push back, and he fell down on his ass. From this position, sitting on the ground, he spit a good looger five feet, splattering the jacket.

I challenged him to a fistfight after school. "Why after school?" this dickhead asked. "Why not right now?" I explained I can't, we would get caught, and I can't get in any more trouble. Unfortunately he knew that, which is why he wanted to fight right away. Everybody started calling me chicken and pushing me around and calling me names and making rude remarks about the jacket. "Morrison's a faggot. . . . You're a faggot," he chided. "It's a girl's jacket. Lookit, it's got fur inside!"

"You got fur inside your brain," I informed him, shoving him away.

We were yelling at each other face-to-face and pushing each other away. I said, "Get away."

He said, "Come on, chickenshit," and he finally hauled off and slugged me with a fist, hard, right on the side of the head, which hurt pretty bad and pissed me right off. I lost control and started really hitting the guy as hard as I could. We were really going at it, and all the guys were screaming for their favorite. I finally got him a few feet away from my body. That's when I took another step and a half back and jumped in the air toward him, left foot first, right foot following, giving him the old flying jump-kick from my wrestling days. It landed right where it should, against his temple, one foot after the other. Whack-whack. He didn't know what hit him. Unfortunately I proceeded to land and fall on my face. But the jump-kick had done its job. He was down and bleeding quite a bit from the region around his nose and ear. I felt myself being picked up, not by supporters but by two of the PE teachers, who dragged me into their office.

They thought I'd been beaten up bad enough already, so they weren't going to beat me up anymore. I knew they were going to report me, though. I felt fortunate not to be getting swats from them, and I was prepared to let it go at that. They had someone from the nurse's office tend to a few of my cuts. Actually I felt pretty good. I'd won my first genuine fight, and everybody had seen it.

In math class, three days after the fight, I was called to the front of the class by the teacher. Smiling, she handed me a pink slip of paper. Orange was from the attendance office. Red was from the counselor. Pink was from the boys' vice-principal, Mr. Tanner. *Oh, shit,* I thought. I may have even said it out loud.

The walk up to his office was the closest I'd yet come to feeling like part of a funeral procession. The march ended at Tanner's office door, the same one I'd sat at before in wait of judgment so many times before. Was this the last time? I was pretty nervous about what was going to happen. I knocked on the door.

"Come in."

And there they were. The tribunal, gathered to cast final sentencing: Mother, Tanner, and Father. I knew this was an action called above and beyond the need for simple administration when I saw both Mom and Dad. The two of them hadn't been in the same room at the same time since the divorce. I felt a little glow of pride, just seeing them together and knowing I was the cause. There was little cause for rejoicing, though, and the glow quickly faded. This was no happy reunion. If the walk up was a funeral march, I was now in the coffin. I tried to concentrate on how good it was to see Mom and Dad together again.

"I hope you're happy," Dad said.

I thought I heard Mom sniffle a little.

Tanner relaxed back in his swivel chair, feet up on the corner of his desk, hands folded over his big belly. In his conservative gray suit he could have been an undertaker. He tried to look stern, but to me he just looked real smug.

He cleared his voice.

Here it comes. This is what you have succeeded in avoiding for so long. Judgment Day is here.

"Danny, I've invited your parents so they may be a part of the decision made here today." He reached in his desk drawer and pulled out a sheaf of paper and unraveled it: my school record. "This will follow you around for the rest of your school days," he said, as the computer paper folded across his desk and down on the floor. There didn't look like there was room for much else in there.

He started reading from the list. "Hair too long, too many tardies, disobedient in class, refuses to cooperate, unexcused absences . . ." He continued for a couple of minutes. "Disruptive, ditching, cussing in class . . . Friday before, you were reported for fighting," he finished.

Dad spoke up, "What were you fighting about?" I knew Dad. He was from the old school. If someone started a fight, he wasn't about to blame me for finishing it.

"Someone spit on me," I told him.

"That's all?" he asked. "How do you know he did it on purpose?"

"Because he's a dickhead."

"You must have done something."

I looked at the ground and said nothing.

"Danny has been having trouble with his classmates regarding some rock group he alleges he knows."

This piqued both parents' attention.

"What's that got to do with this?" my father asked, trying to put together the rapidly dropping pieces to the puzzle.

The hammer was going to fall sooner or later, and the suspense was killing me, so I just let zip: "It's Morrison's jacket."

They were speechless, exchanging infuriated, questioning glances that asked, "Did *you* know he was seeing them? *I* didn't know, did *you* know?"

"I thought I told you to stay away from that guy." Dad started to yell.

"You did."

"And you deliberately disobeyed me?"

I didn't want to answer that, so I didn't.

"You're *still* seeing them? When you *knew* how we felt? *Why?* I don't get you sometimes."

"*Because* I knew how you felt. I *knew* you wouldn't let me see them."

Now Mom spoke up for the first time. "You lied to me, Danny."

"I didn't lie, Mom. I just didn't tell you. I didn't want to worry you."

"I think you owe both of us an apology," Mom said.

"An apology, hell, I want an explanation," Dad said.

"But I haven't done anything wrong! If I thought it was wrong, then I wouldn't keep going there. If I really thought it was so wrong and bad, I wouldn't disobey you. I would have told you if you'd asked."

"All right, what else is going on here?" my father wanted to know.

"Danny just can't seem to obey rules. At school and obviously at home. It's gone too far. You're his parents. Something has to be done."

Oh, shit, this is it. I thought about getting sick.

"So what do you propose we do about it?" Dad asked him.

"I don't think there is anything any of us can do about it," Tanner said.

All three of us exclaimed, "Huh!" at once.

"What are you saying? We should continue to let him run wild?" Dad said.

"No. We can't allow that to continue. But the decision about what will be done isn't ours. It's your son's."

All eyes looked at me.

Tanner continued: "We can provide some alternatives, but the choice is his alone. We can't make him do anything."

I couldn't believe my ears. They were admitting it. I'd been trying to show them this very fact ever since I could remember, and now they were all but confessing defeat. For some reason being right wasn't making me feel any better.

"So what's it going to be?" Tanner, still tilted back in his chair and folding up my record, asked me.

"Um . . . what are my choices again?"

"You can transfer to another school, although I doubt a public school will take you, which means military school enrollment. Or we can experiment with this medication that the doctors think will help you behave."

Dad spoke before I could. "That's the easy way out. The kid just has to learn some discipline. You can't just give him a pill and expect everything to go away."

Tanner answered, "It's up to Danny, though, isn't it? If this is going to work, it has to be his choice. We're all agreed on that, aren't we?"

"So what's it going to be, son?" Dad said.

The answer was simple: I chose the drug.

"When?" Tanner asked.

"Whenever."

"I hope it works, for your sake," Tanner said.

"I hope it works for my sake, too," I told everyone. The question as I saw it wasn't, Was I or wasn't I hyperactive, but rather, Would this get everybody off my back? The doctor told me Ritalin would help the symptoms but wouldn't make all my problems go away. That depended on how one defined the problems. If the problem was doing better in school, the Ritalin worked. If the problem was Clarence, well, the Ritalin had no effect on him at all. It did enable me to concentrate better, though. I was able to sit still longer.

Better living through chemistry, they called it. I've got to admit, boy, I was impressed. One little pill, and almost overnight so many things changed. My grades in all areas (*including* work habits and cooperation) began to rise. The teachers had been apprised of the "experiment" and asked to give me another chance, to watch closely for any change. They were astounded with the results and reported miraculous behavioral improvement. I took all the compliments in stride. Mr. Tanner even called up my mother at home, when he hadn't heard from me in over two months, just to make sure if I was all right.

* * *

Everything was more than all right. I was caught up on homework for the first time in my life. School was getting easier. The Doors were allowing me to listen to their rehearsals, which were the highpoint of my week. When they weren't working or were out of town doing gigs, I was up at Evan's. With the aid of Ritalin, I could pull off school and my extracurricular activities, no problem. Yeah, things were rolling along almost too good to be true. Life was good. Even Clarence couldn't fuck up my mood.

I was sitting on the couch up at the Doors' office, thinking such good and comforting thoughts when Siddons stuck his head out of his office and called me in. Probably to congratulate me on the great poster job. Wrong. "This is a place of business," he told me firmly. "It's not a hangout. It's not a clubhouse. I know how important it is to be able to come up here, but it's gone too far. You're getting in the way of office procedure. You've got to cool it. You can't come up here anymore. You can't just expect to drop in and have everybody baby-sit you, goddammit. I don't like saying this, but you aren't welcome anymore. Now, get out of here."

I walked out of his office in a daze, down the stairs, and out to the bus stop in front. I sat down and started to cry. I put my hands over my face and let it flow. I must have been crying like that for a good five minutes before I felt someone's shadow in front of me. I blinked into the figure before the sunlight.

"What's the matter with you? Who died?" asked Morrison.

"No one died," I stammered, choked with tears. "Bill threw me out of the office. He said I get in everybody's way. He said I can't come over anymore." I was sobbing so hard I could barely speak. And just the thought of paradise revoked sent me into another tremor of convulsive chokes and tears.

"Now, hold on a second, just calm down," Jim said, putting his hand on my shoulder. "Listen to me. Bill Siddons works for us. He can't do anything unless we say so."

"Well, he did." I wailed. "He threw me out!"

"Lookit, will ya, just wait here for a minute." He went off in the direction of the office. Midway there, he turned and said, "Don't get on that bus. I mean it. Just sit there and wait."

I'd never been so embarrassed. Crying in front of Jim Morrison. Like a fucking baby.

I waited, beginning to get scared I might be getting in more trouble. Siddons wasn't going to be delighted about my finking on him to Morrison. About ten minutes passed. The door to the office finally opened, and Jim stood at the top of the stairs.

"Hey, you, come here," Jim yelled to me.

I shook my head, afraid to speak, not trusting my voice.

"Come on! Come on up."

I shook my head again. "Bill says I can't!"

Bill was now standing beside Jim.

Jim said something to Bill I couldn't hear.

"It's okay," Bill said. "You can come up."

With head down I returned to the office. If I had a tail, it would have been shoved between my legs. Once inside the office, I noticed six brown grocery bags filled with mail.

"How would you like to work for us?" Jim asked me.

I was still afraid to speak, but I managed to mumble, "I would."

"We've been discussing the possibility of hiring a fan mail outfit, some professional organization, to handle this for us for some time now. I talked to Bill, and he agrees you'd probably do a much better job."

"Think you could handle the responsibility?" Bill asked me.

"I know I could. You wouldn't be sorry, I promise." I wiped my face and eyes.

"Well, you're hired. That settles it," Jim said. "You'll share my desk with me. You can use the two bottom side drawers for your work, and I want you to set anything especially interesting, poetry, for example, aside for me to read. You read them all first, and then you can answer them, all right?"

It was so all right I nearly started bawling all over again; I really wanted to kick myself. Instead, I just sort of hugged Jim. I couldn't help myself. He seemed surprised and patted my head awkwardly. I never wanted to let go of him. I'd never been so happy in my life. If levitation were possible, I'd have done it right there and then.

I pried myself away and headed toward the door; I was so happy I think I was actually skipping. I was almost all the way down the steps when the door opened and Jim yelled down to me, "Hey, dontcha want to know how much you're getting paid?!"

I yelled back, "Fuck, no!"

All this *and* money, too?

CHAPTER FOUR

• • • • • • • • • •

**Are you experienced?
Have you ever been experienced?
—JIMI HENDRIX**

LIFE was maintaining something akin to an even keel. Most of the behavorial difficulties I'd been experiencing cleared up with the new medication, but not all. I was still going to see the Doors whenever possible, but no one seemed to mind. No one was saying anything, that is, including me. (*At least he's doing well in school*, they figured. *Leave well enough alone.*) I wasn't telling my family, and they weren't asking. Nobody wanted to rock the boat.

And then the boat began to rock itself, gently at first.

A host of new, more subtle, and more sinister problems began sprouting up. My hair was growing long, and I was now simply refusing to cut it. I was going to rock concerts every chance I got, and with Evan promoting a half dozen shows a month, that turned out to be pretty often. It was becoming obvious to all I was becoming enamored with rock 'n' roll in general, listening to records nonstop at full volume in my free time and replacing the blank space in my room with new posters. I'd begun smoking pot on a daily basis, and my parents began to surmise as much (despite my protestations of innocence). I was thrown out of a school dance for being drunk.

The boat rocked a little harder.

In school they'd begun harping on me about picking a major. It wasn't that I didn't want to face the future. I just didn't like any of the alternatives they proposed. I knew I wasn't going to make money at something I didn't enjoy. Just the thought of spending the next ten years becoming a lawyer or an accountant or whatever else they offered made me ill physically.

But they insisted I choose.

The boat rocked harder.

What I eventually wanted to do, though I didn't have the nerve to tell anybody, was manage rock bands. I knew I couldn't start right off at the top, but I was willing to work my way up. It might have been Jim Morrison I had chosen for a role model, but it was Bill Siddons's job I wanted. Unfortunately, choosing the rock business as your vocation in 1969 wasn't considered a wise or mature thing to do. It wasn't a decision one bragged about.

It was frustrating. Everybody was telling me I had to do something, and there I sat with my thumb up my ass, knowing what to do but afraid to say.

And the rocking boat started to lurch.

Then I came to the conclusion school was getting in the way of my education. It just wasn't offering me anything I wanted to learn or could use in the real world. In comparison with what I was learning at the Doors' office and working for Evan, school simply wasn't cutting it. I began thinking seriously about not returning to school after I graduated from the ninth grade at the end of the year.

And that's precisely when everybody foresaw an imminent capsize and the whole crew jumped on the deck and told me exactly what they thought.

"You're lazy," said Tanner.

"You can't do anything right anyway," Clarence.

"You'll find something," reassured my mother.

"You'd better find something," warned my father.

"We're going to find you something," said my school counselor.

"You're doing fine," said Morrison. He sounded impatient. "Christ, you know, you're not the only one—you're not alone—dissatisfied with the alternatives offered. It's not your fault; it's society's fault because the bait isn't good enough anymore. And the punishment isn't enough to deter you. I mean, they can swat you until your skin is gone and you won't change. If anything, it just serves to reinforce your determination."

I'd filled Jim in on the major dilemma and the major depression it was causing me. I was hoping he'd confirm my belonging with him, so I'd be free to leave school and come to work full-time for the Doors. I still hadn't clued him in to the Ritalin compromise, and I felt like a major shitheel about that.

"Anyway," he went on, "the problem isn't one of communication, like they think it is. They think we don't hear them. They've communicated fine. What they've said is just unacceptable, and that's why growing up is so hard because now you have to get it on your own. They're screaming, 'Listen! You don't understand! Do it this way.' And we're saying, 'Yes, yes, we do, and it's still unacceptable!' They can't accept that, and you're made to feel somehow deficient. Don't believe it. The people you thought had the answers don't."

"Great. So what am I supposed to do? Something I don't want to do?"

"You don't need to do that, but you don't have to break away from their values entirely yet either. But you do need to realize that they won't necessarily comprehend yours, and it's going to be a fight, and it's important you don't just give up and drop out. Anybody can do that. Take what they have to offer. You can learn from the bad shit, too, you know. Also, your handwriting is really atrocious. You could take some typing courses and get good at that. Shit, I wish I knew how to type. Pick any major; get them off your back. Try and hang in there until you get to college if you can. It gets better; college is a lot freer."

Now I was really in a jam. I couldn't go and split school and expect Jim to give me a full-time job, knowing how he felt. To make matters worse, Dad had decided it was time for him to make a move again. He asked me to come live with him. I guess he figured he was ready to take me on again. The question was: Was I ready for him?

I wanted to go live with him. The thought of having anything even resembling a family made me dramatically nostalgic. Between Mom's loving me and letting me do anything I wanted and Clarence's hating me and not letting me do anything at all, I was slowly but certainly going nuts.

In a state of depression and confusion and with an almost psychotic need to belong, I accepted my father's offer. Of course, I knew how he felt about my rock 'n' roll activities, but I decided I'd just have to be more discreet about my sojourns. In a moment of insanity I thought I could get away with it.

Clarence reacted with something awful close to glee when he heard the news I was moving out. He'd finally gotten what he wanted from the very start—all of us Sugermans out of the house and Mom free to slave uninterruptedly for him and his kids. Mom, on the other hand, didn't take the news of my departure too well. She went on a prolonged crying rip.

By the time my mental clarity returned, I regained my equilibrium, and enlightenment hit, it was almost too late to back out of the deal. Dad wasn't going to let me off the hook so easily. He figured, All right, we tried Ritalin, and it practically backfired; Now we try things my way. That's what he figured, I figured. His way meant: Cut out the Doors, cut out all the so-called corrosive influences, give the kid some stability in their place—home, family, loving discipline—and he'd be fine in no time. Or, as he put it, "Nothing is gonna get better for you until you deserve it, and so far you haven't deserved anything. You've got to make a sacrifice. That's just how life is. You've got to discipline yourself and get into college. You've been coasting, and now you want to quit. If you put one-tenth the energy into school you put into that rock 'n' roll crap, you'd be a straight *A* student. Well, I've got news for you: The fun and games are over, kid. It's time to get to work. You're going to stop running away and face reality. You've been living in a dreamworld, and I'm going to put an end to it."

Had Dad not telegraphed the blueprint for his rehabilitative plans so clearly, and so early, maybe I would have gone ahead and moved in with him. As it happened, the whole prescription sounded so downright unpalatable, so utterly foreign, I couldn't imagine myself abiding by the projected terms. Staying home was a far cry from anything remotely desirable. What Dad was offering was really quite preferable. Even I could see that. But being deprived of my rock 'n' roll, regardless of how improved the accommodations, was unimaginable. There was not an easy solution in sight. So I did what any red-blooded teenager would do in a similar situation: I stalled.

Then, finally and painfully, I had to admit the least difficult and distasteful move to make was no move at all. That's right, stay right where I was. It was ironic, but in order to stay loyal to rock and roll, it meant I had to stay in school, at least for the time being, until the rock world could take me on a full-time basis.

I took a pass on Dad's offer, a move to which he took no small offense, having already begun the process of having his den torn apart and turned into a bedroom for me. He was pissed on a major scale because I hadn't let him know right away but had waited until the last minute.

My father saw the Doors angle right away and called the shot as he saw it: It was just more irresponsible, selfish behavior, and I didn't know what was best for me. He was not pleased and not about to be placated, so I didn't bother to try. The gap between us widened some more, and the lines on either side of that gap became that much thicker and better defined.

Lest you agree with him and think me entirely selfish, allow me to point out in my defense, futile though it seemed on the surface, I just couldn't stand the thought of leaving my mother alone to deal with Clarence's wrath. I ran interference for her, too. Sure, we both got bruised. But all in all, we made a pretty good tag team. We survived. I just couldn't bear the thought of losing my rock 'n' roll *and* leaving Mom alone in that house, too.

I ended up choosing sports as a major. Since I was still playing baseball anyway, I might as well continue on to high school and play on the school team. This move assuaged my father somewhat, but it would still be some time before we were on speaking terms again. He was so seriously pissed off I got debunked from his not inconsiderable will, one reaction I definitely hadn't counted upon.

Frankly I was sorry the whole thing had come up in the first place. Now all I could do was wait for the boat to stop rocking. And don't think everybody else wasn't waiting for the same thing.

I'd begun sneaking out of the house early in the morning, before school, to avoid Clarence. Actually I can't take all the credit for this move. He'd forbidden me entry through his halls until I looked like a "normal human being." In addition to the hair issue was the dress code: no bell bottoms; no leather jackets; no ripped or patched blue jeans; no boots. As long as I continued to dress the way I was dressing and wear my hair the length I was wearing it, he forbade me to be myself in his house. Fair enough. I liked him and his house probably less than he liked me and my presence. Having to face him wasn't my idea of a wonderful way to start the day, either. I much preferred leaving home early, meeting some friends and smoking a joint on the way to school.

Pot made things more interesting for me. I felt freer, less tied to the hassles at home and the expectations from around and beyond. I'd read some literature and heard the news that drugs gave you a "false sense of well-being," which sounded good enough to me. I was interested to learn "peer pressure" led to the use of drugs. I kept waiting for my friends to put the screws to me, but they never did. If anything, if you didn't pay, you didn't play. My mother had warned me not to let my friends influence me. Dad had been worried about the Doors' turning me on for over a year. "Don't let them make it a condition of belonging" was the warning.

Peer pressure. It's a myth. It doesn't exist. The pressure comes from within. It's *me* pressure. *I* want to belong. *They* don't give a fuck whether or not I do what they do. They're probably too worried about who the fuck they are and how they can fit in to be concerned about who they're gonna give free dope to.

Getting high gave me the freedom to be what I wanted, to escape who and where I was. Just the virtue of being loaded made me feel cooler because then other people thought I was and I picked up that reflection of myself in their eyes. Or maybe it was just easier for me to project cool and they picked up on that. That other people didn't think it was cool, weren't impressed at all, but instead condemned it, only enhanced its overall appeal.

103

I liked getting high; I liked smoking dope. I liked the smell. I liked getting it, I liked talking about it, I liked the action, the whole concept of getting high. I liked other people who got high. I liked myself when I was high. I appreciated music more when I was high. With Ritalin's ability to help me concentrate, I even discovered that with a little buzz I actually liked reading.

The Doors had been in the studio recording their third album. I'd hang at Evan's promotional firm once or twice a week and drop by the office to say hi once in a while. I hadn't seen Jim or any of the Doors for a few months. They were in the studio working on the final recording process, the mix. When they were finished, they'd be back at the office for meetings and rehearsals for some live dates. I timed my visit to coincide with their arrival back at the office.

They'd been too busy for the better part of the afternoon to pay me any attention. By late afternoon the final meeting of the day was over, and Jim came out and asked me if he could sit at his desk. I moved to the ottoman in front of the desk.

I waited for him to say something, but he was immersed in some papers. I waited for him to finish, still hoping for some contact. He finally finished with the contract, got up, returned it to Bill, came back to his desk, and picked up a magazine to read.

"Hey, Jim," I said, trying to sound as casual as possible, "I just finished reading my first book."

He gave a small grin. "What d'ya want me to do about it? Send out a press release?"

I went back to work with some mail. Jim put down the magazine.

"Okay, what did you read?"

I told him *Knock on Any Door*, a novel about a tough kid coming of age in South Side Chicago.

"And?" he asked.

"I loved it. I never thought I'd enjoy reading so much."

"How did you choose that particular book? What attracted you to it?"

"I liked the title."

"I mean, what did you like about the book? What impressed you the most?"

"That kid, Nick Romano, he had no fear."

"You remember the recurring phrase from the book?" he asked.

"You mean, 'live fast, die young and have a good-looking corpse'?"

"Very good." He smiled. "The kid's a learner."

"You read it, too?" I asked. I had hoped to turn him on to something for a change. The problem was there didn't seem to be anything he didn't already know.

"Yeah. But listen, as good as it is, it's still a novel. By that I mean, it's not true. It's just fiction."

Jim seemed to be trying to make up his mind about what to say next. He always spoke slowly, choosing each word very carefully, pausing at length between sentences and thoughts. But this was more than a pause. He seemed undecided about something. He waited, looked at me for a while, and then spoke.

"I might be able to turn you on to some books about some real people. If you liked that one, I mean. What I'm trying to say is Willard Motley's book is taken from a tradition only based in reality, and in this case at least, reality wins. Are you interested in what I'm saying? Should I go on?"

Did I want him to go on? I was practically memorizing every word.

"Yeah, I'm listening, go on. I'm really interested."

He paused again. "Well, there is a certain breed of man that emphatically embraces all aspects of life. They are all for growth and learning and love, but there's more to it than that. They're fearless, you hit it on the head, man. There is nowhere they will not go, nothing they will not do. But the ultimate goal is knowledge; the kicks are just an added bonus. The only way to attain that sort of knowledge is with experience. The more intense, the better. See, experience is not thought. Thinking is bullshit. Experience is where it's at. Knowledge is the end, but experience is the means, see?"

He stopped and paused.

" 'Deliver me from reasons,' " I said, quoting a line from the Doors' "Crystal Ship."

"Right! Exactly! You got it. 'I'd rather fly.' There's a couple of books I can turn you on to if you're really interested. First, there's a sequel to the book you just read you probably should read next. I'll try and have something picked out for you by time you're finished with that."

In school I had devised my own means to divine whom I'd meet and whom I'd have nothing to do with. It went past the school gates and into the general world.

"Is he hip? Do they get stoned?" became a conversational key I used to unlock the only relevant truths I needed to know about a potential intimate. If people smoked pot, then they were probably into music, too, and chances were good we could communicate. A negative response indicated avoidance. An affirmative answer was a confirmation of alikeness, a shared set of values and ethics. But it wasn't that simple. Getting high wasn't just about getting high any more than rock 'n' roll was just about music. It was a whole way of life.

It didn't take long to learn that long hair, dope, and music were attractive to girls. It was a near-delirious discovery, and a fortunate one for me, too, since I lacked the other things that attracted girls to Westchester boys, like a surfboard, or blond hair and blue eyes, or for that matter, the nerve to approach them. Yet it was still a good world, I decided, abundant in many things, if not fair in all.

For one thing Dad and I were speaking again, and I was sick and tired of his telling me, "You can't always do whatever you want!" I understood what he was saying. What I couldn't comprehend or agree with was *why*.

"You're doing everything too fast. Be a kid. Don't be in such a rush to grow up. Slow down. You're not going to have anything to look forward to. There won't be anything left for you to do when you're eighteen years old." That wasn't good enough. Why put it off? What tangible harm was it doing? They said they didn't want me becoming some dope addict living in the gutter with a needle in each arm or a high school dropout turned bum. Which I agreed with. No problem there. "We just want you to be happy, healthy, and successful. We only want what's best for you." Me, too, guys, me, too.

They didn't understand the depth of the attraction and commitment I'd made. They saw only its manifestations, and they didn't like those one bit. The problem was: What could they do about it? They attacked. I dodged.

I was looking over some Doors' press coverage when Bill popped his head out of the back office. I thought he might be pissed I was reading and not working on the mail. I really didn't want another scene with him. I was worried he might still be pissed at me for disobeying him, going around him to Jim. I thought I may have gotten him into some kind of trouble, and I was a little scared of being alone with him. He looked down at the floor, where I'd made a thorough mess with dozens of press clippings sprawled about, in front of the doorway to his office, impossible to walk around. I started picking the clippings up.

"Oh, good!" he said. "Good, you found the press clips. I've been meaning to do something with those . . . to log them into some book.

Good idea." He went to a closet and brought out an enormous, empty scrapbook, at least two hundred pages thick and sixteen by twenty-two inches big. "Why don't you put them in here and just continue it whenever the press packages come in from the clipping service?"

"No shit?"

"No shit." He laughed.

I almost had a real job now, two legitimate things to do. Two good reasons to be there. It didn't feel like work at all. Now if I could just pull off school and do this, too, everything would be shining.

After extracting a solemn oath I would refrain from rifling through their file cabinets in search of goodies and would not make any long-distance calls to different countries around the world (to make sure Doors records were in stock), they eventually came to trust me in the office sans supervision.

The Doors had graduated from the Fillmore-size halls which held about three thousand to Madison Square Garden, the first rock act to do so. Their going rate, according to *Variety*: a hundred thousand dollars per show.

As their popularity increased, more and more fans began congregating around the office. Most kept a respectful distance. Then there were those who felt they were the Chosen Few.

One quiet West Hollywood afternoon, alone at his office, I received an unexpected and unwelcome visit from the lunatic fringe, a frazzled, skinny wench called Crazy Nancy. She claimed to have been married to Jim in a previous incarnation and to have left him because of his womanizing and carousing ways. Now she'd come back to claim what was rightfully hers. I'd heard she could be difficult to get rid of. On occasion someone had to call the cops to come and take her away. Then she stayed away for a few months until her courage or schizophrenic enzymes returned and she popped up again.

A borderline psychotic, Bill said, totally harmless. Not to worry, Ray promised. I'd heard about her but never experienced her first-hand. I knew she was part of what was referred to as the lunatic fringe, the tag given to fans like Cigar Pain, another certified wacko who'd burned his vocal cords with a lit cigar to try to sound like Morrison. When the Doors rehearsed downstairs, Cigar Pain would lean up against the air ventilation shaft outside and croak hoarsely the lyrics to whatever song they were working on inside. The effect was almost an echo on Jim's voice. Cigar Pain was getting quite adept at the imitation. More than once the band would stop and someone would ask, "Did you hear that?"

"I don't hear anything," says John.

Ray: "I could've sworn I heard something!"

They would start again and without warning halt all together, and sure enough there would be this gravelly baritone groaning away, caught mid-bar. "Call the cops," Robby would say.

Cigar Pain walked around with an enormous hunting knife hanging from his belt. Last we heard of ol' Cigar Pain, he'd gone home and murdered his mother, stabbing her thirty-two times in the back, and then raped his father.

Ray chuckled. "Poor Old Cigar Pain—can't even get the Oedipal complex right." Anyway, that was the last any of us heard of him.

Crazy Nancy, however, seemed to bounce back. There I was on this particular afternoon, studiously working at Jim's desk, when, without any knock or warning, in through the front door charged Nancy. She barged inside, slamming the door behind her and suddenly stopping, legs spread and feet planted firmly, prepared for attack, taking in the area, turning her head from side to side, making sure no one was going to jump her.

I'd never been too good at confronting fans—especially older ones, which most of them were. I was always afraid they'd just take one step forward and say, "Yeah, and *who the fuck do you think you are, ya little runt*?" and push me out of the way. And I wouldn't have any idea what to say. I sat quietly at my desk and tried to act cool.

"Where's Jim?" she's yelling. "I know he's up here somewhere!" She opens the bathroom door and slams it shut, jams over to the closet doors and opens them so hard they fall off their hinges, and I think, *Oh, fuck, Siddons is never going to trust me alone here again. I'd better stop her before she destroys the place.* I get up and as calmly as possible stroll over to her. *Remain in control*, I tell myself, *let her know you have the upper hand, show no fear. She'll sense it, like a dog* (which is what she reminds me of, a scraggly, underfed, angry dog nobody loved and nobody fed), *and attack.*

"Listen, Nancy," I say, "Jim's not here. He hasn't been here all day." Up close to her I'm getting a little spooked. "Why don't you wait outside for him?" She gives me a vacant stare and a sniff. Trying to get a grip on myself, I tell her what Bill had used on me, "This is a place of business." I can't think of anything else to say. It doesn't work on her either. I don't think it even registers. She seems unfazed, distracted. She must have picked up on my fear. I repeat my statement.

She moves so quickly I don't even see it happen. In less than a second she's grabbed a letter opener from the secretary's desk, maneuvered herself behind me, and whipped the blade against my neck, just under my Adam's apple.

"I fuck your business," she tells me. This registers. I'm not exactly sure what it means, but I know I don't want to find out.

"Where's Jim? Ya better tell me," she's demanding, pressing the blade a little harder against my skin.

I'm trying to regain some semblance of cool. "I'm telling you, he's not here. No one's here. I'm the only one here." Then, realizing this might not be the smartest thing to say, I try to correct it. "Bill should be back pretty soon, though. He'll know where Jim is." *Stay cool. Let her jump Bill*, I figure, thinking in terms of pure survival.

"Don't give me no bullshit lies, fuckhead, or I'll slice your fucking eyes out," she hisses, tightening her hold on me.

I panic. So much for cool . . .

The phone rings. "I really should get that," I say, but she won't loosen her grip. "It might be Jim," I lie. But it works. She lets me loose.

"Don't try anything stupid, stupid," she warns me.

It *is* Jim. I'm so relieved. "Hi, Jim! Boy, am I glad to hear from you." Nancy's over to the desk in one smooth swoop, and she has the point of the letter opener against my skull, temple region. "Let me talk to him," she yelps. "I know it's him, I know it's him, I know it's him." She's drooling and blathering in my ear. It's too late to try to deceive her. I never should have spoken his name. Now, if she doesn't get to talk with him, she'll kill me, and if he has to talk to her, he'll kill me. I decide I'd rather take my chances with him, which aren't quite as immediate or threatening.

"Ah, listen," I say to Jim, "there's someone here who really wants to talk to you."

Silence. Nancy has really begun frothing; her vibes bouncing around the room.

"Who is it?" Jim finally asks.

"Nancy."

"Nancy who?" Nobody has ever called her Crazy Nancy to her face, so it takes me a moment to figure out how to answer him. He's never met her but he's heard about her and he doesn't want to meet her. It was the office's job to guard him from the fringe.

"I can't say."

"Male or female?"

"The latter."

"Who?" he asks.

"It's Crazy Nancy," I whisper into the receiver.

"Who?"

"Crazy Nancy," I finally say in a regular voice, taking a deep breath and closing my eyes, waiting for the blade to puncture my head. She doesn't even hear me, she's so deep into her hysteria. . . . Ever since Jim got on the phone, she's entered a frenzied kind of trance—a sort of feeding frenzy.

"You've got to be kidding," he tells me.

"She wants to talk to you."

"I'm not going to talk to her."

I don't know what to say now. She presses the point a little harder against the soft spot on the side of my head. "Please, Jim, she's got a letter opener against my head."

"No . . . I don't want to talk to her. You're not afraid of a little girl, are you?"

"But, Jim! She's got a letter opener on me!"

"So, take it away from her."

Nancy starts acting up, trying to grab the receiver, which I'm holding away from her. "Let me talk to Jim! It's me! Nancy," she singsongs, then yells, "Give me that phone!"

I resist.

"Please, Jim, just talk to her. She's gonna kill me."

"Listen, Danny, she's just a harmless chick."

"Yeah, I know, I believe you, why don't you tell her that?"

"Just tell her I don't want to talk to her." I don't want to tell her that. "I'm going to hang up now."

"No, Jim, wait!" I yell. Just before she pulls the receiver from my hand, I hear the line disconnect.

I take advantage of the opportunity to scramble away from the letter opener, her, and the desk. She's talking into a dead receiver. Maybe she won't even realize he's already hung up. She's asking him if he misses her, and he's obviously not answering. She lifts the receiver above her head and with a whip of her hand slices the cord. Now she's coming at me with a departed receiver and the letter opener. She throws the receiver at me but misses, and it crashes against the wall, where it breaks a gold record. She shakes the opener at me. "I'm gonna cut yer fucking nuts off and feed 'em to my cats," she informs me. "Meatballs, yum, yum, my cats *love* meatballs. . . ."

We both hear the doorknob turn at the same time and watch as Evan walks inside. Nancy immediately drops the weapon and skips over to him, flirting hideously. I try to get his attention to tell him she tried to kill me. She keeps waving me away, asking Evan, over and over again, "Where's Jim?" Finally I succeed in getting his attention.

"I'm glad you came in when you did. She was going to kill me!" I'm almost out of breath as I say it.

"Don't be ridiculous, she's harmless."

"Oh, shit, I know that . . . she is the one who has trouble with the concept."

Nancy is still dancing around, singing, "He's lying, he's lying." Then, dancing closer to him: "Where's Jim? Where's Jim?" in just the sweetest voice you ever heard.

And cool as can be, Evan tells her, "If I tell you where Jim is, what will you do for me?" Now he has her full, undivided attention.

"What do you want me to do for you?" she asks, in total earnestness.

"Why don't we step into my office and talk about it?" Evan suggests, leading her into Bill's office.

"You want a blow job, is that what you want? If you want, I'll give you a blow job if you tell me where Jim is."

I wouldn't let my nuts within thirty feet of her, and here is Evan offering them directly to her teeth.

He takes her into Siddons's office, which always seems to be used whenever there's going to be sex in the office, closes the door behind them, and proceeds to have his way with her face.

Ten minutes later she emerges from the office, smiling at me, and then she walks right out the front door. What did he tell her to get rid of her? "I told her Jim was at the Hyatt House."

"But he's not at the Hyatt House. He's at the Chateau," I say, and then it hits me. "Pretty smart, Evan."

"Ya just gotta know how to handle these things," he tells me.

"Yeah, but how could you put your pecker in that face?" I want to know.

You know what he told me? I swear, he said, "What do you mean? All mouths are the same. It's better than jerking off."

I felt queasy for the rest of the day. Even Jim's friend, the Andy Warhol film star, Tom Baker, seemed nauseated when I mentioned it to him, and Baker would fuck almost anything that moved.

I went home about 6:00 P.M., leaving a note: "Don't feel so well. Sorry about the gold record. Crazy Nancy paid a visit; will explain later." I picked up the letter opener and put it back in the drawer where it belonged, carefully locked the door, and hitchhiked back home, happy to get out before Nancy discovered the deception and returned to find me alone.

The Doors were rehearsing for upcoming shows to promote their third LP, *Waiting for the Sun*. The single "Hello I Love You" had shot up the best-seller lists and looked like it would be top ten by the time the LP shipped. To the observer everything looked rosy, but underneath there were problems developing. Morrison was missing interviews so often Elektra Records had stopped scheduling them. He'd also begun to miss rehearsals. Not a lot of them yet, but enough so that the question "Where's Morrison?" was being asked quite a bit. For the first time I began to sense definite tension within the band.

I showed up on the Thursday when a band meeting to discuss the upcoming dates and a rehearsal were scheduled. Later that night Bo Diddley was opening at the Whisky and I was hoping Jim would remember a mention he'd made that he would let me tag along with him to the show.

I skipped school after lunch to make sure I made it to the office early. The meeting was supposed to start at 1:00 P.M.; rehearsal at 3:00 P.M. By 5:00 Morrison still hadn't shown.

Everyone started leaving about 5:30. Bill hung around until 6:30. I asked him if it was all right if I waited a little longer. "Why not?" he said.

After Bill left, I called the Palms Bar to see if Jim had been in. "Hasn't been in all day," English Red, the bartender, told me. He wasn't at the Phone Booth either. I looked up Pamela's phone number on the Rolodex. Her number wasn't listed, only an address. I hesitated. Should I just go over there? The address was only around the corner.

Pamela was a touchy subject around the office. Everybody respected her as Jim's lover, and though Jim had other girls, he always returned to Pamela. The uneasiness came because Pamela didn't respect Jim's relationship with the Doors, and they knew it. Pam didn't want Jim to be in a rock band. She thought it was beneath him; "nothing personal, guys," was her attitude, "but the man is a poet, he doesn't belong in a rock band." The people at the office knew how she felt, and she never came around.

Likewise, nobody from the office went around to her clothing store. Jim had fronted the money for Themis to be built, a sore point with the Doors' accountant. She didn't want Jim in the band, but it was his work with the band that provided the money to build and stock the store. And she could spend. Themis was made with the best oak and cherry wood money could buy, hand-cut and polished; the ceiling was covered with layers of peacock feathers; silk pillows littered the floor, and there was crushed velvet on the walls—a jet-set hippie harem which cost a fortune, paid for by one Jim Morrison, via Doors' royalties. So there was resentment toward her from the Doors as well. It went both ways.

The first time I met Pamela, she'd taken an instant dislike to me.

Pamela usually left the running of her shop to her sister Judy. This time I'd bumped into Pam as I was entering the shop.

"Who's this?" Pam had asked. Judy introduced me.

"How do you know Jim?" she asked.

"From the office," I told her.

She immediately sent me out of her store and back to the office, "where you belong." I watched as she roared away in Jim's Mustang Shelby 500.

I wasn't looking forward to seeing her again.

Jim was probably at her apartment, though. That would explain why he hadn't shown up for the meeting and rehearsal. Or else he was on a drunk, and if that were the case, then only God knew where he was, and since God wasn't telling me, and I really wanted to see him and get into the Whisky, I decided to take the short walk over to Norton Avenue, apartment 2, where Jim sometimes stayed.

Jim answered after the second knock. He seemed a little drunk, but it was hard to tell with him. I'd seen him drunk and not show it at all. Other times I'd heard about his getting awful drunk and showing it an awful lot. Anyway, there was booze on his breath.

"You're just in time for some of Pam's specialty," he told me. Then, yelling toward the kitchen: "We have company, honey."

Pamela stuck her head out to see who it was. "What's he doing here?"

"Listen," I said, "I didn't mean to interrupt your dinner. I shoulda called first, but I didn't have the phone number."

"No, it's all right. I insist, we have plenty, come on in." Hesitantly I stepped into the one-bedroom apartment. Pamela didn't act like it was okay or that there was plenty. "It's okay," Jim said to Pam. "I invited him over to loan him some books." I looked at the apartment walls. They were jammed, floor to ceiling, with boxes filled with books.

Jim went into the kitchen to talk to Pamela. I sat down on the couch. Fifteen minutes later I was still sitting there, getting bored, antsy. I looked at my watch. It was almost eight-thirty. It was Friday night, and I was ready to go out and do something. I'd been psyching myself up for this evening all week long, ever since Crazy Nancy almost knifed my eyes out. I'd never really gone out with Jim, except for the odd lunch at Duke's or down the street at the Garden District. Mainly I saw him at the office or backstage. The thought of going out on the town with him was making me practically giddy. I kept looking at my watch. *Let's get going.* I mean, I figured, what good was it knowing Jim Morrison if you couldn't take him out once in a while and show him off a bit? Meanwhile, I was getting more and more impatient and beginning to wonder if he even remembered making the mention in the first place. He certainly wasn't acting like it. He'd been in the kitchen with Pamela for almost half an hour.

I heard Pamela yelling, something about the two of them never being alone. Jim strolled out and sat in a big purple velvet reading chair. I thought how princely he looked in it with his white shirt and black leather pants against the plushness of the chair. I felt uncomfortable and small.

"You don't have homework to do tonight?" he asked me.

"No. I finished it all earlier in the week," I lied. I wasn't about to let homework get in the way of going out.

"Don't you have anything to read? Ya know, any books, something with pages?"

"Not here."

"Then you have nothing left to learn, huh? You know everything there is to know?"

I was feeling more uneasy by the minute. "I finished that sequel, *Let No Man Write My Epitaph*," I told him. "I've been kinda looking around for something else."

He got up and lumbered over to where the wall of books were. "Hmmmm," he said, "let's see what we have here that might possibly interest the inquisitive mind of a growing fourteen-year-old boy." He smirked, kneeling in front of the books. Jesus, I'd never seen so many books outside a library. He began pulling a few out of this box, a few out of that, going over the spines with his finger, finding what he was looking for and pulling it out.

After he'd picked out about a dozen, he sat back down in his chair, setting them on his lap. "You'll love this one. I read this when I was your age," he said, and across the room sailed Jack Kerouac's *On the Road*. "This'll be good for you," he said, and threw *Thus Spake Zarathustra* over, followed by a Rimbaud biography and a book of Rimbaud's poetry. "He's one of the guys I was telling you about." I was catching the books and setting them down as fast as I could and he was tossing them over as quick as I could catch them: Sinclair Lewis, Jack London, Edith Hamilton's book on mythology.

"Wait a second!" I stopped him. "This is the same shit they teach me in school!"

He just smiled. "Exactly. That's right."

I didn't know whether to be flattered, pissed, or scared. I didn't know how I felt about getting homework from anybody, Jim Morrison included.

He'd just tossed *Been Down So Long It Looks Like Up to Me*

when Pam yelled for him from the kitchen. "I want you to remember what you read, too. That's important. Sooner or later it all fits together, you'll see."

"*Jim!*" Pamela screamed.

"Yes, honey?" Jim said, his voice as smooth as butter.

There was more yelling, louder this time. This time I definitely heard her say, "Just get him out of my house!"

"He's just a kid!" Jim said.

"You're always with your friends. You promised me we'd be alone tonight!"

Jim poked his head out and threw me a beer. "I'll be just a minute." Something told me I should bolt for the door, but I held on to the hope of still getting out to the Whisky, although I have to admit it was getting slimmer and slimmer.

Dinner was ready. I wasn't welcome, and I knew it. For the first time that evening I noticed Pamela was loaded. Her eyes began to close, and then they'd flutter open. She was drinking one large glass of wine after the other and was having trouble speaking. At one point, fork midway to her mouth, her head suddenly went dip and stayed down. Jim dabbed his napkin to his lips and pushed his plate away and looked at me.

"Well, I suppose you want to go out and do something tonight?"

"Well, yeah, sure, Jim, whatever you want to do. I mean, I'd love to."

"Well, get your coat, and let's go out and see what kind of trouble we can get into."

I was up in a flash. "What about the books?"

"Leave 'em. You can get them later." Jim got his pea coat on and we had opened the door to leave when Pamela's head rose back up. It took about twenty seconds for it to register what was happening, but once it did, she didn't miss a beat.

"Quick, take off." Jim opened the door and pushed me out. We were halfway down the stairs when Pamela, wide-awake now and livid, started screaming, "Where the fuck are you going? Jim goddamn Morrison, you *answer* me! You'd rather go out with some fucking *kid* than be at home." She was really shrieking. "*God damn you*, I stay home and fix you a home-cooked meal . . . and *you'd* rather go out and *pervert* some little kid who's so fucked up he'd rather be with you than at his own home! . . . And you're as bad as he is! *Worse!* Fuck you, Jim Morrison. YOU AREN'T LISTENING TO A WORD I'VE SAID! . . . *Jim!*"

Pamela was still yelling as we were running over the lawns and across the street. "Hurry up!" Jim yelled, pulling me along. "Run!

Before she starts throwing things. That chick has an arm you wouldn't believe." And we ran, heading first north toward Sunset, then west toward the Whisky-à-Go-Go.

We were both out of breath by the time we pulled up to the front of the line, which wound around the block. The doorman ushered Jim in with no problem but put his big hand out to stop me. "Got any ID, kid?" he asked.

"It's okay," Jim said. "He's cool," Jim told him. "He works for us. He's been begging me to bring him here for months." At last. I was inside the Whisky.

The opening act was onstage. Jim headed to the bar and ordered four double vodka straights for himself and a glass of milk for me. As I started drinking the milk, being thirsty from the running, Jim nudged me. "Leave some." I thought he meant to leave some for him. I left the glass a quarter full. He tossed a vodka in it. "Okay, now try it." It was gonna be a good evening. Jim introduced me to the manager of the club, Mario. I relaxed. And then we proceeded to get fucked up.

Jim was knocking back vodka straights, encouraging me to do the same, until it was time for Bo to come on. The minute he was announced and his rhythm guitar and jungle drums began, Jim was away from the bar, jumping the railing that separated the dance floor from the bar and the seats, and onto the dance floor, up against the stage, throwing his head back and his arms in the air, dancing. Nobody seemed to recognize him. By the time Bo hit the second song, Jim had pulled one of the backup singers' microphones down from the stage and was screaming along with Bo. The song finished, and Bo leaned over and said to Jim, "Say, boy, you scream purty good. You ever thought of joining a rock 'n' roll band?"

Jim threw his head back with pride and slurred, "Ya ever heard of the Doors?"

Bo said: "Oh, sure, 'Light My Fire' and alla them?"

Jim roared, "Well, I *am* the Doors!"

The audience went wild. Jim spun on the crowd. "Fuck you," he bellowed, "*this* is the man that deserves your respect!" Bo took a step back from the lip of the stage. "You don't know shit," Jim yelled. "You're all a bunch of niggers! A buncha fucking, ungrateful, stupid niggers!"

There was a low, strong rumbling as a thousand eyes glared down on us. Hands were pushing us off the dance floor, down some steps, pulling. I tried to grab Jim to stop, but he was in front of me, so I just tried to hold on. . . . All at once we were outside, shoved out of the fire door, onto the sidewalk alongside the club. Mario gave Jim a final push away. "Ya try that bullshit again, Morrison, and I'm gonna let them cut ya!" Jim spun away from Mario's push and just kept spinning, like a top, down the incline, right into the intersection of Sunset and San Vicente, jacket swinging off his shoulders and at the oncoming traffic, Jim stood in the middle of Sunset Boulevard, playing matador with the cars coming in either direction. *He's gonna get busted, if not killed*, I thought; *one of these cars is gonna be a cop*. Cops cruise Sunset like once a minute. Somebody had to stop him. I looked around furiously. There was nobody paying any attention. I had to go into the street and get him. I'd never been in this position before, having to take care of someone else.

I dodged between the honking, screeching cars, and in the middle of Sunset Boulevard, peak traffic hour, midnight Friday. We held a conversation. "Come on, Jim, this is gonna get you busted." Something akin to recognition registered in his eyes, and he showed no resistance as I led him off the street and back onto the sidewalk.

We had no sooner hit the sidewalk than he decided the Phone Booth, across from the office, was just the place to be. I was too tired to argue. "C'mon, man, it's just a few blocks. We'll walk it," Jim said. I tried to tell him it was too far to walk. I was tired. "I know, I know, it's after your bedtime," he taunted.

I shut up. "But couldn't we hitch?" I wanted to know.

"No." Jim had this thing about not hitching. He didn't think it was dangerous so much as undignified. Fine for him. He could drive if he wanted to. I didn't disagree though, thrilled to be walking anywhere with him at all. . . .

But I was also afraid I knew why he was taking me there. It was a topless bar, and he'd just found out a couple of weeks before I was still a virgin. He tried to get this girl to take me into Bill's office. She was willing. I wasn't. I squirmed out of it with a lame excuse I don't think he went for, something about having to go to Elektra on an errand.

Most of the guys I knew claimed they'd been laid dozens of times. But they were all so full of shit. They lied about everything else; why should they be telling the truth now? Besides, it wasn't for lack of opportunity I hadn't gotten laid. I hadn't found the right girl yet. When I did, I'd know, and I sure wouldn't go around telling everybody. Sometimes I felt like saying I had. But I figured just as it took years before anyone believed me about knowing Morrison and the Doors, it would probably take the same amount of time to convince anyone I'd been laid, and by then I probably would be, so what was the whole point anyway?

"You're gonna love this!" he promised. My sense of dread increased a bit more.

The whole trip I had to keep reaching behind myself and pulling my fucking Jockey shorts out of my ass. It was an annoying and embarrassing situation. I tried not to do it, but sometimes it was impossible not to, it got so uncomfortable. Toward the end of the trip he finally said, still looking ahead, without losing a step, "You know, I used to have that problem, but then I got smart one day and threw them away." I thought he meant my pants. He stopped and looked at me. "No, dumb fuck, your underwear." Then he sort of shook his head and said, "It's just around the corner." I was glad it was dark so he couldn't see me blush.

I needn't have worried about the Phone Booth. I wasn't let in, despite Jim's protests.

The manager had come out. "We can't let the kid in, the ABC [Alcoholic Beverage Control] is in there, and I can't risk losing my license for some kid."

I let out a sigh. "It's okay, Jim." But he wasn't one to take no for an answer.

"Bullshit!" he said. I didn't say a word.

He told me to wait a second; he was going to go inside and look for somebody. Forty-five minutes later, when he hadn't come back, I split.

Now I didn't know where to go. It was too late to go home. Besides, I'd told Mom I was spending the night at a friend's house. It was too late to go to the friend's, and I didn't have enough money to stay at the Tropicana, which I'd done a couple of times before. I crossed the street and checked the door at the office. Just as I figured, it was locked.

A voice barked, "What the fuck do you think you're doing up there?" It was Jim.

"I don't have nowhere to go," I told him.

He checked his pocket. "I don't have the key for the door," he said. He imitated my voice: "I don't have nowheres to go either."

"Can't you go back to Pam's?"

"No way. I'll catch it tomorrow bad enough. I can wait."

"Maybe we can break in," I said.

"How?"

"Is it okay?" I asked him.

"Do you know how?"

"I think so," I said, and stood up, knowing if I just walked straight across the beam until I got to the wall, I could do it. Once there, all I'd have to do is steady myself and pull the slides of glass out of their holders.

We were inside in less than five minutes. Without another word to each other, we both went to sleep—Jim on the couch in Bill's office and I on the floor behind his desk. He threw me an arm cushion for my head and closed the door.

I awoke at five-thirty, still drunk, with a parched throat. Without turning on the light, I put my head under the bathroom faucet and guzzled water from the sink.

Next I hitchhiked home. I caught a ride with an early commuter on his way to Hughes, around the corner from my house. It was a good ride.

As quietly as possible I moved along the walkway along the side of the house, which ran right next to Clarence and Mom's bedroom, and opened the side gate to the backyard. I took about three minutes just to close the fucking gate, trying not to make a sound. That's when his goddamn dog started barking his senile head off. Just after I had closed the gate, I took about three steps toward my room, and before I could take another, I saw him and froze. There was Clarence, his big terry-cloth robe tied around his waist, standing not five feet in front of me. He was holding a lethal-looking fireplace poker in his hand. Sobered me right up. I squinted at him in the dark, smoggy redness of dawn.

"I could kill you where you stand. As a trespasser. I'd be justified. It's dark out, how was I to know who it was?"

I didn't move.

Neither did he. From somewhere in the house, my mom yelled, "Who is it, Clarence? Who's there?"

We continued our stare-down.

"I should just get rid of you once and for all," he said.

"Then why don't you do it?" It was dawning on me I might be provoking him on purpose—trying to make *him* do something since *I* didn't know what to do to get out of an unbearable and seemingly inescapable situation. "What's stopping you?"

"Don't think I won't."

"Go ahead, I'm waiting. . . ."

"What the hell is going on here?" Mom appeared in back of him, soundlessly emerging out of the house. He must have left the back door open, and in her slippers she hadn't made a sound. Now she whacked him in the shoulder and tore into him. "What's the meaning of this? What were you going to do?" she demanded.

He didn't answer her. What did it look like? Like he was gonna congratulate me for staying out all night? He said to me, "Count

119

yourself lucky this time, mister, but you're cruisin' for a bruisin' around here, and I'm just the one to give it to you."

"What are you talking about? What did he do now?"

"He hasn't done a goddamn thing around here!"

I wanted to say that wasn't true, but I knew he'd just accuse me of calling him a liar. He was always twisting what I said. He delighted in catching me off guard, and I was sick of giving him the satisfaction.

"Don't be surprised if you come home one night and find the locks have been changed."

"I don't have a key anyway," I told him. "Go ahead and change them."

"Why doesn't he have a key?" she asked him. Then she asked me, "Why don't you have a key?"

"Your husband took it from me." It was true. Months ago, to keep me out of the house.

"You ring the front doorbell like everyone else," he told me.

"But you told me before to walk around the house."

"No buts, young man."

"You did," I reminded him.

"When? When did I tell you that?"

I just sighed. I was tired of the inconsistency. Not only was it making me angry, but it was making me a little nuts, too. I walked away from them.

"Where are you going?" Mom asked me.

I didn't bother answering.

Clarence hollered, "Answer your mother, young man!"

I kept walking.

"Don't you yell at him!" my mother yelled at him.

"Somebody's got to. I tell ya, Harriet, that kid's turning into a real loser."

I opened the door to my bedroom and slammed it behind me. I slapped a copy of the Doors' latest album on the turntable, turned up the volume, and cued up the last song, second side.

"Five to one, baby-ay," Morrison threatened, "One in five, No one here gets out alive. . . ."*

---

*"5-1" by the Doors

BOOK · II

THE ROCK

CHAPTER FIVE

·   ·   ·   ·   ·   ·   ·   ·   ·   ·   ·

**The truth was obscure,
too profound and too pure,
to live it you have to explode. . . .**
—BOB DYLAN

"WERE you on drugs last night when you came home? I hope not, because let me tell you something . . ."

"Mom . . ." Sitting at the kitchen table after school, stoned on grass, I tried to reassure my mother, who wasn't letting me get a word in edgewise.

"Just tell me it's not true. Please, tell me it's not true. . . . I've got enough to deal with already."

"Okay, Mom," I cut in, "it's not true."

"Listen to me!" she stormed, wiping her hands on her apron. "I just don't know what to do with you anymore; I need to know if I'm doing the right thing letting you have your freedom. I fight everyone for you, and I just don't have the strength anymore. I heard from someone's mother you were using drugs. How did she know? Do you know how I felt? I want to know whether it's true or not."

"If you'll let me speak, I'll tell ya." I almost laughed I felt so awkward. *It's not really a lie,* I reassured myself, *it wasn't pot, it was booze last night.* Nit-picking, I know. "It's not true."

"Thank God," she sighed.

"But, it's not false either," I added.

I've got this weird thing about honesty at the stupidest times. I'm a horrible liar when it comes to people I care about. I really am. I can do it, sometimes, but I really feel lousy about it afterward.

It was a stupid thing to do—she didn't want to hear the truth. A lie she could handle. I was the one who had trouble with the lie.

I knew it because of the look of alarm that rushed over her face.

"I'm just kidding, Mom."

I decided I'd better change the topic.

"What I can't understand is why your husband gets so pissed off when I'm not home enough or when I get home late. The less I'm here, the happier I'd think he'd be. I mean, it's not as if he likes my company." I couldn't shake that image of him, standing there on the walk like some beast ready to eat me alive for walking into his lair.

"Don't pay him any attention," she said. "He's just a lonely, unhappy man."

"*He's* unhappy?" I said, incredulously, "Mom, *I'm* unhappy. *He's sick*. I swear, I wouldn't be the least bit surprised if there were some weird kind of pathological sadism somewhere in his family tree."

"Danny, please," she begged. "Is it honestly that bad?"

"Honestly? Mom, it's worse than bad. We passed horrible over two years ago. We're way into miserable by now. I don't see how you can stay married to him. He hates me."

"No he doesn't." She paused here, then added, "Sometimes he's nice."

"Sometimes isn't enough. Most of the time he's a flaming asshole."

She started telling me how his kids need her and how they have no mother like I have a father and mother. She was telling me how she didn't want to be all alone in her old age, and I'd heard it all before. God, what a couple they made. The biggest sadist and the biggest martyr on the block. Probably the whole city. Maybe the state, even.

The next day I had my blue jeans dyed black to look formal and to the combined relief, surprise, and gratitude of all my elders, I graduated the ninth grade.

The rock portion of the class passed around bottles of vodka and orange juice, got drunk, and stumbled to the beach, where we blasted *Let It Bleed* by the Stones on the cassette deck, got stoned on grass, danced with the girls, and had a real cool time.

"*Oh Children*," Jagger crooned. "*It's just a kiss away . . . it's just a shot away . . . it's just a shot away . . .*"*

My concert consumption was improving radically. The bulletin boards left barren after the wrestling posters had been so rudely removed were now colorfully filled up with Avalon and Fillmore posters, group blow-ups (mostly Doors and Stones), black light posters, local concert posters. My album collection was filling out nicely, too. The money I was making from the Doors which didn't go to dope went to LPs. A big problem was that my rock 'n' roll habits (and the ramifications contained therein) exceeded my income. I needed to get more money. I was tempted to trade in some old LPs for some new LPs, but that struck me as inanely counterproductive. I finally decided I'd just have

---

*"Gimme Shelter" by the Rolling Stones

to sell some drugs. I figured the market was already there, I was personally acquainted with both the supply source and the customers, no problem. All I needed was the start-up money and the product. I'd be flush in no time. It seemed ideal. I'd have drugs left over for myself, enough cash to support my album habit, and a little extra money to boot.

The only problem was I couldn't stop getting high and buying albums long enough to save enough to begin. Just when I'd get sixty or seventy bucks together, some good Mexican would come in, or I'd spend it on cabs coming and going to the Doors' office, or else a bunch of new music would come out and I'd go on an album binge. So why didn't I just start small and work myself up a little bit at a time? I tried! I saved a bit and scored a few lids, and then I smoked it all before I could sell any of it! It wasn't the first inkling I had that I couldn't postpone gratification, but so far it was the most nagging. When it came to something I wanted, restraint went out the window. So that's why I never became a drug dealer, even though I really wanted to be one.

A girlfriend would have been nice, but I figured that was just a matter of time. Girls. It was weird. I liked a few, but I could understand someone like Rimbaud easier than I could a single girl. I wasn't one of those guys like Ladd who said, "Cunts! They all have *cunts*! And they all *work*! What's there *not* to like?" They were still pretty much a mystery to me.

Music and getting high were all I wanted, all that mattered. Good loud music and good strong dope.

"There's a box for you on Jim's desk," the new Doors' secretary told me as I walked in the front door.

Over on my desk was an orange crate, like the type in Jim's apartment he used as bookshelves, filled to the brim with the books I'd left at his apartment a few months ago. I'd been missing him lately. The Doors were recording their fourth LP, to be called *The Soft Parade*, and I'd heard rumblings the sessions weren't going too well. Between my respect for the band while they were working in the studio and my fear of being thrown out if I showed up, I decided to play it safe and stay away and take care of my responsibilities at the office.

Taped to the top of the crate was a note. It said: "Read these— There may be a test. Jim." He'd obviously added some more titles to what he'd tossed my way before. On any other occasion the sight of so many books to read would have depressed me black and blue, but as I began poring over the titles and jackets, I was getting excited almost despite myself. There were about twenty books, quite a few of them new, most of them used.

I set the carton aside on the floor and retyped a form letter I had been working on to send out to the fans. After answering the first batch by hand (which took months and left my writing hand sore for a few months more), I learned pretty quickly that the people who wrote in were happy to get any sort of reply at all; most of them wrote back to thank me for answering them. These letters, combined with the new ones that had flowed in since, made for over five thousand letters in all I had to answer now. Since I'd learned how to type, it occurred to me some sort of form letter would be a whole lot easier than replying individually or by hand.

I took the final draft of the form letter over to Elektra Records across the street and used its Xerox machine to run off the copies. Unbeknownst to me, Elektra had been pestering the Doors' office for months to get it a press release. (Apparently the band hadn't approved of the previous ones Elektra had sent out. "Fine," Elektra had said, "then you provide us with one," to which the Doors said, "Fine, we will." Then, of course, nothing happened.) When the people in the publicity department discovered my original form letter (inadvertently left in the Xerox machine, where I'd forgotten it), they naturally assumed it was the release they'd been waiting for.

The "press release," as it had become, told the reader the Doors were in the studio finishing up work on their fourth LP, that they would kick off their first major U.S. tour, thirty-five dates in all, in Miami, Florida, where the band had won a college popularity contest, and that their first single, "Touch Me," would be released within a month. I'd never seen a press release, but apparently my form letter contained all the necessary information and was just what the record company wanted.

Later that week, as I was finishing up stuffing and addressing the envelopes, Siddons asked me, "Did you forget something over at Elektra?"

I thought for a moment, immediately struck with the old what-did-I-do-wrong-now fear. "No, I don't think so."

He handed me the press release. "Sound familiar?" he asked.

"Yeah, it does. It *sounds* familiar, but it doesn't *look* familiar. I've never seen this before. I didn't write this." He raised his eyebrows. "I mean, I wrote the words, but I didn't type them on this letterhead." The release had been transferred to Elektra's letterhead. I didn't want to get blamed for something I hadn't done.

Turned out he thought it was funny, to my enormous relief. "I don't know why I didn't have you write one up in the first place."

Now that was settled, I just wanted to know one thing. "Do I get paid?" I was learning.

"Sure, you get paid. But from them, not us."

From then on I wrote two form letters, one to the press and one to the fans. The one to the press was a bit more formal, and the one to the fans had more personal stuff in it, like how Ray Manzarek and his wife, Dorothy, were getting into gardening and how Robby Krieger still loved surfing and why Jim preferred living in hotels to houses ("more convenient") and how John Densmore had recently gotten married in a private ceremony at Lake Shrine near the Pacific Ocean.

Down in my bedroom, door locked and reading light on, I was reading the paragraph for the third time: "The innermost nature of Dionysus is madness: the churning up of the essence of life surrounded by the storms of death. Dionysus is the frenzy which circles round wherever there is conception and birth which in its wildness is always ready to thrust forward into destruction and death. It *is* life." No less an authority than Friedrich Nietzsche said that!

I was digging through the books Jim had given me. I set down the one I was reading and picked up *Dionysus: Archetypal Image of Indestructible Life*. I hadn't been reading long when I came across:

> A god who is mad! A god, part of whose nature is to be insane! He who begets something which is alive must dive into the primeval depths in which the forces of life dwell. And when he rises to the surface, there is a gleam of madness and life in his eyes because in those depths death lives cheek by jowl with life. Not the medical definition of madness, but that state in which man's vital powers are enhanced to the utmost, in which consciousness and the unconscious merge as in a breakthrough.

My eyes zoomed ahead. The writer went on to state that the followers of Dionysus are "exclusively a cult of intoxication." I nearly fell off the bed I reached for the blue underlining pen so quickly. "Not just alcohol, all intoxication."

Aldous Huxley, another one of Jim's favorite authors, was quoted in the same book saying the festival held once a year in Greece in honor of Dionysus provoked "ritual dances [which] provide a religious experience that seem more satisfying and convincing than any other. . . .

Audience and actor and god become one. Divine. Under the spell of Dionysus not only is the union between man and man reaffirmed, but nature celebrates her reconciliation with her lost son, man. It is as if the evil of Maya had been torn aside and were now merely fluttering in tatters before the mysterious primordial unity."

It sounded just like a goddamn Doors concert!

Was that what had happened to me?

A feeling of power and certainty filled me as I closed the book and laid it aside for the night. What had once seemed so strange and unknown was beginning to make sense. I'd been delighted with the glimpses of Morrison's, and music's, power and magic before, and it hadn't been enough. I wanted to know about the source. I wanted to locate it for myself, to be able to tap into it at will. For the first time in a long time I felt solidly reassured I was heading in the right direction. I turned off the light and went to sleep.

I didn't understand everything I read, far from it. But I managed to find what I was looking for. I understood what I needed and what I wanted to know. It was like panning for gold. I didn't keep what I wasn't looking for.

From Rimbaud I went to Baudelaire, from there onto William Blake, whom I was already aware of because he was the guy who'd produced the quote that inspired the book from which the Doors had chosen their name: "If the doors of perception were cleansed," Blake had written, "everything would appear as it is, infinite." I picked up a copy of Aldous Huxley's *The Doors of Perception*. What I hadn't known was that the book was about his experiences with mescaline. The whole book was about getting loaded!

Blake also was the one who said, "The road of excess leads to the palace of wisdom," which I interpreted to mean what Jim had told me when we first had really spoken to each other that day at Duke's: Make as many mistakes as you can; don't limit yourself. I checked it out with Morrison and Manzarek first chance I got. Ray gave me an *A* for comprehension. Jim called me a smart ass.

"And," I continued, "what about this constant solicitation to madness I kept reading about? What's that all about?"

Jim and Ray exchanged meaningful glances. Then Jim said, more to Ray than to me, "I've always thought an artist can't just will the muse."

Ray said, "Right, she doesn't always come when called."

To me, Jim said, "There's a school of thought that puts forth the proposition that everything, all accomplishment, is based on will. In some cases it may be true. But I think an artist's real power lies in his ability to receive, not invent. . . . And I also think it's an artist's duty and obligation to do everything in his power to increase his powers of reception. We're all products of the universal mind. The trick is to hear the whispers."

"How do you do that?" I wanted to know.

"How do you do what?" he asked.

"How do you hear it?" I said.

"I was afraid that's what you meant."

I waited for an answer.

"Well," he started, lighting one of my cigarettes (neither Jim nor Ray *ever* had his own), "first it's necessary to get yourself out of the way. First you break down entirely everything that builds up the human personality, all the egoism that forms it. Any means that'll help bring about an oblivion of self is considered good—drugs, alcohol, meditation, chanting, everything that breaks down the control of reason and frees you from your normal inhibitions. See, it doesn't matter if the means are poisonous. They're the fertilizers."

"Rimbaud says the same thing about becoming a seer or a visionary," I added. I just assumed they knew the quote I was talking about. It was underlined in one of the books Jim had given me. It read:

One must make oneself a *seer* by a long, gigantic and rational *derangement* of *all the senses*. All forms of love, suffering, and madness. He searches himself. Unspeakable torture where he needs all his faith, all his super-human strength, where he becomes among all men the great patient, the great criminal, the one accursed—the Supreme Scholar! Because he reaches the *unknown*! . . . and when bewildered, he ends by losing the intelligence of his visions, at least he has seen them. Let him die as he leaps through unheard of and unnameable things. . . .

Or as Jim had once said, "There are things known and things unknown, and in between are the Doors."

I wanted to see the unknown, too! I wanted to go!

"Christ," Ray said to Jim, "what are you teaching this kid?"

* * *

131

Near as I could make out, Baudelaire was the first real rock star. At least he was the first one to smoke dope, stay up all night, and crash in hotels, dress in a dandyish manner that served to confuse "real men" about his gender, frequent brothels, and proceed to fuck around so much he finally got syphilis and ultimately died insane and mad, brilliant as he was tragic. Years later his life made a significant impression on young Arthur Rimbaud, much as Blake had on Baudelaire years before. That's the start of the lineage, far as I could tell. As much as Chuck Berry and Little Richard and those guys shaped the sound of rock and roll, these guys set the standard for its action and behavior, its attitude.

Nietzsche had died of syphilis, too. Over in England, Byron, another maniac poet, got VD as well and so did Oscar Wilde. Morrison said that's how he wanted to go. First you go crazy, then you go blind, get visions, get dead.

Back over in France, years later, Antonin Artaud fitted right in with the rest of these brilliant madmen. He didn't get syphilis, but that didn't stop them from sending him to an insane asylum first chance possible. He was an opium user, a confirmed and admitted drug addict. Jim borrowed a lot of his ideas about theater from him. Artaud's writings sounded like a direct manifesto for a Doors concert. In his book *The Theater and Its Double* he writes: "The theater like the plague is a crisis which is resolved by death or cure. It releases conflicts, disengages powers, liberates possibilities, and if these possibilities and these powers are dark, it is the fault not of the theater, but of life." He goes on to write: "It reveals to men their dark power, their hidden force, it invites them to take, in the face of destiny, a superior and heroic attitude they would never have assumed without it."

He could have been describing the Doors on a good night rather than his much-maligned ideal for the theater in Paris during the 1930's.

Getting to know these men not only helped me understand Morrison, and my attraction to him, but helped me better understand myself and the transformation I was going through. As well as where to head next. What I didn't know, couldn't know, was how it was to affect me eventually.

What all these guys had in common was a natural inclination falling somewhere between genius and madness. Nearly all of them put themselves in the company of those like-minded who had come before. Madness was affirmed as the outward sign of a profound spiritual exile. If it was not a natural product of genius, it could be achieved by other means. "Pure intelligence," said Samuel Taylor

Coleridge, "is in principle madness." The mad know the truth. So much truth that society takes its revenge on these seers by outlawing their behavior, banning their books. Society says no to them. And if you want to make anything attractive to a healthy teenager, then just say no to it. It didn't hurt that the same society that had said no to these guys was also saying no to drugs, sex, and rock 'n' roll. Those nos were based on lies, and I knew it. To my mind, they all were shamans; they all were obsessed, possessed, and brilliant, screaming because they were out of control: immoderate, intense, and totally, wonderfully relevant.

And, I was learning, it's also a damn old process, this rhythm and drugs. It's about action as opposed to thought; dance instead of meditation. It was all about Dionysus and the marriage of man and nature. As long as there has been rhythm, there has been song and dance. As long as there have been drugs, there has been healing, spiritual as well as physical. First there was voodoo. Then there was jazz and R&B, and then came rock 'n' roll. The shaman (ancestor to the philosopher, poet, and prophet) used peyote and rhythm to receive visions and to heal suffering. Morrison used music and alcohol and poetry. Coleridge smoked opium and transcribed his dreams. Huxley took psychedelics. Drugs and words and music have almost always been together—for hundreds and hundreds of years!

Madness. Freedom. Suffering. Liberation. Ecstasy.

The thread ran thick, long, and deep. I followed it everywhere. Sometimes it led into dead ends; sometimes, into revelations. One thing was sure: I was learning about something that meant a great deal to me. Solving a personal mystery. Picking up clues. Not about dead civilizations or abstract symbols or Eli Whitney and some cotton gin or about Presidents I didn't care about and who said nothing that interested me. Instead, I was learning about life and how I wanted to live it. Working on my night moves all the while knowing I wasn't alone.

My schoolteachers were no more interested in what I was learning off campus than I was in what they were trying to teach me on. Keeping my grades up in what I regarded as useless topics wasn't the easiest. It meant twice as much effort, but it was necessary if for no other reason than to keep me free to pursue the stuff I was really interested in. In order to be able to do that, I had to be able to go to Hollywood, the Doors' office, and concerts, unhampered, with no outside interference from parents, teachers, or any one of a dozen people who were practically waiting in line to stand in my way. Outside of math, I was doing okay in school. I wasn't *going* much; but I was going enough, and I read the books, I did the assignments, I showed up and took the tests and answered the meaningless questions, and I passed the classes. Then I promptly forgot everything they'd taught me. I wasn't about to give them the slightest provocation to get involved, and it seemed to be working. I was doing what I wanted to do at a time my old man still didn't want me to so much as set foot on the Sunset Strip, night *or* day.

In fact, I was doing more than I wanted. Like taking acid, for instance.

First I had to try it, just once, to see what it was like. After all, it was *the* drug to do. It was more than a drug. It was practically a counterculture religion or some fundamental belief system. Siddons had told me a year ago to wait until I was ready. Now I felt I was. Also, it was available now, whereas it hadn't been before. I scored two tabs from Ladd, and started off with one when I woke up. I expected *Alice's Adventures in Wonderland*, to see unexpected landscapes and textures, animated architectures, colorful hypnogogic visions, stupendous, awesome, symbolic dramas rich with heroic figures trembling on the verge of revelation. *Psychedelic* is what I expected.

Hell was what I got; it scared the living shit out of me. For the first hour or so it was kind of fun. It happened on one of those screaming hot blue L.A. days when everything looked like it was dipped in alcohol, shining and nearly vibrating, humming with energy. By the time we got around to saying the Pledge of Allegiance in homeroom, things had started to get weird, and I was seriously considering turning back when I realized I couldn't. The stars and stripes started melting, dripping off the flag and turning to flame on the floor, streaming down the rows of chairs and out the doors like some blood and chrome molten lava flow. And that was the fun part. Those cute visual oddities aside, the tone turned ominous, and I was consumed primarily with unholy fear, the likes of which I'd never experienced before, but which I sensed was only the merest tip of an iceberg of an underlying hell, resting just imperceptibly below the surface of my consciousness—ready, able, and threatening to leap out into daily life and stay there with me forever.

Well, no sense of well-being here, I thought, sitting in the middle of the football field, staying as far away from people as possible, trying my best to keep all sensory input at an absolute minimum. I figured the less input, the less chaotic output I'd produce. If no one talked to me, I wouldn't immediately concoct twenty different interpretations and possible answers from every conceivable vantage point. If I didn't see anything new entering my horizon, I wouldn't be so likely to turn it into something it wasn't or something it could be. Then I made an interesting, if unhappy, discovery: When the mind is deprived of external stimuli, it begins generating its own output, its own internal universe. That is precisely what started happening. In the midst of all this madness I came to the remarkable conclusion that what I needed to do to get my head going in a better direction was to take the other hit of Blotter I was still holding. Shake up the course this trip was taking, sort of jar things around, kick the machine a bit, and try to get my money's worth. After all, I reasoned, other people were obviously enjoying it. I probably hadn't taken enough. I'd misjudged the dose. That was all it was. At the time it seemed clear and sane.

I ate the remainder and proceeded physically to vegetize and mentally to terrorize myself, shattering my personality for what I was convinced would be forever, spending the next six hours in this state, enduring what became the most smoggy, unendurably long sunset imaginable. Acid was definitely not the drug I was looking for. It had done *nothing* to make me feel better.

I prepared to check acid off my list of things to do for good. But then I thought, *Hey, wait a second, maybe it's just me; everybody else can't be wrong*. I felt ashamed my experience had been so negative. I didn't want anyone to know. I felt insecure and afraid for weeks. Nothing had ever shaken me up so badly, counterculturally speaking. I'd thought I was ready for it, and I hadn't been. I'd thought I could handle it, and I couldn't. I felt absolutely retarded being afraid of acid precisely because it was a drug that meant so much to so many people.

Before I could check acid off my list forever, I had to do it again, which on the surface probably looks pretty retarded all by itself. I just had to get it out of the way and reclaim my self-respect and sense of belonging as soon as I could.

The prospect of tripping again didn't exactly enthrall me. I wanted to go to Morrison for advice, but I was too self-conscious about the whole ordeal; he was the last person I wanted to know that I had freaked out. He was also the best qualified person to help me. He'd tripped thousands of times. He was called the King of Acid Rock, for godsake; he had the experience and the knowledge that could help me. The problem was I didn't want him to know I lacked it.

* * *

Trying to dig up a drug I enjoyed was getting harder and harder. The distaste I felt for acid only made me all the more anxious and determined to find a drug I liked.

A couple of times I'd taken downers, red devils, and they just put me right to sleep. Falling asleep in the height of an otherwise perfectly fine afternoon was not my definition of a good time, so I took a pass on those, no questions asked.

Everyone had begun raving about cocaine like overnight, and coke was the new drug to do. I read up on it and decided this must be the one I was looking for. "Feelings of superiority and strength," the literature read, and that old, elusive "false sense of well-being" I was still so seriously in search of. True or false, who cared? I'd take it.

Unfortunately the people I was asking either couldn't or wouldn't get it for me. Some were telling the truth; others were lying to me, for my own good. The harder it became to procure, the more my determination increased. As a last resort I called Siddons and asked him if he knew where to get any cocaine.

He said he might. "Who wants it?"

"Who do you think?" I nearly yelled, optimism filling my voice.

"Not you?"

"Yeah! Me!"

"No way."

"Why not?"

"For your own good," he said, and I should have known.

Maybe because I felt guilty about the acid routine or maybe because I was going through a temporary adolescent confessional and stupid period, I finally got around to telling Morrison about being on Ritalin. I'd been putting it off, figuring he'd interpret it as some gross sellout on my part. Not only was he not pissed when I told him, but he wasn't even disappointed. I was so ready for some gigantic expression of condemnation from him I was almost let down when I got what he gave me, which, I was learning, was typical Morrison: unpredictable and quite excessive.

He questioned me about the drug, how many times a day I took it, what were the effects, how many did I take at a time, and could I give him a couple so he could see for himself how it worked.

"Sure, how many do you want?" He looked at the bottle I'd taken out for display purposes, opened it, took out a palmful, and washed them down with a swig of beer.

I decided I was glad he took the news so well, so to speak, after all.

"I heard you're looking to score some cocaine."

He wasn't asking me. He was telling me, so there wasn't much sense in denying it. He didn't sound real excited about my pursuit either. I don't know how I expected he might react, but somehow I hadn't anticipated the way he did. He was keeping me off-balance, but good.

"Listen, I don't like being put in this position. It's not one of my stronger points, taking a moral line with teenagers. It's not good for my image." I laughed. He didn't. "But," he cut in, "I'd rather let you know how I feel about it now and get it out of the way than have to watch you fuck up later and have to deal with it then. I'm going to put it to you as bluntly as possible. No proselytizing, no theorizing, no moralizing, no hypothesizing. I don't do it, and I don't think you should either . . . and if I find out you're getting into it, I'll break your fucking fingers, one at a time. I swear, man, you'll never be able to write a word again, you dig?"

"I hear you," I said, looking at my feet, which were still there. It was a stupid thing to say; I'd picked up the expression from Jim and hadn't even realized it. It was what he said when he wanted to let someone know he understood while not necessarily agreeing with what was being said. He shot me a glance that burned a hole through my skin. I tried to look him in the eye.

"You know," I said, trying to lighten the scene, "between you cracking my fingers in half if I even try coke and my old man breaking my knees for so much as speaking to you, the chances of me making it to sixteen without becoming a quadriplegic first are about slim to none."

"Let's go for a little walk," Jim suggested.

Jim Morrison didn't take little walks any more than NASA took little trips. There had to be more involved. Not that I needed a reason. Being with Jim was motivation enough to follow him anywhere.

We walked up La Cienega Boulevard, up to Sunset, where the street curves up so sharply you can see nothing above its crest. We hung a right on Sunset, walking east, toward the Hyatt House and Chateau Marmont and Laurel Canyon.

It was a crisp, windy day. Broken clouds drifted high overhead. The wind whipped around my baseball jacket.

"Hold on," Jim said.

In one swift motion he took off his coat and started walking back in the direction we had just come from. I trotted along after him. Before I could ask a word, he crouched down in front of a long-haired kid we'd passed, wearing nothing but a torn T-shirt, sandals, and patched jeans. Jim handed him his jacket. "Here, take this." The freak shook his head to clear up a fog, not believing his own eyes.

"Aren't you Jim Morrison?" he asked Jim Morrison.

"Aren't you pretty cold?" Jim asked him.

"Why—why are you giving this to me?" the guy asked us.

I shrugged my shoulders.

Jim told him, "From the looks of it, you need it more than I do. Put it on."

With the wind ripping down the Strip, we walked into the wind, continuing to wherever we were going.

"I suppose it's futile to ask you where you're taking me?" I asked him.

"You know, if you have too many answers, Sugerman, you can ruin the element of surprise life might otherwise hold for you."

We walked, and I thought about what he said.

"That's pretty cryptic," I said, trying to start a conversation.

He said nothing.

"I suppose it's also out of the question for us to hitchhike to wherever it is we're going."

He said nothing, again.

A few blocks later we climbed the stairs to the Chateau Marmont.

We took the elevator to the fifth floor and walked down the corridor to the end. I thought he might be taking me to the room he sometimes kept there. *Maybe he's going to turn me on to some cocaine!* My heart jumped. *Sure, why not?* I reasoned. *He probably figures better him giving it to me in his company than me getting it from some stranger on the street, maybe getting burned or busted.* Instead of opening the door he stopped at, he knocked.

The door opened a peep. I couldn't see a thing inside.

"Hey, Jim," I heard a man say from the darkness as the door opened the rest of the way.

"Hey, Tim," Jim said softly as he walked inside, leaving me to follow.

Tim was horribly thin, naked to the waist, his ribs poking out. Jeans hung on his waist, and he was barefoot. His pants were smeared. There was an awful smell coming from inside the hotel room. "Be careful of the floor," Tim said to us as we moved inside. "I had a little accident."

"Tim Hardin, I want you to meet a friend of mine," Jim said.

He introduced us, but Tim wasn't interested. I recognized the name, though. He was the author of "If I Were a Carpenter," an L.A. songwriter/singer of some acclaim.

"Jim, listen, I really need to borrow some bread. I'm sick, man. I'll pay you back, I swear to God, Jim, I'll pay you back, you gotta help me."

Jim said, "I thought I heard you were going to kick."

"I did, I mean, I have. I just got a meeting, man, I gotta get it together, I just need a little bit to get straight. Then I'm going to get out of town for a while and get it over with for real this time."

He went into the kitchenette to get a Coke.

"Are you taking notes?" Jim asked me.

"What's that?" Tim said from the kitchen.

"Oh, nothing," Jim said. "I was just wondering if you had any toast."

As Tim walked toward us, he grabbed his ass and yelped, "*Oh, God, oh, shit, oh, shit,*" and ran to the bathroom. "I just shit my pants!" he moaned. "I shit in my fucking pants!" he cried.

"We'll see ya later, man, I'm splitting . . ." Jim called.

"No . . . Jim, don't . . . *Wait,*" Tim pleaded. "What about the coin?"

Jim kept walking. I followed, practically in shock.

Before I saw Jim again, the Doors had started their first ever national tour. First stop, Miami, Florida.

As most Doors fans know, Miami was the first, and the last, date on a tour where the rest of the dates were either canceled by city officials or aborted. Each of the Doors escaped, flying to a different island in the Bahamas. Then, one at a time, they returned home to Los Angeles to estimate the damage, to try to sort out what had happened and plot out their next move. When Jim came back, he found a warrant for his arrest waiting for him. He announced he was going to turn himself in to the FBI, an act I considered nothing short of heroic.

The night of the day Jim had surrendered I was back at the house in Deadchester, sitting at the dinner table with Clarence presiding. I hadn't been around much lately, but once again Mom had squeezed a promise out of me to attend dinner and try to get along by bribing me with one of my favorite meals, barbecued spareribs with pecan pie for dessert. What the hell . . .

At dinner I announced to the gathering how Jim had turned himself in.

"For what? What did the freak do this time?" Clarence demanded, since he didn't know how to ask anything nicely.

I took a deep breath and with pride, to the best of my ability, recited the charges I only vaguely understood. "The misdemeanors were public drunkenness, public profanity, and inciting a riot," I said. "And the felonies were lewd and lascivious behavior and simulating masturbation and oral copulation." The misdemeanors I sort of grasped, but the felonies really had me quite baffled. I thought "simulation" meant "a drawing of," like a cartoon, and I thought "oral copulation" meant *saying* fuck, "oral" meaning "mouth" and "vocal," and all, like an oral quiz.

"Not in front of the girls!" Clarence yelled, whacking the table, doing the ol' silverware jump again. He meant his daughters. I didn't know that.

"Yeah, the girls, in front of boys, the whole audience, cops, too!"

"Young man, you have one filthy mouth, and you will leave this table, pronto."

"No." I tried to explain. "*I* didn't say anything; *Jim* said it. I wasn't even there."

He gave my mother his vacant-gape-of-awe look that said, "He can't be that stupid." Toward me his expression melted to hatred. That I understood.

He rose out of his chair and grabbed me by the wrist and hauled me out of the chair.

"Okay, okay, I'm going, I'm going. . . ."

I left the dinner table before I even finished my salad. It wasn't a record, but it was damn close.

I didn't think his reaction was fair; after all, I didn't actually say a cussword. I never thought saying "fuck" should carry the same penalty as saying "shit" anyway. "Fuck" I can understand a parent getting upset about. Even "shit" is pretty bad, but "goddamn" or "hell," those sorts of words, I really think should carry lighter or, even better, suspended sentences in child punishment cases. And I hadn't said *any* of the above.

But to judge from the way he reacted, old Clarence thought the images I'd conjured up with those charges were just about the worst things I'd ever said. I had no idea why he was so pissed off. Of course, I had incorporated cussing into my vocabulary so thoroughly for a minute there I thought I might have let something slip I shouldn't have, but I was pretty positive I hadn't said anything wrong.

CHAPTER SIX

· · · · · · · · · · ·

Stand
In the end you'll still be you
One that's done all the things
You set out to do
Stand
For the things you want are real
But you have yet to complete
And there is no deal

     —SLY STONE

CLARENCE invited himself into my bedroom without knocking, as usual, and announced Mom and he weren't getting along so hot. My hopes rose. For a minute there I thought he might be telling me that he was actually going to leave her. No such wild luck.

"What's that got to do with me?" I asked, giving him a chance to clarify the situation.

"You're the reason we're always fighting," he told me.

"I can't help it."

From the angle I saw things, he could help it a lot more than I ever could.

"Hell's bells, you can't."

"What am I supposed to do about it?" I asked, an edge of helplessness creeping into my voice for dramatic effect . . . totally lost on someone so insensitive.

"You can leave. If you had any guts, you'd just get the hell out of here."

What did he think staying took? I mean, besides a keen sense of the absurd.

He tried again. "If you really loved your mother, if you cared one bit for her happiness, you'd leave."

Was he right? If my presence was making things harder on her and I hated it here anyway, then what was the use in staying?

"Do we understand each other?" he asked me.

To avoid further conversation, I nodded. I had no idea one simple gesture could ever be so misunderstood.

I was still tossing out feelers for cocaine wherever and whenever possible. It was turning out to be a real first-class pain in the ass to score. The harder I tried to find it, the farther away it moved. The more I looked, the more evident it became it wasn't in the cards to be had, and the clearer it became, naturally the more I wanted it.

Until finally I gave up looking. Not because I didn't want it anymore, but because I had run out of places to look.

When it became sneeringly obvious there was no cocaine to be found, at least for the time being, I took it as a high sign it must be time to go another round with LSD, an event I'd been hoping to postpone for as long as possible.

Typically I had absolutely no problem whatsoever finding any acid.

Ladd the Bad scored me three hits of Orange Sunshine, and I ate them down during morning nutrition with my sweet roll and milk. It was lousy timing, I realized, midway through math class, when the numerals written on the blackboard refused to stay put, turning faster and faster, spinning apart and reassembling until it was impossible to identify any of them. I was beginning to feel pretty hectic.

Some of the kids started resembling different animals. Ladd, with his blond goatee and skinny neck, began turning into a billy goat. Saddolwright, for example, looked just like a big, fat bullfrog waiting for a fly. Mr. Carrigan, whom we all called Mr. Cardigan for obvious reasons, began turning into a chimpanzee. He was pretty hairy to begin with and with his short sleeves and long arms was becoming increasingly apelike by the minute. When he spoke, giving directions, I assumed, I couldn't make out any of the words. I decided I'd better get out of there before he called on me or recognized anything was wrong with me (which I was sure was obvious to everybody). Math class was not the ideal setting for a good trip, I concluded, and with a preponderance of zoo-type chatter filling my head, and chalk figures turning razor sharp and threatening to zoom off the surface of the chalkboard like some strange kung fu hieroglyphic cum airborne weapon spinning wickedly toward me, without so much as a wave or raise of the hand, I upped and split, quicklike.

The books became too heavy to carry, so I tossed them in the first garbage can I passed, figuring the printed numbers filling the pages might turn against me at any time and the more distance I could put between me and them, the better. Then I started the journey to Hollywood.

Slowly, almost delicately, I moved through the Doors' office to my desk in the corner. Nothing seemed solid or dependable. The whole world seemed to be perched on the very edge of disaster. At any moment I fully expected to fall straight through the second-story floor and hit the ground, whereupon I'd simply shatter into a zillion particles of dust. The traffic noise from outside, combined with the office noises of phones ringing and typewriters, was unbearable. It seemed essential I remember to breathe. My whole organism was unraveling as I sat down, determined to hold it together. Suffice to say, I was pretty ripped.

I heard Siddons call my name, but I couldn't begin to move to get up. I opened my mouth to speak, and nothing came out. He came out of his office to get me. He leaned down, eyes level with mine, and said something. I heard his words, but they didn't seem to come from him but from some other dimension. They appeared inside my head, but I couldn't tell if they emanated from his mouth.

"Are you okay?" he wanted to know.

I shook my head, slowly. Talking seemed impossible. Thinking I'd forgotten how, I panicked.

"Grass?" he asked.

I shook my head again.

"Mescaline?" He guessed again.

I reached way back into the very depths of my willpower and managed to squeak out the word "close."

"Acid?" he asked.

Ah, relief. I nodded.

"You're peaking."

The word "close" came out, but it didn't sound nearly as serious as it should have.

Ray came by and patted me on the shoulder. "Hang in there, man." His touch was warm, reassuring. I didn't want him to leave.

I heard Jim's voice. He was laughing, talking to somebody in another room, another world. What if he got pissed at me? I'd seen him get pissed at other people, and it wasn't pretty. I once saw him ridicule two fans, leaving one of them in tears, both speechless. I wasn't real sure how he'd take the news of my tripping at the office during school hours. I tried to maintain as he came into view, walked by me and into Bill's office. Tony, previously Mick Jagger's bodyguard and now Jim's, a friendly, gentle six-foot-six black man, asked me if he could use the phone. Now he just looked plain mean. I tried to tell him to go ahead but could only shrug.

"How's it going?" Jim stood before me, grinning. Did he know? Had Bill told him anything?

"Okay," said a voice I thought was mine.

"It's a perfect day," Jim said.

I nodded. *He doesn't know*, I decided.

"I'm going to the beach. You feel like coming?"

I nodded. *He knows*.

Maintain, I told myself, but I was shaking instead.

145

We climbed into his blue Mustang Shelby. Jim swung the car onto Sunset Boulevard and headed west, toward the beach. At the stoplight in front of the Whisky, a beautiful blonde walked in front of us in the crosswalk. She ignored us.

Jim sighed. "Now that's what I call art."

I nodded. *Maybe he doesn't know.*

He turned up the music. We listened to the radio for a while. The scenery blurred by. I couldn't focus. About three miles into the drive Jim turned off the radio and looked at me instead of at the road.

"How much did you take?"

It was no use lying to him. I was having a pretty hard time by now. The whole drive I had been working myself into quite an elevated state of paranoia. I could really use his help.

I told him the truth. "Three hits."

"That's a purty good dose for a kid your age. How ya doin' so far?"

How was I doing? Good question.

"Not too good." I felt like a totally useless, pathetic, sniveling wimp. There I sat, freaking out in front of the King of Acid Rock.

"You'll be okay," he reassured me.

"I hope so."

We were coming to the part of Sunset Boulevard known as Dead Man's Curve. It had been widened recently, but cars still occasionally flipped off the road and into an adjoining estate's pool. As we approached, Jim accelerated into the turn. I held on.

"Don't reject what's happening. Don't fight it. Go with it. I want you to pretend. Imagine you're a hitchhiker. Someone you don't know, never met before has picked you up. You don't know who he is or where he's taking you, but you get in the car anyway because you intuitively trust him. It feels good. You recognize goodness within the driver, so you go along with him. Can you picture that?"

"I just want this to be over."

"It will be. You know this driver, this new friend, maybe you've met him somewhere before, is taking you someplace good. You really trust this guy. You *know* he won't hurt you. You know everything is going to turn out okay. Just enjoy the ride. Okay?"

I felt a little better—calmer. I nodded.

"You know, in Sri Lanka a sect of Hindus believe that God is actually closest when danger is nearest. They have many gods, for good and evil that must be appeased, but there are three main ones: Brahma, the creator; Vishnu, the preserver; and Shiva, the destroyer. The believers confront danger, invite it, by doing rituals like walking over hot bamboo coals or placing razor-sharp hooks through their skin and hanging from them. When someone is sick, a member of his community will manifest the darker powers to cure him, reconfirming his faith in the process. Sometimes God *is* closest when danger is near. . . ."

Only a few blocks from the coast, we drove into a fogbank. In a few minutes the car swung through two large gates into a deserted parking lot. Even though I'd driven along Sunset Boulevard to the beach dozens of times before, I'd never noticed this turnoff. The whole area was filled with trees; through the tops I could make out a shining blue, gold, and white Eastern temple. A windmill sat at the edge of a lake.

Silently we both got out of the car and stepped off the gravel parking lot onto a path of smooth, flat stones that led through a clump of tall trees. The sound of a waterfall came wafting through the air. We walked down a path through a bamboo grove; moss clung to the large, damp rocks which made up the wall to our left against the mountainside. To our right were tall reeds, cottontails. Beyond them lay the lake. At the far end was a tall waterfall. A smaller waterfall ran down the hillside in front of us, and the path we were on became a little bridge. The water spilled down the hillside and splashed underneath our feet as it flowed into the lake. A painted turtle slid off its rock in the sun into the water. Brilliantly colored ducks paddled in a group along the shore while parrots glided above. A multiarmed dancing god(dess), playing the flute, stood on a tree stump along the path. I wasn't convinced I wasn't dreaming the whole thing, about to wake up back at the office or in the classroom at any second.

The path wound its way around the lake. Everything was moist and green, quiet, serene. We came out of the trail into a clearing—a small meadow of manicured grass at the end of the lake. Overhead were the borders of the temple, marble columns holding them aloft. There was no floor or ceiling, earth and heaven in their place. The walls were invisible, too—trees and nature. Fog blanketed everything. I looked at Jim, who was squatting, staring into the water.

I crossed my legs and sat down in the middle of the outdoor shrine, trying to focus on the scenery and ignore what was going on inside. I could smell the ocean.

"How you doing now?"

I looked up. Jim was standing beside me.

"I'm not sure."

"The driver is you," he said.

"Huh?" I blinked.

"I said, 'The driver is you.' Whatever is going on inside your head, whatever trip you're on, there is nothing to be afraid of. You're traveling inside yourself. You're the driver, passenger, vehicle, and horizon. The reason you were able to trust that driver before is that you were able to get in touch with that aspect of yourself."

We both sat. Jim played with a clump of dirt, found a worm inside, and was letting it crawl through his fingers.

"Mystery and pain always precede an act of creation. You're in the process of creating yourself today. Try and enjoy it.

"Accept the unacceptable. Whatever happens, embrace it. Resistance just brings persistence. You've got to fully experience all your emotions, all the suffering. Go through it. After you go through it, you come out the other side a free man."

I felt a little better. The confusion was evaporating. Everything had begun to assume a clarity and brilliance. Even the fog had begun to burn off.

"That's what real liberation is. Freedom. It's really the only thing that's worth dying for. Not the kind of liberation they talk about with wars, dying for a cause—that's all concept and no reality. That's not what the Constitution was originally about. Personal freedom . . . life, liberty . . ." He was almost whispering. I had to lean forward to hear him. "It's a much more personal war, and in some ways it's more difficult; but it's no less real. Death, real or imagined, is always there. And what's more unacceptable than death? Name one thing. You can't. Once you accept death, then you're home, man, then you're free. Nothing can touch you."

I could have sat there and listened to Jim forever. The fear had vanished and become confidence. I felt positively radiant. We sat in the sun. He talked, and I glowed.

"Total acceptance," he said, nodding to himself, rubbing his hands in the grass, "that's the key. To go beyond good or bad, you have to destroy all your previously established values. Forget the Ten Commandments. Invent your own commandments, become your own God, create yourself, develop your own personal set of values."

Finally, I had something to say.

"I was reading that Nietzsche book you gave me, and he said, 'To raise a new sanctuary, the old sanctuary must first be destroyed,' that it's a law."

"In other words," Jim said, "destruction's not necessarily a bad thing. We've been programmed, brainwashed into believing it is, which isn't surprising, especially in a society which values materialism as much as ours. But you have to see through that bullshit and try to see that destruction is really necessary. All being is a state of perpetual perishing. As we grow we're also dying. By the same means, if we artificially stimulate the death process, by introducing a destructive element, we stimulate the growth rate. So what I'm saying is it's actually possible to accelerate the life force with self-destructive behavior. There can't be birth without death first. Even the Bible says so: 'Whosoever will save his life shall lose it; and whosoever will lose his life shall find it.' But there's no guarantee after you've lost it you'll be able to find it. That's the risk. There it is. It's incredibly ironic: You really have to risk dying to live. It's an incredible gamble. The stakes are your life. You have to be willing to die for it. If you lose, then it's all over. But if you *win*, if you win, man, then you'll know. The unspeakable becomes *known*. That's the other side. It's the doors of perception cleansed. That's where I'm trying to get."

"Me, too," I said, whispering now as well, "me, too." Nothing else ever mattered so much.

I was actually enjoying the postacid glow, sitting in my room waiting to be called for dinner, listening to *Tommy* by the Who, and feeling a real sense of accomplishment.

Dinner turned out to be a surprise. Clarence made a definite, undisguised attempt to be nice to me. He wasn't ever what you'd want to call a subtle guy, so this move was as obvious as the rest. But in comparison with the rest of humanity, he wasn't being what you'd call inconsiderate either.

"What did you do today?" he inquired.

I didn't bother answering. Then Mom kicked me, and I looked up to see Clarence smiling at me. I blinked and almost looked behind me.

"Well, what are you waiting for?" He was still smiling.

"Uh, well, school was okay. They were laying new blacktop, so we played basketball in the gym"—I was improvising desperately—"and in English literature I gave a verbal essay on 'Subjective Narration and Its Usage' by John Updike and"—I added the final touch in this creative tapestry—"then I came right home, went to my room, and did all my homework."

"Don't you have anything else you want to tell us?"

I thought for a moment. "I don't think so."

"Tell your mother what you told me the other night," he said. "Danny has an announcement to make. Go ahead, tell us." His grin tightened.

I had no idea what he was talking about.

"I do?"

"A farewell statement." He prompted me. "Tell your mother what you told me."

I looked over at Mom, who looked as if she were ready to toss her cookies.

I patted her leg under the table.

"I didn't tell him anything."

That got that ridiculous grin off his mug quick.

"Are you calling me a liar? *Well?*" he demanded.

What I really wanted to say was: "Goddamn right I am. You're a liar, and a fucking asshole on top of that!" It's no fun being a chickenshit. It's not great for one's self-esteem. But I didn't say anything.

"You answer me now, goddammit!"

Ah, his true colors had returned.

Now I smiled. I was back on familiar ground. "No, I'm not calling you a liar," I calmly replied.

"*No what?*"

I repeated myself.

"I heard you the first time," he yelled. "*No what?*"

Instead of saying, "*I* heard 'no what?' the first time," which was what I wanted to say, I gave him what he wanted to hear instead.

"No, sir," I mumbled. Before anyone could make me say anything else I didn't mean, I got up and sent myself to my bedroom without dessert for being such a pussy.

Jesus holy duck fuck! What a rude awakening.

What was he so pissed about now?

It was just a little after dawn, and my whole bedroom was rattling from top to bottom. It wasn't a sturdy room to begin with, and with the thousands of louvered window slides, the thing was really making a terrible racket this morning. Before I even opened my eyes, my first thought was it must be Clarence at the door, trying to get in, furious at being foiled by the lock I'd secured the night before. I figured he was getting me up early to lay into me for my behavior the other night, or the pool, or some such shit.

"All right, all right already! I'm coming, I'm coming."

I rolled out of bed and right away was tossed to my knees.

He must be really pissed. The whole room was shaking. My eyes shot up to the front door window. He wasn't even there.

150

Holy shit . . . a fucking earthquake!

It stopped as quickly as it had started.

Coming out of the subconscious as it had, I'd ascribed the whole force, the total wrath of nature to a goddamn stepfather. The shaking had stopped, but inside, I was still trembling. The fucker really had me snowed.

Slowly I recovered.

And then I got mad. First at him. Next at myself.

In between trips to Miami for the trial the Doors were back in rehearsal. The Miami "incident" was turning out to be a mixed blessing. While it was a major curse in terms of lost concerts and court costs, it also slowed things down. The Doors had time to rehearse, working up material in a manner they hadn't had time for since the very early days before their first rush of success. They luxuriated in the process, growing confident and tight. Gone were the horns and strings. They'd returned to their roots, back to the randy carnivalesque classic Doors sound of yore.

Jim had changed, too. His leather pants didn't go into the closet, they went into the trash, and he'd taken to wearing black jeans or, as was more often the case, baggy blue-and-white pinstriped cotton engineer pants with loose, billowing pockets. Because of the lack of concert activity and an overabundance of food and drink, he'd grown a paunch, which dropped onto his jeaned hips. Perhaps, to cover the weight, he'd begun wearing Mexican wedding shirts—white muslin garments which flared out under the neck yoke.

The beard he'd begun during the days just prior to Miami had sprouted into a wild and woolly bunch of whiskers covering his face and neck. His hair had begun to turn gray in places. He didn't appear intense or threatening anymore; instead, he had become almost gentle, serene.

But he was missing rehearsals on the average of two or three a week, and if he didn't miss them, he was still late, drinking more than ever and worrying everyone around him.

Personally I didn't see anything wrong with anything he was doing. It was obvious the whole Miami situation was a real thorn in his side. The audience was still expecting Jim to do something outrageous. On the other side were the cops, the government waiting for him so much as to twitch or say the F word, ready to lock him up. Stuck in the middle was the whole group, which more than ever just wanted to make some good music.

Jim wanted to confess his innocence, and his opinions, about the whole mess, but his lawyers forbade it, afraid he'd just make matters worse. Jim wasn't about to be so easily dissuaded.

I was tossing back beers, chain-smoking joints and cigarettes simultaneously, and reading *Creem*, a little rock magazine out of Detroit I'd never seen before. One of the editors had written a review of the Doors' latest album, *Morrison Hotel*, which had just been shipped to the public. It was a total over-the-top rave, and I had never read anything in the rock press which had affected me so directly.

I took the review over to Jim. "Read this," I told him. "I could have written this. This is *exactly* how I feel."

After reading for a few minutes, he handed the magazine back to me. "Did you see this?" He pointed to a little ad at the front of the magazine that invited readers to send in manuscripts. "Boy howdy," it started. "Nobody who writes for this rag has anything you ain't got," it said, and printed the magazine's editorial address and phone number.

"Great," I said. "What am *I* supposed to write about?"

Jim smiled a smile that pointed to himself.

He'd finally found a way to get his feelings about Miami into print. Jim picked up the telephone and dialed the number. He asked for the editor who had written the piece. "This is Jim Morrison," he said after the guy got on the line. Obviously the person at the other end of the line didn't believe it was him because Jim said, "Well, I could sing you a few bars of 'Light My Fire.' " Apparently allaying the guy's doubts, Jim told him he had a kid sitting next to him who was turning into quite a writer, and was the guy interested in an article, an exclusive about what was happening with the Miami trial?

Jim hung up and told me, "Congratulations. You've got your first assignment." We set a date for him to help me with it.

The Doors had begun gigging again, albeit sporadically, so I had some good reasons, if not bona fide excuses, to be away from home. With Mom covering for me, all I had to do was get the transportation together. One weekend I hitchhiked 150 miles north to Bakersfield on Friday night for a show, then south 300 miles to San Diego for the Saturday night concert.

The band was in the dressing room, but Jim was nowhere to be found. The Doors were scheduled to take the stage at eleven-thirty and even though it was only eleven, everyone was already getting nervous because Morrison hadn't been seen since the afternoon sound check despite his promise not to disappear. Siddons saw me and told me to go outside and look for him.

"What am I looking for?" I asked him, thinking maybe a limo or something like that.

Bill wasn't feeling real patient and just yelled, "Anything, something, *Morrison!* A cab, a car . . .'"

I took off, ran twice around the arena within ten minutes, and then started banging on the backstage door to get back inside. I must have pounded that door for a good ten minutes before someone opened it, just a crack. "Yeah?" a bouncer/security guard asked.

"Let me in," I told him.

"Where's your pass?"

"Shit, I don't have one. Just ask Siddons, he'll okay me."

"Don't know Siddons," he said.

"Well, ask Evan Parker, for chrissakes, do ya know who he is? He's the goddamn promoter here."

The door closed in my face.

"Ya handled that with your usual tactfulness and aplomb," a voice said, startling me from behind. I spun around. It was Jim. Boy, was I relieved. I really was. I told him so. I had visions of spending the night waiting to be let back in.

"Great," I said, "now we're both stuck out here."

The door opened. The guard said, "Can't find no one named Evan." But he saw Jim and immediately corrected his demeanor to one of more respect and let us in. I felt like a real champ walking backstage with Morrison following me. But before anyone could congratulate me on a job well done, they just took one look at Morrison and clapped their hands and proceeded to parade right past me, enveloping Jim and marching him back to the dressing room.

When Jim found out I'd just finished hitchhiking almost five hundred miles in under twenty-four hours, he was outraged. Siddons wasn't anywhere to be found, so Jim took the matter into his own hands, handing me everything that was in his pockets, which included about a hundred bucks, a couple of backstage passes, and a dozen tickets. Then he cornered the Doors' booking agent and ordered him to make sure I got home safely after the show. "He's your responsibility from here on out. You understand what I'm telling you? I want this kid taken care of."

Then he pulled me aside and said, "Look, they don't have any beer. Why don't you see what you can do about it? But be discreet."

Within fifteen minutes I had sold the tickets, half the passes, pocketed two hundred bucks, sold the airplane tickets the agent had given me, and talked a flabbergasted over-twenty-one-year-old fan into helping me buy Jim Morrison two cases of Coors and a bottle of Jack Daniel's with the money I gave him and a backstage pass. I stashed the booze in the bushes after unloading it out of the guy's van and, with my own all-access pass, went back inside the hall to find Jim.

The lights went out, and the audience was stomping for "Morrison, Morrison" and the standard Doors announcement, "Ladies and gentlemen, please welcome the Doors," boomed out over the system. Ray, Robby, and John took their places with their instruments, and I crawled to my place right behind the PA.

This time I was ready for Jim's delayed entrance, but he still got to the microphone without my seeing him.

"WAKE UP!" he screamed as the spotlight hit him. "YOU CAN'T REMEMBER WHERE IT WAS/HAD THIS DREAM STOPPED?" His face contorted; his head turned in a thousand different directions, left to right, up and down, as his hand cranked, throttled the microphone. It was new material, stuff I hadn't heard before, not even in rehearsal. You could tell the audience wasn't expecting it. Suddenly everyone stopped; the music, Jim, the audience froze. Not a sound. Then there was the crack of the snare drum, and they took off into "Light My Fire." The audience erupted. Jim's body became a piece of cord to the music's wind, bending from it, leaning backward into it, ready to rise right off the stage.

That night, even though I'd heard it over a thousand times already, "Light My Fire" took on a new meaning.

"You know that it would be untrue / you know that I would be a liar / If I was to say to you / girl, we couldn't get much higher. . . ." He started the second verse, into the second chorus, and when he yelled, "Try to set the night on fire," I knew exactly what he was singing about. It might have been Robby's lyrics, but it was Jim's song.

As I continued to watch from my perch ten feet away from where he stood, I was hypnotized once again. Emotionally I ran the gamut from exhilaration to terror. When Jim leaped off the stage and ran up the aisle, the audience cleared for him. Then he turned around and fled face first over the lip of the stage and fell to the ground. I was certain he was knocked out cold. He just lay there, the music pounding. I thought about jumping down to help him just as he rose and effortlessly lifted himself back onto the stage. Then he finished "The End."

"Come on baby take a chance with us, and meet me at the back of the blue bus. . . ."

That evening I understood the chance. And more than ever I'd booked my ticket on that bus.

"Driver where are you taking us?" he sang.

It was a very good question. The possibilities were more tantalizing than anything else I could think of.

This is what I'll be doing for the rest of my life, I promised myself, confirming what I already knew.

It was a great show. The Doors performed for over three hours, played songs that hadn't been performed live in years, came back for three encores, and Jim danced and told jokes and was in great spirits all night long. What nobody could figure out was how he'd managed to get so drunk when there had been only one six-pack in the dressing room.

I ended up getting a ride home with some of the people I'd met outside when I'd been scalping the tickets and passes.

The day I went up to the office to do the story about Miami with Jim, he wasn't around. The band was downstairs rehearsing without him, the atmosphere was tense, ready to snap. No one was talking to anyone else. Nobody, it seemed, was in a good mood. Jimi Hendrix had just died and no one was sure if Jim knew or not. I was sitting at the desk reading the story in the paper, waiting for him to show up, when Siddons came out of his office; his face white. "Jim's been picked up by the cops."

Jim had gotten fucked up the night before and at about 4:00 A.M. stumbled up to the wrong apartment. Thinking he was a Charlie Manson type, the elderly couple whose residence it was called the cops. They picked up Jim, who had passed out on the front porch. It wasn't a real cool thing to have happen while the Miami trial was coming to a finale.

A few weeks before, Jim'd been arrested by the FBI during a flight to Arizona to see the Rolling Stones. He'd gotten drunk and disorderly on the flight and been arrested promptly upon landing and, along with Tom Baker, thrown in jail, missing the concert and further jeopardizing his freedom and the group's future as well.

This latest bust was bad news. As Bill gave us the lowdown, Ray hung his head and gripped the desk sides with both hands. It almost appeared Jim was intentionally trying to ruin everything he had worked so hard to establish, hell-bent on bringing the whole house down with him. Bill was on his way to the lawyers, then the bank, to go downtown and bail Jim out of county jail.

I didn't figure he'd feel much like doing my interview with me when he got back.

I showed up the next day, after school, hoping maybe he'd want to go to work on the article, but I was hesitant to bring it up. He was there, but he was plainly not in a very good mood. He was drunk and looked horrible—unclean and dirty. He even smelled lousy.

I figured I'd just keep my mouth shut and hope my silence would be a conspicuous enough reminder for him. Unfortunately it was.

"So, what do *you* think we should do? Compromise with the establishment or slide with reality?" he asked me. Not in a nice way either.

After a moment's deliberation I answered, "I don't know. Slide with reality, I guess."

"*You don't know, you guess.* What the fuck *do* you know? You don't know shit. What are you doing up here all the time anyway? Don't you have anything better to do? It's really pathetic, ya know, just hanging out here all the time like you do, getting in everyone's way. I wouldn't even come here if it weren't for all these people. What's *your* excuse?"

I wanted to say, "I work here! What I do is important!" I wanted to stand up to him, but I didn't know how.

"I don't know," I mumbled in a slightly quavering voice.

"Nobody needs you. You're just a loudmouth punk who doesn't know his mouth from his asshole."

I hoped he was finished with me.

He wasn't. "Oh, yeah, I forgot," he said, his voice dripping sarcasm. "We were supposed to do an *interview* today, right? This is what it's come to," he announced to the whole room. "Rock star Jim Morrison, in a blind career plummet following a concert in Miami, gets interviewed by a fucking high school punk!"

He was staring to see my reaction. I bit the inside of my cheek and tried not to cry. I just sat there, staring at him through watery eyes.

"I gotta go meet some people," I mumbled, and was gone.

* * *

I stayed away from the office for quite a while after that. I'd called once, and when my call was never returned, I couldn't understand it. I couldn't believe he really didn't like me anymore. I didn't know how much longer I could stay away. I had to find out if the Doors were still open to me or if they were shut, and locked, forever. Over two months later I returned, timid and uncertain. I felt like I barely knew Jim anymore and had to ingratiate myself all over again.

I wasn't feeling real cozy, more like someone was going to throw me out of the office any second. I sat down at my desk and dug out the latest batch of mail. I could hear a meeting going on beyond Siddons's closed office door. More than an hour passed before the band and some other people emerged, saying their good-byes to each other and shaking hands. I concentrated on reading the mail.

My heart was pounding as the office emptied, leaving just the Doors, Bill, and myself.

"Well, well, look what the wind blew in," Morrison said.

Oh, no, here it comes. I prepared myself for the verbal onslaught.

"Where have you been? I thought you might have been kidnapped." He grinned. "I've been half expecting a ransom call."

Boy, was I relieved. "I called, ya know." I told him.

"Yeah, I guess so. Only I'm not real good at talking on the phone. You should know that. . . . If you don't believe me, just ask Crazy Nancy."

I laughed even though I didn't want to. "That's true," I said.

That was it. There was no reference to the confrontation we'd had. It was back to business as usual or as close to usual as it got working for Jim Morrison.

"Aren't you supposed to have some questions ready for me?" he asked, browsing through a magazine.

"I didn't want to bother you with that."

"Well, it just so happens . . ." He came over to the desk and pulled out a piece of paper with a list of questions written on it. "Now, here's what you do," he told me, handing over the questions and a Sony portable cassette recorder. "You ask me those questions and be careful not to interrupt me. That's the first rule an interviewer should know. Wait till the subject is finished with his answer. Once he's done with what he's saying, either go to the next question, or ask me one of your own if you think it's suitable. You think you can handle that?"

"Yeah, I guess so. I mean, yeah, sure, I can handle it." I was trying to be careful and not say anything that would blow up in my face. "When do you want to do this? There's no rush."

"I thought we could do it now. I'm starving. Let's go down to the Garden District, and we can do it over lunch. That is, if you don't have any other plans?" He walked toward the door.

I was out the door, tape player and questions clenched tightly in my grubby little hands, hot on my subject's trail.

I continued with the avoidance strategy around the house. But I knew I couldn't go on avoiding Clarence forever. It was a lousy way to live, always hiding, leaving early, coming home late, intimidated and running scared.

What I could and did change was the degree to which the discomfort registered. I deadened it. In my mind I ran away as far as I could. However, I also knew it was just a matter of time until there was a confrontation and I would have to take that trip on the ground, in reality. I couldn't continue living there and avoid him forever. Oh, my mother had a great idea. She thought maybe if we all spent *more* time together . . .

Within a three-day period I fucked up royally in school twice and got busted both times. My class counselor said if he didn't know any better, he'd think I was acting like I wanted to get caught. "Why would I want to do something like that?" I wondered.

"There're reasons," he told me, "and you can either find out someday or keep heading the way you are and end up in jail or dead."

The first fuck-up was for being drunk. During the preschool cigarette, someone pulled out a bottle of Southern Comfort, and it tasted so sweet and good that before I knew what hit me I was drunk. Add to that some healthy tokes off someone else's bomber to get rid of the taste of the booze, and I was staggering off to first period. Lucky for me, it was creative writing, Mr. Kortick, and rather than turn me in, he gave me cab fare to go home and "sleep it off." I, of course, did no such thing.

I went to Hollywood instead. Elektra Records was holding an open house party to celebrate its new office space.

Me and Morrison and his friends Babe Hill and Tom Baker were standing across the street, on the roof of Themis, watching everybody go in. Jim really didn't want to go over. All of us were bugging him to go mainly because all of us wanted to and none of us wanted to go without him. He finally relented. "Hell, I paid for the fucking place, I might as well go over and have a look at it and see where the money went."

Right after we walked in, a whole crowd of people swallowed up our little group, handing us drinks and pumping our hands. I was busy getting drunk at the bar when I saw Baker leading Morrison down the hall toward the new executive office suites. I moseyed over to see what they were up to, not wanting to miss out on anything but careful not to butt in either. I hung a ways back down the corridor, sipping my tequila sunrise, just close enough to overhear.

"You're really an asshole, you know that, Morrison?" Tom was telling him. And to my surprise, Jim was listening to him, taking it.

"You paid for all this corporate bullshit! You're a fucking corporation, Morrison!" It was one of Tom's favorite games—to antagonize Jim. He was the only person I'd ever seen get away with it.

"All this doesn't mean a thing to me," Jim maintained. "All I'm doing is helping some good people out."

"You're a fuckin' hypocrite, Morrison!" Baker baited him. "You're financing the very authority that you claim interest in overthrowing!"

"I'm not attached to any of this, Tom. It's not my trip. I can't help it if my music helped create it."

"Oh, bullshit, Jim, you can, too. Don't even try to bullshit me. Take some responsibility. I *know* better." Baker sounded convincing.

"It's the truth, Tom—none of this stuff means a thing to me."

"Oh, yeah? Prove it then. Prove none of this expensive equipment doesn't mean shit to you. Don't prove it to me. Prove it to yourself. Prove it to *them*." Baker waved his hand in the direction of everyone in the party room.

"I don't have to prove anything to anybody," Jim insisted.

"You're a chickenshit, Morrison." Baker laughed. "A no-count barefaced chickenshit."

Jim swung into action—knocking Baker across a desk, knocking down typewriters and pushing over desks and file cabinets, throwing papers into the air and to the floor, kicking the freshly painted walls, and yanking telephones out of their sockets before a dozen people ran down the corridor right past me to see what was going on. It took about ten of us to subdue him.

"Get him out of here now!" someone from Elektra told us as we were being shoved down the hallway and outside. We piled into a waiting limousine.

"Get him away from here!" an executive VP of Elektra told the driver.

"Go, go . . . *Andele! Andele!*" Jim yelled in a husky voice as we roared off into the Hollywood night.

Suffice it to say I did not wake up early the next morning and go to school.

The second fuck-up fell on the third day of the three-day period, and it had to do with that old menace to society I carried around with me, my hair, which I'd been wearing behind my ears and pushed down under my collar to avoid getting caught. The school rule was, If they could see the back of your hair from a front view, or if it touched the ears, it was deemed too long and disruptive. I still didn't get how something like my hair could be considered disruptive any more than a piece of chalk could, or a tree or even my left foot, for that matter.

It's hard to hide anything, let alone your hair, in the shower. Old Mr. Dean pulled me out of the stall by my hair and dragged me bare-assed into the phys ed office, with no towel on me or anything. "Lookee what we have here," he bragged, holding my wet hair way up in the air to emphasize the length. The other PE teachers gathered around to witness their long-haired, dripping wet catch. They gave me the choice of letting them cut it then and there (they showed me the scissors) or facing Mr. Tanner, who I already knew from experience would just march me right across the street to the worst barbershop in the state. At least with the latter I stood some chance of escape. I chose Tanner and, without even bothering to dry off, got dressed and then got away from them in a hurry, before they assigned me an escort.

Having bolted off campus, I hitched up to the Doors' office, where I worked on the scrapbook for a while and then remembered I had to go home early. Mom had extracted a promise from me that I wouldn't miss a special dinner she was preparing for her old friend Hanna, the one who had the dubious honor of introducing her to Clarence. I had absolutely no interest in seeing her and told Mom as much.

"But she's the one responsible for setting me up with my husband."

"Yeah, I know," I told her. "She should get a jail sentence, not some special dinner."

Mom pointed out how she never asked me for any personal favors and if I appreciated that at all, I'd do this for her this one time.

"How about if I give you credit now and you can ask me a favor some other time and I promise I'll do it, no questions asked?"

She wasn't biting and went right ahead until she guilt-tripped me into promising her I'd attend the 5:00 P.M. hurrah. I was absolutely beginning to loathe that dinnertime, I tell ya. Judging from the way things had been going, I had a real intuitive feeling this one had the potential to be a genuine humdinger.

Sometimes I really hate being right.

It started getting intense the moment I walked into the house.

Clarence told me to get in the bathroom and wash my face and comb my hair. I did better than that. I went downstairs to my room and took a whole goddamn shower, shampooed my hair and combed it back, like I did in school. Oh, fuck, I'd totally forgotten about what had happened in school!

Once I'd taken my chair at the dinner table, he told me to go back and wet my hair down and get it off my ears and out of my face again. I took a deep breath, got up, and brushed my hair back, to the best of my ability following his instructions. Returning, I took my seat.

"You forgot to be excused."

Since I just got back and was already seated, it seemed a little stupid to ask now, so I ignored the comment.

He had us all bow our heads while he said grace. Christ, I hated that part of the meal maybe the most.

When he finished, he started back in on me. "You didn't close your eyes during the service."

"How do you know?" I grinned.

"What do you mean, how do I know?" He was getting pissed off. "I saw you."

"Oh, I see," I said, and asked his youngest daughter to pass the baked beans.

"Wait just one goddamn minute!" he hollered.

Everybody stopped everything.

"I thought I told you to get that hair out of your face."

"I did."

"I say you didn't. It's too goddamn long anyway."

The telephone rang. Thank God. "Nobody move!" he screamed. Nobody moved.

"I already did, three times since I got home. I've washed it, I've brushed it, and I've combed it."

The ringing continued.

"Well, I'm telling you to do it again. Plaster it back and spray

161

it, and don't come back to this table until it stays. Or I'll take care of it personally."

"It doesn't need it," I said, pushing it back off my forehead with my hands. "There."

"Oh, hell, why hasn't anybody answered that goddamn phone?" As he got up, he warned me, "I'm not through with you yet, young man."

Under my breath I said to Mom, "I'm telling you, I can't take this much longer."

"What did you say?" Clarence, midway to the phone, spun around at me.

"Answer the phone, Clarence," she said to him, and to me: "Please do what he says." To Hanna she managed a weak smile.

I didn't budge.

Clarence came storming back to the table, and before I knew what hit me, he'd yanked the chair out from under me and was shoving me toward the bathroom. "I've warned you about that goddamn hair of yours. You move when I tell you to move. . . ." He pushed me to the floor.

My mom was up in a flash. "What the hell do you think you're doing? Leave my kid alone," she ordered him just as I was regaining enough of a grip on myself to fight back. She grabbed his hand and pulled him away from me and back to the table.

"Do you know who was on the phone?" he yelled, throwing her hand off. He was really screaming now. Nothing compared with what my own father could get up to, but not bad at all.

Mom didn't say anything. Of course, she didn't know who was on the phone. But *I* knew who had been on the phone.

"It was your precious son's school! He was sent to the boys' vice-principal for the length of his hair!"

"That's no concern of yours," Mom told him. "The school can handle it."

"The school *can't* handle it! *That's* why they called! He was sent, but the freak never went! They looked all over the school for him, but he wasn't in any of his classes! And do you know what your wonderful son did the day before yesterday?"

"No, I don't, but I'm sure you're going to tell me."

Oh, shit, here it comes. My instinct was to get the hell away, but morbid curiosity held me in place.

"He was drunk! At ten o'clock in the morning! I tell ya, Harriet, the kid's no good! When are you going to be able to admit that to yourself?"

"Stop saying that," she said, her head down. "It's not true."

"Oh, you two are a real pair—you're both pathetic. I thought I told you to take care of that goddamn hair of yours. I'm *not* going to tell you again," he yelled at me.

"And I told you I've already taken care of it," I yelled right back at him.

His nostrils flared and vibrated. He looked like a bull ready to charge. I stood my ground, not sure whether I was paralyzed with fear or just too proud to be pushed any further. I didn't know if I could finish what I'd started. I only knew I was finished backing down.

"Are you saying *no* to me?" he demanded, leaning across the table, eyes drilling into me.

I didn't know what I was saying. I hate to admit it, but I was having serious second thoughts. Maybe it wasn't too late to back down. I'd never seen him so pissed off. He was so much bigger than I was. Should I say no? Which was, after all what we weren't supposed to say. Or should I say yes? Which in this case meant no, too.

I started to giggle. It was nearly enlightening. There was nothing to say. Either way I was fucked. He waited for an answer, growing impatient. The whole dinner table was looking at me, waiting.

I slowly walked back over to the table. I figured I might be able to do this only once, so I might as well take my best shot. It was time to tell him exactly what I thought—not what he wanted to hear or what my mother wanted me to say—and I told it to him in as few words as possible. I put my hands on the back of the chair to steady myself.

"You're really a fucking asshole, you know that? I'm so sick of your bullshit I can't even put it into words."

His youngest daughter giggled and said, "Oh, m'God," and as his face went flaming bright red, Mom's went dead white. He lunged across the table, trying to grab me and just missing, knocking over the table instead. Tacos, tomatoes, onions, dip, baked beans, everything went flying.

That was my cue. I was off, adrenaline flooding, legs pumping. I think I did a little midair skip as I flew out the door into the backyard. I should have used the front door to make my getaway, but I was not in the habit of it. Cindy tried to grab her father to hold him back, begging him to leave me alone, and Mom was yelling at him to stop; but he knocked his daughter aside, ignored my mother, and came chugging after me.

The door to my bedroom couldn't keep a hard wind out, so

locking myself in there was out. If I only had the time to hop the backyard fence, I could make it into the fields, but I didn't want to get halfway up the fence and have him pull me back down. I came to a stop at the far end of the pool. Either he'd have to swim across to get me, which wasn't likely, or he'd have to chase me around to try to catch me, which was more likely. At least the chase scene would give me time to figure out my best escape.

Clarence headed straight over to the pool shed, pulled down the aluminum pool broom, which was about fifteen feet long with a three-foot-wide metal brush at the end.

"It's not too late," he shouted. "You just stop this asinine behavior this minute and take this broom from me and get to work and I'll forget about the whole thing."

I wasn't going anywhere near that brush.

"*No!*" I screamed. It felt so damn good I yelled it again. "*No! I ain't forgetting jackshit!*" I was hot as a pistol.

"You shut your filthy mouth!" he yelled from the other side of the pool.

"*No! You can't make me! No more! No way!*"

"You don't know what you're talking about . . ." he yelled.

"*I* don't know what I'm talking about?" I screamed at him. "Don't you understand? I'm done working for you. Go hire a pool man to clean your fucking pool. You're the only one who ever uses it, you clean it. You pay somebody to do it 'cause I'm done. Fuck you! No more!"

That got his juices back up. "I'll kill you this time," he thundered, coming after me, but I jogged to the other side of the pool where he'd just been standing. He kept coming, so I kept going. Around and around the pool we went. At one point he thought he was being really clever by suddenly shifting directions on me, but all those years of baseball training, changing directions on a dime during pickle practice, and running laps around the field, were paying off. I was young, strong, and plenty mad, whereas he was just over the hill, out of shape, and mean.

"You're going to regret this," he puffed, "when I get my hands on you . . ."

"*If* you get your hands on me. You gotta catch me first, Clarence. You're losing it."

"You little piece of shit." And he came after me again.

I dodged him easily, trotting around the pool again.

As a last resort, he aimed the broom at me as if it were a spear and threw it over the pool, where it flopped harmlessly to the deck in front of my feet. Then I made a stupid move. I stopped to retrieve it while he took full advantage of my delay to charge. Hurriedly, I picked the broom up and held it like a knight's lance, and as he rounded the pool, coming at me, I ran toward him, hit him squarely on the shoulder, and knocked him on his ass. If I was ever going to make a break for it, this was it. I took off for the fence.

In the background I heard his daughters screaming me on. I hit the fence on the run and was up and over it with a jump and scramble in a flash. As I dropped over the top, I took a chance to peek back into the yard, where I saw Clarence, up and charging. I hit the ground and kept running, down the face of the hill, getting up too much momentum. I took a fall which I turned into a roll, hopped to my feet, and commenced flying down the mountainside. He was still coming after me. I kept running and never looked back again.

The pathetic fuck never caught me.

But where was I running to? I knew only what I was running from. Where could I go? I kept running. I hit Centinela at the bottom of the hill and headed west before the cigarette smoking got the better of me. Winded, I slowed into a jog, then a trot, holding my thumb out, headed toward the beach.

On my way I stopped at Marina liquor, which never checked for ID, and picked up a gallon bottle of Tyrolia wine and a pack of Marlboros.

The sand was cold and damp from the recent rains, and the sunset was blood red streaked with orange. I took a seat on the jetty rocks and smoked and drank and thought. What was going to happen next? Anything was possible. I was filled with a real sense of adventure, excitement, and for the first time in a long time, hope.

I woke up under the lifeguard tower, wondering for a moment what I was doing there. It was still early, too early to call the office. I walked around the Marina peninsula over to Venice and went to Olivia's Café, the real Soul Kitchen, for eggs and coffee. It was Thursday morning, October 4, 1970. In seven more days I would turn sixteen years old. I wondered where I'd be sleeping.

The office was locked. I walked over to the Alta Cienega Hotel. Jim had checked out. After calling the Tropicana and the Hyatt House, I finally found him at the Chateau Marmont. I apologized for waking him and we arranged to meet at the office.

Siddons's black BMW was in the office driveway, parked alongside Ray's burgundy Citroën and Jim's lime green and white-top Dodge. The colors didn't go so hot with the Tyrolia.

"Christ, you're a sight," Jim said when I arrived upstairs. "What were you doing, playing in a sandbox?"

"Close. I slept at the beach," I told him.

"Is that what you woke me up to tell me?"

"I've run away from home."

"It seems to me you've done that before."

"Not like this."

"Yeah," he said, "what's so different about this time?"

"I told Clarence to fuck off. The shit really hit the fan."

"Did any of it get on you?"

"It went *everywhere*. I just couldn't take it anymore. It was so cool."

"Good for you. But remember that there's a big difference between rebellion and defiance or just refusing to go along with something. Rebellion involves a demand to be treated as an equal. It involves values and a sense of identity, dignity, and from what I know about what's been happening, that's the same conclusion you're coming to."

Siddons wasn't thrilled with the news I'd left home for good.

"Oh, that's great. So what are you planning to do now?" I think he was afraid I harbored a secret ambition maybe to move into his office full-time. "Why can't you move in with your father?" he asked. "Doesn't he live somewhere around here?"

I'd never gone into much detail about my father's disapproval of my being at the office. I was afraid they'd take it as an insult or maybe worse, sympathize with his point of view and comply with his desires by not letting me come around anymore. Now I had to say something.

"We're not getting along too swell right now, but I was thinking of apologizing about that."

"About what?" Ray asked.

"I was gonna move in with him about a year and a half ago. He went ahead and had the house construction guys over to demolish his den and begin turning it into a bedroom for me. I backed out just before I was supposed to move in. Things have been pretty tense between the two of us ever since. He got kinda pissed off about the whole thing."

"Gee, I can't imagine why," Bill said.

"That is a pretty understandable reaction," Jim pointed out.

"Anyway, I'm not too excited about bringing it up again with him. I'm not too sure he'd even consider it."

166

"You've got to live somewhere. . . ."

"Shit, we can't adopt you, ya know."

"I don't expect you to . . . I just don't know where else to go."

"You can't sleep in the streets," Ray told me.

"You could at least ask your old man," Jim ventured. "The worst that could happen is he could say no."

Jim didn't know my old man. He could go into one of his yelling tirades on me, which was much worse than a common no. He wouldn't just say no. Assuming that would even be his answer, he'd definitely accompany it with a good ten-minute diatribe about what an ungrateful, selfish, rotten, expectant kid I was. That is, assuming he'd say no at all.

"No," I told Jim, "there are worse things than no he could say."

"Like what?"

"Like yes, for instance."

"I don't follow," Bill said.

For the first time I told them all about how my father tried to keep me as far away as possible from Hollywood and the Doors. "My mom lets me get away with it. She knew she couldn't stop me, and I guess she trusts me enough. My stepfather didn't care enough about me one way or another; he basically forbade me to do anything I liked. But," I continued, "if I moved in with my dad, there's no way I could ever get away with coming here. You don't know him. He'd never let me get away with it."

Nobody said anything. I still felt I had more to say.

"He hates rock 'n' roll. He thinks I'm too young to come around here. He thinks you guys just use me. He doesn't understand what it means to me. If I moved in with him, I'd have to give up everything, 'cept maybe baseball; he really wants me to be a ballplayer," I reminded Jim. "I mean, I really love him a lot, I really want to live with him, it would be so much easier than where I've been. You don't know half the shit I put up with from my stepfather; he really went out of his way to make my life hell. But at least I could get away from there and come up here. As bad as it got, and it got *very* bad, it could never be as bad as not being able to see you guys."

I think for the first time they understood how much they all meant to me. Nobody said anything for a while. It didn't seem there was anything else to say. The room fell still, and my chest felt tight and heavy. Bill walked away into his office, shaking his head. Jim stared at his hands, which were on his knees. Then he looked at me.

"Maybe if I spoke to your old man, it would help."

"You'd do that?" I asked, incredulous.

"I said maybe."

Ray had to leave, rubbing my hair as he went by. "It'll be okay."

Siddons came out of his office and handed me two hundred dollars. "An advance. Get a room at the Tropicana until you figure out what your next move is gonna be."

Now that the question of where I was going to stay was settled, at least for the next few weeks, I had another question to answer, like, What the fuck was I going to do now? I was paid up at the Trop for the next month, so I knew where I'd be sleeping. As to what else I was going to do, I had no idea at all. "Take it easy baby, take it as it comes,"* whistled through my head.

During the first few days a new pattern began to emerge. With no pressure and no outside interference, I began to feel a curious, new sense of freedom, and with it, an even more startling sensation emerged: responsibility. Not fully developed or anything dramatic like that. I just found myself doing things on my own I wouldn't have ordinarily done without someone standing over me, making me. Stuff I didn't like doing, and didn't have to do, I was doing anyway. Different, huh?

To no one's greater surprise than my very own, I continued going to school. And you want to know what really flipped me out? I even got my hair cut. I did! Not real short or anything too severe, just a trim. It was still an incredibly traumatic experience, but it wasn't too bad because I knew it was something I had to do and nobody was making me. I *chose* to do it, so I could get back in school. Hell, I even paid for it *myself*! Strange stuff.

I wasn't proud of it or anything weird like that. I just found it interesting, that's all.

Things were going okay. Mom wasn't taking the news well that her sixteen-year-old son was living on his own at an eleven-dollar-a-night hotel in Hollywood known primarily for its hooker raids and drug busts, but I called her a couple of times a week and put her fears to rest and reassured her I was eating okay and my clothes were getting cleaned. Speaking of clothes, she was real concerned because she hadn't found any underwear in any of my drawers, and she knew I hadn't

---

*"Take It As It Comes" by the Doors

taken anything with me 'cause she'd seen me running, and now that she thought about it, she hadn't seen any underwear in the hamper for a long time. On top of that, she told me, she found a book that had her quite worried. I couldn't imagine what she might be talking about; she was pretty liberal when it came to what literature I read. When she asked me if I was "seeing any girls" lately, I knew exactly what book she was talking about. Boy, the two things—the absence of underwear and John Rechy's *City of Night*—combined to shake her up but good.

"Don't worry, Mom, I didn't move out 'cause I'm turning weird," I told her. "I moved out so I wouldn't."

She told me how horrible she felt for not being able to provide me with a real home. And I couldn't help feeling horrible, too—not for leaving her; I stayed as long as I could take it—but because she should have seen it coming and done something. Whenever she brought that stuff up, I couldn't help feeling like reminding her that all she had to do was leave the bastard—but I never did. I bit my tongue and protected her from both of us.

I made her absolutely promise, to swear on my own life, she wouldn't dare tell Dad where I was under any circumstances. I knew he wouldn't take the news well at all. He wouldn't feel guilty. He'd feel pissed. I figured if she promised me that, I'd let her guilt off the hook about what had happened with her being so stupid and blind. It seemed like an eminently fair deal to me.

Good ol' Mom kept her promise and didn't tell Dad where I was exactly, but she told him sort of, which was worse because then he went and assumed the very worst. After he had put the screws to her, and turned them for a while, she finally told him all she knew was that I was living "somewhere up in Hollywood." That was all he needed to hear to spring into action. As I said, Dad was no fool. He knew what Hollywood meant. Hollywood meant the Doors and you already know what the Doors meant.

My sister, Nan, called and told me Dad said he was "through fucking around." That's a direct quote. I had the distinct impression what he really meant was I was to be the one "through fucking around" if he had his say in the matter. He responded by having warrants issued for everybody's arrest. Overnight I was a wanted runaway, and everybody else was "influencing a minor" to leave home and "harboring a runaway," neither of which charges was true, but since Mom saw fit neither to confirm nor to deny it, that's how it came down. It came down fast, and it came down hard. I thought the whole thing was ridiculous, a gigantic misunderstanding, as Cool Hand Luke once put it, a failure to communicate.

Needless to say, those at the office were not delighted with the paperwork Dad had sent their way via the West Hollywood sheriff's division. Now they were pissed, too. With the Miami trial and Jim's other legal hassles, this was the last shit they needed. They gave me the word in no uncertain terms: "Get your ass away from here *now*." They didn't care where I went so long as it was away.

Everyone knew what was best for me, what I should be doing, and where I should be doing it. Now *I* was pissed off, too. What about what I thought?

"The whole thing is groundless! I'm not even staying here," I told them, really getting worried they weren't going to let me come around ever again.

"Tell your father that."

I hadn't talked to him since before I'd moved out, over two weeks ago, mainly because I didn't know what to say without irritating him more than he already was.

"Maybe it's time for us to meet him." Jim finally spoke. "Maybe if I talked with him, he'd lighten up."

That got everybody speaking all at once.

"You can't do that. You don't have to do that—"

"I won't allow it, Jim."

"No way. This isn't your responsibility."

"It's not necessary. There're other ways."

Dad showed up in his white convertible Corniche Rolls-Royce, sober in both appearance (he was wearing a blue suit with a light-blue shirt; he never wore a tie, and he sure wasn't going to start today) and behavior. Jim and I came downstairs to meet him. I have to tell you I was beginning to think this might not be such a good idea. I introduced the two. "Dad, this is Jim. Jim, this is my father."

Jim said: "Pleasure to meet you, sir."

That was good. Definitely a good start. Maybe I was wrong to worry. Still, I had a nagging suspicion Jim wasn't real serious about this. There was something just a little off. I was really afraid he was in one of his moods. He had been known to test people before. It wouldn't have been the first time. He wasn't what you could call a predictable guy.

"I've heard a lot about you, Jimmy," Dad said.

God almighty, would you look at that? A term of endearment! Dad was trying, too, I gotta give him credit. He really was.

"And I've heard a lot about you," Jim said.

I hoped God was watching and paying very close attention.

We were going to my favorite restaurant, the Luau in Beverly Hills, on Rodeo Drive, for dinner. I said a prayer and got in the front seat, Jim in the back.

"Nice car," Jim said, stroking the leather.

"The way I see it," Dad started, "is we both have one thing in common. We both want what's best for Danny."

"That's exactly how I feel, too," Jim told him. Boy, was I feeling optimistic. "What's this?" Jim asked. I turned around. He'd picked up a book.

"Oh, that's Danny's government book from school," Dad told him.

Jim said, with an edge of shock in his voice, "*Government!* Don't tell me they're still teaching that bullshit in school." Then he put down the window and threw it out. I don't think my dad appreciated that gesture too much.

It was all downhill from there.

It was disastrous. If I had tried, I couldn't have imagined feeling more embarrassed, more uncomfortable, or more torn apart.

Jim got sloshed on every exotic drink the restaurant offered, which was pretty abundant, basically drinking his dinner while I suffered in silence. Dad tried his best to ignore him. At one point early in the "meal" Dad turned to me and said, "You don't get hobbies; you get obsessions." He sounded thoroughly disgusted. I felt lousy for putting him through all this.

"That's off base, Dad," I said as calmly and as nicely as I could.

"Oh, yeah?" he practically snarled. "What would you call it then?"

Jim spoke in my defense. "Being a teenager?"

"Teenagers don't spend half their life with rock bands twice their age. Teenagers don't live in hotels."

"It would be cool if you could acknowledge that and still support him."

"I'm not cool, I'm his father."

"I admit he's an unusual kid, but he's really doing surprisingly well," Jim told him.

"Well, c'mon, Jim, that's not altogether true either," I said, trying not to appear ungrateful for his support. "Rock and roll isn't just a hobby," I tried to explain to Dad. "It's much more than that. It's more like it's the only thing that means anything to me. I can't help it. I just don't care about anything else."

To which Dad gave me one of his patented you're-absolutely-nuts looks.

"And you believe this kid?" Dad asked Jim, who was the wrong person to ask that question.

Jim looked at him with total innocence. "I know exactly what he means."

Dad just glared at both of us. "You know, when you die, you don't go to the Great Rock Concert in the sky."

I said nothing to that.

Jim ordered a double Singapore sling and asked me why I wasn't drinking.

Dad said, "So you're drinking now? Big man."

Before I could think of an answer, Dad asked Jim if he always drank this much, and Jim answered, "No. Sometimes I drink more." So Dad told me right in front of Jim that my hero was a drunk. Jim responded by asking my father what he did to unwind. Dad told him he enjoyed sports, healthy interests. "Ever go to Vegas?" Jim asked. I thought he might be starting to try again, but I thought wrong.

"Yes," my father told him. "So?"

"You like cards?" Jim asked.

"Yeah, gin, so what?" Dad asked.

"Craps?"

"Sure, so what?"

"Ever bet the games?"

"All the time. What are you getting at?"

Jim turned and said, "Great role models, kid, a gambler and a drunk, ya really know how to pick 'em."

That's when Dad finally stood up and announced he'd had enough. "Let's go, son."

He expected me to get up obediently and leave with him.

I expected me to get up and leave with him.

Then how come I wasn't moving?

Fuck if I knew, but I wasn't.

Dad made the next move. I wish he hadn't, but he did.

"This is your choice then?" he yelled at me, everyone in the restaurant spinning toward us. "You're going to stay with him for the rest of your life? He's gonna take care of you when you're sick? He's gonna support you?"

I started to tell him I'd never said that.

172

"Well, make up your mind already. You can't have it both ways anymore. It's either rock 'n' roll and this creep or your family and school. That's your choice. Now, you pick one."

"Don't make me make that choice, Dad, please." I couldn't even think straight. I was still trying to figure out what had gone wrong. I was too busy thinking I shouldn't have ever set this whole thing up.

Dad wasn't waiting around for me to figure anything out. He was up and walking out of the restaurant.

"Dad, wait a second," I pleaded.

I turned to Jim, and I turned back to my father. Dad was already gone. I ran out to the parking lot in time to see his Rolls burning rubber up Rodeo Drive.

Being independent, fully on my own, was sort of overwhelming at first, but when I looked around, I saw I wasn't alone. There was the Doors family; it was still there, and I felt more a part of it now than ever before. Over the phone Nan told me Dad had forbidden either her or my brother to speak with me, but she just wanted to let me know they still loved me. She also told me I'd made a big mistake. "Dad's really pissed this time," she told me. "He's dropping the charges. He says he doesn't want you enough to go through with it." I wasn't sure if this was good news or bad, but I was relieved anyway. To make everything nice and official, he also dropped me out of his not inconsiderable will again. I didn't even know I'd been put back in.

The Doors had begun work on their new album. It had been quite some time since their last LP, and the record company was screaming for Christmas product. The Doors were taking their time. They'd parted company with their producer and were rehearsing in the same area they intended to record, the Doors' Workshop, the downstairs rehearsal room. If they recorded at the office, I'd be able to see the whole process! They decided they'd produce the album themselves, using their old engineer as coproducer, and rent a sixteen-track board from Elektra, which they eventually installed right in Bill's office. Bill wasn't overjoyed about that.

While Elektra readied for release what would be called *13* (thirteen of the band's best-known songs), the Doors rehearsed what would be the songs for *L.A. Woman*. It was the best summer I ever had.

The Miami trial, which had been dragging on, finally began to wrap itself up. Jim was found guilty on two of the misdemeanors. Bail was raised from five thousand to fifty thousand dollars to make sure he came back for sentencing. He faced six months to three years in Raiford Penitentiary, the toughest prison in the South. When he returned to L.A., Janis Joplin OD'd, and Jim really hit a funk. I'd never seen him so low. He was missing more rehearsals than ever. He was taking on some disturbingly strange friends no one had ever seen before. One night I went with him and some of these so-called friends to the Palms Bar. He lifted his glass and made a toast: "First Jimi, then Janis. You're drinking with number three." His new friends all guffawed and slapped his back and clinked glasses with him. I got up and left the table and went home to the Tropicana and got drunk alone.

School resumed in the fall. By now I had nothing in common with those people in Westchester. I hated going back there. It was like a trip back in time. But I didn't feel like transferring either. After all, I had only one semester to go. Life would have been a hell of a lot easier with a car, but no one around was leaping at the chance to buy me one, so I hitched, took a lot of cabs, and, when all else failed, took the bus.

I'd made some new friends at the Tropicana. Black Dawn and White Dawn, two of the resident hookers, looked in on me at night, made sure I was in my room when they went out to work, then woke me at dawn when they came off work so I could make my trek to school. On the weekends they helped me with my laundry. Fast Freddie, their pimp, didn't take too kindly to me at first, but when he found out I was still a virgin, he turned into a real nice guy. He ended up giving me a great cassette player for Christmas so I could have music in room 103.

On the weekends, when the band wasn't rehearsing, I hung out by the pool at the hotel, which was becoming, more and more, a stopover for bands playing in town, especially at the Whisky. Not only had I met Andy Warhol and Bob Dylan, but I'd become friendly with the J. Geils Band and especially their singer Peter Wolf, who were just starting out, and Alice Cooper, who was a great drinker and a big fan of Jim's. Eric Burdon, another great boozer and buddy of Jim's, stayed there all the time, too. All in all, I was having a pretty cool time. Knowing Morrison was opening doors all over town. People at Barney's Beanery, the Whisky, Palms Bar, and Garden District all knew me and treated me swell 'cause they'd seen me around with Jim.

Pamela, who had been out of town, returned to L.A., and Jim's life began to stabilize. The recording sessions were going smoothly. I was at the office every day, and by now the school was giving me work credits. That meant I could leave school at noon and receive for working at the office the same credit two afternoon classes would give me. The tension that had been so obvious just a few weeks before began to evaporate. For the first time in a while you could describe the environment as "happy," a word one wouldn't ordinarily choose to describe the Doors. No one knew the reason, and no one was questioning it.

In February we found out. Jim announced he was going to Paris with Pamela. Pamela was enthralled. Pretty soon she would be departing to find them both an apartment and ready it for Jim's future arrival. She was going to have Jim all to herself. She must have felt like she'd won.

The band's contract with Elektra was up with the delivery of *L.A. Woman*, so there was nothing really keeping Jim in L.A. He had already made it abundantly clear he would not tour the album. He was tired of the audiences' expectations as well as the cops' limitations. In L.A. he was fed up with the hangers-on, the so-called friends. He found it difficult to say no in Los Angeles. He was sick of being a rock star. He craved anonymity. Paris had been home to so many of his literary heroes, from Rimbaud to Hemingway. It was the locale of Henry Miller's *Tropic of Cancer*, and Baudelaire's Hashish Club. Jim wanted to write, poetry, perhaps a book, and Paris seemed the natural choice. The Doors could finish the mix of the album without him.

Everybody thought it was a good idea for Jim to get away, to take an extended vacation. Everybody, it seemed, but me. I was depressed at the idea of his leaving for so long. I couldn't picture what life would be like in L.A. without Jim around. Yet I couldn't announce my displeasure either. Who was I to say anything? It wouldn't make one bit of difference one way or the other what I thought, 'cept maybe piss someone off. I'd just be told to keep my opinions to myself. It was the job of those of us who worked for Jim to shield him from unpleasant confrontations, not to provoke them. My job and my needs were in obvious direct conflict, and I hurt. I took it personally.

Jim reacted to Pam's early departure to Paris to find them a flat with unreserved abandon. He took to the town, stopping in every bar he'd ever been in to have a drink and say good-bye. He went on a monthlong bender, during which time he called every phone number he had to say "so long," crashed two cars, and kept going until he was slowed down by a fall from the second-floor window ledge at the Chateau Marmont. Usually Jim avoided doctors if at all possible, but this time he was in so much pain he had to go. The doctor told Jim he'd punctured his left lung. I'd heard the news in a confidential way, and I was sworn to secrecy. Jim either didn't want to worry anyone or didn't want his trip to Paris jeopardized, I couldn't be sure which. The doctor had given Jim specific instructions to take it easy. Jim, meanwhile, seemed bent on disobeying and continued his farewell drunk as if uninterrupted. All the while he never slept in the same bed twice.

Every time I saw him, I wanted to beg him not to leave, but I knew how unrealistic that was. On March 15 I walked into the office to help him clean out his desk. Later in the afternoon there was going to be a little going-away party, and he'd invited me to come by if I felt like it. I thought about not going just to let him know I didn't feel like it. He probably wouldn't notice whether I came or not anyway, and I really did want to see him off, get a chance to say good-bye, even though I was still pissed at him for leaving (me). I figured I might even be able to engineer a little sympathy from him and maybe whoever else was there. At least he knew where he was going. I had no idea what I was going to be doing. I tried to peer into the future, and it just looked blank and depressing. It was going to be a long wait for him to come back home.

Jim must have sensed something was off. He was going through the desk drawers, and I was going through the scrapbook I'd been working on for the past four years, when he stopped what he was doing and leaned down next to me. We were the only two in the office.

"Ya know, you're always working on this thing. I've never really had a chance to see what you've done with it. Slow down."

For the next forty-five minutes we silently pored over the material: from the Doors' first review in the Los Angeles *Times* panning the group at the Whisky, the beautiful pictures of shirtless Jim, the raves for the first album and *Strange Days*, the put-downs of *Waiting for the Sun*, the riotous concert tour of '68 headline coverage, the best-seller lists, gold record press releases, and award photos, the hateful reviews of *The Soft Parade*, on through the controversial press surrounding Miami, including the wanted poster of Jim *Rolling Stone* had printed on its first page, to the "comeback" claims for *Morrison Hotel* and lastly to a glowing review of *13* from *Rolling Stone* with a letter the magazine had printed praising it for "finally catching on." It was signed Denny Sullivan, which was the name I used. Every time some magazine would give the Doors a bad review, I'd dash off a letter giving the paper a bad review. Siddons had suggested if I wanted to help the band, I should consider using a pseudonym on account of the total lack of objectivity I'd projected for my real self via the letter columns.

"What a trip!" Jim whistled. "Where are you going to take it from here?" he asked me. "How is it gonna end?"

Oh, shit, I thought, *I can't hold it in anymore. Why does it have to end? Why can't it continue? Isn't he coming back and starting again?* Instead, I simply said, "I don't know."

Jim persisted. "Come on, you must have some idea?"

It spilled out. "Aren't you going to tour when you come back? After vacation? I mean, after a rest, maybe you'll feel like touring." It was the days of big tours and big money now, and the Doors had never done one. The music business had changed a lot, even since Miami. And now I was old enough and, more important, free enough to go out on the road with them. I knew Jim was tired of touring, but I figured a vacation was just what the doctor ordered. He'd lose some weight, write new lyrics and poetry, get a rest, get in shape, and come back ready and raring to go.

Jim cut into my thoughts.

"Listen to me, Danny. You know that fall I took out the window at the Chateau the other week? You know, usually I just sort of bounce, pick up, and hop along unscarred? Well, that one really hurt, man. I must be getting old or brittle or something. I think that's some sort of sign. All the other times nothing happened. I don't know if it was just luck or my constitution or a guardian angel or what. But I was thinkin', ya know that nine-lives trip? Well, I'm like that cat, and that fall was my last chance. Next time there'll be no next time. Next time it's over."

"What the fuck are you talking about?"

I was trying to sound tough. I never heard Jim sounding like this before, this vulnerable. Then again he always talked about dying. One nice sunny Sunday I'd stopped by his Laurel Canyon house only to find him sitting alone in the dark, curtains drawn.

"What do you think happens when you die?" he'd asked.

"Christ, I don't know, Jim. C'mon, let's go play some pool at Barney's."

"Anyway," he was saying to me, "the point I'm trying to make is, I might not ever come back from Paris. And you gotta be prepared for that, man. And if I don't, then you'll know the cat ran out of lives."

"I don't like it when you talk like that," I said, looking away from him and at the scrapbook instead.

"Why not?" He laughed.

"I don't know what I'd do without you."

"Well, listen, there's probably nothing to worry about. I'm just going on vacation and everything'll be fine. You know how teachers go on sabbaticals? Midway through their career, for rejuvenation and vacation, they take some time off and usually go somewhere that coincides with their vocation. That's exactly what I'm doing—a semi-sabbatical, a career break. I'll be back in no time.

"I want you to write to me whenever you get a chance and tell me what's going on in L.A. when I'm gone. That way I won't feel like I'll be missing out on so much, and we can still be in touch, okay? I'll be back. I'll see you in June."

I thought I was gonna cry, but I didn't. I held it in. I didn't want Jim to see me cry.

Fortunately people started arriving for Jim's farewell party. I wiped my nose, closed the scrapbook, and looked for a place to stash it.

"This is for you," Jim said, handing me a new, private edition of *The New Creatures*. He'd written: "See ya at the Big Rock Concert in the sky. Your brother of laughter and freedom, Jim."

After a few beers and a couple of hits on some dynamite opiated hash, I was feeling fine—downright snappy, in fact. Good thing, too, 'cause no one was about to notice how I was doing. Jim Fucking Morrison was leaving town.

I drained my fourth Coors and headed toward the back office to get another out of the refrigerator. The office door was closed, but I knew there couldn't be a meeting going on, not now. Otherwise, I wouldn't have just walked straight in without knocking.

Jim was sitting behind Bill's desk, pen in hand. His head, down, jerked up. "Haven't you ever heard of knocking?" he barked. He dipped his head and put the pen—no, it was an empty pen cartridge—to his nose and ran it along an album cover, sniffing up a long, thin white line of cocaine.

I didn't know whether to be mad (at him for being so damn hypocritical), sad (for the same reason), or glad (thinking he might offer me some). I ended up just standing there, no doubt looking like a completely astounded nincompoop.

"You shouldn't walk through closed doors unless you're prepared for what you might find inside," he told me, handing the pen cartridge to Babe. One part of me wanted to turn and leave, but another, larger part of me was too fascinated by what was happening to make a move. There was still plenty of the drug left.

"Can I go next?" I asked Babe, afraid to ask Jim.

Babe looked at Jim. Jim looked at me. I fully expected him to say no. I think I wanted him to say no.

"Sure. Why not? I guess you're old enough, go ahead."

I took the Bic pen cartridge and put it to my right nostril, bent down, and the way I'd seen Jim do, I snorted up the line, sniffing hard, making it disappear as I went along. I felt it hitting me somewhere under the eyes and behind my nose. It made me twice as hyper as ever. But I felt something else, too: It made me excited, confident. The whole effect lasted only about twenty minutes.

During second period, physical education, the class was sitting cross-legged listening to somebody from the drug rehab house Synanon lecture us about the danger of drugs. A guy with a shaved head was telling us about how marijuana led to harder drugs, about how he first started with grass and ended up on the hard stuff. A guy from the police department was with him. They passed out three joints for us to pass around and look at. They traveled through all sixty-five of us. When they were turned back in, the cop counted an extra three joints.

Out of nowhere I felt an undeniable, overwhelming tug of longing, loneliness, an impending sense of doom. As the laughter died down, I became conscious of a vaguely familiar sound. Through the din of the class noise, a plane droned somewhere overhead. I looked at my watch. It was ten-thirty. Jim had taken off for Paris exactly fifty minutes ago.

A month passed before I finally got around to writing Jim. I figured I'd wait until enough time passed so maybe he'd be wondering why I wasn't writing, or maybe he'd worry, or something. Also, waiting awhile gave me a chance to be able to tell him what was actually happening outside of how much I missed him and all that sort of emotional shit.

It was a long, rambling letter. I told him that Ray, Robby, and John were in rehearsal, getting some great songs ready for his return. I thought that might be a subtle enough reminder he had something to return to. I also told him what books I was reading (*Steppenwolf*) and all about the favorable press *L.A. Woman* was getting, and I even included some of the reviews, figuring that would cheer him up. I thanked him for setting me up so well with Bob Gibson and Gary

Stromberg, two publicists in L.A., who together handled about 90 percent of all the big name rock groups, including the Doors. They'd arranged interviews with Rod Stewart and Jethro Tull already. They were working on a Mick Jagger interview. I didn't tell Jim about the Jagger thing 'cause I was afraid it might piss him off. I'd once asked him if he'd score me some Rolling Stones tickets, and he asked me what I needed Jagger for when I had him. I never did know if he was teasing or what, so I just thought that would be better left unsaid. I included the article we did together for *Creem* magazine about Miami. I told him a little about school, and then I told him to hurry up and get home because everyone really missed him a lot.

He never did respond, which was okay 'cause I didn't really expect him to. The deal was I'd write him and tell him what was going on; nothing was ever said about his writing back.

He did call the office, though I wasn't there when the call came. He told Bill everything was going great and he wanted more money, enough to spend two months longer than he'd originally planned.

Which didn't exactly thrill me. I'd been counting the days until he returned. I still went to the office and hung out and did my jobs, but I was lonely. It wasn't nearly the same without Jim around. For the first time in a long time life was getting boring. All I did was wait. For the past four years my life had revolved around Jim, and without him I felt distinctly lacking in both direction and purpose.

To alleviate some of the boredom, in March I got a job playing the music broadcast over the senior lawn during nutrition and lunch, if I wanted to stay late before going to work. It looked like I was actually going to graduate high school. My grades had been good on my last report card. After a recent ballgame I had been approached by a baseball scout from UCLA, who said if I graduated with no less than a *C* average, he would extend a baseball scholarship to me. He had been watching a couple of us for a while without our knowing it, and despite being warned by practically everybody he talked to that I was a troublemaker, he still wanted me for his team.

All I had to do was graduate, then take a foreign language at a junior college. I hadn't ever taken one, and you couldn't get into a university without one. I tried, but I'd flunked Spanish two times already, so I'd stopped trying. I wasn't really eager to go it again. In fact, I wasn't one bit sure I was gonna take UCLA up on its wonderful offer. I always assumed I'd go to work for the Doors full-time after I graduated. I hadn't really considered college. That was Dad's dream for me, not mine. I almost considered calling him with the scholarship news. He'd be delighted and I sure could have used some approval, but I resisted, and the temptation passed.

In May I played the eleven-minute uncensored version of Chuck Berry's "My Ding-A-Ling" (from his new *London Session* LP) over the school PA system. The song had yet to be edited into its three-minute single form and contained some rather racy, but still relatively harmless, lyrics. Tanner heard its broadcast and immediately sent me back on probation, effectively banning me from ever playing any more records at school. "You've got to learn some responsibility." He warned, "I'd suspend you, but I know how much this scholarship means to you." As usual, he was wrong. After all, how could he know what it meant to me when I didn't know what it meant to me? And then he proceeded to give me a lecture on morality and the single teenage male, not a word of which I deemed relevant to my case.

I'd been walking around with a real chip on my shoulder anyway, pissed at the world, bored and impatient, just daring someone to cross me. Mr. Tanner was the lucky one. I thought he had grossly over-reacted. Taking away my music, however small a piece, was not a move to be taken lightly. The song was harmless. It wasn't serious or slanderous. It was funny. You know the one, where Chuck sings, "I want you to play with my ding-a-ling, oh everybody sing," and the audience chimes in: "My ding-a-ling, my ding-a-ling, I want you to play with my ding-a-ling?" Practically a nursery rhyme. If he thought that was obscene, he hadn't heard nothing yet. I'd show him obscene. I'd show him irresponsible. I'd show him . . .

Since he hadn't remembered to take the broadcast room key away from me, I had no trouble sneaking back in when no one was looking. A week later, during lunch, I brought in a brand-new mint-condition copy of the three-disc *Woodstock* sound track-album, locked the door behind me, turned the public-address system up to 8+, as loud as it would go without feeding back, and cued up the stylus to Country Joe and the Fish's "Fuck" cheer. Then I stood back, prepared to watch all hell break loose.

"Gimme an F . . ." Country Joe McDonald sang out.

I looked out the window onto the senior lawn.

The whole class of five hundred stood up and hollered, "F," along with the half-million voices on the record.

Country Joe screamed, *"Gimme a U."*

The class yelled back, *"U!"*

And so on.

"*What's that spell?*" Country Joe bellowed.

"*Fuck!*" shouted my whole class.

"What's that spell?" he sang.

"*Fuck!*" they shouted again. And again and again.

Through the trees I could just make out Tanner standing stonestill for a beat and a pause, his jaw hanging down past his tie knot, before he took off in my direction. I really didn't want to chicken out and stop the song just so I could get away and save a twentydollar record. Then I got a bright idea: Forget the album, save yourself. I left the song on, unlocked the door, went out and locked it behind me, so he'd think I was still in there, and seeing the coast was clear I took off. When I made it off campus without being detected, I could still hear the fading chorus of Country Joe's "I-Feel-Like-I'm-Fixin'-to-Die-Rag" which closes the cheer. Then I ran like the Beast.

The outcome of this event was threefold:

1. Come June I did not graduate with the rest of my class, by verdict of the Student Council and boys' VP.
2. I received my high school diploma in the mail.
3. And the strangest of all, no one even bothered to ask me if I'd done it. So I wasn't even able to protest or declare my innocence. Everyone just assumed it was me since I was the "only one" with a key, which wasn't true, which just pissed me right off all over again.

Another and perhaps even more interesting outcome was that Chuck Berry's "My Ding-a-Ling" eventually became the number one song in the country, his first top ten single in over ten years and his first number one song *ever*. I considered it nothing less than a total vindication of the missed festivities, if not my whole senior year.

Then I got back to the unpleasant task of waiting around for Jim Morrison to come back from Paris.

CHAPTER SEVEN

· · · · · · · · · · ·

How does it feel?
How does it feel?
To be on your own
with no direction home
Like a complete unknown,
Like a Rolling Stone. . . .
                —BOB DYLAN

IT was a lousy morning. For one thing, it was too hot, almost in the nineties and not even 10:00 A.M. yet. Summer. Sunday. Smoggy. My head hurt, I was hung over. My mouth tasted like a swamp. There was a line at Duke's. I needed coffee and a smoke. What also made it lousy was that I had nothing interesting to think about. I was bored. I wished Jim were back already. I hated the waiting. Jim had already extended his stay twice. I had an awful feeling in my gut. It was like waiting for my father to return home all over again.

I went into the lobby at the Tropicana to buy a pack of Marlboros out of the machine. Maybe after I did that, there would be an opening at the counter at Duke's.

"So your buddy's dead, huh? I guess you're gonna be leaving us." The desk clerk was speaking to my back. I didn't think he was talking to me. We'd never gotten along. He didn't seem too crazy about anyone who stayed at the hotel who wasn't a tourist, which excluded all us regulars.

"You talking to me?" I turned around to face him. He was really an ugly, sour old shit.

"I guess you're gonna be movin' on," he said.

"Oh, yeah, why's that?" I asked.

"Dontcha listen to the news?" he said. "Your buddy Morrison, he's dead. I heard it myself just this morning on the T.V."

Rather than be shocked or surprised, I looked at him doubtfully. I didn't believe him. Once upon a time maybe I would have. But Jim was always dying. . . . By now I was used to it.

There had always been Morrison death stories. Either he was going out a window and doing himself in that way, or he was dying in a car crash after a night of serious drinking; he was always OD'ing on some unlikely drug (like acid) or in some bizarre sexual escapade or any combination of the above. But then Jim would always show up later that day or the next, saying something like "Rumors of my demise have been greatly exaggerated." And we'd all laugh and feel relieved.

"How'd he go this time?" I asked Bukowski look-alike, curious.

"Heart attack is what they said, but if ya ask me, he probably OD'd like the rest of 'em freaks."

"Yeah, heart attack, huh? That's a good one. I haven't heard that one before." I thought I'd heard them all. I went back down to Duke's for some coffee to wake up and ordered some breakfast.

At the counter, I lit up a smoke and drank my coffee, while the radio played "Riders on the Storm." When the song finished, the DJ, B. Mitchell Reid, came on and with his deep, smokey voice told us who the song was by. Then he paused and continued talking.

"I don't know quite how to say this. . . . In case you haven't heard, it's been confirmed by the Doors' manager, Bill Siddons, that Jim Morrison died yesterday, July third, in Paris. . . ." BMR went on to say what a great guy Jim was and how much he'll be missed, but I didn't wait to hear any more or for my breakfast order. I leaped up, threw some money out of my pocket onto the counter, flew out the door, and ran straight for the office, up the stairs, and through the open front door straight into a meeting. . . .

Siddons, Ray, John, and Robby were sitting around in a circle. They all looked at me. I was out of breath; I implored them with my eyes. I wouldn't have known what to say could I have spoken.

Bill spoke first. "I'm sorry, I just got back in town. I've been meaning to call you. . . ."

Now I knew what to say. "What the *fuck*'s going on! What am *I* supposed to do now? *Huh?*" I panted.

They all looked at me like I was crazy and they were nothing but sorry.

"I can't go home! I can't go back! I have no place to go now. What am I supposed to do?" God, I really thought I was gonna cry. "Say something!"

John cut in. "That's really crass. You're really thoughtless some-times, you know that? Our best friend, our singer just died, and all you care about is what are you gonna do."

Bill spoke up again. "We were just sitting here, trying to figure out what we're going to do. . . ."

Ray, who hadn't said a word since I barged in, finally spoke. He stood up and came over to me, put his big arm around my shoulder, and walked me to the door. "Don't worry, as long as I live in this city, you've got a gig. I know it's gonna be hard for a while; it will be on all of us. I don't know what I can say that'll make it any better, except I'm sorry. I know how much you loved him."

I looked up at Ray. He was a good head and a half taller than me. "I can't deal with this. I don't know how to deal with any of this at all." Without saying good-bye, I left the office and walked out into the day.

I kept on walking, up one block and down another, first northeast toward Sunset Boulevard, then southwest. I tried to sort out my feelings, but it was useless. There were too many, and they were moving too fast for me to grab, hold, and look at. All I could do was let them fly by and hope sooner or later they'd tire and lie down. I felt like I was gonna bust. I couldn't stop walking. I had to keep moving. Stopping, even for a moment, was unthinkable.

I bought a six-pack of Old English, which is what I drank when I wanted to get drunk rather than just drink, I took off to Poinsettia Park, and while a bunch of college students played softball, I sat under a tree and rested as I drank, one can after another, and chain-smoked cigarettes, feeling again that if I stopped, something horrible would happen. The thoughts just kept coming.

Jim's dead. He's really dead. I had no idea how to process the information. Everything backed up and overflowed, overwhelming me.

I got up and walked around and let the thoughts come some more.

I was trying to make myself believe it. It was torture. *Jim Morrison is never coming back from Paris. You've been waiting for him, but he's not coming back. You're never going to be able to see him, or talk to him, ever again. He's gone for good. And there's nothing you can do to change it.* And the impatience and sadness and anger began rolling together. In waves. As illogical as they were unstoppable: *It's not fair! How could he do this to me? The asshole. Yeah, dying is real easy for him. What about me? He should have known it was going to happen someday.* Christ, was I getting mad. It was just like Dad's leaving all over again. And then I'd left my Dad and my family for Jim. I'd sunk all bets on him. *I gave him everything I had to give, and he left me! God . . . They did it again! The bastards! I depended on them, I loved them, I trusted them . . . and they left me! The insensitive fucks!*

What else could my reaction be? Maybe John was right. Maybe I was just being selfish. But what choice did I have over how I felt? I couldn't help it. Besides, getting angry felt a whole lot better than the other feelings that were gnawing inside and now came ripping up through my heart. *What's wrong with me? What did I do wrong? I'm fucked. Is that why they left? If I love them, they go away. If I trust somebody, he leaves me.* God, I missed him already. The loneliness. And fatalism. *I'll show them. They can't get away with this.* Impatience. And then, the rage. At them, myself, the whole fucking world. *I will never trust or love anyone or anything ever again.* They ruined it for me and everybody else forever. I swore as I stomped the sidewalk under my feet.

What do you do when you love and you hurt so fuckin' much you want to die? You can't take it; you're so scared and frightened and pissed off you don't even know where you're going. What school teaches you how to handle it, and what book can you read that tells you how to stop hurting? How long does it last? How do you make it go away? There's got to be a way, or do you just have to feel it? What do other people do? Do they get it this bad and how bad is this 'cause I can't imagine any worse.

The sun had set, and I finished the beer. I walked into Hollywood and into the night . . . and I kept walking. Cursing the whole fucking world. So alone . . . so fucking alone.

I must have walked twenty miles that night. I never stopped. When dawn broke, I headed north, into the flats of Beverly Hills. I was on automatic. I didn't dare make any decisions. I didn't trust myself. My feet made all the decisions. It was easier like that. It was easier for my feet to hurt than my heart.

At 6:00 A.M I found myself walking up Beverly Drive in Beverly Hills. By 7:00 A.M I was standing on the sidewalk in front of my father's house. I hadn't planned it this way. Nevertheless, there I was. I wondered if Dad was home. I wondered if I should go up and knock. It seemed like a stupid thing to do. And it seemed stupid not to.

I walked up the brick driveway to the front door. His Rolls was in the garage next to his blue Ferrari.

The house looked good—secure and welcoming with its big trees and wide lawn. Suddenly I knew this was where I was supposed to be. That there was no place else in the world for me to be right now. I needed a home. I needed time to figure out what to do next. I needed to be held and hugged and reassured. I needed love.

I knocked on the big cherry-wood door.

It swung open. Dad stood there in a pair of baggy cords and his

sleeveless UCLA sweatshirt. His big, hairy belly poked out between
the two garments.

He didn't look surprised to see me. But he didn't look real pleased
either.

"Jim's dead." My own voice sounded strange to me.

"Yeah, so what? What did you expect?"

I don't know what I wanted him to say. We both stood there in
the doorway. Him inside and me outside. I was hoping for some
compassion; forgiveness would have been great. Or was that asking
for too much?

Neither one of us was speaking. At this point I would have settled
for "hello."

What was he waiting for? Did he want me to ask him the obvious?
Did he want to hear me say it? That I was sorry, and can I move in
with you? Or what? Then it hit me for the first time that he *could*
say no. He didn't have to let me move in with him. That really shook
me up. Staying at the Tropicana, waiting for Jim to return home, was
one thing. The prospect of living there for the rest of my life was a
different matter entirely, especially with Morrison gone.

I was prepared to beg. If I had to, I was ready. And Dad still
hadn't said anything else.

Finally he spoke to me. "You think you're ready to move in
here, get your long hair cut, take your role as a member of this family,
and begin acting like a responsible human being?"

I swallowed. Now *I* had the option of saying no. It was a bit
more comfortable, but not a whole lot more. Saying no meant saying
yes to a whole lot of other things I wasn't sure I could handle. On
the other hand, saying yes meant saying yes to a lot of things I wasn't
too sure I could handle either.

"I can try," I told him.

"That's not good enough anymore."

He started to close the door in front of him.

"Okay, okay, I'll do it. I'll do whatever you want. I want to fit
in, Dad. . . . Jesus, I don't have anyplace to go anymore."

"Oh, I get it. This is your last choice?"

I became aware of how much I wanted to please him, how much
I needed him. The question was, How much of myself was I willing
to forfeit to get that approval and how much good would it do if it
weren't really me he was accepting?

"This is my only choice, Dad."

The door pulled back open, and with my head down, I stepped in.

"Welcome home, son," my father said.

I hugged him. I fell against his big barrel chest, and I could barely fit my arms all the way around him; but I tried. I hugged him with all my might. But I didn't cry. I never cried through the whole ordeal—not then, not before, and not after. Maybe I was afraid if I started, I'd never stop. Maybe I just didn't want to feel all that pain, all that loss. But mainly I just didn't want to deal with anything that hurt so much. Dad had always told me that when no one else would help me, my family would be there. Well, I needed him, and he was there 100 percent. I had a lot to make up for.

Dad had it all figured out nice and clean: As I entered UCLA in two years to begin playing baseball, brother Joe would be graduating medical school in Chicago and coming west for his internship and residency. My sister, Nan, would be graduating UCLA and entering law school at that time. It was Dad's dream for all his children to go to college, graduate, and become professionals. I had been the only unknown element capable of screwing up the plan; now that I was squared away he was real proud.

Compared with what I'd been through at Mom's house, life at Dad's estate was nice and easy. He had a gardener to take care of the lawn and gardens, a pool man to clean the pool, even a housekeeper to take care of the house and make breakfast. All I had to do was continue playing baseball in junior college and get Spanish out of the way. You'd think that wouldn't have been so difficult. You'd think my part of the bargain was easy enough. Yeah, you'd think so, wouldn't you?

After I got my hair cut, he bought me a brand-new white Corvette just like my brother's. I even thought it was worth it.

We went out to Jerry Magnin's on Rodeo Drive, just down the street from the Luau, and he let me pick out a whole new wardrobe. Since I'd finally begun to grow, it was easier finding clothes that fit and Magnin's had a real cool selection. I picked out a half dozen faded prewashed French-cut blue jeans, some black jeans, a few leather jackets (one brown, one black), a few pairs of boots (red cowboy, brown suede, and cool black Cuban-heeled zip-ups, like Beatle boots but higher), and a couple of pullovers. When he paid the bill, he opened a charge account for me so I could come and shop whenever I wanted.

Before the Plan went into action in the fall, he'd opened charge accounts for me under his name all over town, from Joe Rudnick's (the best sporting goods store in town), to Nate 'N Al's (the rich man's deli on Beverly Drive).

He put me back into the will.

Then he pulled me off the Ritalin. One evening he just took the bottle out from the medicine cabinet and poured its contents down the toilet.

"You won't be needing these anymore," he said, tossing the empty container in the wastebasket.

On the outside everything looked real smooth. It was on the inside things were beginning to go wrong.

The depression I'd been fighting off washed over me. I was the opposite of hyper, lethargic and down instead; my body dragged, but my mind ran and dove. I couldn't concentrate on anything. I felt raw and vulnerable; hot and cold flashes came over me unexpectedly. I got a lot of dizzy spells and had to lie down.

When those symptoms cleared up, I saw that junior college and I weren't getting along too well. Everything I had heard about it led me to believe I'd like college more than high school, and I wanted to believe it. But I'd heard wrong. It was just as bad, if not worse, because it was that much harder. Schools still made you take stupid classes that you didn't want to take and that had no bearing whatsoever on Life in the Real World and barely any on your major (in this case sports) or your minor (law). More nagging. What did *any* of this have to do with rock 'n' roll? Not one fucking thing. Had I given up all my dreams to make a living outside music? Was I really going to turn myself into a jock? A lawyer?

It wasn't working at all. This wasn't what I wanted. I knew it every day I went. It had been stupid of me to think I could make it work.

When Jim was alive, I always had something to look forward to. I knew where I belonged. I felt like I didn't need anybody else. But now I felt nobody else needed me. And I felt frustrated because I felt trapped. To the best of my ability, I stayed away from people and ignored the rest of the world. I tried to do the work that was expected of me, but it just got worse. The future looked bleak. The past depressed me. The present was unbearable. As depressed as I was, that's how pleased Dad was. He only saw that I was living at home, going to school, and on my way to becoming a professional ballplayer.

One night at the Whisky, while I was reliving the old days with some rock and roll cohorts, Doreen, an editor from *Scene* magazine, handed me a rather large chalky white pill. I washed it down with a tequila sunrise and proceeded to get more plastered than I'd ever gotten before in my entire life of trying. I called up Doreen the next day to find out more about what she'd given me. The name of the pill was Quaalude. I'd never heard of it before. How exciting to be on the cutting edge of drug discovery and chemical research. "How does one go about procuring another?"

She told me she had a renewable prescription. From that day forward she became known as Doreen-from-*Scene*-the-Quaalude-Queen.

The weeks passed like a dream. When Quaalude was combined with alcohol, the effects were almost miraculous. Of course, exercises like walking up a flight of stairs with little or no muscular coordination, or navigating a car while your eyes played Ping-Pong in their sockets, became treacherous. But these were minor obstacles as far as I was concerned. I felt better. The end was being achieved. Almost.

It was as if I wanted to be the one who had died; I wanted to be the one who had left everybody behind for a change. I stopped smoking pot altogether. It only made me more aware of the horror of my situation and more insecure than I already was. By accident I discovered how well a couple of lines of cocaine could straighten me out and set me talking and walking once I already had a few too many drinks and Quaaludes laying into my system, also how nicely a lude took the speedy edge off a cocaine zip. It was a precarious balance, rarely achieved, mixing up all the elements just right, but I had a lot of fun trying.

Usually the ludes proved to be more influential (especially when reinforced by the booze), and since they lasted longer than cocaine anyway, the combined effect usually overrode the cocaine, and I'd pass out. If I did too much coke, it would win, and I'd be zipping along a mile a second, teeth clenched, breathing heavily labored, quite uncoordinated and sloppy from the residual effects of the Quaaludes. But those magical minutes when everything balanced out and complemented each other just right were truly something to behold.

I'd been snorting cocaine ever since Jim left, whenever it was available. I'd just wanted to try it, to really experience it; then, I'd promised myself, I'd leave it alone because I knew how I could be with something I liked. It's odd the way these moral promises one makes to oneself drop away so quickly in the face of an attractive adversary. Once you step over that line, it's gone, erased forever, and you can never go back. I wasn't using coke on any sort of regular basis, but whenever it was around, I'd do it. I didn't go out looking for it, but there was so much around I didn't need to. If it wasn't offered, you just looked for a coke spoon around a neck and found out that person's name, then introduced yourself. To be honest, I wasn't really that crazy about it. The last thing I needed was something to make me more hyper. Maybe that's why I hadn't gone characteristically overboard with it yet. I didn't go broadcasting the fact, though, on account of if I did, who'd want to give it to me anymore? They'd think it was just a waste.

As far as my father knew, everything was fine. All I had to do was stay in school, do reasonably well, play ball, and be home by midnight. He was asleep by then anyway, so when I stumbled in, drunk and drooling, at 2:30 A.M., no one was the wiser. In the morning he left before I was up. Unless I told him how miserable I was, how was he ever going to know?

There was another rule, unwritten and unspoken but no less expected to be abided by than the others. *No Doors*, meaning no extreme interest or indulgence to be displayed in rock 'n' roll. Since Jim was presumed dead, the Doors per se weren't an obvious target anymore. What Dad didn't know, 'cause I hadn't told him, was they still were. During my second semester in college the post-Morrison Doors, with Ray handling the lead vocals, were in the studio rehearsing for a new LP as a threesome.

Needless to say, it wasn't the same. First of all, the temptation to risk everything I had in order to see them wasn't nearly as great as it had once been. Not only because I now had more to lose but also because the sad truth was they were worth less. After I snuck back to the office a few times to wrap things up, I stopped going entirely. It wasn't that I disagreed with their decision to continue. After all, everyone in the Doors family knew all along the Doors were more than just Jim. What no one had reckoned on was that the group was always greater than the sum total of its parts. The Doors were more than the four of them had been and certainly more than the three of them now were.

But that's not why I stopped going to the Doors' office. I stopped going because it was just too weird, too quiet. I kept expecting to see Jim walk in and say something like "Fucking-A-Rudy, what is this, a business office or something?" I missed not hearing his voice with the music rehearsed there. Most of all, there were just too many memories. And while I didn't want to forget, I didn't necessarily want to remember either if I didn't have to.

It wasn't easy maintaining the balance required between my night and my day activities, but since I really didn't see any other choice, I did it. I didn't think about how long I might be able to carry it off. All I knew for sure was I wasn't heading in the right direction. I was headed in two directions at once, and I knew damn well one of them wasn't right.

You know the feeling you get when you're on a roller coaster and you're just starting into the first climb on the track? When the car suddenly downshifts and you begin the first long, steep climb up the first big hill on the course? Then you know when you get right to the top there? Right at the crest? And you take a deep breath with a mixture of terror and excited anticipation just before you plunge almost straight down? You know that very feeling? That's how I felt. Practically every day when I woke up. Part thrill, part dread.

I guess the downshift just before the climb in real life began the morning of baseball practice when my coach informed me he wasn't ever going to play me in a game again until I got my hair cut short. There was a lot of controversy and even some lawsuits concerning long hair and the kids' rights versus the authorities (or the establishment, as they were known back then). Although he'd made it pretty obvious he wasn't in favor of my hair hanging over my ears and down toward my shoulders, he'd never come right out and said, "I'm not playing you because your hair's too long."

I'd gotten sick and tired of sitting on the bench and had started bugging him because he wasn't playing me and I'd never had to sit on the bench before. Not only was I getting impatient, but it was humiliating. It wasn't because of my playing. When he had played me before I was batting .325, so it wasn't like I was in a slump or anything, and if I wasn't getting a chance to play, then what the fuck was I doing there? To add insult to humiliation, we'd been losing, and he still wasn't playing me. . . . He was putting in players who were last string before me. That's when I asked him why he wasn't playing me, and that's when he told me, "Your attitude stinks. You haven't been supporting the team, you've missed practices, and besides, that goddamn hair of yours is too long."

"Sorry I asked."

It wasn't too long by my father's standards, but it was too long for this guy. Still, I was only too aware if my old man got wind I'd been asked by my team coach to cut my hair and I'd refused, he'd side with the team any day, anytime.

The next time I showed up for practice, hair pulled behind my ears, I was changing into my uniform, about halfway into the pants, when the coach came up to me and said, "Don't bother."

"What? Whaddya mean, don't bother? I'm here to support my team."

"You're not on the team anymore. We don't need your type."

"Oh, and what type is that?" I was curious, "Do we have a name, my type?"

"Candy ass, you're a real first-class candy ass."

"Yeah, you're just saying that 'cause you want to eat it."

I grabbed my clothes and left. He threw my glove after me, bouncing it off the lockers. Some coach, couldn't even throw straight.

I might have gotten in the last word, but somehow I wasn't real consoled about it. Dad was gonna shit a baseball bat when he heard. That was my first reaction. My second reaction was, you don't have to tell him.

But inside, where it counted, I knew this was the start. I could either pull it together in one huge, heroic effort or let it fall apart in one glorious, dramatic finale. This was the beginning of the end. I chose the path of least resistance. I let it fall—mainly because it was too late to pull it together anyway. The coach was going to report my behavior to the team manager at UCLA, who'd asked to be kept abreast of my progress, and they'd never let me on their team after that. And if they weren't gonna let me on their team, then what the hell was I doing in junior college trying to learn Spanish?

At this point you might be wondering just what it was I did want. To do, or be, or to have, it didn't matter because I didn't know, though I myself was beginning to wonder seriously. Actually I did have a clue, a little one, but that's all. I didn't have what you'd call a goal and a plan of how to get there. I was sort of playing everything by ear—reflexes primed and ready to respond at a moment's notice, winging it. A few days later I found out I was flunking Spanish.

That's when the uphill climb really started and the tension kicked in for real. You'd think the logical move here would be to buckle the seat belt, maybe say a serious prayer or two, and hold on for dear life. You'd think so. But not me, no, sir, that was way too easy. That was no fun. You want to know what I went and did?

I took my fucking seat belt *off*, stood up in the car, and started yelling my fool head off.

And that's precisely when the ride really got rough.

*   *   *

Ever since Morrison had helped me get that article on Miami published, I'd been writing free-lance for a couple of different rock papers, among them *Creem* and *Rock*, plus a few papers in Canada and England. The PR firm Jim had fixed me up with, Gibson and Stromberg, was continuing to arrange interviews with choice subjects and helping me place the pieces as well. I didn't make much money off it, but the perks, as I would soon discover, were unbeatable. The main reason I bothered writing at all, besides the desire to express my feelings about rock 'n' roll and share them with other people who cared, was I started getting records in the mail. For free. At first I thought it was some kind of mix-up, and I kept waiting for a bill to arrive. But when I asked the editor at *Creem*, he explained the deal to me. It turned out the record people did expect something: more writing. I was supposed to find a record I felt strongly about, positively or negatively, get an assignment, and then review it. If I did that, and the review got printed, they'd keep sending me records. The unspoken part of the deal was if I said too many bad things, they could drop me from their list, so I usually ended up reviewing only what I liked, which didn't exactly do wonders for my objective critical credibility. What would you prefer, free records or some vague notion of respect from some kid in the boondocks you'd never met?

When I explained the arrangement to Dad, he thought I was a first-rate fool for doing work for free. The name in print and the free vinyl didn't impress him one iota.

The Kinks were coming to the Hollywood Palladium for a concert. I contacted their record label and scored tickets and a backstage pass. I ended up going to the show alone. I didn't know it then, but I was about to learn lightning can strike the same place, and sometimes even the same person, twice.

The night of the Kinks concert, backstage in the banquet room, I met a person who (to take the roller-coaster analogy one step further) was about to jump into the runaway car with me and not only stand up but throw away the brakes in the process and then proceed to put us both on an entirely different track.

His name was Jim Osterberg, but he was better known, notoriously, you might say, as Iggy Pop.

The Ig and I hit it off from the gate. Pat from Epic introduced us, and rather than shake my outstretched hand, Iggy jumped into the air and onto me, like a little kid, legs around my waist, arms wrapped around my neck, planting a big wet kiss on my cheek and sending both of us toppling over backward against one of the banquet tables, sending all the cold cuts and salads sailing every which way.

When he got off me, he wiped his hand off on the belly of his T-Rex shirt, put out his hand, and said, "Pleased to meet you. My name's Jim."

What could I do? I took his extended hand and shook it. "It's a real honor, Jim."

Which it was. I'd seen him work once at the Whisky years ago, and I had since read all about him in *Creem*. "If you like Morrison in concert, then you'll absolutely love Iggy Pop," writers and friends alike had promised. They were right. It was getting almost impossible for me to go to concerts anymore because I'd inadvertently end up comparing whomever I was seeing with the Doors and there was just no comparison forthcoming, which meant I was in for a lot of disappointments. Iggy, however, had been the real thing.

Rather than the standard two sets a night, his band, the Stooges, did only one show, starting at midnight. During the performance Iggy dived headfirst into the audience, grabbed a candle off a table, returned to the stage, and proceeded to pour hot wax over his chest as the band cranked out a blitzkrieg *Sturm* and *Drang* at an ungodly volume. In the audience Andy Warhol thought it was so hilarious and laughed so hard he split open an old wound. I didn't see what was so funny. I was mesmerized. This guy was no mere act, this was uncensored raw power, naked dangerous reality alive on stage. Later, I'd caught Iggy on a TV special, *Mid-Summer Rock*, during which a member of the audience handed him a jar of peanut butter. He took the jar and spread the contents over his torso and then continued his stroll atop the sea of hands his followers provided.

Now standing in front of him, experiencing him even offstage, I could tell we'd all be right. He just felt right. We used to call it vibes. The vibes coming from him, between us, were real good.

I asked him what he was doing in L.A.

"Nothing," he said.

"Nothing?" I asked. It didn't sound like a real good career move to me.

"What I want to do is make music and perform, but I can't."

"What do you mean, you can't?"

"These people won't let me."

Unquestionably, immediately, I believed him, or *in* him would be more appropriate. "I want to do a story on you," I told him. We set a date and place.

"Have you ever read Lao-tzu or Cocteau?" he asked me.

"Why, no, I haven't. Why do you ask?"

"Before we talk, read 'em. For research. I can't talk to anybody who hasn't read those guys."

I promised him I would. Lao-tzu, I would learn, was an ancient sage of the mystical Eastern Tao, and Jean Cocteau was a dope addict/artist/writer. And Jim Morrison, somewhere, was smiling.

The timing, combination, and force of the recent events conspired to force me to make a move. Not only was I off the team, but I had dropped out of college. I suppose it was inevitable. I'd given it my best shot (now I knew what was meant by the "old college try"). I hung in there for a year and a half until I couldn't hang anymore. Now I'd let go, and with that letting go came a flood of relief.

There was some unfinished business to take care of, however. I still hadn't told my father anything. I was a bit hesitant to clue him in to what was going on. The relief was short-lived and quickly replaced with apprehension. In fact, I became absolutely panic-stricken when I realized the true awfulness of the situation I found myself in.

I put it off until one day I could put it off no more. I just didn't feel comfortable deceiving him, living what had become a lie. Every day he'd ask me how school was going, and I'd have to come up with some bullshit line. He was always saying how proud he was of me, how much I'd turned my life around. It wasn't just me he told that to either. He'd told everyone who'd listen. "Danny this and Danny that." I was never comfortable with his praise to begin with, but now that it wasn't true anymore, I was downright miserable about it. I hated lying to him. I might have wanted his approval with near desperation, but I at least wanted it honestly.

I considered writing Dad a letter, spelling it out and apologizing for disappointing him; but that was chickenshit, and I knew it. I had to tell him face-to-face, man to man, although I didn't know why I wanted to do that. I really had tried it his way. And I'd blown it. I'd blown college, and I'd blown the baseball scholarship. I'd blown my big chance at the Big League and the straight life. I just couldn't be what he wanted me to be, what a big part of me wanted to be, if for no other reason than to please him, to gain his acceptance. I knew he was going to be disappointed in me. It was just one more piece of pain I had to deal with.

When Dad was disappointed, he didn't get sad. He got mad. That's why I waited so long to tell him. I put it off and I put it off.

But I just felt lousier. So one night just before dinner, with my bags already packed and just inside the door (just in case) of my beautiful bedroom, I walked into his room, and standing as far away from him as I could while still remaining in the room, I told him.

There was no way to soften the news. The best approach was to be direct, quick, and get it over with. Then be ready to run like a rabbit.

He was lying on his bed, watching the seven o'clock news with Walter Cronkite.

"I dropped out of college." I didn't say when I'd done this.

He pushed the mute switch on the remote control.

"Beg your pardon?"

He'd heard me fine. He just wanted to see if I had the nerve to say it again. I took a deep breath and said it again despite my lack of nerve. And then I braced myself.

If I hadn't been so scared, maybe I could have appreciated the sheer shock value the statement had on him. Maybe if it were happening to someone else, I could have appreciated the look on his face; but as it was directed at me, and it was me he was getting off the bed and coming at, it was sort of difficult to remain objective.

I backed against the wall.

"You fucking moron," he snarled. He spun around and began to pace the room. I didn't budge I was so scared. That's when the eruption started. I could actually feel it inside him, building, simmering, getting ready to blow. I prepared myself for the delivery.

"WHAT DID YOU DO THAT FOR? WHAT THE FUCK DO YOU THINK YOU'RE GONNA DO NOW? HUH? YA THINK YOU'RE GONNA LIVE UNDER THIS ROOF AND BE A GODDAMN BUM? YA THINK I'M GONNA SUPPORT YOU?"

I didn't say anything. They were what's known as rhetorical questions. He didn't really expect an answer. I was too scared to answer him anyway.

"YOU MUST THINK I'M A FUCKING IDIOT. IS THAT WHAT YOU TAKE ME FOR? YA LITTLE RUNT! I OUGHT TO HAND YOUR FUCKING HEAD TO YA." He walked up to me and raised his hand, and I ducked; but he didn't swing.

Instead, he walked away and yelled, "I'LL KILL YA. I SWEAR TO GOD, I'LL KILL YA! I TAKE YA BACK INTO THIS HOUSE AND GIVE YOU EVERYTHING IN THE WORLD A KID COULD WANT. *THIS IS HOW YOU REWARD ME?* YA KNOW HOW MANY KIDS WOULD GIVE THEIR LEFT NUT TO HAVE WHAT YOU HAVE HERE? DO YOU HAVE ANY IDEA HOW LUCKY YOU ARE? *AND THIS IS THE THANKS I GET?* I MUST BE

A SCHMUCK FOR BELIEVING YOU IN THE FIRST PLACE. YOU USE PEOPLE, THAT'S ALL YOU DO, YOU USE THEM, AND THEN YOU GO ON YOUR OWN GODDAMN SELFISH WAY AND LEAVE PEOPLE WHO LOVE YOU LAYING IN YOUR WAKE. . . ."

He was right in front of me. I'd never seen him so mad. For a second there I felt like answering him, telling him I hadn't meant to use him, that I really loved him, that I tried, that it wasn't his fault and it wasn't mine—but I didn't dare. Then I thought, *This is good for him to express his anger on account of if he doesn't, his ulcer'll just get worse.*

"AND I KNEW IT! I KNEW WHAT YOU'D DO! 'HE'S NOT GONNA DO IT TO ME AGAIN,' I SAID TO MYSELF, 'I WON'T LET HIM DO IT TO ME AGAIN,' AND *YA DID, YA DID DO IT AGAIN, YA LITTLE PRICK!*" He swung out and whacked me up against the head so hard I flew onto the bed and all the way across it, falling onto the carpet on the other side. I jumped up, ready for anything. I was really shaking, and I guess I must have involuntarily clenched my fists because he said, "COME ON, YA WANT TO HIT ME? I'LL GIVE YOU ONE SHOT, ANYWHERE YOU WANT, COME ON, PUNK, TAKE YOUR BEST SHOT, THEN I'LL FUCKING BREAK EVERY GODDAMN BONE IN YOUR BODY. *DON'T YOU DARE MAKE A FIST AT ME.* COME ON. I BROUGHT YOU INTO THIS FUCKING WORLD, I TURNED YOUR LIGHTS ON, I'LL TURN 'EM OFF!"

Frozen where I stood, I looked down at my hands and unclenched them.

I guess he reconsidered his offer, which I wasn't about to take anyway, because he changed his mind.

"G'WAN . . . GET THE HELL OUT OF HERE . . . I DON'T WANT YOU AROUND ANYWAY, GET OUT AND *DON'T YOU EVER COME BACK!* GET OUT OF HERE BEFORE I KILL YA. . . ."

I still couldn't move. I must've been in shock. I thought I was gonna have a heart attack, or pass out and faint, or something. I wished he had just beaten me up and gotten it over with instead of yelling at me like that. He was really quite an impressive yeller, I tell you, boy; he'd yell at his dog Champ so bad for crapping on the rug Champ would go all over again. I knew what "scared shitless" felt like now. I knew almost intimately the meaning of that phrase.

"GO ON, GET OUT, WHAT ARE YOU WAITING FOR? THAT'S WHAT YOU WANT, ISN'T IT? *BIG MAN!* YOU WANT TO BE OUT ON YOUR OWN? WELL, GO GET THE HELL OUT, AND DON'T YOU EVEN EVER THINK ABOUT CALLING ANYONE IN THIS FAMILY AGAIN. YOU ARE NOT GOING TO DRAG US DOWN WITH YOU. I WILL NOT ALLOW YOU TO HURT ANYBODY

ELSE WHO LOVES YOU. *WHAT ARE YOU WAITING FOR? I SAID GO!"*

And I *got*. I got out of there so goddamn fast. I flew into my room and grabbed the bags and dashed out to the Corvette before he could take it away from me. I fully expected him to jump into his Rolls and take off after me, to tell me to get the hell out of his car. As I floored it down Beverly Drive, I kept looking back over my shoulder. I was still looking back, expecting to see him screech alongside me in a blaze of white, when I pulled up in front of the Palms Bar. I was still shaking.

But he never came. I had the car. I'd made good my escape. And I didn't fool myself for a second that he hadn't let me.

At the bar I called up five double tequila sunrises to Red, the same old grizzled bartender Jim had introduced me to almost four years ago. The drinks came, and he leaned over and inquired what were the haps. I proposed a toast: "So much for compromising with the establishment. Here's to sliding with reality." Red shook his head and went back to cleaning glasses while I started swallowing and tried to stop shaking.

I confess I did feel a twinge of remorse that accompanies any realization that you've blown it, that one era has ended and another begun. But it was only a slight twinge, because with it came a real optimistic anticipation of what would be coming up next—better things to follow. Mostly I was relieved it was over. I was free.

My first move was to get a place to live, then to hook up with Iggy Pop and, as soon as possible and to the best of my ability, to practice a complete and total absence of any and all available limitations. To live in a way I hadn't, except in my dreams.

I felt better already.

I fully planned to go at it with the same zeal and commitment which characterized the best of my past indulgences. True, I hadn't been exactly moderate while I'd been staying with Dad, but I had shown some restraint. No more. No longer was I aiming for his concept of security. Excitement was my goal now. I'd wasted too much time already. If what my parents' world represented was considered normal, healthy, and sane, then where I wanted to go was immoral, unhealthy, and insane, I admit it. I couldn't wait to get started.

Not only would Morrison have approved, he would have applauded.

* * *

The past two years hadn't been what anyone with any taste would want to call a high-water mark in the annals of rock 'n' roll history. The pathetic reality was (with the possible sole exception of the Rolling Stones) rock 'n' roll was getting boring, which should be a contradiction in terms but unfortunately wasn't. Cream had released its last album, *Good-bye Cream*, and gone on its "farewell" tour. No more Creedence. No more Beatles, even (moan, sob).

The Doobie Brothers, Chicago, the Eagles, and the Allman Brothers simply didn't get it on. They sold plenty of records and all that, but I didn't like 'em. They were the epitome of everything I hated about the way music was headed. There was no dramatic reality. There was no transcendence. They couldn't even rock. Fast alone was not rock, no more than loud was rock, but either one of these traits should be there, and these bands, for the most part, lacked both. Even when they did get loud and fast, it was still gutless. The whole scene had become gutless. Before, one or two folk singers, like, say, Donovan, was fine. But now they were tipping the goddamn scale as far as I was concerned. Who needs a dozen Simon and Garfunkels? That's the problem with change; it fucks with the balances. James Taylor (not to mention the rest of the clan, Livingston, Alex, and Kate), Carole King, Crosby, Stills, Nash and Young—these were the new heroes, and it was sickening. The new wimps were more like it. It was the end of one era, the start of another.

If the sixties were a party, a time for self-discovery and exploration, an era marked forever by its sense of celebration and experimentation as reflected not merely by the musical world but by the drugs it took, then the seventies were bedtime. It was only fitting then that the drug of choice in the early to mid-seventies was Quaalude, basically a sleeping pill if you want to get right down to it, and the music appealing to the cultural palate was just as much a downer. Using drugs wasn't merely recreational anymore; it was mandatory. There was nothing else to do.

The revolution was over. We lost basically. The establishment said, you can have your long hair and you can have your bellbottom slacks, and you can even have your marijuana cigarettes, but you get your rebellious asses off our streets and get back home inside with your families where you belong. Now we were back inside, off the street as it were, and we didn't want to rock anymore. No one wanted to be inflamed; everyone wanted to be sedated. It's no accident "laid-back" was the operative word of the day.

And here comes Iggy Pop, flying in the indolent fat face of all that was considered popular, tasteful, and commercial singing:

I'm a street-walking cheetah with a heat fulla napalm
The runaway son of the nuclear A-Bomb
I am the world's forgotten boy
The one who searches and destroys. . . .*

"Hotel California" it was not. Iggy represented all the pent-up energy I couldn't express, all the anger I couldn't verbalize, all the unpredictable excitement I craved. He was a breath of fresh air, a tornado of energy in a desert of boredom and lethargy, and a hell of a nice guy, too. He was everything I looked for in a hero. Mischievous, innocent, truthful, excessive and outrageous. Of course, possessing the traits it seems must always accompany genius, he could also often be infantile and vulgar.

I considered it nothing less than destiny, a born duty to do anything possible to aid him in his mission. Hell, it was an honor.

That's what I thought. I truly believed in him.

Other people had other ideas. My friends in the business thought I was nuts for taking him on (some already knew it; for others it was simply confirmed). Still others (like the Doors' business manager, Gabe Reynolds) said it was an insult to Morrison's memory, I owed him a better follow-up. Rock 'n' roll had become big business in the past couple of years, and Iggy wasn't considered a "good investment." He was an insult to the lawyers and accountants who were now in power and running the music business. For one thing, he had already gone through two record companies; he'd had two chances to make it and failed (in purely commercial terms of success) both times. He was currently without a contract again, up for a third chance in a business where most people are lucky to get one and even fewer people get a second. His previous manager, who was also David Bowie's, had spent most of his hundred-thousand-dollar record advance on putting him up at the Beverly Hills Hotel. Now that money was gone, and everything else with it. While Bowie was out becoming a star in Japan and readying a second attack on America, Iggy hadn't performed in over a year and wasn't exactly in a good mood about it.

In summary, this singer I wanted so badly to work with had no recording deal, no manager (not necessarily bad news as far as I was concerned), no band, no agency, no equipment, and no money, and, in two more days, no place to live.

What he did have was one gigantic heroin habit.

All in all, not what you'd call a Grade A prospect. But, then,

---

*"Search & Destroy" by Iggy Pop

neither was I. Maybe that's why we got along so well. We needed each other; neither one of us had anyone else.

"You don't know how frustrating it is," he told me, "to live to be onstage and be denied the opportunity. Do you have any idea how much it hurts to be prevented from doing the one thing you love to do?" I did, or at least I could imagine. I believed him. Fuck everyone else.

I told him not to worry, I'd take care of him, I'd do everything I could to get him where he wanted to be. And in the meantime, he could live with me.

He raised his eyebrow into an arch. "Where is that?"

Which was a good question, since I didn't have anyplace to live either.

"That's my problem," I told him. Then we proceeded to get sloshed poolside on his last paid-up day at the swank Beverly Hills Hotel. After we'd gotten to the point where the Cabana Club bartender wouldn't serve us anymore, Iggy leaned over to actress Tina Louise (remember *Gilligan's Island*?) and asked her if she'd care to buy us a drink. When she said no, he asked her if she'd like to see his cock ring. Her jaw went agape as Jim reached down and extracted his rather large penis out from beneath his baggy gym shorts and proudly displayed his goods. Ms. Louise was not impressed. We were immediately thrown out.

I took all the money I had out of the bank and put it down on a ninety-dollar-a-month apartment in Venice Beach—an old dilapidated bleached-out wooden structure that probably should have been condemned, a single apartment, right off the beach. And Iggy kicked heroin then and there. We scored some sleeping pills for him to make it easier. For three days he looked horrible. He tossed and turned and sweated and shivered. But he never complained. He dragged himself down to the ocean every morning and, while I was afraid he'd drown, proceeded to swim out into the horizon; then his blond head would reappear, bobbing up around a mile out, and teeth chattering, he'd swim back to shore, where I'd put a big towel around him and walk him back to the apartment. His reserve of strength was amazing.

Within four days he was fine. He was great. He wasn't sleeping really well yet, but he looked, and sounded, incredible. His physique looked like a rugged, but young, brawny, muscular sailor's. His eyes, large and blue to begin with, were now a shining aqua blue. Best of all, he was being Jim all day long.

He was essentially two separate and distinct personalities. Jim Osterberg, the straight, considerate, pleasant, charming, endearing, intelligent, well-mannered, well-read, conversant, loyal friend; and Iggy Pop (né Stooge), the stoned, inconsiderate, uncouth, indulgent, selfish asshole who took all he could get, never said "thank you," and then, if you were still around, took from you some more. Onstage this latter character might be intensely satisfying and entertaining; offstage it could be a real pain in the ass. But for the time being, he was being just Jim, and he was being just great.

For exactly one more day, at which time he asked for fifty dollars, which I gladly gave him, to get his laundry done. He returned two days later with his pupils pinned, his speech slow and deep, scratching his nose and arms.

He was stoned.

Fuck.

Heroin.

Double fuck.

"You don't understand. You can't." He pleaded his case, telling me not to judge him because I didn't know what he was up against. "If you haven't walked a mile in my shoes, don't expect me to be able just to step out of them and walk away" is what he pretty much told me, without inviting me to step into those shoes, while not exactly discouraging me either.

I hadn't tried it, so I couldn't understand, no matter how much I wanted to. If I didn't understand, then I couldn't possibly help him, was the message. That's where I drew the line. I thought of Tim Hardin. No way. Oh, sure, I was curious, but I was never suicidal. I was afraid I might like it. I knew once I stepped over that line, I might not be able to make it back so easily. The farther I went, the farther I'd go. It wasn't common sense or discipline that kept me away. It was fear.

But he was right, goddammit. I couldn't really help him and I felt left out. Not enough to try it, but enough to wish I had. It was both horrifying and intriguing, the way he couldn't seem to stay away from heroin. I had to readjust and loosen my thinking about heroin enough to allow Iggy to squeak through. I felt like a parent with a beguiling child. How do you say no to somebody you love who is asking for something that means so much to him?

The next day I drove him to score.

Two days later I had to go to the used record store to trade in some LPs so we'd have enough money to eat. At the record shop I bumped into an old friend.

"Hey, Danny! How ya doin', man? How ya been?" I'd recognize that voice anywhere. It was Ray Manzarek.

"Gawd, Ray, I can't tell you how good it is to see you!" I really had to restrain myself from running up and jumping into his arms. "I thought you were in Europe." The Doors were supposedly in London, looking for a rhythm guitarist, maybe even a new singer.

"We were. Robby and John are still over there. I quit."

"You what?"

"I quit."

"That's fantastic, Ray!" I was really proud of him. "Why?"

"It just wasn't the same without Jim."

"How come no one knows?"

"I haven't told anyone yet."

"You should send out a press release, have a press conference, you should tell everyone. Do you know what you're gonna do next? Are you gonna put together another band? Do you have a solo deal set?"

"Whoa, boy! Slow down. Listen, I'm meeting Dorothy for lunch. Why don't you drop by the office tomorrow and we'll talk about it?"

"What time?"

"About twoish?"

"I'll be there," I told him.

"Hey, I almost forgot, what are *you* doing? How's that baseball scholarship coming?"

"I fucked it. I'm working with Iggy Pop."

"That must be interesting."

"Interesting is exactly the right word."

"Well, see ya tomorrow then, Danny."

"See ya tomorrow, Ray."

I got $69.30 for the twenty pounds of records I brought in. That night and the next day Iggy and I ate at McDonald's.

After lunch we drove to the Doors' office.

En route Iggy turned to me and said, "Ya know, it was after I saw the Doors in a university concert in Detroit that I decided to become a singer? I'd been playing drums up until then. Seeing Morrison . . . I never felt the same after that, ya know what I mean?" I knew exactly what he meant. "Anyway," he said, "I'd sure love to play with Manzarek someday. That," he said, smacking his lips at the thought, "would be very appropriate."

That, I thought, was an awfully good idea. Iggy needed a band. Ray needed a singer.

We pulled the Corvette into the Doors' office parking lot.

I sure coulda used this car three years ago, I said to myself as I climbed out of the car and headed upstairs. It was eerie. Nothing had changed. Same furniture. Same gold records. Plus a new one for *L.A. Woman*.

A moving man emerged from Bill's back office, carrying a large box. Another came through the front door.

"What's going on?" I asked one of them.

"What's it look like?" he asked.

"The office is closing," Ray said. I turned around. At least the refrigerator was still there. With three shelves packed with beer. I took one out and cracked it.

"How come?" I asked Ray.

"The lease is up."

I'd always assumed the Doors owned it.

"It's just as well," Ray told me. "Time to move on."

Just like that? I hadn't wanted to admit it for a long time, but now it was impossible not to. The Doors were over.

"What are you gonna do now?"

"I'm gonna make a solo album."

"First, aren't you gonna let everyone know you quit the Doors? That's news, Ray. I think everyone would really respect that. All you have to say is exactly what you told me, 'It wasn't the same without Jim.' That's what everyone thought. You should acknowledge that. You should get out a release."

"I was thinking about letting you do that for me."

"You mean, write the press release? Sure." I could use the money. "What about the mailing?"

"Without a contract, Elektra isn't going to do it. Are you signed?"

"Not yet, no."

"Well, I guess I could get a mailing list together and get it out for you and handle any questions that came in."

"You mean, like a press agent?"

"Yeah, sure, why not? I mean, I know how it's done. I've dealt with enough press agents to know what they do."

"Good. That's what I had in mind, too. All right, then, it's settled. You know what to do first."

"And next we announce your intentions of going solo. You're gonna need some individual photos, too. I'll set up a photo session. Then the record contract release goes out, and the musicians you'll be working with get announced—"

"Sounds good. How much you want?"

"Whatever's fair, Ray."

"Say a hundred a week?"

A hundred dollars a week! A salary! "A hundred a week sounds fair," I said, staying as calm as possible.

"All right! We got a deal."

"Hey, Ray, if the office is closed, where are you going to rehearse? You need a rehearsal room, don't you? A place to store your equipment?"

"Ah, good point," he said, giving his best Henry Fonda no-teeth grin, lips pulled back over his teeth, deep in thought. "I hadn't thought about that."

"What about Siddons? Where's he going?" I asked.

"Wherever he's going, he's going without me," Ray told me. "I don't want to work with Siddons anymore. I think Robby and John are going to keep him on."

I had assumed Bill would still be managing Ray.

"So you don't have a manager?"

"Nope. Not anymore."

"Does Bill know?"

"Nope. Not yet."

"He's gonna be pissed."

"Most likely."

What I didn't tell Ray is that I meant he was going to be pissed at *me*. Ever since I'd gone behind his back and Jim hired me, I'd felt I wasn't his most favorite person in the world. It was difficult to consider myself a threat to his position, but I also knew that was exactly what he'd think when he heard he was out and I was in with Manzarek.

"I guess we're gonna need a new office," Ray said, "a place where I can rehearse and compose and you can work."

"Yeah," I said, "and I'm going to need to find a new place to live pretty soon."

"Uh-huh. A regular office wouldn't do; we need a place like this that doesn't feel like an office, where no one will complain about the noise."

"There aren't too many places like this around, isolated two-story buildings."

"So we need a place where we both can work and you can live."

"You mean, me live in the office?" I shuddered at the thought. We were outside now, on the steps, and I looked through the sliding glass doors, into the rehearsal room, to the small back room where the equipment cases were stored. I tried to picture myself living there.

"No." Ray stroked his chin. "I wasn't thinking of that, but along those lines. Something a little more appropriate."

"Like a house!" I asked, all shade of depression vanishing.

"It's not a bad idea," Ray said. "Could be a good investment."

"Whereabouts?"

"I don't know, somewhere around here, West Hollywood somewhere. . . . Why don't I leave that up to you? Look around. See what you can come up with."

I agreed and promised him I'd be in touch as soon as the press release was written up. We exchanged phone numbers. I collected my scrapbook and autographed copy of *The New Creatures*. Then I turned around and walked away from the Doors' office for the last time.

Once out of sight I ran to the car where Iggy was waiting for me. I jumped in, grabbed his neck, and planted a big kiss on his cheek. "I've got a job! Ray hired me! We're rich! We're rich! We're getting a house! I've got a job!"

"Awright!" he said, pushing me away. "Awright, I heard you the first time. What are you gonna do, answer his fan mail?"

"*Fan mail!* Fuck, no! I'm his press agent!" I cranked the key over, and the engine kicked in, humming at an idle.

"You're no press agent," he said, effectively popping my bubble.

"Whaddya mean? I can be a press agent. You don't have to go to school to be a press agent; all a press agent has to do is send out press releases and set up interviews. . . . I can do that."

"If ya shut up for a minute, I'll tell ya what I mean," he said. I shut up. "All I'm saying is that you're too smart to be a press agent. I think you'd make a much better *manager*."

"What?"

"Besides, you're Jewish," he continued. "I think you'd make a great manager."

"Bullshit," I said.

"No, I'm serious. You're enthusiastic and dedicated and smart, and you're Jewish. You've got all the qualifications."

"I'd rather be your press agent." It seemed more plausible to me. Being a press agent I knew something about. I knew next to nothing about management. I thought he might go for it. It wasn't as if he had one already.

"And what am I supposed to pay you with, my good looks?" he asked.

"You don't have to pay me until you make some money."

"Why not?" He nodded. "The price is right."

Did you hear that?! Two jobs in one day! Not just any jobs. I was working with two of my heroes! Two of the most talented people in the world. And, they were also good friends. This wouldn't be work; this would be fun. And I'd even get paid for doing it! This was how things were supposed to be, I thought as we pulled out into the traffic running on Santa Monica Boulevard.

Now all I had to do was find a house and set up shop.

I was so happy my ears were ringing. Never had the future looked so promising.

"Feel like house hunting with me?" I asked Jim.

"Sure, why not? It's a nice day for a drive," he commented before asking, "Can you afford a house?"

"No, not exactly, but Ray Manzarek can."

Ever since my father had taken me for long Sunday drives with the top down on his Rolls, I'd always known where I wanted to live if I ever had the chance. I knew right where to go look.

As if magnetically attracted, the car headed onto Sunset Boulevard, took a left on Crescent Heights, and continued. Straight into the foothills of Laurel Canyon and the Hollywood Hills.

CHAPTER EIGHT

· · · · · · · · · · · ·

I woke up this morning
Got myself a beer
I woke up this morning
Got myself a beer
The future's uncertain and
The end is always near.
                    —THE DOORS

IT was the fall of 1973, and things were beginning to jump.

Within a few weeks after Ray and Iggy hired me, Iggy had a booking agency, his band, the Stooges, re-formed and in rehearsal, a tour in the process of getting booked, and a good start on reestablishing his addiction to heroin. He was away from the beach apartment more than he was home. That was fine with me since there was barely room for one person there, and if Iggy Pop needed anything besides an audience, it was space. I was also having a difficult time supporting both of us. My record collection had suffered a serious depletion already, and despite the income I was receiving from Ray as a publicist and the pittance I was getting as a free-lance critic, I could no longer afford the twenty-five-dollar-loans (or advances, as we called them, the idea being someday I'd get paid back) he was constantly hitting me up for. Twenty-five dollars to take care of the laundry, twenty-five dollars to buy hair bleach or to go shopping or any other reason among the myriad he came up with. It didn't take me too long to figure out a balloon of heroin also cost twenty-five bucks.

He knew I didn't approve of his doing smack, hence the bogus reasons. Lately, however, he wasn't even bothering to come up with a cover-up. He didn't seem to care anymore what I thought. If I gave him the money when he asked for it, fine. If I was willing to drive him, even better. If I didn't front him the money, then I was a Jew, and I wouldn't hear from him for a few days. He owed me no explanation in either event. His tour was slated to kick off in the not too distant future, and he was scheduled to be out of town for almost two months. I was going to miss him.

The landlord delivered an eviction notice, and I was given thirty-five days to leave the premises.

Every day I went for long drives through the twisting, turning, slender, tree-shaded streets of Laurel Canyon, eyes peeled for For

Sale signs. Two different realtors were covering the area and setting up appointments for houses to see.

It's been said there is a gold record for every acre of land in Laurel Canyon, which is another way of saying a hell of a lot of rich musicians live there. Alice Cooper was living somewhere in the canyon, and Keith Moon was rumored to have recently purchased a house. Doors drummer John Densmore used to live there before his divorce, but his ex-wife, Julia, stayed on, eventually having Allman Brother Berry Oakley's son a short month before Berry followed Duane Allman to the grave in a motorcycle nightmare accident of his own. Frank Zappa lived in Laurel Canyon, and Carole King had a house in the hills there. David Crosby owned a big brick estate tucked atop the canyon just under Mulholland Drive. Joni Mitchell, another resident of the area, had recorded an album soaked in the canyon's ambiance, called *Ladies of the Canyon*, and John Mayall, still another local, had one of his first best sellers with *Blues from Laurel Canyon*.

Harry Houdini built his castle in Laurel Canyon, and its eroding structure sits alongside Laurel Canyon Boulevard like an ancient ruin, alive and smothered with miles of ivy, almost prehistoric monstrous palm trees jutting up and above the jungle and decaying architecture; marble stairways twist and rise and disappear into nowhere. On Halloween bands of freaks hold séances to contact his spirit. Stories of his ghost's being sighted among the crumbling walls and ruins abound in the canyon. Anyone who tried to redevelop the property or made an indiscreet psychic trespassing had, it was said, met with a violent and untimely death. The canyon was supposed to be magical. But it was also said to possess a curse. Stories of unsolved deaths were abundant. The canyon attracted many of the nouveau riche artists, yes, but less known and more curious was the fact that no one ever seemed to stay long, and most almost always left in a hurry, under dramatic and even mysterious circumstances.

Laurel Canyon was funky, naturally woodsy and wild, musical, artistic, and endlessly hip. Even the cops were cool. The hillsides were lush and green with an abundance of vines, wildflowers, and trees— pine, oak, palm, and the laurel trees from which the area took its name. Summer nights smelled of jasmine while the days were filled with the scent of eucalyptus. Houses were pushed up on the hillsides, hundreds of tiny stairs winding, stretching up to reach them. Some of the hillsides were so steep, and houses so precariously perched atop them, outdoor elevators had to be installed to make the climb. Quaint cottages sat next door to Spanish adobe residences; redwood cabins and mini-Tudor castles sat on streets with rustic-sounding names like

Lookout Mountain Road, Appian Way, Kirkwood Drive, and Outpost Avenue.

There was nowhere else I wanted to live, nowhere else I would even consider. I was sure it was just a matter of time until I found the right place. The only problem was I didn't have much time left. Ray needed a place to rehearse, and I had to find a place to live.

By night I got drunk or stoned, usually both, going around to the nightclubs around town, reviewing shows or interviewing the bands, often getting too wasted to do either. The J. Geils Band and Humble Pie had done back-to-back three-night engagements at the Whisky, and I hadn't missed a show. There were also a lot of record company-sponsored events and parties going on, with lots of good food and free booze and it was almost a full-time job hitting all those. If it was a nightclub show, we'd be given a tab to sign and drink off, courtesy of whatever record company had the band playing there that night. Each tab had fifteen lines, one drink per line. I felt nothing short of obligated to fill up each line, with a double. If the event was a party or press conference held in a reception room or a restaurant, then no one counted anything, and the only limit on how much you could drink was the body count at the bar and your own capacity. The philosophy behind this sort of behavior was nothing short of bribery. Record companies knew writers didn't have money, and by getting them to feel indebted or grateful or, failing that, drunk half the battle of getting a sympathetic write-up was achieved. Personally speaking, it worked on me.

Not only did I feel motivated to attend these events for the music and perks, but they gave me an opportunity to work the room for my new clients. I had sent out a press release announcing Ray Manzarek's departure from the Doors and his intention of pursuing a solo career. The resulting media attention was even better than I had hoped for, and the item was picked up in news columns and gossip sheets around the world. Ray was currently in the process of assembling a new band, and I was preparing a new release to send to the trades. I was already looking forward to throwing a party of our own. He had given me a fifty-dollar raise in the meantime, and everything was moving right along.

A month after I was hired, and three weeks before I was due to be thrown out from where I was living, I stumbled onto a real dream house. I called up the realtors from a phone booth, and we arranged to meet back up at the house. Everything about it was just right.

Besides being in Laurel Canyon, it had the right number of rooms and a fair-size backyard with a pool *and* hot tub, and even the price was in the right range. It was a definitive canyon house, pushed back a little ways from the streets among a small glade of pine trees, a rustic two-story Spanish adobe, what classified ads refer to as a "charmer." I called up Ray that afternoon, and we made plans to meet there the next day. Since I had no credit and couldn't afford it even if I had, Ray would have to sign the appropriate papers, if it met with his approval.

"Where is it?" he asked me over the phone, ready to write down the address.

"You're gonna love this," I said, hustling him. "It's on Wonderland Avenue."

"Wonderland Avenue," he said, "how appropriate . . ."

"That's what I thought, too. You're gonna love it, Ray. It's a perfect place for us. It's not too big, and it's not too small."

"Well, I like the street name," he said.

"It's only a mile off the Strip . . . Ben Franks, the Rainbow, the Whisky are right around the corner, but you wouldn't know it, it's so quiet and beautiful up there."

The next day, standing outside, he was practically sold before he set foot inside. Once he saw the floor plan and the backyard, all he said was "How much?" as he pulled out his checkbook.

"You can move in any time after the first of January," we were told.

Merry Fucking Xmas!

I was so happy I couldn't stop jumping up and down, hammering and yapping away at Ray. "You won't be sorry, this is gonna be so great, this is exactly the right kind of place we need, there's plenty of room for both of us to work, you can have the living room for your rehearsal room, and I can live upstairs, we can use the dining room as the conference room, and there's even a guest room upstairs for Iggy when he gets back. . . . I really feel good about this. . . ."

While I proceeded to work on Ray's new solo career and coordinated advance coverage for Iggy's upcoming tour, I also anxiously awaited the first of the year, at which time I could take up residence in my new home.

My report card from junior college arrived in the mail. Three *D*'s and two *F*'s, including Spanish. I wasn't real broken up about it.

Pamela Morrison was back in town. Reportedly she'd flown in

shock to Sausalito from Paris after Jim died and had been resting at some posh clinic up there. Now she was supposedly back in Los Angeles. She'd been seen at the Whisky and at the Greenery on Melrose Avenue, a jet-set eatery. Someone had spotted her playing pool at Barney's Beanery with three big bearded Hell's Angels. I'd heard stories that she had become part of a pimp's stable, that she was addicted to tranquilizers and had been put in a rest home, that she'd never recovered from Jim's death and had become a downer freak. Some people just said she was psychotic, plain and simple. She looked fine, but the motor was misfiring.

It wouldn't be long before I bumped into her. No sense in looking for her; the way things were falling into place, if we were supposed to find each other, it would happen soon enough.

Cheech and Chong were playing at the Troubadour on Christmas Eve. The place was packed. The idea was to watch the show and interview the guys backstage afterward, but I'd gotten a good start on a decent drunk at the outer room bar and was working on my sixth kamikaze when I heard someone talking to me.

"Aren't you even gonna offer to buy me a drink?" Pamela Morrison was standing by my side.

Right away I felt uncomfortable. We'd never gotten along before. Why should now be any different? If she wanted a chance to yell at me for taking the Doors' side, I didn't want to listen to it. However, I also felt sorry for her, and I felt an obligation to spend some time with her, out of loyalty to Jim if nothing else.

"What're ya drinkin', stranger?" I asked her.

"Southern Comfort, on the rocks," she said.

Barney, the bartender with the big, drooping mustache, overheard her and brought her drink over. Pamela took a stool next to me and stared at the poster of Jim behind the bar, over the register. I tried to take her mind off it.

"You really look good. It's good to see you," I told her.

"Oh, Danny, you haven't any idea how good it is to see you."

I was caught off guard by that remark, and I told her so. "I thought you hated me."

"I hated everybody who tried to take Jim away from me."

"I never tried to take Jim from anybody."

"I know. I was just being selfish. You know, he let me read the letters you wrote to him. He hardly got any personal letters. It really made him happy when you wrote."

"You mean he didn't get a lot of letters?" It was hard to believe. I thought of all the mail he'd received every day at the office.

"No, not many. Nobody had our address 'cept the office, and you know how paranoid and protective Siddons is. None of the guys wrote to him. Siddons sent only business papers. Your letters really made us laugh. I never get any mail, so he let me open yours, and then I read them out loud to him." She looked into her drink.

"I know he spoke to the office once or twice," I told her, "and I heard he called John a few days before . . ." I didn't want to refer to his death.

"Whatever." She sighed.

"I'm glad you're back in town," I reassured her, only realizing it as I spoke. "You don't know how much I missed him." Fuck. That was really stupid of me to say. I really didn't want to upset her. She seemed so fragile, vulnerable. I doubted the stories about her were true, but I wasn't about to take any chances.

She leaned her head on my shoulder.

"You don't know how good it is to be with someone who knew him. He really liked you. He told me I should give you a chance, that you were a good kid."

"I never knew. I always hoped he did, but I never knew for sure. I always felt so insignificant compared to everyone else around him."

"Maybe that's why," she said.

"What do you mean?"

"Well, maybe because you didn't demand anything of him. I don't know, maybe you didn't need him the same way other people did."

"But I did, Pam, I needed him just as much as anyone else." I felt it was important she know how I really felt.

"No, you didn't. You couldn't. It wasn't the same. You were so young. You're still just a kid. How old are you anyway?"

"I just turned nineteen."

"God, you're not even old enough to drink."

We drank and talked and talked and drank some more. It was great to be carrying on a conversation with her, to be treated as an equal. When Pam said, "My old man would be so proud of you," I just swelled.

We toasted the past and we toasted the New Year and we toasted the future. We confessed to each other how much we missed Jim until we both were practically in tears, and we reminded each other of things he'd done until we laughed so hard it was difficult to drink. By the time the clock struck twelve, I was drunk enough to ask her if I could kiss her.

"You're blushing!" she said.

"I'm not."

"You are! I think it's cute."

"Forget I asked," I said.

She leaned over and kissed my cheek. "I think you're a sweet-heart."

By the time Barney announced "last call" we were practically falling off our stools but straightened up enough to order a double Rémy Martin and drain the rest of our beers, before staggering out of the bar arm in arm, head against head.

We drove back to her apartment on Norton Avenue in West Hollywood, where we fell asleep, fully clothed and in each other's arms.

The night before Iggy was to leave on tour, the two of us responded to an invitation for the opening of a new club on Sunset Boulevard, Rodney's English Disco, owned and operated by Rodney Bingen-heimer, the cherubic munchkin-about-town/self-declared mayor of the Sunset Strip, best known for his part on "The Prince and the Pauper" episode of the Monkees' TV show where he played bassist Peter Tork's twin. Rodney had a snaggle-toothed grin and always greeted you with a "What's happening?" He wasn't the town's most raving intellectual, but what he lacked in critical facilities or verbosity, he more than made up for in sheer commitment to and spirit for the local scene. Rodney made sure his club had no age limit (and no hard liquor, either), so the young girls of Hollywood would have no trouble getting in the front door.

Rodney's was dedicated to the new metallic dance music scream-ing its way over from England, a crude, yet awkwardly glamorous style of music the critical establishment had quickly rushed in and dubbed "glitter rock," essentially equal parts heavy metal and pop, purveyed by such self-styled androgynous musicians as Slade, T-Rex, Gary Glitter, and a truly great singles band, the Sweet, whose "Little Willy" was perhaps the best dance song of the year. At the very top of the bunch was David Bowie, the reigning king of what was being hailed as the second British invasion. It was a weird, transitional time for the music world.

If "peace" and "love" were the buzzwords for the sixties, then decadence, at least in rock 'n' roll Southern California, 1973, was the pronounced goal of the new era dawning. It conjured up images of decaying mansions, cracked Roman columns, maybe a broken statue or two, an uncleaned pool, palm fronds afloat, cluttered with smaller and dirtier debris both adrift and sunken to the bottom, gin out of the bottle, dark sunglasses, a filterless cigarette with a very long ash, and a complexion pale, better if verging on translucent. Sunlight was out. Nightlife was in.

Roman, Greek, Byzantine imagery was heavily associated with the concept of decadence.

"I like the word decadent," Rimbaud's buddy/lover/writer Paul Verlaine had written over a century before, "all shimmering with purple and gold, it is made up of unhappy flesh and carnal spirit and all the violent splendors of the Lower Empire. . . ."

Byron and Shelley were regarded as decadent. Thoreau and Emerson were not.

Keith Richards was decadent; Paul McCartney was not. Lou Reed was decadent; Neil Young was not. Iggy Pop was; Neil Diamond wasn't. Cocaine and Quaaludes were; marijuana and LSD weren't. Bisexuality was; innocence was not.

Decadence meant world-weary and self indulgent, effete and depraved, luxurious and degenerate. The ripe before the rot. Yeats wrote that "suffering is the greatest decadence of all." Dangerous stuff to play with. Appealing? Maybe. Glamorous? Usually. Fun? Occasionally. Ironically, fun was out, bored was in. You get the idea.

Iggy and I had been ushered into Rodney's past the line of people waiting to be admitted and were sitting at the VIP booth, getting wrecked on champagne, snorting cocaine out of a vial behind the menu, surveying the scene from our place of privilege. We both had begun asking around for drugs, and in no time the coke had landed on our table.

I checked out the scene, looking for a familiar face, debating whether I wanted to stay or leave, when my vision came to a halt.

I saw her sitting at the bar. The most perfect-looking girl I had ever seen. I noticed her face first, darling, rare, dovelike, a Southern California version of a young Lauren Bacall. Perched high atop a barstool, sitting next to a blond girlfriend, she was wearing a brown and white cowboy shirt, unbuttoned midway, and worn blue jeans with brown suede patches on the knees, and her booted feet reached clear to the ground. She was cool and distant—as unapproachable as she was desirable.

"See that girl." I bumped Iggy.

He nodded. "Yeah, so?"

"She's gorgeous."

"Yeah, I know. She's also unavailable. Forget it," he advised me.

"How do you know? Do you know her?"

He looked bored. "Yeah. Her name's Tiffany. Forget her. She doesn't fuck. I already tried."

"What do you mean, you already tried?"

"She was at some party, I don't remember, everybody was hitting on her. She shined everybody on. I think she's a virgin or maybe a dyke."

"Just because she wouldn't let you fuck her?" I was already pretty impressed. Iggy usually got whomever he wanted, more than he wanted. Maybe this girl had some dignity. On the other hand, maybe he was right. A tantalizing dilemma.

"She wouldn't let anyone fuck her; she wouldn't let anyone near her. She's probably frigid."

"I don't believe it."

"Well, is she frigid or is she a dyke?"

"I don't know! I don't know her socio-sexual proclivities."

He just shrugged. "I don't believe it." I couldn't take my eyes off her.

"What else do you know about her?" I pestered him.

He shrugged again. "Nothing. That's it. I don't even know her. I just happened to hear her name and remembered it."

"I'm going to meet her."

"Good luck. If I were you, I'd save my strength."

I got up.

"You're a real glutton for punishment sometimes, you know that?" he told me. Coming from him, it was a comment I probably should have taken seriously.

I walked to the bar. On the way over I bumped into Rodney. Grabbing his elbow, I asked him, "Ya see that girl over there? Do you know her?"

"Oh, yeah, sure, Tiffany. What about her?"

"Rodney, listen, this is important, you gotta introduce me to her."

"Forget it, why should I introduce you? I've been trying to get her to go out with me for weeks."

"You're a real compassionate guy, ya know that, Rodney?"

I forced my way through the crowd to where she was sitting. "Forget it!" Rodney called. "You'll never get her." Boy, all this reassurance was really beginning to get on my nerves.

I moved to her side and tried to figure out what to say. I would have been content just to stand there and stare at her all evening; she was even prettier up close. She turned to me after I had been standing there like a jerk for about four minutes.

"Yeeeaaasssshh?" she drawled, sounding vaguely Southern or maybe just drunk.

"I think you're really beautiful." I stumbled for words. "I mean, you look nice." It wasn't the most original thing to say, but it was honest.

She did a double take. Then a slow look up and down.

I was ready to beat a hasty retreat and lick my wounds when she spoke up. "You're not so bad yourself, sailor." That did it. I was gone. Over the top.

I ordered two pitchers of beer, sat one down in front of her, and I sat down next to her with the other. She had a shit-eating grin all over the lower region of her mug. It said, "I don't want you, but I want the beer, so I'll let you stay, but don't take it too seriously." She could have no idea how seriously I already was taking it. It occurred to me she was just hustling me for the drinks, but I didn't care. It gave me time with her.

Also unspoken but implicit in her expression was: *You can't have me. No one can have me. Not for beer, not for anything; I don't have a price. But you're welcome to try.* Tiffany's expressions, I would learn, always said more than her mouth. With a come-hither look and a forty-tooth sterling grin, she had looks that said things there weren't even words invented for. Her eyes were the color of jade, elegant green, and were topped by thin blond eyebrows. Her neck was long and invited stroking. I was thoroughly, completely, and willingly hooked.

She reached straight for the pitcher, ignoring the glass, without the slightest sign of resistance or obligation. In one continuous series of large gulps she downed the entire pitcher of beer, then wiped her mouth and smiled. "Another?" she asked.

I happily obliged and ordered two more. I didn't know it then, I couldn't have, but it was the beginning of a relationship to be based, precipitously, on chemicals. When she finished the second pitcher and I was still working on my first, she turned to me with a doe-eyed smirk and said, "Let's ditch this beer and wine scene and go somewhere that serves real alcohol."

I didn't need to be asked twice.

I told Rodney to tell Iggy I had left and if he needed a ride to leave word on the service and I'd come and get him. Wherever he ended up.

In the car I asked Tiffany if she'd ever been to the Rainbow Bar & Grill, hoping, maybe, to impress her.

"That dump?" She smirked.

"Yeah," I said dully, "that's the place."

"Why not?" she said, bored.

"Your excitement overwhelms me."

"Asshole," she mumbled.

"Beg your pardon?"

"Fuck you," she said.

These two expressions and the three words that constituted them, I would soon learn, were the cornerstones of Tiffany's verbal vocabulary. Occasionally she'd become creative or get the impulse to express a full sentence complete with verb and noun, and she would throw them all together and I'd get "Fuck you, asshole." Some days that was as close to having a conversation as we ever got. It didn't make for very lively discussions, but I guess it did cut through the superfluous bullshit pretty well.

"That's not a real ladylike way to address your date," I told her.

"Oh, yeah?" she said, giving me a look that told me she was not concerned with my judgment calls.

I just giggled, absolutely charmed, to the heels of my cowboy boots.

Once we got seated at the Rainbow, I asked her if it would be all right to have her phone number.

"I don't give my phone number out to strangers."

I gave her mine. We split a bottle of champagne and a pizza, and after a few Jack Daniel's, I was tapped out; I didn't have enough money left to tip the parking attendant.

"Well," I said, trying to sound as casual as possible; "that was fun. What do you want to do now?" I felt expansive, open to suggestions.

"Find someone to buy me another drink," she said, and was up and away.

I thought she was kidding. When she didn't stop and return, I jumped up after her and, grabbing her elbow, told her to get her own ride home.

"I thought you were different," I said to her.

"That's because you're an asshole," she said to me.

I sure felt like one. Depressed, drunk, and dejected, I drove home alone.

The telephone woke me up at 10:00 A.M. A hysterical young girl was on the line. Not being able to understand a word she was saying and not recognizing her voice, I hung up the phone and rolled over to go back to sleep.

The phone rang again. I picked it up and put it to my ear without saying a word.

A calmer version of the same voice asked me if I handled Iggy.

"I try," I said, refusing to commit myself. I hoped this would be short. I was hung over and wanted to get back to sleep.

"Well, you better get over here," whoever it was warned me. "He's at the bottom of the driveway chopping up Daddy's Mercedes with the garden ax."

Now she had my attention. "What do you want me to do about it?"

"You better come and get him before Daddy gets home from the airport, or else my mom is going to call the police. He's totally crazy. Please come and get him before we all get in trouble; I'm in enough already."

I got her address and pulled on a pair of jeans, and dragging my red cowboy boots and a bottle of beer with me, I lit out to the car. It took me about fifteen minutes even to find the car; I couldn't remember where I had parked it when I came home the night before.

Iggy had the knack of attracting countless young, pretty, and rich Beverly Hills debutantes, the lights of Daddy's life. Not your obvious Iggy Pop fans. Yet they must have thought he could be molded into their boyfriends. I couldn't believe these girls actually wanted to take Iggy to meet their fathers. What kind of resentment and hatred must exist in these nymphets' hard little hearts I couldn't begin to estimate. They knew he had a reputation as one of rock's last legitimate bad boys, a human destructo machine, but they came to him just the same. Whether to tame him, mother him, help him, or offend their parents I don't know. Maybe they just wanted an adventurous fucking. I can only say they continued to show up from the first day I knew him. In their BMWs, Porsches, and Mercedes-Benzes, they chauffeured and pampered him. He went along with it, and he remained docile and lovable and restrained and agreeable until the day came when he refused to be cuddled and used anymore and he rebelled. So far it had resulted in nothing more than some hurt feelings and a good deal of resentment on both sides. He'd written a song about them called "Rich Bitch." Among the lyrical highlights: "When you're so big/they drive through you with a truck/and everybody knows you already been fucked/ Daddy ain't around to pay your bills/nobody wants to buy you pills. . . ."

As I pulled into the driveway, I passed a bright candy-apple red

Mercedes convertible with wide gashes in its tires and sides, windows splintered out, chopped up and gouged with some sort of large blade. Feeling a distinct invasion of dread and not seeing Iggy, I raced up the driveway farther, into a clearing before a six-car garage. Inside stood a fleet of cars—a Jeep, a station wagon, a Mercedes-Benz sedan—and over in the corner by the lawn was a shining black customized Maserati. Standing on the hood was Iggy, ax swung over his head and brought down with a loud crash into the bumper, over and over again, ripping the shit out of the steel frame.

I honked the horn, and he ignored it. *He must be really into it,* I thought, getting out of the car and walking over to the spectacle, watching him, careful to keep my distance. The display was awesome. He was truly pissed.

The young girl ran up to me and pleaded with me to stop him. "But he's got an ax," I pointed out.

"Please, you've got to stop him, my father is on his way home, and Mom's up and calling the police." Then, to Iggy, she screamed, *"You're such an asshole. Why are you so mean to me?"*

Without missing a beat, his voice dripping hatred, he yelled, *"You think you're such a hot shit! None of this means anything! They're symbols! Just 'cause you can buy the most expensive toys in the world doesn't mean you can buy me!"* He readjusted his footing and whipped back into action, cutting up the windshield and dashboard.

"Why don't you do something!?" she pleaded.

"I'm not a fucking toy! You can't buy me with your daddy's money. I'm a goddamn man," he told her, momentarily resting. He leaped off the automobile, which looked as if its front end had gone through a car wash equipped with razor blades instead of cloth and brush.

"I'm sorry," she sobbed. "I'm sorry, I didn't mean to, I didn't know—"

The mother came up and announced the police were on their way.

"Hey, Jim, come on, let's go. You got a plane to catch, or didja forget?"

He wound up and took a healthy swing at the passenger door. I was still hesitant to approach him.

"Jim, come on, man, I'll give you a ride to the airport. Let's get out of here."

He was having trouble pulling the ax out of the car door. I rapidly walked over and tried to pull it out for him.

"It's stuck, forget it. Don't you think you hurt the car enough? Look," I told him, "I think you killed it. It looks dead to me. And you killed its baby down the road, too. Let's get out of here before they get you on a multiple assault charge for killing cars."

"I swear to fucking God I hate this fucking city," he snarled. "Get me out of here."

We got into my car and got out of there, quick. I drove him directly to the airport, where he hooked up with the rest of the Stooges, to start his tour.

My head felt as if it had gotten bashed in instead of the cars. It was a bitch of a wake-up call, and my hangover wasn't any better for it. I drove home and tried to sleep. I'd just gone under when the phone rang.

After five minutes of ringing, I pulled it off the receiver and down under the covers to my ear.

"Yeah?"

"Where the fuck are you?" a girl's voice asked.

"Pam?"

"Nooo. Who's Pam?"

"Who's this?"

"You sure have a short memory."

"Who is this?"

"You don't even remember last night."

"I'm trying not to."

"Thanks a lot."

"Oh, hi, Tiffany. That was a real first-class move you pulled last night."

"Me? You're the one who ran out of money on our first date. Don't blame me."

"Lookit, what do you want? I've had a rough morning."

"Aren't you happy to hear from me?"

"I can't stop jumping up and down."

"Thanks a lot, asshole."

"Now I recognize your voice." She ignored the comment.

"Can I ask you a favor?" she asked.

"I don't have any money."

"I know who your father is."

"Great. Go ask my father for some money, and while you're at it, get a loan for me."

"I don't want money."

"What do you want?"

"I need a place to stay for a while. I was wondering if I could crash at your place for a few days."

Maybe this day wasn't going to be a total bummer after all.

I sat up in bed, trying to get my brain started. Without any coffee in me, it wasn't going too swell.

"Ummm, I think I'm going to be moving pretty soon."

"Where?" she asked.

"Laurel Canyon."

"Sounds nice."

"It is," I said.

"Great, I can help you move. I'm great at moving. I helped my mother move about a hundred times already."

"Sounds stable."

"It's fucked."

"Sure, you help me move, you can stay with me. Is it all right if I ask why?"

"I'm not going to sleep with you."

"That's not what I asked."

"Yeah, maybe not yet, but you will."

"What makes you so certain?" I wanted to know.

"Because you guys are all alike."

"Whatever you say."

"I'm just telling you so you know," she warned me.

"You will. Someday." She might as well know, I decided. Planting the idea couldn't hurt.

"What makes *you* so sure?"

"Because from what I can tell, I'm the only guy not trying to."

That stumped her for a second. Then she regained her poise.

"When can you come get me?"

"You didn't answer my question," I reminded her.

"Oh, and what was your question?"

I'd forgotten.

"Never mind, it's not important. What's your address?"

"You forgot?"

"Listen, do you want me to come get you or not?"

"Don't do me any favors," she said, and hung up.

I looked at the receiver, not entirely certain of what had just transpired.

I hung up the phone and rolled over and tried to go back to sleep.

The phone rang again. I grabbed it after the first ring.

"You know where Poinsettia Avenue is off Santa Monica Boulevard?"

"Around the corner from Danny's Okie-Dog."

"You got it, bunkie. I'll meet you at Okie-Dog."

"No, that's all right, I may not have enough class to have enough money on a first date, but my parents didn't bring up no slouch. I'll come to the front door to get you."

"You sure you want to do that?"

"Why, is there something you're not telling me?"

"There's a lot I'm not telling you."

"Is it safe?" I inquired.

"For you it is."

That alarmed me. For her sake, not mine.

"Are you okay?" I asked.

"So far." Pause. "Not really." Pause. "I'd rather meet you somewhere else."

"I'll see you in an hour at Okie-Dog."

"Thanks. I mean, I barely know you. Why are you being so nice?"

"Maybe because I think you deserve it. Maybe not."

"Thanks for the vote of confidence, asshole."

"I guess I'll find out soon enough if you're worth it."

"Boy, are you in for a wait!"

"I can't hardly stand the suspense," I told her, and hung up.

An hour later I collected her.

"Hello, sailor," she said as the car pulled up, throwing her travel bag in before climbing in next to me. She smelled fresh, clean, and shampooed.

Later in the day I came to the conclusion she wasn't real bright. Stupid people don't like it when you imply they're not smart. After all, it's not like they're insensitive, too. They'll admit to being lazy, or scared, or dishonest, or practically anything else. They'll admit to being ax murderers probably, before they'll admit to being a feather-brain, a rattlepate, or a dumb fuck. Fortunately one of the reasons I wanted a girlfriend did not include conversation. If I wanted to talk to somebody, there was Ray, who was a great conversationalist and whom I talked to every day anyway.

What she lacked upstairs, she more than made up for in heart—big and solid gold. You could feel it from across the room. Just because she had a good heart I don't mean to imply she was a softy by any means. Just the opposite was true. She was one tough cookie. Nobody pushed her around, she told me, she did not take any shit from anyone, so don't try, she warned me, and I believed her.

At bedtime she offered me a Quaalude, flipping it up in the air like it was a coin and catching it. I sauntered up and swiped it on the decline, tossed it in my mouth, and swallowed. "Very clever," Tiffany said. "I'm going to bed."

She stood up, stretched, and then let rip one of the most gigantic belches I'd ever heard. It kept coming out of her as she strode away from the couch.

"I thought you were going to bed," I asked her.

"Yeah, so?"

"You're headed toward the bathroom," I pointed out, thinking, albeit briefly, she might intend to throw her roll down there.

She paused. She wanted to come up with a zinger, I could tell from her expression, but none was forthcoming. Exasperated, she glanced at me and said, "I'm going to change."

"Oh," I said.

Then she belched again, closing the bathroom door behind her as she did so.

She sure didn't look tough when she came out of the bathroom, all cuddly and cute in her baby blue cotton pajamas with little Winnie-the-Poohs and Christopher Robins stenciled on. It was all I could do not to get all gushy and hug her tits off.

I settled for telling her how cute she looked.

Her eyebrow on the left arched itself up into a question mark. "Cute?" she asked.

"Yeah," I told her, "cute, you know, soft, huggable . . ."

"Ugh. Don't make me puke." She got in bed and under the covers.

"No, I'm serious, I mean it as a compliment. You look real cute in those things."

"Just don't get any ideas," she said, sitting up in bed and shaking her finger at me.

"Don't worry," I said, turning off the light and getting into bed next to her and my ideas.

"*Hey, asshole!*" she yelled, turning back on the light. "What the fuck do you think you're doing?"

"Going to bed?" I suggested.

"Not with this girl, you're not."

"Wait a second. This is my bed, my apartment."

"Yeah, I know, and there's a couch over there that belongs to you, too, so why don't you go sleep with it?"

"C'mon, I won't touch you. I won't move from this side of the bed."

"Sure you won't." She didn't sound convinced.

"I have a good idea," I told her. "Why don't you sleep on the couch?"

"Oh, you're a real gracious host, aren't you?"

"Okay," I said. "I'll make you a deal: I'll let you sleep in my bed with me if you let me sleep in my bed with you."

"Just shut up and go to sleep," she said, turning off the light and rolling her back toward me.

Over the course of the next few days I found out more about the new girl in my life. She'd saved some money from working as an actress in a string of B movies, but acting wasn't a goal of hers. It was something that had come along, and paid well, so she'd accepted. She'd done some modeling and wanted to do more but didn't have the time to pursue it because of school. She was just fifteen years old and in the tenth grade at Hollywood High School.

Tiffany had been living with her mother, a waitress, and her mother's second husband, Dallas, an ex-con, on probation. He'd been out of the can for just over a year and had another two years on his probation to go. Dallas was in his mid-twenties compared with Tiffany's mom, Marilyn, who was in her late thirties. The three of them lived together in a small West Hollywood one-bedroom bungalow apartment. Her mom worked during the day; her stepfather tended bar at night at a pretty hard-core Sunset Strip billiard and bar dive. He sold dope under the counter for extra money. When I asked what type, Tiffany said, "Any type as long as he can step on it with cut and rip off whoever is stupid enough to buy it."

"Sounds like a real charming guy," I said.

"He's not. He's an ass!!"

He also hassled Tiffany. The lock on the bathroom door was broken, and when Tiffany was showering, he'd stroll in to take a leak or shave.

"Can't you ignore him?" I asked her. "I mean, it isn't like he touches you, is it?"

She let out a short, sarcastic "Ha!" and told me the night before I met her he'd undressed and climbed into the shower with her.

"Where was your mother? Still at work?"

"No way. She was passed out, drunk."

"Didn't you tell her, later on?"

"She doesn't care. I told her before. She just blamed me for the whole thing. She said I musta provoked him. Next time he tried it, I told her again, and she thought I was just trying to get him in trouble."

The morning she called me to come get her, he'd done it again,

230

this time pushing his naked body against hers and trying to kiss her. This time her mom was awake and sober; she thought it was funny. Tiffany fled.

On Monday morning I got up with her at seven to drive her to school.

"I thought I was through with this getting-up-at-dawn-and-going-to-school bullshit," I told her.

"Fuck you," she said as she finished getting dressed.

When we arrived and saw no one there, she remembered school was out for two weeks' Christmas vacation; I turned around and drove us back to the apartment.

On Tuesday we slept late. Later in the day we drove into West Hollywood and scored a gram and a half of cocaine from a friend of hers. Good, smooth, strong coke, not too speedy. Perfect for moving.

The next morning we woke up at our leisure, about ten forty-five, snorted a few lines of cocaine, cracked two beers, and began packing my few possessions, the stereo, clothes, a small box of kitchen utensils, and about twenty boxes of records and books. We finished loading up and down the car, got in, and drove away from the beach, headed for Hollywood. We kept going until we pulled up in front of our new home on Wonderland Avenue.

BOOK · III
THE LIFE

CHAPTER NINE

· · · · · · · · · · · ·

**The man in the back said
"Everyone attack"
And it turned into a
Ballroom Blitz
—SWEET**

THE realtor waiting for us in front of the house handed me two sets of keys. "One for you, one for me?" Tiffany asked.

"For some reason I don't think Ray would appreciate that too much," I told her.

The movers brought Manzarek's musical equipment out of storage and up to Wonderland, and Tiffany and I brought my few belongings along with us in the one trip. There wasn't much left to do except walk through the front door and move in.

The house except for the living room where there were baffles, amps, microphones, and keyboard equipment, was already furnished. The previous owners had taken out the den furniture, and we'd transformed the room into an office. Ray and I had gone out shopping and picked out an off-white couch with a chrome and glass coffee table for one wall and a mahogany desk and chair set for the other side of the room. Ray brought his Doors gold records over and hung them on the wall behind the couch, and the pinball machine from the Doors' office stood in the corner near the file cabinet.

First thing I did was install the stereo and turn up the music.

Everything else was already in place. Upstairs the guest room was mainly Moroccan pillows, and a little alcove for the bed was tucked into the wall. Down the hallway was a door leading to the master bedroom. The room was enormous, high-ceilinged with a combination dressing room, walk-in closet, and hardwood floors. Behind the large wooden bed frame was an all-mirrored wall. Facing the bed was a natural stone fireplace. Two big windows opened out onto the backyard, the pool, and the hillside rising behind us. A large oak pushed itself up against the side of the house and right up to the window. The room was big, cool, and airy, but cozy and cute at the same time.

"Nice joint you got here," Tiffany said. "Not bad, not bad at all. Where's the bar?"

"Wherever we sit is the bar."

We left the master bedroom and headed back downstairs, where we heard Ray and Dorothy. As we passed the guest room, Tiffany said, "This'll do just fine for me. I always wanted my own room."

"Wait a second," I said.

"What for?" she asked, flopping onto the bed.

For a second there I was going to tell her if she thought I was going to pay her rent and have her sleep in another room, she had another think coming. Then I realized, for one thing, I wasn't paying any rent—it was a mortgage, and I wasn't paying that either—and two, perhaps it was best not to push the sleeping-together issue just yet.

"We're not done moving in yet," I said.

"Oh, okay," she moaned, pulling herself off the bed.

Downstairs Ray and Dorothy were just coming out of the kitchen and met us at the bottom of the stairs. I introduced them to Tiffany.

"Well, what do you think?" Ray asked.

"Not bad," Tiffany answered, "except it could use a wet bar."

I wanted to belt her.

"Oh, well"—Ray laughed it off—"you can't have everything."

"I love it," I told Ray. "I love the office. I'll get the phones in as soon as possible."

"I like my room just fine," Tiffany announced to nobody in particular.

Ray looked at me, and I just shrugged. "How do you like the rehearsal room?" I asked him.

"Great, the whole house, everything's going to work out fine. I can't wait to get to work. Everything's perfect." He looked around. "Anything else?" he asked, getting ready to leave. If everything was perfect, how come I felt I was thirteen years old again and should say something to reassure Ray that everything would be okay if he left me there alone?

After all those years of insisting on doing everything my own way, and everyone telling me how wrong my way was, I guess I was surprised to discover I'd been right. Now I had what I wanted and had no idea of how I'd done it. I couldn't believe it had been so easy. Something was amiss. I felt compelled to say something to Ray that would justify his setting me up like this.

"Are you satisfied with the job I'm doing?" I asked, searching for reassurance.

"Are you kidding? You're doing a great job. I've never seen so much coverage. You just keep doing whatever it is you're doing and I'll make the music and everything will be perfect."

238

"Oh, before I forget, these are for you." I handed him the keys.

"That reminds me. I have something for you, too. Here." He handed me a credit card.

"What's this for?"

"Look at it. It's for you. If you're going to be a publicist, you need an expense account. Old Gabe says we have to unload some cash."

"You're kidding, right?"

"No, I'm serious. When you entertain from now on, put it on this."

I looked at the card. "It says the Doors on it," I pointed out.

"Yeah, the corporation is still going; the partnership still exists."

My name on a credit card with the Doors' name right under it. I felt better already.

"Are you sure?" I asked.

"Yeah, I'm sure. If I can't trust you by now . . ." He laughed. I couldn't decide if he was a saint, so rich he didn't care anymore, or just foolish. "I'm not saying go wild with it, but enjoy yourself, get the job done, go out, be seen, you know how to do it. Don't be shy."

"Don't worry," I said. "Hell, I love to spend money. . . . I never went for that antimaterialistic hippie head trip anyway."

"Well, don't go bragging about it," Ray warned me.

Before Ray decided to take the card back, I pulled out the vial of cocaine and offered everybody a couple of celebratory hits.

"A toast," I said, "here's to us."

Ray agreed. "To us."

Ray and Dorothy left to go get a bite to eat. They were always doing little things like that, going out for lunch or a little drive, or to do a little shopping, or to see a foreign movie, or to spend the day at the beach. They were quite a couple like that. I got the distinct impression they were each other's best friend, not just husband and wife. Dorothy was seven and a half months pregnant, and Ray was real cute in his attentiveness to her. Together they coordinated what they wore, always in the latest fashions by the best designers.

Tiffany and I were alone in the house.

"What else do we need to do?" she asked.

"I guess we're done. There's nothing else I can think of."

I couldn't help smirking. Too fucking much. A house! Not bad. And I was down as a co-owner. Ray's business manager and I had worked out a deal whereby a portion of the mortgage payments were also a piece of my salary, making it a unique and suitable tax deduction for Ray and a credit-building device for me. Tiffany had gone upstairs to "her" room while I stayed in the foyer of the house and eyed my new surroundings: the wicker kitchen dining set to my left, to my right the rehearsal studio, straight ahead the office, and past that the backyard and pool.

I felt like an idiot, standing there all by myself, grinning my head off. *You did it! You fucking did it! Far-fucking-out!* I wasn't exactly positive how I'd done it, but the results were impressive. Of that I was certain. A real house, not a rental, not an apartment, not a lease, or a condo; a solid, genuine two-story Spanish-style "charmer" in fucking Laurel Canyon! With a goddamn swimming pool and gold records on my own goddamn office walls! And a beautiful girl! Living with me! Plus a job! Two jobs! And a salary! None of this working-by-the-hours bullshit. What more could a guy want? What else could I ask *for*? They'd all been wrong. Dad and the hick teacher dumb fucks at school and Mom and her asshole dickhead of a husband and those butthole surfers at school—they'd all been wrong. I didn't have to do it their way. I hadn't failed like they predicted I would. I'd won! I was living as good as them. Better! I *liked* what I was doing. I could work when I wanted and have time off when I wanted. I could say, "Fuck it," and go to the beach for the day if I were so inclined. I didn't have to get out of bed if I didn't feel like it. I didn't even have to worry about making the house payments; they were already taken care of. There was money coming in, and after Ray's record was out and Iggy had another contract, hell, I'd be making a fortune. Who knew how much? Who cared? It'd be plenty. I had already started making plenty. And a credit card with the Doors' name on it under my own and a place for my signature on the back. I didn't even need money! I had everything I ever wanted, and more than I needed, right here, right now! I was fucking *set*.

I almost broke out singing "(I Did It) My Way."

For a quick flash there I felt content. It must've lasted for all of a hot minute before it passed. Then a bit of reality sunk in. Everything wasn't fine. What the fuck was I supposed to do now? How was I going to continue deserving all this luxury? Now that I had it, it wasn't likely I'd ever want to give it up so easily.

Sure, I'd done some work. What I did basically consisted of sending out a press release every other month and getting drunk and buying writers drinks, going to every party in town, and blabbing my mouth off about whatever it was I'd written in the last release. If that were all I had to do, I could do that. I could type and I could drink and I could talk. It just didn't seem like enough to merit all this. It just didn't seem right to be compensated so well for something I liked doing. Something was out of balance. There had to be more to it. I really wanted to feel like I had earned it. Ray obviously thought I had; how come I didn't feel the same way? Why did I feel like any minute someone was going to walk in and say to me, "Lookit, excuse me, there's been a mistake here; we thought you knew what you were doing; you can't have all this"?

Ray really trusted me, and I, in turn, felt a sense of dedication and loyalty proportionate to that trust. I didn't want to let him down. I wanted to show him I deserved that trust. By some immeasurable stroke of strange luck I had secured a recording contract for him with Mercury Records. The lawyers had just finished closing the deal. The next step on my end, as anyone who ever read two issues of *Billboard* magazine knows, was to coordinate a signing photo between the artist and label executives, and the step after that was to make sure the publicity department had an updated biography and recent photos. I tried to reassure myself that that took care of the next month or so. But then what? What was I supposed to do after that? When Ray was in the studio, what was I supposed to be doing? What was I going to do when he went on tour? I didn't even want to call anyone I knew to ask because I didn't want to risk the possibility of word leaking back to Ray I didn't know what the fuck I was doing. Just because I questioned my worth didn't mean I wanted him to as well.

But I knew. I wasn't about to admit it to a soul, but I knew. I tried to convince myself if Ray was pleased, and the coverage was being delivered, whatever else I was telling myself was bullshit. The job was being done, and the employer was pleased, so shut the fuck up. Nothing else matters. Nobody is going to find out jackshit because there is nothing to find out, so enjoy yourself and stop worrying.

And I also knew something else was wrong but I couldn't name what it was. I only knew that I felt an almost paralyzing sense of unexplainable guilted fear. Flying in the face of so much good fortune, I was also at a loss to know the cause except that something had begun to go, or was about to go, very, very wrong.

After a couple of laps around the house, admiring the territory, marveling anew at the magical way it had all transpired, trying to regain that intense moment of contentment, but instead just getting more confused, I called out to Tiffany, who was in "her" room. "C'mon, let's go out somewhere and test out this plastic."

She bounded out of the room and down the stairs two at a time, in long strides with those great long legs of hers, pulling on a denim jacket, wrapping a long scarf around her neck, and pulling out of her pocket a Russian fur cap, which she adjusted on her head.

"That's the best idea I've heard all day," she said. She was real happy, smiling her face in half. She looped her arm through mine and pulled me out the front door.

"Let's go get shit-faced, bunky," she whispered, nibbling on my ear.

Arriving on the West Coast amid a roar of hype and heralding, were the New York Dolls, the new critical darlings, reputed to be just the thing for those rock 'n' roll fans caught between the pretentious pomposities of stadium-filling supergroups and the equally pretentious cut-rate plaintive introspective warblings of the supersensitive singer songwriters. They epitomized the whole new movement struggling to give birth to itself, giving it not only a look and sound but lyrics, voice, and a state of mind. Trashy, brassy, and sassy, all painted up, pouting lips and ratted hair, standing up on six-inch platform heels, wrapped up with five-inch Leatherette belts with enormous (doll-like) buckles, decked out in ladies' frill and lace blouses and leather jackets. All reds and blacks and pinks. They were hot, and their music was even hotter.

The Whisky had dropped its age limit down to eighteen years old, although you were still ID'd at the front door if you wanted to drink. Since I'd been coming there for so long already, the doorman (whom I called Pimp—Tiffany called him Superfly—with his big, white, fuzzy hat and a knee-length phony fur coat) always gave me the okay-to-drink stamp without any investigation. I never questioned him, but I wondered how come I got away with it. Certainly not because I looked twenty-one. I barely looked the nineteen I was. As Tiffany and I walked past the doorman to the guest ticket window, I heard the owner, Mario, tell the Pimp, "That kid drinks his weight in booze every time he comes in here." I guess he figured I was worth risking the wrath of the ABC (Alcoholic Beverage Control).

We stepped over the purple velvet-swathed rope that cordoned off the public seating from the VIP section. One of the bouncers rushed to stop us, recognized us, and ushered us straight to a reserved booth. Betty Lou, the lanky blond waitress for the booth area, came over to take our drink orders. Betty Lou and I had developed a close, friendly, if lopsided, relationship over the past few years. She'd driven me home and tucked me in on more than a few occasions when I'd gotten too drunk to drive. Lately she'd shown signs of losing her patience. "The usual?" she asked, setting down two double Kahlua and creams with two shots of tequila gold and a record company tab for me to sign.

I wasn't going to get a chance that night to use my new Master-charge with its thousand-dollar limit.

When the last notes faded and the Dolls had left the stage, I told Tiffany to wait where she was while I went upstairs with Denny from Mercury Records, who was responsible for the Dolls while they were in town and had also been influential in signing Ray to the label. A crowd had backed up and flowed down the stairs as those vying to get backstage jammed together with the regulars trying to get out. The guard at the door was losing his cool as everyone tried to get past him at once. "One at a time," he snarled.

From somewhere in back of me I thought I heard my name called. I didn't bother turning around. Standing ready to go backstage, know-ing your name is on the list, when there're all these people pushing and crowding around to get to the very same place you're about to be privy to, frantically vying for position and dropping every name they've ever heard to gain access, you tend to overestimate your im-portance. I wasn't in a real hurry to turn around and find out who was calling out. What could anyone possibly have I could need? On the other hand, I knew what I had he could want, like backstage access. When I heard my name yelled again, I ignored the call, again.

When the line still wasn't moving five minutes later and my name was shouted out one more time, curiosity got the best of me, and I moved my eyes down a few rows where a guy was waving at me. I'd never seen him before in my life. Just as I was about to turn my head away, I caught a glimpse of him handing a vial of cocaine back to a guy with long dark hair sitting next to him.

"I'll meet you upstairs," I told Denny from Mercury, and walked over to say hello to my two newfound buddies.

"Hey, man, how you doin'? Man, I didn't think you'd remember me," said the first guy I didn't remember.

"All right, how you doin'?" I asked him back.

"Remember us?" said the guy with the dark hair. "San Diego?"

"Sure, I remember you," I lied. "I just don't remember your names."

"Blake," said the guy who'd waved, "I'm Blake Foster; this is Shane."

I shook both their hands. I still didn't remember either of them.

"Yeah, sure, good to see you again," I said. His friend handed him back the vial. "Ahhh, I sure could dig a hit of that," I told Blake.

"You know what this is?" he asked me.

"Of course, I know what it is." What a stupid fucking question. No wonder I didn't remember these guys. I figured I'd cop a toot and then make a quick getaway before anyone saw me talking with them and mistook these yokels for friends of mine.

"All right." He handed me the yellow vial with the little spoon and white powder. "Knock yourself out." I pocketed it into my jacket. The line had thinned enough for me to get backstage, and I got my pass from the security guard and walked upstairs, heading straight into the upstairs bathroom before going back into the dressing room to meet the band. Inside, I locked the door, took out the vial, and filled each nostril up four times.

I checked out the mirror over the sink to make sure none had gotten on my face, put the vial back inside my jacket pocket, unlocked the door, took a step outside into the hallway, looked in the direction of the dressing room, which was overflowing with people, decided it was too much of a hassle to get inside, figured I'd kept Tiffany waiting downstairs long enough, turned to go back downstairs, took one step down onto the first top stair, and then it hit me. Everything went black, my knees buckled, and I tumbled down the stairway, past the door leading back to the balcony, rolling all the way to the fire door Mario had thrown me and Jim out of four years ago for being drunk at the Bo Diddley show.

I didn't want to open my eyes. I'd never felt more peaceful. I heard voices and, through my eyelids, saw light. I smiled. Something, a hand it felt like, slapped my face. I could feel the impact, but it lacked sting. My eyes fluttered open. I was lying on the bed back in my bedroom at Wonderland. There were four people looking down at me: Betty Lou, not looking entertained but very impatient, and next to her Tiffany, actually looking concerned. I focused in on the two guys with them. They were the same two I'd spoken to just before I'd gone backstage.

Gradually it came back to me. They must want their dope. I didn't blame them. Whatever it was was the best thing I'd ever done. I felt inside my jacket, but the vial was gone.

I tried to explain to them I was sorry, but when my voice came out, it didn't sound like mine. It was froggy and hoarse. I closed my mouth. As I began to sit up, I was flooded with an incredible feeling of serenity and contentment.

I slipped back down and closed my eyes.

"Oh, no, you don't, not again," Tiffany said, dousing me with a glassful of water.

"That was completely unnecessary," I sputtered.

"Just keep your eyes open," Tiffany said.

"Talk to me," Betty Lou said, squatting at the bedside. "Say something."

"I'm sorry about your vial," I told the guys. "I don't know what happened to it." Keeping my eyes open was very difficult. I wanted to close them and dream. That was either the weirdest cocaine I ever had, or somebody had spiked my drink, or . . .

"How do you feel?" Betty Lou asked me.

"I feel"—I nodded for a brief second—"wonderful." Everyone looked worried. "Why?" I asked. "What's wrong?"

"I thought you knew," Blake said.

"Knew what?" I asked.

"That wasn't cocaine."

Aha, I thought, managing to keep my eyes open. *Now we get some answers.*

"We tried to tell you." The other guy, Shane, apologized.

"I thought you knew," Blake whined.

Tiffany shook her head in disgust.

"Knew," I croaked, "knew what? What was it?"

One word was all he said. "Heroin."

"No shit?" You remember that old cagey and elusive sense of well-being I'd been so well-intentionally looking for but never able to find? *Eureka!* I found it.

I let my eyes close, shutting myself in a warm and wonderful comfortable land.

Everyone started talking at once, telling me to get my eyes open. "You scared me," Tiffany said. "Don't ever do that again."

"Okay, okay," I said, lifting my eyelids before I was doused again. "Leave me alone."

Everyone was staring at me. I was sopping wet, fully dressed, and didn't care at all.

"Heroin, huh? Very interesting." This wasn't what I imagined heroin would be like at all. I always suspected heroin would be like acid, but a thousand times worse. Or maybe like a superstrong sleeping pill. This was exactly what I'd always been hoping some drug would feel like but never had. The one drug I'd promised myself I'd never do was the one drug I really liked. The Big Meanie was a pussycat.

"Did I lose it?" I wanted to know.

"No, don't worry about it," Blake told me, patting his chest pocket. "I have it."

"Can I have some more?"

Which got everyone talking all at once all over again.

"I don't believe it," Blake said.

"You're nuts," his friend Shane said.

"I'm leaving," Betty Lou said, "if you do any more."

"You almost died, you asshole," Tiffany remarked.

I didn't say anything for a minute or so. "Is anybody going to please answer my question?" I looked at Blake. "*Is* there any left?"

He spoke up. "Yeah, sure, I got some more. And there's plenty more where that came from."

It was difficult for me to talk. I didn't feel it was necessary. What a bother. How come he wouldn't just do what I wanted and give it to me? I wanted to close my eyes and have some more heroin when I woke up, and then prolong this state for as long as humanly possible. I'd never felt like this before. My whole brain slowed down and relaxed, calm and certain. No need to talk! I was amazed. Totally relaxed! The kid who couldn't sit still! Imagine! The cure for hyperactivity!

When I didn't say anything else, Blake started speaking. "I sell the stuff. I'm up here from San Diego, looking for a room to rent so I can transfer to UCLA." He didn't exactly fulfill my image of a heroin dealer. He looked like what he was, a nice young Jewish college student who just happened to sell heroin and was also balding prematurely, a little pathetic in a cute sort of way. I couldn't have been happier with him if he were a magic genie.

"We might be able to work something out to our mutual benefit," I told Blake. "I have an extra room. . . ."

"I'm leaving," Betty Lou announced, walking out. "You're crazy."

"He's not moving into *my* room," Tiffany said.

"He can have the guest room until he finds a place to live or Iggy gets off tour," I told her. "Whichever comes first."

"You know Iggy Pop?" Blake gasped.

"Whoopee whoopee," Tiffany snorted, twirling a finger in the air.

I continued where I'd left off. "And you can sleep in here with me," I told Tiffany. I didn't really care whether she stayed or left.

"And you"—I turned to Blake—"can pay me with that nifty white power you got stashed somewhere between your jacket pocket and San Diego. Bring it over, my man! Move in! Tomorrow, if not sooner. And you can skip the deposit. I already did that, and we can get right on to the first and last month's rent."

Still miffed about the sleeping arrangement I'd proposed, Tiffany went off to stay with some actress friend.

For the next week I did heroin every day. I wasn't too worried about when or if Tiffany was coming home. Blake had moved right in, and we were getting along fine. I wasn't worrying about anything anymore. The insecurities I'd experienced shortly after moving in had completely vanished. I was intuitively handling the business on a daily basis effectively and confidently. In the past I'd always hated to go to bed for fear of missing out on something important. I'd never been a good sleeper. Now I slept like a baby. Time, which had always been so unbearable to endure, simply melted away. Heroin killed time, almost like that folding-time process in *Dune* with the spice mélange, but instead of eyes becoming blue, they became pinned, reptilian and lizardlike. Who cared if it was addictive? Who'd want to stop long enough to find out? Not me.

That first time I did it, I knew. This is it. People go to jail for this, and it's worth it. I knew why people would rob from their families, lie to their best friends, or risk freedom and even their lives to get and do it. This is how I always wanted to feel, but couldn't, because I didn't know how, until now.

You get paralyzed into a feeling of well-being, cast into a witness role. You just dig what is happening, detached. You don't even have to move or get in the way of the world. Everything's fine, and you feel benevolent. You contain the universe. Sometimes you just want to talk. You just quack on for hours about anything because nothing matters. You make wonderful and elaborate plans, picnics at the beach or forest, restaurants to dine at, plays to attend. You have an endless capacity for enjoying everything but in mind only. When it comes right down to it, you don't even want to be bothered to get up to do it. Why bother when thinking about it, stoned, is just as good, if not better?

You feel absolutely no compulsion whatsoever to venture out into the real world with other people. They don't know what you know; they haven't found what you've found. There is nothing to do and no place to go. Or you can do anything and nothing bothers you. It doesn't matter whether you stay in or go out. Heroin brings it all home to you. It removes the need and replaces it with contentment. It takes the pain and turns it into pleasure. There's no other high even slightly like it. It explodes in your head like a silver Roman candle and thumps your chest and flows down your arms and limbs and

through the rest of your body like warm liquid gold. All you can do
is scratch and groan, "It feels sooo good." It is enoughness in the
extreme. You don't even want any more dope right after you've done
some, unlike coke, of which you always want more. There is absolutely nothing you need or desire. It is a spiritual encounter with
yourself in a detached, euphoric, composed, contented state. It is
completeness and warmth and serenity, security, and ultimate peace.

Blake had left Wonderland early to look for a more permanent place
to live. Then he was headed down to San Diego to replenish his
depleted heroin supply. I hadn't had any junk all day, the first time
in almost three weeks I had gone any measurable period of time
without it, and I felt fine. A little jittery, maybe, but otherwise okay.
It didn't seem possible snorting something that felt so good could be
that dangerous, and now I was convinced it wasn't.

Ray had expressed some concern over my recent dalliance, but
I'd reassured him it was under control. "It helps me work better," I
told him.

"I thought you worked fine without it," he replied.

"Well," I told him, "it helps me sleep."

"Wait a minute, I thought you just said it helped you work."

"It does. It helps me work *and* sleep." Then I offered him some.

"No, thanks," he said, "I can live without it."

Pamela was dropping by to meet with Ray about a lawsuit the Doors'
accountant had filed on the Doors' behalf against the Morrison estate
for moneys the Doors had lent Jim during the Miami trial and during
his stay in France. For Pamela it must have felt like the final injustice
in what had become a long string of battles she had fought, and lost,
since Jim had willed everything he had to "my wife, Pamela," and in
doing so bequeathed more trouble than protection.

The two fell into each other's arms like long-lost friends in the
Wonderland office. Ray assured her he'd help her, he placed a call to
the accountant and lawyers, and the matter was dropped.

When their meeting was over, Pamela and I had a date to go to
Westwood to see *The Battle of Algiers*. Pam had taken it upon herself
to continue the education Jim had started and the first class she
wanted to enroll me in was foreign films, which I had no desire
whatsoever to attend. "Don't complain," she warned, "and when we
get there, don't read the captions. Concentrate on their expressions."

When the movie let out at 9:00 P.M., we went back across town into West Hollywood to her favorite bar, the Bullshot. Jim used to call it the Bullshit. It was a gay bar, and I'd never been to one of those before either. "What's this, second period?" I asked her.

"No," she said, "this is recreation."

She knew half the people there, and her mood escalated as we made our way through the crowded room. I was glad to see her feeling so good. We drank bottles of wine side by side with Singapore slings, and the more drunk we got, the more gay she became. We pulled each other onto the dance floor while the band hammered its way through "Bits and Pieces" by the Dave Clark Five. One minute we were fast-dancing and the next minute, when the band downshifted into "Spooky," we were slow-dancing, hugging, and rubbing against each other.

While the band took its break, we went back to the table, where the drinks kept coming, and Pam leaned across the little round table-top, took my head in her hands, and kissed me long and wet. One of her gay friends came over and gave us soft pats on our heads.

"Now, you know we don't allow that sort of behavior in here." He laughed, dipping himself into the third chair at our table. Pamela laughed and introduced me to her friend Hector. Hector wanted to know if we knew anybody who was interested in buying any Quaaludes.

"Have a drink, Hector, my friend," I said, pouring him a glass of wine.

Pamela handled the business transaction while I looked on at the peculiar Puerto Rican redhead with the red sweater and tight red leather pants.

"How much money do you have?" Pamela asked me.

I pulled a wad of cash out of my pocket. "About two hundred and thirty bucks, before drinks."

"And I've got about twenty dollars," Pam said, collecting all our cash together in a clump at the middle of the table.

"Why don't you get some dujé?" Hector asked us. I didn't know what dujé was, so I kept my mouth shut and let Pamela answer for us. I figured it might be some new-fangled fag drug like amyl nitrate. Whatever it was, I was game.

"So do we have enough to get enough for both of us?" I asked.

"I'll be right back," Hector said. "Let me check on it."

When he was gone, Pamela asked me, "Have you ever done heroin?"

"Funny you should ask . . ."

Hector returned, and we copped four ludes apiece and a quarter

gram of Mexican heroin, handed over to us wrapped inside four dif-
ferent-colored balloons. I'd never seen it come like this before, only
in vials or wrapped in folded paper.

"What's this for? What are we having? A party?" I said, referring
to the colored balloons.

"Haven't you ever gotten it like this?" Pam asked.

I shook my head.

"It's so you can swallow them if you get pulled over."

"Don't they just dissolve in your stomach with all the acids in
there?"

"You just shit them out," she explained.

"Oh, that's charming," I said, taking them and putting them in
my pocket. "But I think I'll carry it the old-fashioned way."

"No, give it to me. I'll hold it. It's safer." She put out her hand.

I handed over the balloons. She shoved them down inside the
front of her jeans, then took two of the ludes off the tabletop and
washed them down with a glass of wine. I followed suit. "Are you
okay to drive?" she wanted to know.

"I'm always okay to drive."

Since Pam lived closer, we drove over to her apartment.

During the ride "Light My Fire" came over the radio. Pamela
flipped it off and her mood suddenly darkened.

"What did you do that for?" I asked, half mad/half curious.

Pam gave me a look of passive angst. "I killed him," she said.

There was no need for me to ask who. I knew exactly whom she
meant.

"What do you mean you killed him? Come on, Pamela, don't
talk like that. . . ."

"You don't understand," she said.

"Then tell me," I asked her. "I mean, no one could have stopped
Jim from doing what he damn well pleased. You can't blame yourself . . ."

"I know!" she cut me off. "You don't get it, do you? I killed
him. It was my dope."

That shut me up. I had a thousand thoughts at once and said
nothing at all.

Pamela took a deep breath and let it out. "He found out I was
doing dope," she quietly recalled, "and of course"—she gave a slight
laugh—"you know Jim, he just had to try it," and here she tried to
laugh again but instead only managed a weak grin. She pushed her
long strawberry-red hair out of her face and I could see her green
eyes filling with tears. "And I gave it to him! Don't you get it?" she

yelled, sounding thoroughly disgusted with me. "He'd never done it before and I gave it to him. Then he said he didn't feel well, that he was going to take a bath. I should've gone in and checked on him but I nodded out. I didn't think it would hurt him," she said, sounding full of remorse. "He could take anything, you know that. Jim Morrison was always so strong, nothing ever could hurt him."

She looked over at me and paused to see how her words were registering. I wanted to console her but I did not know the words. I just drove and shook my head, afraid to look her in the eye, afraid to know the truth. On a good day Pamela changed moods like most people changed channels on the TV. And today certainly could not be described as one of her better days.

"When I woke up at dawn," she continued, "I went in the bathroom and there he was in the tub. You know that cute little boyish smile he had that was so serene? He was smiling like that and I thought he was putting me on. Then that's when I freaked out and called Bill."

"And you only told Bill the part of the story from Jim telling you he didn't feel well and going to take a bath?" I asked her.

She nodded in the affirmative.

"Pamela," I said as firmly yet gently as I knew how, "are you telling me that you gave Jim smack?"

"Of course not!" she snapped, turning indignant as if it were me who'd just proposed the whole scenario. "You think I would let Jim find out I was doing heroin? I'd be the dead one!"

Now I didn't know what to think. With Pamela reality and fiction were blurring with a rapidly developing consistency and it was difficult to know if it was because of drugs, just the pain of losing Jim, or, now that I thought about it, perhaps the guilt she felt as the result of what she'd just told me.

"Pull over here," she instructed. As I parked the car she came over and took me by the hand, leading me up the walk.

Inside her room, sitting on the bed, we broke the balloons open onto a mirror. It wasn't white; it was brown.

"Shit," I said, "we got burned."

"What are you talking about?" she protested. "Look at all those rocks. . . ."

I looked closer. "It doesn't look like any heroin I've ever seen before."

"Well, that's what it is," she said, taking out a small leather pouch and opening its contents onto the bed. Inside were a blackened spoon, a syringe, some razors, and a woman's nylon. "Don't tell me you can get China White?" she asked.

"I guess that's what they call it. You're not going to use that, are you?" I said, referring to the needle.

"No, I wish I could. I don't know how to hit myself. See?" She held out the crook of her arm under my nose. "No veins. They're like thread. You snort it?"

"Uh-huh, I'd never shoot it. I hate needles."

"Sure, that's what I thought once upon a time." She selected a razor blade from the paraphernalia on the bedspread and wrapped the rest back up in the leather. After a few minutes of being chopped, the little rocks had turned into a fine light brown powder. The Quaa-ludes were getting into the booze in my system. My skin felt sensitive; I felt good, compassionate, protective, and caring. We snorted three thick brown lines apiece. Within five minutes a warmth folded over me, nausea hit my stomach, and I jumped to the bathroom, where I threw my guts into the toilet.

Pamela stood at the doorway, giggling. "That's how you know it's good dope."

After washing my face and gargling with some Scope, I went back into her room and tumbled onto the bed. My skin itched terribly. I pulled my shirt off and scratched my chest and the area around my shoulders.

"Here, let me," she said, climbing around me on her knees, gently scratching my back.

Within minutes we were naked, lying on top of the spread. Her skin was a milky cream color dabbled its length with soft cinnamon freckles; her eyes were closed; her strawberry red hair was swept to the side.

"Jim would be so glad I'm with you instead of some stranger. He'd want us to be together, I know he would. . . ."

"There's something you should know," I said, beginning to panic as she climbed on top of me. She ignored me. I was inside her.

"What should I know?" she asked, pushing herself further onto me.

"Forget it," I moaned. "It's not important anymore."

I was awoken by a crash accompanied by the sound of shattering glass. Then I heard something whistle past my ear. There was another crash. Bolting up, I saw Pamela taking a windup, getting ready to let fly a coffee cup in the precise direction of my head. *"Get the fuck out of my house!"* she shrieked. *"Get out of my bed!"* As I ducked, the glass shattered against the headboard. *"Out! Get out of here now!* If my old man knew you *fucked* me, he'd fucking *kill you!"* she yelled, ready to let sail a plate. "He'd slice your fucking *balls off!"*

I jumped into my jeans and didn't even bother looking for anything else except my jacket with the car keys, flew out the front door, and hauled ass into the middle of the street, frantically looking for the car I didn't remember parking.

Tiffany was sitting in the middle of the Wonderland lawn when I pulled up in the driveway. She'd decided to accept the living conditions and returned home. With typical grace she greeted me: "I've been waiting here for over an hour, asshole. About time."

"Couldn't stay away from me, huh?" I smiled.

"Don't flatter yourself. Anything's better than living in that shithole. What a slob, I tell you." I took it as a good sign she didn't like a mess. Perhaps she possessed some untapped potential as a nest builder. Still, there's a mess and then there's a shithole.

Within an hour Blake was back from San Diego with a fresh batch of good, clean dope, over an ounce of heroin, the dull white powder wrapped in a condom, and a dozen grams of morphine stored in a film canister. Even though I'd already snorted about six months' worth of rent, and he was scheduled to be staying only another two weeks, he continued to supply me with all the drugs my nose could hold.

Tiffany had tried it once, with a friend, and gotten violently ill, but that didn't stop her from wanting to try it again. I was stuck between wanting to protect her, to keep her away from it, and wanting to turn her on to it so she could join me in the experience.

The lines were on the mirror.

"If you're going to do it, I want some, too," she told me.

"Tiffany, that's an idiotic statement. If I shoved rhinoceros shit in my ear, I suppose you'd want to try that as well." I wasn't being greedy or selfish. To the contrary, just because I didn't care about consequences in my life didn't mean that I had no conscience when it came to people I cared for.

"I don't know," she said. "Would it get me loaded?"

"The point is, it's not good for you."

"Oh, you're a fine one to talk, sitting there with a straw in your hand."

She had me there. I was in no position to argue. So I agreed with her.

"That's right. I know. I know if you do it this time, you're just going to want to do it again later tonight, and if not tonight, then tomorrow. I know it's so good you shouldn't even try it."

It caught her only momentarily off guard.

"Oh, you're an old pro at it, huh? I told you already I've done it before. I know what I'm doing. If you don't give me some, then I'm leaving. I don't want to sit around and watch you stoned."

I didn't want her to leave. "I just don't want to hurt you."

"C'mon, don't give me that shit. Lookit, I'll pay you for it."

"That's not the point," I said.

"If you don't give me some, I'll go get some from Dallas. He'll sell it to me. He doesn't give a shit."

I felt I was arguing with a child. I hated being put in the position of authority. It felt supremely awkward. She was going to do it anyway, and it would be nicer to be high with her than without her. I gave in and gave her some dope.

We both got sick to our stomachs at the same time and raced each other to the john to puke. This time she didn't mind getting sick. On junk it doesn't bother you; nothing does. You just upchuck and get it over with; it even has a cleansing effect afterward. I took it as a positive sign. As Pam said, you only get nauseous if the dope is very strong, and this latest shipment Blake brought in rushed like a runaway locomotive.

"Who's this Pamela?" Tiffany wanted to know.

"You'll find out someday," I answered.

"Oh, I get it, a mystery girl."

"Don't worry about it," I said, wanting to allay her jealousy somewhat, while not exactly wanting to put it to rest either. "She's somebody's wife."

After the Ten-Yard-Bathroom-Dash-and-Puking Competition we lay on the bed and watched television, snorted a few more lines later that evening, and spent the rest of the night watching our dreams drift in and out of the television shows, finally slipping from a nod into sleep sometime around 4:00 A.M.

She woke me up at 7:30 *in the morning* to drive her to high school.

"It's Christmas vacation, go back to sleep."

"That was a month ago."

"Then it's Easter vacation."

"Come on, get up," she said.

"Take a cab," I mumbled.

"Come on," she said, shaking me awake. "I'll be late for school. You don't want me to be late to school, do you?"

"I really couldn't give a fuck," I said, rolling over to get back to sleep.

"Oh, great, what am I supposed to tell them? I overslept because my boyfriend gave me heroin last night?"

I got out of bed and pulled on my jeans and slid into a leather jacket.

"Oh, so now I'm your boyfriend?"

She thought for a moment, not wanting to commit herself to something she might regret later. "Well," she said, "maybe you aren't, maybe you are."

I drove her to school.

We hardly saw Blake at all, except in the evenings. He was off to college and into his drug delivering before we got up. Before he left, he'd leave a generous helping of heroin in the upstairs bathroom.

Ray would show up at Wonderland around noon, the time of the day I was usually getting up and having my coffee, go into the rehearsal studio and work for an hour or so, come into the office, where we'd go over any new business, go back to work, stay until three or four, and then return home to his wife and newborn baby, Pablo. Tiffany returned from school about four, on those days she went, and we'd go up to the bedroom, snort some smack, and rest up before getting ready for the night, which was when we'd cut loose, basically ricocheting from one end of Sunset to the other, from the Rainbow to the Whisky to Rodney's back to the Rainbow, to Over the Rainbow, over to On the Rox, above the Roxy, and so on.

During this period an interesting phenomenon began. Someone over at his new record company had my name, address, and phone number down in the "Artist Roster" as Manzarek's contact, and the result was I started getting calls from not just the publicity department but practically everyone. The A&R department was calling, wanting to know when Ray was going in the studio and what studio was he going to use. The art department wanted to know about our album-cover plans; the vice-president called to inquire about any tour plans.

It wasn't only Ray's solo career I was fielding calls about. Ever since the Doors' office had shut down and everyone had gone his separate way, more and more inquiries regarding the Doors were flooding into Wonderland on a daily basis. The press still wanted information, pictures of the band, quotes regarding Morrison's death (which was taking on a curious life of its own), and miscellaneous PR materials. Elektra Records had begun referring all calls pertaining to the Doors to the Wonderland offices. Elektra itself had been calling;

it needed a constant, dependable contact on behalf of the Doors. After a dramatic rise in sales immediately following Jim's death, there had been a momentary decline before the Doors' record sales leveled off. The Doors' albums were doing a good, steady business for the company, and Elektra wanted immediate access to at least one Door at all times, and while neither Robby Krieger nor John Densmore wanted to be bothered with the past, preferring to concentrate on the future, and Siddons felt the past too painful, I was only too happy to oblige and do whatever I could to accommodate the callers and requests.

In a relatively short time it had become obvious to both Ray and myself I was no longer simply doing publicity anymore, but something more. Ray hadn't made any plans regarding management, and I hadn't made any conscious or overt moves to handle that role, but the way it was happening that was exactly what I was doing.

One day I was feeling confident enough to propose, only half-jokingly, that Ray should make me his manager. When he agreed, however, I was unprepared.

"Are you serious?" I asked him.

"Are you?"

"Yeah, I guess so. I mean, I'm doing it already anyhow. We might as well make it official. It would make me more effective on your behalf. People tend to take a manager more seriously than a press agent."

"I see what you mean," he said. Then he offered me a choice between a salary or a percentage.

"Of what?" I asked, meaning, How much of how much?

"Of everything."

"Everything?"

"Well, aren't you handling everything? Hell, no one else is seeing to it the Doors are taken care of."

"Yeah, I guess I am." I paused. "But you mean, your Doors money, too?" I asked, incredulous.

"That would fall under the general heading of 'everything,' wouldn't it?"

I nodded.

"It's settled then." We shook on it and agreed on a salary against percentage situation, after expenses.

"Do we need a contract?" I asked Ray.

"I don't if you don't."

"No," I said. "I don't if you don't. . . . I trust you."

A piece of the Doors. I couldn't believe it.

I was in such a good mood I drove over to Hollywood High to

pick Tiffany up from school. She was so surprised to see me standing in front near the flagpole, waiting for her, she walked right by before she turned around and walked back.

"And to what do I owe this honor?" she asked.

"Money."

She extended her hand palm out. "Gimme."

"For me. Money for me, not you."

"That's what you came by to tell me? Your generosity over-whelms me."

"I thought you might be persuaded to go out and celebrate."

"What are we celebrating?"

"Life, happiness, good vibes, us . . . good drugs, good music, and a whole shitload of money."

"Boy, you had me going for a minute there, I thought you were having a nervous breakdown or going wimp on me or something."

While Tiffany had been away at her friend's, she'd scored a prescription for Quaaludes. While I showered, she took one. During the course of putting on her makeup and getting dressed, she put away an entire bottle of wine. On the way to Dan Tana's for Italian food, she gargled down two cans of beer and another lude. Waiting for dinner, she downed two double Bloody Marys. By the time the pasta arrived, Tiffany was having trouble keeping her face above and away from the plate until, finally, her eyes drifted shut and her head lolled back and then dropped straight down onto the table—clunk. Not a graceful move. Pamela had done it so much more delicately. Gary Stromberg was in an adjoining booth entertaining some clients. I turned around to face him questioningly. He just shook his head, got up, and came over to put a vial of cocaine in my hand. "Blow this up her nose; that oughta bring her around." I put some blow in a straw, lifted her head up and back, made sure no one was watching, inserted the straw carefully into one nostril, blew as hard as I could, and then repeated the procedure in the other.

Her eyes snapped open, looked dazed and confused for a moment. Then she proceeded to blabber on a thousand words a minute about absolutely nothing, not eating another bite, gulping her wine, and not shutting her mouth all the way through dinner, not in the car, and not when we got into the Rainbow, where Warner Brothers Records was throwing a party for Jethro Tull. "God, I feel GGRRREAT!" she kept yelling like a tiger.

When the drinks arrived at the Rainbow, I got a lude out of my pocket and swallowed it. Tiffany polished off her double White Russian and then excused herself to go to the ladies' room.

As she got up to leave the table, I made her swear on her life she'd be back within ten minutes. It was past eleven. She promised me, without fail, she'd return promptly to the table so we could be home in time for Johnny Carson. Don Rickles was guest hosting, and I didn't want to miss his monologue.

Exactly ten minutes later, expecting her return momentarily, I looked at my watch and took the other two Quaaludes I'd brought along, believing I'd timed them to come on just as we arrived back home, in time to snort some smack, climb into bed, watch a little of Johnny, and, maybe, make love. Tonight, I was hoping, would be the night. We'd been getting closer and closer every day. A definite affection had been developing between us. She'd slowly stopped seeing her other male friends. Only a few nights before she'd let me kiss her good-night. It turned into quite a kiss, but before I could take it any further, I nodded or maybe passed out. I'd saved a little cocaine this time, back at home, as a precautionary measure.

Ten minutes later, no Tiffany. Fifteen minutes, no Tiffany. I knew if I didn't get out of that place fast and safely home within a matter of minutes, I would be too fucked up to drive and very unlikely to be in a state of mind where I'd be willing to admit it. I had to either find Tiffany and get out of there quick or score some cocaine to sober me up and keep me alert. It was a toss-up. I'd take either.

With a tinge of desperation creeping in, I got up from the table where I'd been sitting and began making my way through the crowded restaurant. I made two trips around the floor, grabbing everyone I thought I recognized, demanding, "You seen Tiffany? No? Got any coke? No? Fuck, you're a big help." I began to get more frantic after the second lap and took a detour, heading upstairs to the private disco.

There she was, on the dance floor, a glass in each hand, dancing with a Marina swinger in a satin Porsche racing jacket who was drinking out of a champagne bottle. There was no time for niceties. It had to be a quick and effective exchange. Sneaking up behind him, I pulled the bottle out of his hand. He spun around. "Hey, what the fuck!"

I held the bottle up in my fist.

"We're going," I told Tiffany. "Get going, get the fuck out of here!"

She just stood there looking at me like I was out of my mind. "Now!" I screamed. "Move!"

She moved. "You!" I yelled at Parnelli Jones. "Stay out of this;

make one move on me, and I'll put the front of your face out the back of your skull."

I dashed out of the club and out of the restaurant, champagne in hand, catching up with and dragging Tiffany after me out the door into the parking lot, desperate to get home before the ludes hit.

So far so good.

The Strip was the fastest, most direct route to Laurel Canyon from the Rainbow, but Sunset Boulevard was packed with Friday night cruising traffic. I U-turned, zigzagged across the canyons up to Mulholland Drive, a longer route but tonight, I hoped, quicker than Sunset.

"Why are you driving so fast?" Tiffany asked.

"You wouldn't understand . . ." I told her, not wanting to explain myself.

"If you're pissed at me for just dancing with that guy, forget it, you don't own me. . . ."

I looked at the car clock and pushed down on the gas pedal, spinning out as I turned onto Mulholland Drive.

"Will you please slow down?" she begged.

I sped up. The car almost flipped around a turn, but I regained control and straightened it out, turning the wheel into the skid.

The road began blurring before my eyes. I couldn't feel the gas pedal beneath my foot. There were bright lights coming at me. . . .

The car hit a bump. There was a sudden jerk, the swish of a bush. We were airborne. The valley lights spread out in front of the windshield.

"What do we do now, genius?" Tiffany said.

"Hold on!" I yelled as the car came to a crashing halt. We seemed all right. The car landed right side up, on all four wheels. I looked out the window but couldn't see anything but night. "Wait here," I told Tiffany, setting the parking brake and opening the car door. I stepped out onto the flat gravel roof of somebody's house. "Hey, Tiffany," I called. "You'll never guess where we landed. . . ."

She opened the passenger door and took one step out, and before she could hazard a guess, the whole thing caved in, and me, her, and the car all fell away into space.

I landed on a couch. Tiffany hit the TV. The car made a perfect four-point landing smack in the middle of what looked like the living-room floor.

I grabbed her, unlocked the front door, and, pulling her along, scrambled up the hillside we had just flown over. All the way up she kept bitching something about her leg hurting.

"Screw your leg," I told her. "My automobile is sitting in the middle of some stranger's living room!"

"There's a new invention they got these days," she puffed, "They call 'em driveways, ya know, as in *garages?*" she finished, with a somewhat caustic, sarcastic emphasis on the last word.

By the time we reached the top and were back on Mulholland, I was too wasted to do anything else but sit down. Tiffany went and stood in the middle of the street and stopped the first car that came along. Actually it was a little pickup.

"We were held up," she reported breathlessly to the driver, "by these Mexicans with guns and they stole our car. . . . Can you take us home, please? We just live down the hill."

"What's wrong with him?" The driver pointed to me, still trying to sit up on the edge of the street.

"He's in shock," she reported.

"Sure, why not?" he said.

Tiffany climbed in the front seat. I staggered over to get in next to her.

"You," he said, "get in the back."

I tumbled into the back.

Back at Wonderland, I pulled myself upstairs, got out the quarter gram of blow I'd been saving, emptied a generous helping of China White, and put both drugs out into two long lines on the nightstand. I snorted about two inches of each, asked Tiffany to save some for later, handed her the straw, and went into the bathroom to take a bath. I was enjoying the warmth of the water and the commingling of the drugs in my system, my eyes closed. The cocaine lifted me up while the smack kept the edge off, changing the quality of both highs into something different, a third, even more satisfying experience, if that was possible. I'd heard it said if God invented anything better, he saved it for himself. Ever since I'd heard that, I had wanted to try it. Now I knew why, and I had to agree. It was the best of what both drugs had to offer—the best of both possible worlds.

"C'mon, stop hogging the whole thing. Make room." Tiffany walked in, pulled her shirt over her head, stepped out of her leather pants and into the bath.

She asked for the soap, and I handed it to her.

"Did you have fun tonight?" I asked.

"Oh, yeah, I had a great time." She laughed. "We gotta go out like that more often." I felt her soapy hands on my back.

"Wash it off," she said. I slid down under the water. Next she washed my hair, playing with the lather, rubbing her hands over the slickness of my skin, putting her hands around my waist, her fingers stretching over my belly.

"C'mon, your turn," I said, reaching for the shampoo bottle and turning to face her.

"Aw, shucks, I was just beginning to enjoy myself," she said.

"So was I," I told her.

There was a moment of awkward silence as her hand reached under the soapy water and fondled me. We leaned toward each other and gently kissed.

I was becoming aware of how comfortable I felt with her, how much I was beginning to love her, and I had no doubt she was feeling the same way. Whether out of uncertainty or respect, I had been careful to keep my distance. But tonight she was making the first moves.

We split the last of the cocaine and smack and climbed into bed. I stayed on my side of the bed and put on the TV and turned the lights out. It was a little after 2:30 A.M. Tiffany snuggled up against my back and laid an arm over me. "Hey, don't I get a good-night kiss?"

I rolled over to face her, she pulled her warm, naked body against me, and we were off. I got on top, she wrapped her arms around my neck, and everything went great. For the first time in my life a girl told me she loved me, and for the first time I told a girl the same. Now I knew why they called it "making love." Never before had I felt so close to anyone. We lay nose-to-nose in the dark.

"I lied," I whispered.

"What about this time?"

"I'm not a virgin."

"No shit," she said, "not anymore."

"No," I told her. "I mean, before I wasn't one either."

"Oh," she said, not sounding too disappointed. "That's okay."

"I just thought you were entitled to know."

"Don't worry about it. Neither was I."

"You're kidding, right?'

"Would I lie to you?"

"You did," I reminded her.

"Well, so did you," she pointed out.

"So, then, it didn't hurt?" I asked.

"Shut up and come here." She laughed, leaning over and pulling me toward her. And we were off again.

Somewhere between 3:00 A.M. and when the sun rose, I saw and fell deeply in love with another side of the girl I was living with,

hidden beneath the sarcastic and often humorous, gruff exterior—
open and playful, innocent and trusting.

The next day the cops were on the phone. They wanted to know if
I knew where my car was.

"In the garage?" I asked, figuring asking a question is not the
same thing as lying.

"You better meet us," they said, and gave me the address. "Your
car must have been stolen sometime during the night."

"You're kidding me."

After taking a cab up to Mulholland Drive to meet with the cops
and the insurance representative, we stood at the side of the road to
watch the biggest helicopter I'd ever seen lift my car out of the middle
of the house. The car came out of the crash relatively unharmed. Too
bad the same thing couldn't be said for the house, which looked as
if it had been bombed sometime during the night.

Eyeing the busted guardrail where the car had jumped the road
and the rest of the destruction fifty yards on down the hillside, one
of the cops standing beside me remarked, "Whoever was driving that
car is lucky to be alive." He wasn't smiling when he said it.

I, however, couldn't stop myself from grinning. *I'm still here*, I
thought. *Not even a scratch.*

"You seem to be enjoying yourself," Tiffany remarked.

"Oh, I am," I said. "I'm having a good time now."

"Oh, you are, are you? I'm so glad."

"Me, too," I replied, kissing her cheek, "me, too."

Maybe if I'd really known what I was doing, I wouldn't have
been in such a cheerful mood. Maybe if I'd clearly seen what was
happening and what was about to happen, I would have thought twice
about continuing. As it was, continuing was all I wanted to do, all I
knew how to do, and for the time being, that suited me more than
fine.

C H A P T E R T E N

· · · · · · · · · · · ·

**Mama always told me not to
look into the eyes of the sun
But Mama, that's where
the fun is.**
—BRUCE SPRINGSTEEN

THESE were good, high, crazy times. We were proud to the point of arrogance, reckless to the point of being dangerous, and filled to overbrimming with a careless faith that told us everything was possible and anything would be survived.

We were young and in love, wealthy, arrogant, reckless, and stoned—a potentially deadly combination. But in the meantime, we were having one whole hell of a lot of fun.

In some ways Tiffany was much older than her fifteen years indicated. She knew independence in a way I was just learning to, and she had street smarts, intuitively and in spades. In other ways she was still a child, an innocent, craving dependence and protection, delighting in play. Yet the playground she had chosen to romp and frolic on was not the asphalt of her high school or the grass or fields at a local park. Tiffany loved Hollywood and its parties and dance floors, the endless nights and unlimited intoxicants. She inhaled chemicals with a swiftness, thoroughness, and delight I had never seen a girl possess. In turn I was delighted, inspired, and encouraged.

We became stoning buddies, forever and always, not only getting high together but copping and scoring together, looking out for each other, and sharing our bundles with each other.

It was a fun and important game, including all the ingredients a game should possess—danger, teamwork, excitement, and reward—to say nothing of agility, ability, cunning, and a lot of luck.

We made a good team. And so far we were winning. In fact, you might even say we were on a roll. What guts we lacked, we faked, and our bravery astounded even ourselves. Our luck streaked like lightning before us, and our faith was enormous. We predicted the future and then proceeded to make it happen.

We were going to the best parties, and we never had to wait on line at any nightclub we went to, two, sometimes three times a night. VIP booths sat empty in jammed clubs, awaiting our arrival. Promoters and record companies supplied us with backstage passes; most concerts we watched from the stage. Everywhere we went, Tiffany and I were treated like royalty.

I say we were *treated* like; I didn't say we *acted* like.

Four out of seven nights a week we went out, into the night, to dance to the music and get as fucked up as humanly possible, not necessarily in that order either. Some of the time we started to go out but got too loaded before even setting foot out of the house and ended up staying in, and that was okay, too. Once in a while, we actually stayed in on purpose, getting high, nodding out, and fucking till dawn. Heroin is a great drug for sex. You just want to hug and kiss, and you can fuck forever without coming. The only problem is you keep nodding off. Or one of you is always going soft or drying out. We'd spend hours trying to get each other ready and then stay ready long enough to get it on. We weren't always successful; but when we were, it was unbeatable, and when we weren't—we still had an awful lot of fun trying. I can't remember how many nights I awoke with my face buried between her legs, fighting for air, or vice versa.

The nights we did make it out, we stayed out, using cocaine to fuel our wakefulness, to keep the other drugs at bay while not so significantly diminishing their effectiveness. Speedballing. A 100 percent, fuel-injected euphoria; a junkhead with a Phil Spector production.

Whenever we'd begin to lose our energy, or the junk would begin to take over and gently close our eyes, out would come the vial of coke, and within a matter of minutes we'd be alert, ready for action, game for anything, anywhere, until anytime.

By dawn, after everything wound down, we'd head over to the Old World restaurant on Sunset Boulevard across the street from Tower records, only a short mile west of Laurel Canyon, and have a champagne and waffle breakfast and watch the sunrise before heading home to Wonderland, where we'd put away the up, if there was still any left, snort a few lines of heroin, maybe take a downer or two, curl up in each other's arms, and sleep through until one or two o'clock, when Ray's piano would drift upstairs and awaken us.

Tiffany was going to school less and less, most mornings preferring to stay home and sleep in. If we'd gone out the night before, chances were she'd ignore school. If we'd stayed home, she'd probably go, usually arriving late by an hour or two. I tried to be a good influence on her and persuade her to go to school on a more regular basis, but if it meant giving up some of our more meaningful time together, well then, I confess, it didn't mean that much to me either. I mean, it's rather difficult taking the tenth grade seriously when you're pushing the bounds of reality on the average of four out of seven nights a week.

＊ ＊ ＊

I knew this sort of behavior wasn't exactly conducive to prolonged health and welfare. If it didn't kill me right away, someday it would. You live by the sword, you die by the sword, right? Right. Well, I knew that.

I knew it put me on a collision course with death, but at least I knew where that path led. It wasn't uncertain—unsafe, maybe, but that just made it all the more interesting as far as I was concerned. I'd come to the conclusion I much preferred mystery with my life and certainty with my death to mystery with my death and certainty with my life. At least it put me in control of my destiny (at a time when I felt out of control in relation to everything else), however short-lived that destiny might become.

Besides being interesting and fun, it feels good, too. Who wants to live to an old age anyway? That was never one of my priorities. Hope I die before I get old; better to burn out than fade away and all that. What would you rather do? Live a slow, boring life to eighty years old only to die of some unknown cause, maybe cancer, slowly and painfully, first the hearing gone, then the sight, then the mind, a burden for family and friends? Or live to twenty-one but have eighty years of experience and action packed in tightly under your belt, looks and pride intact, and be in a position to choose your own means to an end?

Besides, *dying* didn't scare me. Growing *old* scared me.

I was scared of growing up and becoming the authority, the society I loathed. I couldn't conform to those ideals anyway. Those ideals rejected me, and I didn't care anymore because those values didn't work. I'd tried and failed. It was easier to say, "Fuck it," and turn up the music. It was a gigantic relief. Ah! You've made up your mind about this death business, you've left all those people with that petty morality behind, their judgments can't touch you anymore, now you can really get on with the business—no! the *pleasure* of living. Try everything! That's the only rule you have to follow, and if you don't want to follow it, you don't have to. Do what you want and nothing else. If it feels good once, do it again, and again and again. Then do some more! Then mix that with something else you enjoy, and see how well they go together. Increase the quantity, alter the dose, combine the ingredients, mix it up, experiment. . . . Have some fun! After all, you're young only once.

If rock 'n' roll is about personal freedom, then drug use is nothing less than a declaration and celebration of its existence.

And this was something I was really good at. I was like a pig in shit. I knew I'd die there, and I didn't care. Just when I go, God, let me be spent. Please, God, just let me have no regrets when my time is up. Then I don't care how or where or when death comes. I just don't want to feel as if I've missed out on anything. I just don't want to have any thirst left; I don't want to have any wants left.

The promise as I got it was that financial security, material abundance, and the "good things in life" would be enough, would take care of the insecurity, the fear, and the pain and would make you happy. But they don't. It doesn't work because it's never enough. And once you get to this distant point, where you feel utterly hopeless and you know there is no other way out, you are willing to try absolutely anything, and *drugs kill pain, new cars don't*. Where people hurt, drugs comfort. Friends may come and go while drugs remain reliable and loyal.

But it's illegal. Surely that should be a warning. It's dangerous; it can kill you.

Fuck the law; the law is wrong. So it doesn't have society's endorsement or approval, *so what*? At least dope delivers relief, which is just down the street from happiness. I'll settle for relief. I'll take it. Something is radically wrong. Heroin is too dramatic a step not to know why it's being used. *It's a painkiller!* It all but says so on the bottle. Everyone knows this simple fact. And for once the literature was right! It does do all those great things they say it does, and so far I haven't so much as glimpsed any of the negative horrors they warn àbout and even if the worst possible scenario does occur, it'll be worth it. Because it works where nothing else even comes close.

If you sit around enough junkies long enough, you're bound to hear talk about a conscious desire to return to the womb, that homeostasis condition, that only heroin provides them with. They are aware of it and not ashamed of it.

The logical extension of this tendency is, of course, death. *That's* what the death wish really is. It's not a conscious decision to self-destruct. It's the survival mechanism gone haywire. Because pain is perceived as a direct threat to our survival. Pain opposes life, the elimination of pain is all we really want. *That's* the pleasure principle. All instinct is geared not toward long-term survival but short-term survival. Prevention of suffering or anything that will aid in its elimination, thereby ensuring immediate survival, the brain perceives as good. Look, here's the formula:

Life is suffering. Buddha even said so; it was his first noble truth.
Painkillers kill pain. Heroin works.

Buddha's second truth tells us desire is the only cause of suffering. His third truth instructs, "Rid yourself of desire," which is exactly what heroin does. It eliminates the desire, the need, for everything but heroin and as long as you gratify that one, you're free. Which neatly brings us to the Buddha's fourth noble truth: "Be free."

If religion is the opiate of the masses—then it's only fitting opium itself is nothing less than the religion of the individual addict. Heroin is *something* to believe in.

Once you realize nothing material works, and spiritual discovery eludes you, you are free to turn to drugs without guilt or remorse. You trade off. You concentrate the ache, the desire for something on drugs. Happiness is a cruel myth, whereas addiction is a reasonable alternative to suicide. It is not done out of ignorance or stupidity; it is done out of necessity. It's a way out. Desperate people take desperate steps. Drugs win by default. Nothing else works.

Narcotics were a deliberate and final elaborate step away from the world into which I had been born and the first step into a new, thrilling unknown. Where *they* weren't allowed. Where the ideals rejected *them*.

In addition to all these neat reasons, I was just nineteen years old, and teenagers, contrary to popular belief, do know right from wrong. I did. I just didn't care anymore. You're indestructible at eighteen, nineteen. Nothing can hurt you. Besides, they can do amazing things in medicine these days. If something goes wrong, if it can't be fixed, they can replace it. If you do manage to get strung out, there's always some doctor somewhere who'll be able to cure you.

Blake had found his own place to live and took all his drugs with him. Fortunately he moved just down the block and around the corner. Unfortunately I now had to pay money for the drugs he gave me. Fortunately I was making enough to cover it. Unfortunately I was beginning to notice it took me more heroin to get the same high. Talk about mixed blessings. Still, it was more than worth it. Besides, what else did I want or need? All the essentials were already taken care of; what entertainment wasn't comped went on the expense account, and the house was paid for automatically. All the cash went for drugs.

Shane, Blake's partner in crime, had moved up from San Diego and was rooming with him. They'd decorated their entire house into a semishrine to the Stones, in particular Keith Richards, who, in case you didn't know, is sort of a patron saint of all white middle-class junkies under the age of thirty. A big blowup of "Keef" at the Canadian border was prominently featured right over the stereo. There was a sign right above Keef's shoulder reading, PATIENCE

PLEASE, A DRUG FREE COUNTRY COMES FIRST. We all got our yayas off on that one.

Iggy had finally gotten in touch and given me the rundown on his tour.

At Richard's in Atlanta he'd taken a handful of hash and acid, hung from the rafters by his ankles, and when he dropped to the stage, Elton John bounded onstage in his "Crocodile Rock" costume.

"Have you ever been on six hits of acid and had a fucking alligator jump in front of you?" Iggy wanted to know.

At Bimbo's in San Francisco, during a show with the Tubes, he had sat down on the lip of the stage, gorkeld on Quaaludes, taking a breather, when a lady slid down his bikini underwear and proceeded to administer a "very, very professional blow job." Nonetheless, Iggy was on too many drugs to come and told her as much, yelling in the microphone, "*You can't make me come. . . . You won't believe this,*" Iggy told the crowd, "*but I'm getting my cock sucked!*" Much applause. After the show the girl came backstage, and to Iggy's chagrin and the band's delight, on closer inspection, it became clear the lady wasn't a lady at all but a guy in drag.

On the other side of the country, upstairs at Max's Kansas City in New York, after scoring some junk, Ig took a dive into a pool of broken glass onstage. "And I was hurting so bad," he said, not from the glass, just from the hell of touring without a record contract and therefore no tour support, the whole burden of the tour on his back, forced to perform almost nightly, without the benefit of airplanes or advertising, without any new record to draw the people, who nevertheless still came. Two shows a night! From a man who gave more in one performance than most groups gave in ten. Holding back was unthinkable, totally contrary to his whole being. He *had* to give it everything he had. It wasn't only what the audience expected; it was what he demanded of himself. By the time he arrived onstage in New York he was already in so much pain he didn't even feel the sharp shards of glass ripping into his skin. "So I ground them into my chest with my hand, making it bleed, making it hurt, ya know? Because I *had* to feel something. . . ."

The press had a field day with that one.

In Washington, D.C., five minutes before showtime, he snorted a gram of THC. The announcer introduced the band, and Iggy walked right out of the dressing room, toward the stage, onto the stage, past the microphone stand, and straight off the stage, dropped ten feet, right into the audience, and passed out, face first in the cement.

During the gig in Wayne, Michigan, "a real pit, a farm town . . . I was wearing this woman's floppy hat with three flowers on it and a

dancer's leotard with these little blue ballet slippers and a blue sarong."
Everything was flying toward Pop. "Everything from paper clips to
grapefruits and bottles of Johnnie Walker Black." And eggs. Someone
wouldn't stop throwing eggs. "Not just one or two but dozens, one
right after the other. Have you ever tried to perform under a barrage of
eggs? On Thorazine? Anyway, I said, 'Stop the show,' and I just stopped
the show and jumped into the audience to confront the guy who was
doing it, you know, 'cause it wasn't cool anymore."

Ig walked into the crowd, which parted like the Red Sea for him,
and he walked right up the clearing they made, right up to a seven-
foot biker/farmer with long red hair, leather jacket, filthy Levi's, biker
boots, the whole getup. He was standing among a circle of abandoned,
empty egg cartons wearing a big grin.

He was also wearing a knuckle glove with inverted inch-long nail
spikes pointing out, up to his elbow. Iggy came up to him like David
against Goliath, and not being one to chicken out, he had started
Muhammad Ali-like sparring, throwing feints and punches at the guy,
dancing around, his feet a blur, when this big guy took one poke and
decked the Ig. Bleeding and sore, Ig dragged his ass back to the stage,
where the band performed "Louie Louie."

Next day he went into Detroit for a radio interview and on the
air challenged the guy's entire motorcycle gang, the Scorpions, to
come down to his show that night and "do their worst." As it happened, they were initiating a new member that night and had been
having some difficulty coming up with an initiation project. Iggy gave
it to them. The guy's assignment was to knock out Iggy Pop before
the end of the first song. Iggy finished the set. Barely. It was the last-
ever Stooges performance.

Now (for lack of anyplace else to go) Iggy was coming back to
L.A. I wasn't really looking forward to his suffering through the
posttour boredom and drug syndrome at my house. On the other
hand, I had my own defense now: I was on drugs, too. That gave me
three alternatives, whereas before I had none. I either could use the
drugs to buffer me from whatever surprise behaviorisms he had in
store or I could have the pleasure of behaving like a zombie shitheel,
too. Or we could get high together and have a party! Hell, I had a
whole arsenal of coping strategies at my disposal.

Besides, I couldn't very well let him sit in Detroit.

I told him about the house and he was welcome anytime. "Just
call me when you're leaving, and I'll be at the airport to pick you
up." I felt if I didn't go and get him, I might never see him again.

I expected to hear from him within a day or two. When he didn't

call, I started to worry. I called everyone I could think of, but no
one else had heard from him. I knew he had a lot of drug buddies in
Detroit from the old days when the Stooges were one of the biggest
bands on the scene back there, and I was worried he had jumped back
into smack with both feet and just maybe gotten in over his head.

There was nothing I could do but wait for him to call.

One night at Rodney's I met a petite fourteen-year-old blonde named
Suzette, a beautiful young thin white girl with the plum-shaped bum
of a black woman, close-cropped bleached blond hair à la David Bowie
circa Ziggy Stardust, and full, Betty Boop lips painted a bright red—
vivacious, alive, bright and ready to raise hell with a moment's notice,
and one of the best dancers on the scene. During the week she lived
an average life in Orange County with her mother and stepfather, but
on the weekends she'd transform herself from an obedient daughter
and schoolgirl to a feline Baby Bowie vamp and head up to Hollywood
with a carful of friends. It had been getting harder for her to tolerate
her straight schoolmates' ribbing along with the mundane straight life
down south, and I'd been letting her crash at Wonderland.

We went to Slade's concert at the Civic Auditorium together,
got drunk, and promptly lost each other. I figured she'd hooked up
with some of the Hollywood gang and we'd see each other sometime
later that night. So I wasn't too worried about her when I accepted
the road manager's invitation to ride in the band's limousine to a
postconcert bash at Rodney's.

We were on our way from the concert in Santa Monica back to
Hollywood. I was in the front seat with the driver and Rodney Bingen-
heimer, who had MC'd the show, while the four members of the band
were in the back, one of them making out with a very underage and very
cute girl. Everything was going fine until the girl started protesting the
guy's attempts to go a little further. I tried to ignore the scuffle, not being
one to ruin a party, but I was beginning to feel sorry for that girl back
there, who was obviously drunk and just as obviously no longer enjoying herself. The more she resisted, the more the guy persisted, and pretty
soon another band member joined in and another and before you knew
it, someone yelled out, "Gang bang!"

Rodney cried out, "Wait for me," and, putting a five-inch heel
into my groin, leaped into the back seat. The driver, no doubt ac-
customed to such goings-on, looked straight ahead.

Unable to ignore it any longer, I yelled, "All right, cut it the
fuck out!" I fumbled for the overhead light and flicked it on. Caught

in the glare, the members of Slade, a little bit mad and a little bit embarrassed, looked up and pulled themselves off the teenager. One by one they cleared away, revealing the girl, who had been pinned beneath them, holding onto her tiny tube top with one hand and clutching the waist of her black velvet pants with the other.

"Stop the car," I told the driver. "Pull it over." The car stopped at the side of the road, and the girl climbed into the front seat with me.

"Hi," she said glumly, "my name's MacKenzie Phillips, but my friends call me Laura."

American Graffiti had been released a few months ago, and MacKenzie had become a star. She was the daughter of John Phillips of the Mamas and Papas, and we discovered that despite the difference in our ages (she was fourteen to my nineteen), we still had a lot in common. We both had practically grown up backstage at concerts, where, without fail, we had been the youngest in attendance, she with her father, I with Morrison. We both had been raised in L.A. And where Tiffany had a hard time staying close to me when we were out on a date, MacKenzie was the perfect lady, holding my hand, listening attentively, agreeable, polite, and respectful. I'd been having a hard time getting Tiffany to cooperate on business dinners and outings; she insisted on getting sloshed and saying the first thing that entered her mind. MacKenzie, on the other hand, had been having a difficult time persuading her aunt Rosie to let her go out with the boys she chose to see or stay out with her girlfriends to go partying around Hollywood. We discovered we made a good cover for each other. And because of my recent success, her manager approved of and even encouraged our seeing each other. If she needed an escort to an opening, she invited me. If I needed a well-behaved date, she helped me out. Whenever we went out together, the gossip columnists would write us up. We also learned, much to our mutual satisfaction, we shared a taste for drugs. Recently she'd been contacted by the successful producer of *All in the Family*, Norman Lear, who was assembling a new situation comedy for TV and was interested in her for one of the leads. The show was to be called *One Day at a Time*.

We were all fucked up, junked, quacked, and drunk. It was about 3:00 A.M., and we all were sitting around the Wonderland office, drinking champagne out of the bottle. Tiffany was reeling; I was reeling; we *all* were reeling: Laura, Suzette, Tiffany, and Nigel, Suzette's new pretty English boyfriend. We'd been out drinking, eating, and dancing all night, but for some reason we all were hungry again. You know that hunger you get when you're drunk?

I volunteered to go to Canter's, the twenty-four-hour deli on Fairfax in Hollywood, about ten minutes from Laurel Canyon. "You're drunk!" Tiffany told me. "You can't even walk, you can't even—" and before she could say "drive," she kind of fell. Her legs just sort of crossed at the knees and bent outward, and she plopped down on her ass, leaving her sitting on the office floor, cross-legged and cross-eyed. Tiffany's body tended to get loaded hours before her mouth. As she sat on the floor, unable to rise, she delivered a sermon to me on the dangers of drinking and driving.

Which I probably should have listened to but unfortunately did not. I tied a long scarf down across half my face and over one eye so I would not see double and stumbled out the front door, leaving my friends behind as they shouted their orders.

"Don't forget to get some coffee cake!" Nigel yelled.

"Something sweet!" Suzette yelled.

"Jew food!" Tiffany yelled. "Just get some Jew food." She'd never seen a bagel until she met me, and now she couldn't get enough of the stuff.

I made it to Canter's all right, with scarf still wrapped around my face, and ordered a dozen bagels with cream cheese, lox, sliced onions, sturgeon, coffee cake. Everything looked and smelled so fresh and good. Boy, there's really nothing like the smell of freshly baked bread. I got some more cakes and pastries, some onion rolls and chopped herring, a six-pack of cream soda, and then loaded everything into the Vet I'd parked in the red zone directly in front of the restaurant.

I was about a mile away from Canter's when I could no longer resist the food sitting on the passenger seat. It smelled so good and I was so hungry I couldn't stand it anymore. Keeping my eye on the road, I reached into the bag and felt around for a bagel. Unable to locate it, I momentarily took my eyes—I mean, eye—off the road and looked inside the bag, found what I was looking for, and peeled out a bagel, cream cheese, and lox sandwich. Just as I was about to put the fucker in my mouth, my vision returned to the street in time to see the crash, as I rammed the car right into the traffic light posted on an island in the middle of the Fairfax and Santa Monica intersection. I was running at a pretty good clip when I rammed it, and the car stopped right in its tracks. The impact of the crash, coming unexpectedly the way it did, right when I was about to take a chomp, shoved the whole bagel in my face. Half of it (it was cut in half) went right into my uncovered eye, and the other half compacted itself straight up into my right nostril, temporarily blinding *and* choking me at the same time. My whole nose was engorged with a deli bagel, and when they get done putting all that cream cheese and lox inside, those things are thick. My head had smashed against the windshield, so it was really hurting, and my nose hurt, and I could barely breathe without inhaling gobs of cream cheese.

I tried to back the car up and get the hell away from there, but it wouldn't budge. I staggered out and backed away from the car, pulled out what bagel I could, and surveyed the damage. The traffic light was at a serious angle, and the car looked like it was totally crunched. At that moment a Foothill Security patrol car slowed down and pulled alongside of me. "You all right?" he asked.

"I'm one of your customers. I need a ride home." I caught my breath and said, "Wonderland Avenue."

In the morning I didn't remember a thing.

I went outside to collect the paper. "Where's the car?" I screamed, bounding back into the house. "Who stole my fucking car?!" Then I found the keys and figured it must have been hot-wired and ripped off. I also noticed my nose was unusually clogged, but I just chalked that up to a lot of powdered drugs. I dialed the police and reported the infraction against my personal property. "It was there when I went to sleep last night," I told them, which I was pretty sure was the case.

Another cop from another division called me back within the hour.

"We're calling to inform you your car has been found, but it doesn't look like it's in very good shape."

"What should I do now?" As I spoke, a piece of lox flew out of my nose and landed on the side of my coffee cup, and like the final piece of a puzzle falling to place, the whole night before came back to me like a bad dream.

Without any warning whatsoever, Blake disappeared. After renting a dark-blue Mercedes 450 SL, I drove over to his house (something I'd been doing at least once a day for the past three weeks) to make my usual pickup. Shane answered the door.

"You'll never guess what the prick did last night," Shane said.

"I give up. Went to a Peter, Paul, and Mary concert?"

"Close. He checked into *Synanon*."

"You're kidding, right?" Synanon was a drug-rehab house, at the time practically the only one in Southern California.

He shook his head.

"Did he leave anything for me?"

"Nope, that's one of the reasons why he went in. We're out of dope, and we're out of money."

"What about all that dope you guys had?"

"Gone."

"What the fuck are we gonna do?" I asked, hoping he'd at least have a referral for me.

"Fuck if I know," he said. "I got an old connection in San Diego I was thinking about dropping in on . . . if I had some money."

"*I* got money," I said, thinking it wasn't much good without any drugs to spend it on. "If I give you the money, can you score from him?"

"I think so."

I didn't have any other choice. I gave Shane five hundred dollars for the gram I'd been planning to buy from Blake.

He took the money, and we made plans to meet at the Wonderland house at six o'clock that evening.

At three o'clock I started sweating, first hot, then cold, then clammy and then hot and then cold again. When I walked around, my muscles and bones ached. I couldn't get comfortable in any position, couldn't sit still or lie down for more than a minute or two.

"Oh, fuck," I thought out loud, "I feel like I'm getting hyperactive again.

"Ha, you wish! You're strung out," Tiffany informed me.

"Yeah?" I asked her. "And how would you know?"

"Because I feel the same way you do."

"Oh." Pause. "I guess it's not a hyperactivity relapse then?"

" 'Fraid not."

By six o'clock I was sitting at the kitchen table, staring out the window, counting the cars coming up the street, trying to guess what number car Shane would be driving, just the way I used to do, waiting for my father to pick me up back in Westchester on the weekends.

"When he gets here, I'll kill him," I told Tiffany. "No, first I'll get the dope, *then* I'll kill him."

A bit past seven-thirty I'd counted twenty-seven cars and still no Shane. I was feeling pretty uncomfortable and had begun thinking how similar it was to coming down with the flu. By now I was counting the various methods I could come up with to hurt him when he arrived.

An hour and twenty-two cars later the phone rang. "Where the fuck are you?" I answered.

"I'm sorry," the voice said. It was Shane.

"Sorry! Do you know what time it is? I'm fuckin' sick! What the fuck are you doing? Get the fuck over here immediately! Where the fuck *are* you?"

"In jail." Those two words shut me up long enough to listen to him tell me what happened. He'd found his dealer friend both home and holding. Shane bought one gram for me and got seven fronted to him. He was back in business. Just the thought of it made me break out in a sweat again. He must have gotten pretty excited at the prospect, too, because with eight grams of pure Mexican smack, Brown Sugar, stuck inside his boot, anxious to return and already running late, he sped up as he hit the turn leading onto the San Diego Freeway on ramp, accelerating upward from sixty miles an hour. A pedestrian was just stepping off the curb into the crosswalk as Shane gutter-balled his Camaro, knocking the guy about fifteen feet into the air all the way back off the street and onto the sidewalk. Shane panicked, took off, and continued speeding north.

A witness called the cops, and within five minutes Shane had been pulled over, frisked, cuffed, and busted. Hit and run, vehicular assault, possession with intent to traffic . . .

"I'm fucked," he finished.

"I'd say that's a pretty accurate conclusion." I couldn't have cared less. Not that I didn't care for the guy because I did. But he had no drugs, and it wasn't likely he was going to have any anytime soon. And I needed drugs.

"Wish I could chat," I told him, "but duty calls."

"I understand," he said. And you know something? I think he did, and I wasn't surprised at all.

Now we were really in a jam. No connection and no money. I was beginning to get more than a little frightened of what the night might hold in store. Tiffany and I huddled around the kitchen table and tried to figure a way out of this mess and toward some heroin.

Tiffany called her coke dealer friend Jesse, who lived up the hill. While she made her inquiry, I went into the office and placed a call to Pamela. Pamela wasn't home, and Jesse said he didn't and wouldn't fuck around with smack. "Dealing junk's bad karma," he told Tiffany.

"I'll show him bad karma. What does he think turning down friends in their moment of need is? A blessing?"

We leaned back in our chairs, feet on the table, and racked our brains, trying to figure out a way to get some heroin. "We could break your arm or cut off a toe and try to get some painkillers from an emergency room," I suggested. We went through our phone books and called anyone we knew who might know where to get heroin or might know someone who did. It wasn't going too well.

Then I had a brainstorm. Well, not quite a brainstorm. Like most truly good ideas, this one was there the whole time, but no one had recognized it.

"Dallas!" I nearly screamed. "Dallas! Yeah! You once said you could get it from him, remember? You told me he'd give it to you. Call him," I said, pushing the telephone across the table to her.

She crossed her arms and sat back. "Forget it."

"What do you mean, 'Forget it'? Forget 'Forget it.' Call him."

"No, I said."

"*Why not?*"

"Because I won't."

"Come on, he's our only hope," I begged.

"No way, unh-unh. I don't want to go near that guy."

"You don't have to. I'll go near him."

"Forget it. He won't do business with you; he doesn't even know you . . . I'm telling you, the guy's paranoid."

"Well, introduce me then."

"Forget it. He'll just burn you."

"Yeah, maybe, but he wouldn't burn you, would he?" She didn't say anything.

"He wouldn't, would he?" I continued harping. "He'd sell it to you. You could even flirt with him a little to get a better deal. . . ."

"Yeah, he'd sell it to me. *If* I were willing to buy it from him."

"Will you? Please, come on, I've never asked you for a favor, but I'm asking you now, I'm begging you, I'll do anything, come on, name it. . . ."

"I don't want anything from you—"

I breathed a sigh of relief.

"Give me the phone," she said, and began dialing, then stopped and hung up.

"What's the matter?" I asked. "Why'd you stop?"

"What are we supposed to do about the money? He's not going to give it to us."

"Oh, fuck, I completely forgot! Won't he give us credit? Or how about collateral?" I asked, looking around for something of value. "Maybe a check?"

She shook her head at each suggestion.

"Well, call him anyway and make sure he at least has some."

"What are we going to do about the money?"

"Don't worry, we'll get the money. I don't know how, but we will. If he has the dope, we'll figure out a way. We'll hock something. We'll sell the rent-a-car—"

She called her mother and stepfather's apartment.

I was getting more impatient and desperate by the minute.

After saying hello to her mom and apologizing for not calling sooner, she asked for Dallas. "Does he have any?" I whispered. She held up a finger to her lips, indicating I should shut up.

"A friend of mine wants to go downtown," she told him. Downtown was smack; uptown was cocaine.

"Uh-huh," she said.

"Does he have any?" I whispered again.

She ignored me. "Uh-huh, uh-huh." She nodded her head. "Right, yeah . . . Okay . . ." She hung up. She just shook her head at me. My face went long.

"You're in luck," she said. I brightened up immediately.

"I don't know why I should do this for you," she said, "but let's go."

"Wait a second," I said.

"Oh, now you want to wait."

"What are we going to do about the cash?"

"We can cash it at the Rainbow," she told me.

"I don't think the Rainbow cashes checks."

"Yeah, they do."

"How do you know?"

"Because Mario has let me cash checks there lots of times. I just told him I was your girlfriend and you'd vouch for it."

"You used my name to cash checks?" I asked.

"Don't worry, they won't bounce."

I was trying to decide whether I was mad or pleased.

"Well, do you want to go get high or stand here with that stupid look on your face all night?" she asked. I decided to be pleased, and we left in the rented Mercedes convertible to go gather the cash and the dope.

At her mom's flat Tiffany and I split half a gram and pocketed the other half.

Neither one of us felt the dope we bought. I started complaining. I wasn't necessarily sick anymore, but I was far from where I wanted to be: I wasn't *high*, and I certainly wasn't close to loaded. After all

that waiting and waiting and looking forward to the stuff and then
. . . like, nothing.

I went to check out my eyes in the mirror. "I don't even feel
this shit!"

"Well, what do ya expect, sniffing it?" Dallas asked. "It's like
throwing half of it out the window."

"Don't listen to him," Tiffany said.

"Fine, don't listen to me, I don't care. I'm high, I feel it."

"He's got a point there," I told her.

"I got a point here," Dallas said, holding up a syringe. "Why
don't you shoot it, man? Come on, I'll bet you don't even know how
to do it. You're lucky you came to see me tonight." I was staring at
the tiny needle. I'd never seen one so small—not nearly as large or
threatening as the other hypodermics I'd laid eyes on.

"It's an insulin syringe. You don't even feel it when it goes in."

"*Don't*, Danny," Tiffany warned, dead serious.

"Come on, lighten up," I said. "I just want to get high. What's
it matter how it gets inside me?"

"Okay. But if you're doing it, then I'm going to do it."

"Forget it," I said. "No way."

"Why not? It's okay for you to try it and not me?"

"Never mind why, drop it. Forget it. Let's go . . ."

"Wait a second," Tiffany said. "I changed my mind. I want to
do it."

"No!" I yelled at her.

"Why not?" she screamed back. "Come on, I want an answer,
tell me."

"Well," I said, "I don't have any answers anymore."

"Okay, kiddies," Dallas said, "time's up, have it your way. But
you don't know what you're missing."

"Well, maybe we're better off that way," I said, and, taking
Tiffany by the hand before we did anything stupider than we'd already
almost done, left the apartment. Once I'd promised myself I'd never
do heroin. Then I'd promised myself, with even more commitment,
I'd never shoot up. It was a line I'd drawn and intended to keep.

The next day I met with the executives at the L.A. branch of Ray's
record company to go over the recording budget and billing proce-
dures and begin a publicity file on him. Soon I'd have to fly to the
headquarters in Chicago to ensure that the album would not be ignored

when it was released, and equally important, to get tour support. I had no idea how to manage that one.

I called Tiffany from the record company, and we arranged to meet at the bar at Tana's for dinner at nine and take it from there.

While I waited for her, I got drunk, and the drunker I got, the madder I got until by ten thirty I was ready to fight or fuck the next girl who walked through the door. No single girls were walking through, and I chose to go to Rodney's to get in some trouble.

Within fifteen minutes I'd located some drugs. Not heroin, only pills, but an awfully nice assortment of pills they were: Seconal, Lotusate, Tuinal, Quaalude, Placidyl, a few Percodan, which would come in handy if I didn't find some heroin soon, a whole Baggie full of colors, capsules, pills, and tablets, in exchange for a hundred-dollar bill. I sat at the VIP booth all alone and proceeded to get drunker, going from mad to depressed rather quickly.

I called Pamela, hoping for some consolation. Her service picked up, but I thought she might be home anyway, and since she was less than a couple of blocks away, I took the chance and drove over. I was too drunk to drive all the way home anyway.

I banged on her front door, and wearing just a nightgown, she opened it. There was someone standing just inside.

I didn't like the guy on sight. She introduced me to Sammy. He used to be Jim's chauffeur and had driven him to Mexico on several occasions, or so she claimed (he claimed). I didn't believe a word of it. She was just an easy target, and he was just a hustler. Then I noticed her eyes were pinned, and so were his. There was a tiny bloodstain on her sleeve.

I was having a hard time standing up, the room seemed to be tilting on me, and I still wanted to get higher. They weren't really happy to see me; that much was obvious from the cold treatment I was receiving. I started demanding they give me whatever they were on.

"What are you saying?" Sammy asked.

I ignored him, addressing Pamela instead. *"Give me some!"*

"I don't know what you're talking about."

"Don't give me that bullshit. You know exactly what I'm talking about."

She ignored me. "Don't be such a child. If you need a place to crash, you can use the couch." She walked to her bedroom, following Sammy, and closed the door.

Feeling dejected, rejected, depressed, and pissed, I opened the

Baggie of pharmaceuticals onto the coffee table and started eating one of each color. "Fuck you!" I yelled toward the closed door. "Ya know, I never liked you either! GIVE ME SOME HEROIN!" I yelled. "I WANT SMACK!"

Sammy emerged from the bedroom.

"Maybe you better leave," he said.

"Maybe *you* better leave," I retorted.

"Come on, man, you don't wanna make me hurt you."

"I WANT HEROIN!" I yelled past him.

"Come on, let's go, get up, you're going. . . ."

"Who says? Who the *fuck* are you? Get your fucking hands *off* me. . . ."

I wouldn't give him the pleasure of throwing me out. I collected my pills and stumbled out on my own.

Fuck her, I said to myself, *I didn't want to sleep on her couch while she's screwing some spic bullshit artist junkie in her bed. . . ."*

Since everything was closed by now and Wonderland seemed too far away to chance driving, I headed toward Tiffany's mom's. Besides being less than a mile away, I figured if I couldn't find Tiffany there, maybe I'd bump into Dallas and be able to score some smack. Technically I wasn't supposed to show up to cop without her, but no one ever said anything about not coming over just to see who was around.

I rang the doorbell for at least five minutes before Marilyn, Tiffany's mom, let me in. Tiffany wasn't home, and neither was Dallas.

"S'okay 'f I wait f'er?" I slurred.

"Sure, Danny," she said, taking my arm and leading me inside the apartment.

"I wuv 'er," I tried to say.

"Sure, I know you do. She wuvs you, too. Come on in and sit down." She showed me to the couch. "What have you been taking?" she asked. "You're pretty out of it."

"I'm fine," I said. Then I passed out.

I felt someone shaking me. Thinking it was Tiffany, I pretended to be asleep still, thinking she'd lie down next to me and go to sleep. Then something *hit* me hard. She didn't need to get violent about it. I opened my eyes and saw it wasn't Tiffany. It was Dallas, and he wasn't hitting me: He was kicking me awake.

"Let's go, meathead, go home, get out of here, this isn't a hotel, ya know. . . ."

I tried to sit up, but coordination was extremely difficult. I wasn't necessarily stoned anymore, but I was far from sober either. It was more like a downer hangover with half the downers still somewhere at work in the back of my brain and the other half coursing through my limbs like lead. I tried to sit up.

"Attaboy," Dallas said, grabbing my hands and pulling me up. "Go home, sleep it off. . . ."

I felt like a spastic rubber band as I staggered out and tried to unlock the car door. I couldn't see straight and was having a hard time with my hand-and-eye coordination and fell to my knees a couple of times, trying to get the key in the door. After spending about ten minutes on my knees, I managed to put the key in, open the door, and fall inside . . . right into the passenger's seat, which I'd mistaken for the driver's side since I'd parked the car facing the wrong way on the wrong side of the street. Rather than attempt to get out and walk around the car and open the other door, I simply, well, not simply, but instead, climbed over the stick shift into the driver's seat and rested a bit before starting off.

The car clock said it was 5:50 A.M. I steered the Mercedes onto La Brea and very slowly and very carefully merged with the oncoming traffic, of which there were maybe three or four other cars. It was becoming more and more of an effort not to pass out from the downers. All I was in the shape to do, really, was go to sleep. But I resisted, slapping myself awake every thirty seconds with a harsh open hand to my face. It wasn't like nodding out on smack. This was just being unbearably tired, groggy, *drugged*. With smack it was more like "Oh, I feel so wonderful I just want to let my eyes close and dream," as opposed to sleep. I guess they don't call them "sleeping pills" for nothing, huh?

Thinking about heroin reminded me I should have remembered to ask Dallas for some before I'd left. He most likely wouldn't have sold it to me anyway, only to Tiffany. I had to find her. Pretty soon I'd be needing heroin. Maybe she had gone back to Wonderland. I had to make it back there, but I had to get there carefully.

One minute I was concentrating on my driving, slowing down and stopping for a red light, and the next thing I knew, a policeman was rapping on my car window with his nightstick.

I woke up. He opened the door, and I tumbled out into the middle of the street.

"Whatcha doin', son?"

"Goin' home, Officer," I said, getting up and leaning against the stopped car.

"Didn't look like you were going there too quickly to me."

I tried to think and talk coherently. "I was being *careful*," I managed to say. "I was going a little slow, I guess."

"You weren't going *period*."

"I was waiting for . . . da light 't change," I told him, I think.

"The light changed a dozen times, and you didn't move an inch."

I thought he was putting me on.

"Come on . . ." I said.

"Why don't you come on over here," he said, walking to the curb, "and show me how well you can walk a straight line?"

After taking a couple of shaky steps, I slumped down on the curb to rest. "How about if I just told you what I took?" I asked the cop.

"Well, that would make things easier."

I pulled the Baggie out of my inside jacket pocket. "These," I said, holding the bag out to him.

His demeanor immediately changed for the worse.

"All right, kid"—he laid me facedown on the grass—"I'm going to have to cuff ya." He pulled my arms behind me and cuffed me.

"Ouch!" I cried. "That hurts."

"Don't move and it won't hurt," he said.

"What am I supposed to do, just lay here?"

"Don't get wise with me," he said, lifting me up and pushing me to his patrol car. On the way I tripped and, unable to break my fall, crashed forward onto my face. The cop dragged me up and shoved me into the back seat of his car. My wrists were killing me. My face was killing me. *Boy,* I thought, *I sure could go for a painkiller now.* Then my thoughts returned to heroin. And I got scared. Not because I was going to be arrested and booked but because I wasn't sure how, when, or if I was going to be able to score again.

I kept complaining about the cuffs the whole ride to the station. "Can't you just take these off?" I asked him.

"Nope."

"Well, how about lettin' me wear them in front?"

"Nope, regulation, can't take any chances . . ."

"What do you think I'm gonna do, try and strangle you with my wrists chained together?"

"Might."

"I can barely walk!"

"Could be on PCP, no telling what might happen . . ."

"I just gave you what I took!" I cried. "That's what I get for being so honest. Handcuffed, like a common criminal? If I wanted to make trouble, ya think I woulda just handed all my drugs over to you?" I was indignant. PCP! "I've never done angel dust in my life!"

I told him. I was actually offended he thought I would even use the stuff—basically a hog tranquilizer, without a doubt the most classless drug in the whole country. It's funny the little prejudices and loyalties one develops sometimes.

At county jail they put me in the drunk tank at which I took major offense, then they herded me into the medical examiner's waiting room so the doctor could make sure I didn't die when they tossed me into a cell. It's fairly standard procedure, taking someone who's in a questionable state to be examined before getting booked. That way, if something terrible does happen to the person, the county isn't liable.

I finally hit a sympathetic ear with one of my complaints about the cuffs and got them reversed to the front. Then I slouched back on the hard bench and went to sleep.

"Danny!"

I looked up, my eyes vacant, a look of surprise melting into relief taking over my face.

"*Joey*? What are you doing here?" For a second I thought, how ironic, both my brother and I had gotten arrested at the same time same day. I was happy to see him; now I wouldn't be in jail all alone.

"I was about to ask you the same question."

I hadn't seen my brother, or anyone else in my family for that matter, in almost six months, and I figured now was as good a time as any for a reconciliation.

"I asked you first," I pointed out.

"I work here," he said.

"I thought you worked at County Hospital. This isn't the hospital, is it?"

"I work here one night a week. Now it's your turn. You tell me, what in the hell did you get yourself into now?"

"I fell asleep at the wheel," I told him. "Think you might be able to use your influence and get me out of here?"

"I'll see what I can do. Though I'm not sure why I should." I got the distinct impression he wasn't thrilled to see me.

He came back about five minutes later, dangling my bagful of pills. I reached out my hand to take them back.

He withdrew them. "What the hell did you do? Knock off a pharmacy?"

"No!" I withdrew. Getting accused first of taking pig tranks and now of armed robbery. "Of course not. I wouldn't do that. I *bought* them."

"Oh, I see, so that makes it perfectly all right?"

I was taken aback again. I kept forgetting buying drugs was against the law, too.

"Well," I said, trying not to appear the total fuck-up, "it's not armed robbery, ya know? There's a difference there."

He looked at the bag in his hand. "I don't even know what half these pills are."

"I know," I said, interested and relieved the conversation had taken a change in direction. "Those are Lotusates, and those big white ones are—"

"I know what those big white ones are—"

"And those big fat green ones are Placidyls, which are just like ludes, the blues are Valium tens, and see those brown ones? Those are Percodans—"

"All right, shut up, I'm not impressed, I don't care what they are. . . . You seem totally oblivious to the fact you're in trouble here. You're under arrest. You're on your way to jail for this stunt! Do you have any idea how serious this business is? You coulda killed someone, driving the shape you're in."

"Wait a minute, Joey, I haven't even taken anything since last night."

He looked at me dubiously. "Besides," I told him, "I wasn't driving. I was sleeping when they arrested me."

Good ol' Joey got me off, got all the charges dropped, and the evidence, to my mixed emotions, got lost. Then he insisted on personally taking me on a guided grand tour through the entire county jail facility, about a whole square mile of nothing but jail cells, to show me where I would have gone had I not had the good fortune to get arrested on the one night a week he worked there. I think he saw it as a shock treatment, and his duty as my big brother demanded it. Midway through the walk I was beginning to question seriously how lucky I'd been. I was so tired by now I could barely take another step, but he kept prodding me and pulling me along, continuing his recitation, pointing out cells of interest: the gang cell, the cell where they put the hookers, and so on. "There's where they put the transvestites, and this one is where they hold the transsexuals, and that's where they put the ones no one's sure about . . ." and all I wanted to do was go to sleep. I was beginning to think being locked up anyplace and at least being still and able to lie down would be preferable to being hauled around on this hiking expedition. Then Joey showed me the cell where they put the drug addicts. "This is where they were going to bring you," he said, pointing out a big pen filled with the sleaziest, sickest, most whining bunch of scum you'd ever not want to spend a night with, the pen that had *alla the above* in it. I got the point, and I told him. Then we got the hell out of there as fast as I was capable of walking at the time.

Customs telephoned from Los Angeles Airport to say they had a "Jim Osterberg" in their custody whom it would not or could not release on account of he looked nothing like the picture of the person that was supposedly him in the passport he carried.

"Oh, it's him," I assured the agent. "He colors his hair once in a while."

"That's not the only thing he's gone ahead and colored," I was informed. "He painted his entire torso during the flight from England."

I didn't even know he'd been in England. I had no time to ponder the surprise. They wanted me to come down, snappylike, to make a positive identification.

"I'm on my way."

Sure enough, he'd used his body as a canvas and covered himself with paint from forehead to toenail in camouflage streaks, black and pinks, an exotic green and Day-Glo orange. We washed him off and made the identification. The tour had definitely taken its toll. Under the paint he looked a hundred years old.

During the drive home he was unusually subdued. Then, when he did speak, I wished he hadn't.

"What's this I hear you've started dabbling with heroin?" He said it casually, like "So I heard we've got potted palms on the balcony now."

"Who said?" I tried to sound equally relaxed. Despite myself, though, I was instantly on guard.

"I'm not going to say who said." All pleasantness was gone from his voice. "It doesn't matter *who said, I heard.* I'm not asking you if it's true or not. I figure it probably is. . . . Just do yourself a favor, just stop now, before it's too late. . . . Don't even think twice about it, just do it. It'll never be easier to quit than it is right now. I know what I'm talking about. You'll do what you want to do in the end, just like I did. I gotta tell you: If I heard about it, other people could hear about it, too. You're not just a rock critic anymore. What you do now affects other people. It affects me; it affects Ray. Whether you like it or not, you've got a responsibility now toward people other than yourself. I mean, if you were still a rock writer, would *you* believe you if you said I was straight?"

"Isn't that a bit of a double standard?" It pissed me off. It was like Morrison with the cocaine. These people I really looked up to, whose word and advice were better than gold to me, telling me one thing, then doing another.

"Yeah, I guess it is," he started, then changed his mind. I guess it hurt him because he got defensive, too. "*Hell, no*, it's not. Besides, I'm the singer, not a businessman, so what if it is? It's my job to entertain. It's your job to handle my image as a performer."

But we both knew it wasn't a smart career move for either of us. I told him I hadn't been taking heroin, only cocaine and Quaaludes, and everybody was doing those. Perhaps, I confessed, I'd gone overboard a bit and given the *appearance* of being on heroin. I didn't think he believed me, but I also knew he was as uncrazy about the conversation as I was and would be more than willing to let it drop.

It was dropped.

But the next time I took him to score, I wasn't going to wait in the car. I was going to insist on being allowed inside. As things turned out, I didn't have to insist on a thing.

After picking him up from the airport, I dropped him off at his guitarist's apartment on Sunset Boulevard, and by 10:00 P.M. I had received a call asking me if I could come pick him up and bring him back to my house. I asked him where he was, and he told me I'd been there before, the house near the freeway, just off Robertson. "There's a black Porsche in the driveway; the license plate says 'ROCKS.' " I knew the house. It was where I'd taken him before to score.

Inside, I tried to adjust my eyes to the darkness and the flickering candles. Iggy was sitting on a couch, watching a soundless TV. He introduced me to Zola, the handsome young black man who answered the door. The Porsche in the driveway belonged to him as did the house. I could tell he liked the idea of having a bona fide rock star in his house just fine. He couldn't stop telling Iggy how happy he was to see him and how worried he'd been about him.

"I was wondering if we might be able to do some business," I told Zola.

He asked Iggy if I was cool, and Iggy told him, "If you mean is he a narc, the answer is no." I could read between the lines enough to know he didn't approve of what I was setting up one bit. I hated myself for what I was about to do, but that didn't stop me from doing it. If anything, I wanted to get loaded even more.

"Am I wrong in assuming you would prefer I not go through with this transaction?" I asked him.

"Hey, I did my bit. You're a big boy; you do what you want.

Besides, like you said, I'm not in any position to tell you not to, right?"

I had an impulse to tell Zola to forget it; but it was fleeting, and there was nothing I wanted more at that moment than to score some good heroin. After living on Dallas's crap for the past few days, I imagined my tolerance had dropped, and if the stuff Zola had was half decent, the probability of catching a nod was definitely in my favor.

Zola asked me to wait for him in the living room. Five minutes later he called me back into his bedroom, where I explained my situation to him. He asked me how much I wanted to buy, and I asked him the price.

"Twenty-five bucks for a balloon. If you buy four, for a hundred, you get one free."

"How much do you get in a balloon?"

"A quarter T."

"How much is that?"

"A quarter teaspoon." He showed me the teaspoon and the balloons. I put a hundred bucks on the table, and he handed me five colored balloons and then scribbled out his phone number and handed it to me.

"Don't give this to anybody," he warned me, but nicely. "I'm very careful who I do business with. If Iggy says you're okay, I take his word for it. I don't do business after ten P.M., and always make sure to call before you come over. Don't ever come over unannounced, or else I won't answer the door. I don't step on my drugs, and if you let me know enough in advance, I can always get them."

"You don't know how good that is to hear."

"It's true . . . I'm easy to do business with, and I expect my customers to be the same."

"I don't think we'll have any trouble whatsoever," I assured him.

So that was how I met Zola. And not a day too soon. By the time we made it back to Wonderland, the back of my shirt was soaked with perspiration, and it was a cool evening plus I'd been driving around with the top down. The good brown heroin rocks first put me straight and then on the nod.

The insurance company agreed the Vet was a total loss. It had taken only three weeks to come to that difficult conclusion. "Oh, so that's what you guys call it when a car is compacted to half its previous size."

Ray and Tiffany and I went down to Beverly Hills Coach the very next day and picked out a classic royal blue Cobra, complete with a baby roll bar and the top of the line Blaupunkt sound system complete with a fifty-watt power booster. It was, as they say in the Valley, cherry. I didn't even have to wait until the insurance company got around to compensating me for the Vet. Ray put the whole thing down on his gold American Express card, and I signed a note his accountant had prepared, promising to repay Ray the day the check came in.

A new car and a new dealer within twenty-four hours. Talk about good luck! What more could a guy ask for? To come to terms with the massive good fortune I'd been a recent recipient of and to cultivate faith and avoid insanity, I'd been developing a rather perverse bit of logic that went something like this:

As long as I keep fucking up, as long as I don't try to make things better, as long as I demonstrate faith and keep depending on God (to bail me out), things will continue getting better, and God will keep watching over me and keep me out of harm's way.

But, I was certain, the moment I started to get my shit together and demonstrate my ability to go it alone, God would take one look, see I can take care of myself, interpret it as an insult, or worse, faithlessness, conclude I don't need Him anymore, and split, leaving me to fend for myself.

How else could I explain what was happening to me? It seemed I couldn't fuck up if I tried. And to the outsider it could very easily look as if I *had* been trying to fuck up. And everything was *still* working out. Hell, if anything, it was getting *better*. I could only conclude that if I went in the opposite direction and tried to make it better, things would get worse. Makes sense, doesn't it?

Perverse logic or not, something definitely was happening in my favor. Somehow, for *some* reason, I was still on a roll.

After we completed the paperwork on the Cobra, Tiffany and I went over to Tower Records and picked up a slew of tapes—Springsteen's *Born to Run*, almost the whole Dylan and Stones catalogs, plus various and sundry not-to-do-withouts such as Blue Cheer's *Vincibus Eruptum*, the Dave Clark Five's Hits package, the Animals, Mott the Hoople's *Mott*, and a dozen or so others. As soon as I could, I'd go over to Elektra, raid its tape library, and score the Stooges' LP, the MC-5, and, last but certainly not least, all the Doors albums.

But it was *Born to Run* and *Exile on Main Street* by the Stones that most often found their way into the Cobra's tape deck.

There was something about the times, the mood, and the environment that made them appropriate. Both albums, though extremely different, were somehow alike. Both artists had made LPs that were guiltless celebrations of escape and transcendence, provoked by desperation and the will to rock.

> Baby, this town rips the bones from your back
> It's a death trap
> It's a suicide rap
> We gotta get out while we're young
> 'Cause tramps like us
> Baby, we were born to run. . . .

The music was the sound track to the scenes of our life, by turns complementing and inspiring, firing us forward, giving sound to our thoughts, texture to our feelings.

We'd climb into the new car, zoom out of the driveway, slap in *Born to Run*, and head to our new dealer's . . . down Wonderland Avenue, over to Lookout and onto Laurel Canyon Boulevard, heading south into the city, down to Zola's, down to score. We'd have already talked to him on the telephone, and he'd be expecting us. We had money in our pockets, and the drugs were waiting. We'd be anticipating the connection, filled with desire. I'd gun the engine and turn up the music, ready to storm the gates of heaven.

> The highways jammed with broken heroes
> On a last chance power drive
> Everybody's out on the run tonight
> But there's no place left to hide
> Together Wendy we can live with the sadness
> I'll love you with all the madness in my soul
> Someday, girl, I don't know when,
> We're gonna get to that place
> Where we really want to go
> And we'll walk in the sun
> But till then . . . tramps like us,
> Baby, we were born to run.

And we arrived to leap out of the car, laughing and careless and free, run across the front lawn, stop at the front door, knocking briskly, calling out, "It's us, we're here!" Zola swung the door open, and we were so happy to see him. Tiffany gave him a peck on the cheek, and I walked in, clapping my hands together, asking, "Okay, where's the drugs? Where's the drugs?"

Tiffany would wring her hands together while chanting, "Oh boy, oh boy, oh boy, oh boy. . . ."

"Okay, okay." He laughed, departing for his bedroom, where in some secret box in some mysterious corner or bureau he kept his stash. The energy stayed high while we waited for him to bring it out to us—pure Brown Sugar—Mexican smack, hard golden brown rocks just waiting to be crunched and snorted. I could almost taste the bitterness of the dope as it dripped down the back of my throat.

Candles flickered in corners and on the coffee table, where anyone who wanted could use the fire to cook up his dope. We laid our three hundred bucks down, and Zola dropped out a handful of colored balloons.

"You're so lucky, you two," he said. "You don't have to hustle for your dope. I hope you never have to, but, baby, you two could make an absolute fortune together. I could just eat you up."

Gabor Szabo, the infamous jazz guitarist, gave a snicker, and at the kitchen table Jenny, the hooker, used one of the legs of her nylons to tie off the blood dripping down her arm. Gabor had to hide out over at Zola's because he had to hide his habit from his wife.

He was tying off in front of us, relishing the freedom, using a silk stocking and an old set of works, the kind with a needle slammed into an eyedropper that registers automatically when the vein is pierced. He slid the needle into the mainline, and a thread of blood curled up into the dark brown liquid, like a rose. Then he squeezed the little black bulb at the top, gently, and the mixture of blood and dope rushed under his skin. He untied the tourniquet, ashed his Pall Mall, took a drag, leaving the cigarette in his lips, closed his eyes, and laid his head back to savor the rush.

When he opened his eyes about ten minutes later, he started telling me about the old jazz days in New York.

"Ever since Mess Mezzrow wrote *Really the Blues* back in 1946, white folks be thinking it cool to do dope," he rasped in that cool/jazzy funk/junkie baritone of his. "Then they didn't separate Mr. Jones from grass . . . but they are *soo* different, you know. . . . Smack's just a little powder, you see? It can even go bad and lose its goodness if you let it just sit and don't use it up soon 'nough, though I can't picture no human doin' that. It needs to be inside another living thing, a human being, to come alive, to do its thing, to take the trip, man." He nodded out a little, his thick lips parting a tad, eyelids going down to half-mast, head bobbing.

Then his eyelids fluttered open, and he went on: "It gets you, man, I swear, it gets you, and it kicks your ass. It kicks, man; it becomes the horse. At first, when you ain't use t' it, it kick ya so hard you puke, heh, heh-heh-heh. Then you *know* you got some dope. They call it jazz 'cause a that time thing . . . It be so cool to nod on, see? Jazz takes you over the back of time itself, just like the stuff do; there ain't no time drag atall with neither, ya dig? Jazz is so free-form, the improvisation . . . the musicians be jammin' away, and the audience, their instrument be on Bo, or Horse, or maybe the Lady, be doin' it too right with them! That's right! The musical cats be doin' that cocaine, riding that one 'cause it give them the *life* thang, too . . . and Horse, jazz man, so that jes' perfectly fine. That's why they call her-o-in jazz, ya see? You just jump on the Horse, and ya ride over the backbone of time . . . you follow that musical thread, man . . . and before you know it . . . ya see . . . be . . . for . . ."

Gabor just nodded off, cigarette dropping out of his fingers, into the ashtray propped up beside him on the couch. His eyes closed. He tried to speak again, but I couldn't make out a word he said. It was just mumbling or maybe clear enough, but apropos of nothing, like "I don't like coleslaw," totally in his own world.

"Hey, Gabor? Gabor, you okay?"

"Oh, man, I am *so* sorry, man, where *was* I?"

Nobody outside these walls has any idea this world is turning in here. It's a whole 'nother universe, and we're on the inside of this secret society with its ecstatic rituals and special smells and secret members.

Tiffany and I scoop up our dope and split to worship back at Wonderland Avenue. The tape kicks in, and the motor turns over at once. Adrenaline is pouring through us, and the anticipation of getting the dope inside us is almost unbearable; but we've purposely put it off until we get home, and the suspense is tangible and unbelievably exciting. It's in our pocket; we've got it; nothing can stop us now, except the cops. You have no idea how great it feels, the power it gives you, carrying a half gram of pure heroin around on your body, ready to be used. It's enthralling, better than having a gun or a rifle by your side, better than a million bucks in a suitcase, thrilling, but scary, too: "Well the night's bustin' open/These two lanes will take us anywhere/We got one last chance to make it real/To trade in these wings on some wheels . . ." We want to feel, more than we've ever felt before, never allowed ourselves to feel before because we were scared to go that far, but now it's happened and we each feel the need to confirm that the other one knows, that they know and feel the same way: "I want to know love is wild/I want to know love is real . . ."*

We know we shouldn't be doing it, that's obvious; but we also know damn well we're going to do it anyway, and that ain't nothin' but tragic. But at least we got each other; at least we're gonna make the most of it while we still can. . . .

"Thunder Road" begins, a mix of sadness and sorrow: "You can hide 'neath your covers and study your pain. . . ." A verse later strength and hope are building, as we get closer: "With a chance to make it good somehow/What else can we do now. . . ."

We're side by side, heading home, where we'll step inside a wonderful, warm womb room just waiting for us. The night's coming on, the hot city day is cooling off; it's only a question of time now, assuming we don't get pulled over en route. I accelerate, into escape and on to celebration: "Heaven's waiting on down the tracks/Oh-oh come and take my hand/Riding out tonight to case the promised land/ Oh-oh Thunder Road, oh Thunder Road/Lying out there like a killer in the sun/Hey I know it's late/We can make it if we run/Oh Thunder Road, sit tight, take hold. . . ."

And we know someday there's gonna be a bill for all of this, it's got to have a cost, and we don't give a goddamn, except for the harm and hurt it might cause the other, and even then it's still worth it. "From the front porch to my front seat/The door's open but the ride ain't free/And I know you're lonely for words that I ain't spoken/ But tonight we'll be free/All the promises'll be broken . . ."

I slow down, deciding the risk of getting stopped for speeding is not worth it. But I can't stay slowed down for long; something is pushing us onward, to hell with the risks; the speedometer drifts up again. I look over at Tif; she smiles; I smile back. "Night" is playing. I turn up the volume. The celebration begins: "And she's so pretty that you're lost in the stars/As you jockey your way through the cars. . . ./And you're in love with all the wonder it brings/And every muscle in your body sings/As the highway ignites. . . ./Tonight you're gonna break on through to the inside and it'll be right. . . ."

And it is. We make it home, again, safe, relieved, excited. We dash into the house, scrambling around like two chipmunks, gather the paraphernalia, chop up and snort the dope, and jump on each other, and it is so right there is nothing else to do because nothing else *will* do!

---

*"Born to Run" by Bruce Springsteen

* * *

During the past month, while Ray was still in the studio working on his solo album, and I had plenty of free time on my hands, a peculiar late-morning ritual had developed. I'd go outside to collect the *L.A. Times* to discover my car missing. I'd call the cops and report it stolen, only for it to be found later outside Zola's house or in the Rainbow or Whisky parking lot—in other words, right where I'd left it but gotten too fucked up to remember leaving it. I was in the process of developing a very strange, and strained, relationship with the cops with whom I kept filing the theft reports. It had gotten to the point where they felt obligated to inform me they weren't my personal lost-and-found car agency.

There were the mornings when I did remember being too fucked up to drive and knew why the car wasn't in the driveway out front but still couldn't remember where I'd left it. Then I'd have to call a cab and comb the streets all over Hollywood, looking for it. That's not so bad, considering I knew a party girl who once forgot where she'd left her *baby*. You have to keep these things in perspective.

Then there was the morning I woke up and found almost all of my precious record collection gone. Thousands of records gone, vanished, into thin air. Convinced I'd been robbed during my sleep, I dialed the police and reported the theft. Two hours later they were at Wonderland, and I was giving them my version of what I thought had happened. By then Tiffany had groggily made her way downstairs in her bathrobe and patiently listened to me giving my take on how my records had migrated while we'd been asleep upstairs.

"I think we should talk," Tiffany said at one point during my testimony, but I paid her no mind. Instead, I told the police which albums were gone and how the thief had only left me with all the Doors and Iggy albums. "I don't know how to interpret that," I told them. "Either the guy has lousy taste, or else he was being very considerate."

"I *really* think we ought to talk," Tiffany insisted, but I continued to ignore her and answered the rest of the cops' questions before thanking them for their time and showing them out.

Now Tiffany didn't request a conversation. She just started one.

"You're really an asshole sometimes, you know that?"

"What?" I asked her, somewhat incredulous. "I just got ripped off for thousands of dollars in vinyl and you call me an asshole. You're real compassionate sometimes, you know that? What the fuck did I do?"

"You," she practically snarled, "ripped off your own record collection."

I have to admit that caught me off guard.

"I what?"

She took a breath and told me, "Last night some new dealer acquaintance of yours dropped by with a buncha dope and turned you on, but you wanted more, obviously. I tried to convince you you'd had enough, but no way—"

This was all news to me. She went on. "He wouldn't give you any credit, and you didn't have any cash, as usual. You didn't need anything else; God knows you were wasted enough already. Anyway, you took your records to Rhino Records and traded them for cash."

"I don't believe it."

"Don't believe it, I don't give a fuck," she said, "but you should at least remember doing it. It took about twenty trips for you to carry them all to the car."

I thought hard, trying to keep track of, or to remember, what she was saying.

"So, then, if I traded them in, where's the money?" I asked her; it seemed an ultimately sane question.

She looked at me like I was certifiable.

"You spent it on the drugs," she said as if it were the most obvious thing in the world.

"All of it?"

"Yup." She nodded.

"How much?" I asked out of morbid curiosity, but also hoping some definite sum, a number, might jar some recollection loose.

"About eight hundred bucks."

"Jesus. I don't remember any of this."

"Obviously."

Then I got an inspiration. "The drugs!" I exclaimed. "So where's the drugs?" It, too, seemed the logical question to ask.

She just shook her head. "We did them all."

"*We* did them all?"

"Yup."

"Both of us?"

"Uh-huh."

"No one else?"

"Nope."

"All of it?"

"Yup."

"Eight hundred bucks' worth?"

"Well, you did most of it, obviously."

I was stunned.

"Were they any good?" I asked.

"Obviously," she said. She liked using that word on me, delighted in it, gave her a real feeling of superiority. "Judging from the condition they put you in, I'd have to say so."

Everything is getting unreal. For example, I'm sitting in the backyard at Wonderland, staring into the pool, listening to Sky Saxon, who's now calling himself Sunlight, telling me about his new band, not the Seeds (which he used to sing with) but Universe. Sunlight and Universe. He's telling me how I'm a godsend because I booked him a gig at the Whisky (partly as a tribute because the guy was at one time a great, but mainly to get him off my back) and have been letting him rehearse at the Wonderland studio. He's become a member of the Source Brotherhood and was living in Hawaii, he's telling me, but then their guru/leader, Jim Baker, jumped off a cliff without his hang glider because he thought he didn't need one to fly, mind over matter, he thought, but he thought wrong and plummeted to his death. So now Sunlight is back in Hollywood, ready to make a comeback and spread the word of the Brotherhood through the light and love of music, and he's going on about how I'm going to reap fantastic karmic benefits by helping him with his musical mission and how spiritually gifted and qualified I am, and he's telling me how saintly I am, and meanwhile, I'm trying not to nod out from this junk I just did.

Gypsy Boots has just run into the yard with his latest trap of health-food candy, long black and gray hair and beard blowing in the wind, tan legs pumping from his tie-dyed orange muslin outfit, sandals flapping on the brick, saying, "You are what you eat," as he's shoving these turd-looking organically sweetened mush bars in my face and I'm trying not to puke.

Richie the Dwarf, a Doors fan from New Jersey, is running, well, hobbling, around all over the place, taking pictures of everything from the ivy to the gold records, while these three bodyguardlike thug/buddies of his kept watch over him, lifting him up and setting him down and fetching him beer and rolling his joints, meanwhile making me feel like some sort of ward in my own house. Iggy has just come back from a visit to the gay chapter of his San Francisco fan club, hair slicked straight back, big black and white earrings, high heels, black lipstick, and black nail polish. He's been feminized. He's going on about the CIA and bonfire parties at the bottom of the cliff at the beach, where there were real men "who knew how to treat a real woman." And I find the whole thing, personally speaking, very unnerving.

Tiffany's ordering gallon bottles of Smirnoff silver label hundred-proof vodka from Greenblatt's, and Pamela Morrison is locked in the upstairs bathroom for the second hour straight with her spic junkie "chauffeur" trying to find a vein. A militant gang of Jesus Freaks from the San Fernando Valley have started a campaign of harassment. They are convinced and try continually to convince me that I am doing the "devil's work"—that is, spreading the Word of Morrison, who was, in their opinion, the antichrist. They drive mysteriously by Wonderland (no one ever sees them) and leave unmysterious, vehement anti-Morrison slogans daggered into the front door with these razor-sharp crucifixes they use.

For Tiffany's sixteenth birthday I buy her 150 long-stemmed roses and lay them over her and the bed as she sleeps. When she wakes up, she starts hollering something about "Look at all these fucking thorns." A hundred and fifty perfect rosebuds surround her, and all she sees are the thorns. It was a statement not unindicative of our overall perception.

Morrison, meanwhile, refuses to stay dead. In the past few weeks we've received a telegram from someone in South Africa who says he needs three thousand dollars wired immediately so he can fly a helicopter upriver in the Congo to rescue Jim, who is lying crippled with two broken legs, helpless, somewhere in the wilds of pygmy country. Reporters have been calling nonstop requesting information, a statement or denial about Jim's opening a bank account at the Bank of America in San Francisco. Then someone keeps calling Wonderland collect from Australia's outback region, claiming to be Jim himself and leaving an address to forward his portion of the royalty checks. A *Rolling Stone* reporter calls and informs us Jim was spotted ripping off a can of diced peaches at the local A&P in Atlanta, Georgia. It was not an *un*weird time.

Add to all this madness the usual gaggle of weirdos and parade of girls, druggies, roadies, musicians, music-industry types, and fans, and maybe you can begin to understand how and why heroin was becoming less a luxury and more and more a necessity. Maybe you can begin to understand why I (1) figured if you can't beat 'em, join 'em and (2) decided to stay as loaded as possible for as long as possible. It kept the party going and in the meantime numbed me to all that was unpleasant. The one disturbing question I had: If I did go out, would anybody even notice? Or, to keep the party going, would this reality also be denied?

CHAPTER ELEVEN

· · · · · · · · · · · ·

I'm always hearing voices on the street
I want to shout but I can hardly speak

Heading for the overload
Splattered on the dusty road
Kick me like you kicked before
I can't even feel the pain no more. . . .

The sunshine bores the daylights out of me
Chasing shadows built on mysteries. . . .
—ROLLING STONES

THE time had come to get some work done.

The record company, Mercury, had been hollering for the final parts to Ray's LP so they could start the presses and get it out onto the marketplace, where they could recoup the investment they'd already laid out. So far they hadn't heard so much as one song, and they weren't being patient about the whole thing. The calls coming into Wonderland from the Chicago headquarters had gotten downright nasty in the past few weeks, and they were threatening to fly out themselves, or worse, stop the checks, unless I got them a hear/listen real quick.

Ray and I had already agreed it was best to put them off until we could play a finished product rather than something half baked where they might have to use their imagination (God forbid). That was why I'd been pedaling in reverse after the sales job I'd given them a few months ago, trying to stall them off. Now I'd run out of excuses for them, and there was nothing I could, or would, say to Ray to hurry it up. I refused to tell him about the pressure the record company was exerting, not wanting to put even more pressure on him than he was already putting on himself to get the thing finished and out.

When he was finally done and the work was ready to be heard, but before I took a tape back to Chicago for the company to hear, Ray thought it might be a good idea for me to hear the thing myself and invited me over to his luxurious, cozy West Hollywood home for a preview of the goods. Even though I'd been down to the studio on a number of occasions, I'd still heard only snatches of songs, and while I'd heard maybe enough to go ahead and reassure the record company it was getting an album which both lived up to the reputation Ray'd earned as a Door and established him with a new crowd of people, I was still in no way prepared for what he played me that afternoon.

The whole album was about ancient Egyptian folklore. This

was a good five, six years before the whole King Tut phenomenon landed stateside and made the whole Egyptian mystique palatable for Western tastes. No one knew King Tut from King Lear, including, especially, me.

Okay, so Ray was ahead of his time. What's so bad about that?

Ray basically had made the album for himself. He'd already demonstrated to himself his instincts were both commercially and artistically accurate. If he listened to his truest heartfelt motives, if he pleased himself, he'd learned with Morrison and the Doors, the rest would assuredly follow. And even if it didn't, no big deal. At least he'd be happy with what he'd done. Plus the Doors albums were continuing to sell, so it wasn't as if he had to worry about money. He was a musician who had his pride, and he damn well wasn't going to compose and play just to make a buck when he didn't have to. So the guy had integrity, too. What was so awful about that?

Well, for one, I had no idea how to sell the thing. Besides the Egyptian angle, he'd tossed in a healthy dose of Eastern concepts, a smattering of psychological hipness, a dollop of metaphysical trappings, Zen leanings, and a bit of astrological horseplay, along with references to solar boats, astral travel, "The Purpose of Existence" (one song title), Moorish idols, and lines like "Buddha's eating ice cream and so is Lao Tzu/Freud & Jung are holding hands and saying I'm wid you!" And just to make absolutely sure all the bases were covered, he added in a healthy shake of good old-fashioned LSD-soaked Aquarian-age hippie ethics.

Okay. So the thing appealed to an interesting cross section of people. What's so wrong with that?

Nothing. Not a thing at all. 'Cept I was the one who had to find those people.

And just to make sure he wasn't making things too easy on anyone, he went and called the album *The Golden Scarab*.

"What's a scarat?" I asked him.

"A *scarab*." He corrected me. "It's a beetle. In Egypt the beetle will lay its eggs in a ball of its dung and then roll the ball along in front of him on the floor of the earth, warming the unborn under the glow of the sun. It's actually a little ball of life, see? Under the rays of the sun the eggs begin to warm and hatch. The early Egyptians believed this was how the sun actually rose and set, a giant beetle in the heavens pushing it across the sky. Those Egyptians were as dependent on the sun for life as the beetle was, and they worshiped the sun, not some abstract deity nobody could relate to but something real, something everybody could see and feel, something that really mattered, something their lives depended on."

"Holy shit," I muttered.

"Exactly." Ray smiled.

A concept album about a giant ball of shit floating in the air somewhere over Bum-Fuck, Egypt, with monster insect power sometime way before Year One I didn't expect would exactly cause dollar signs to go flashing off slot machinelike through the record company executives' orbs when I previewed it for them. Like I said, we were in 1974, the Year of the Eagle. Bachman-Turner Overdrive was Mercury's biggest and most treasured act, and the music world was in such a state of doldrums that within a few short years disco was to sweep the nation like a locust swarm and become the biggest thing since the Beatles. Mindless music was in; thinking was not. I didn't expect an album pondering the mysteries of the universe via an Egyptian perspective circa ten thousand or so years ago filtered through the head of a twentieth-century Aquarian-age Pole from Chicago would be a real high priority for any self-proclaimed rock fan, Doors fans notwithstanding.

I forgot to tell you Ray was Polish. I'd only recently found out myself. In fact, I found out Ray was Polish the same day I switched from Marlboros to Kools, not that the incidents are related. The cigarettes don't explain much—unless you buy that line about only blacks and junkies' smoking Kools, in which case my situation became pretty obvious. But finding out Ray was Polish explained a hell of a lot. Like his attitude toward money, for one thing; his tolerance of me, for another; and this album, very, very much so. Plus he was an Aquarius. You take those things and add them together, and you get Ray. God, I really loved that guy.

I responded to the album's preview in a way that befitted a professional of my caliber and a personal manager of my standing: I went out and got shit-faced and mourned my dilemma. And then the next morning with a hangover that resembled a mescaline high, I tucked a tape under my arm and flew off to Chicago, drinking every tiny bottle of booze I could charm out of the first-class stewardess.

The whole executive front line of Mercury was assembled in the conference room. Besides the publicity director, whom I'd already done battle with on several occasions, there were all the VPs of all the departments, a lot of whom I'd already talked with before on the phone. I'd never seen so many straight people in one room before in my life. I thought this was supposed to be the music business! I had to restrain myself from looking under the conference table and counting up the wingtips.

Now before I go and write something I might later regret (like in court, for instance), let me pause here to say all record companies go through their up phases and down phases. In retrospect, it's not real difficult to ascertain which period Mercury was going through.

I learned a new word that day. The VPs used the word when referring to music. This word is "viable." It means "commercial" or "successful." They say something like "I really don't think this record will be viable in the marketplace." The "marketplace" means you. And they call the music the "product." One of them said, "We have to justify the viability of this product to our shareholders before we issue it in the marketplace."

"In language someone who isn't a business school graduate can understand, what are you trying to tell me?" I asked. "What are you saying, that it's no good?"

"We can't make any commitments at this time." The VP of something told me that.

"When do you think you'll be able to make some commitments?"

"Not at this time."

"You mean you're just going to forget about it?" I asked, trying to drag out of him what he wasn't willingly offering up, which was that they didn't intend to do a fucking thing with it.

"Oh, no, not by any means. We'll release it. It's just beyond that I'm afraid we'll have to wait and see."

"Wait and see? Wait and see what? Of course, nothing'll happen if you just wait and see! What do you expect? How's it going to sell? How is anyone going to buy it if they don't even know it's out?"

He just shrugged. "We'll have to get back to you."

"Maybe you don't even want to release this record. What would you do if I just refused to give you the master?" I could do that. It definitely was a possibility; I'd brought along only a copy to play, while the original was back in L.A., securely tucked away in the studio's safe.

"You mean you're interested in buying it back from us?"

That wasn't one of the possibilities I'd just considered, but I decided to play along and see where it might get us.

"I don't know, maybe . . . it depends . . . it depends on whether you're going to do your job promoting it."

"Listen," one of the other VPs said, "don't *you* tell us how to do *our* job. Our business is selling records, and we're damn good at it." Which was a patent line of bullshit; everyone in the industry knew there was about as much science and know-how connected to what Mercury did as throwing the shit against the wall and seeing what stuck. "Don't you ever tell us we don't know how to do our job," the veep went on, but the pres patted his back to calm him down and interrupted him.

"We will respond to this record however we deem most appropriate," he told me, "and when we make that decision, I promise you you'll be among the very first to be notified."

I went back to L.A. to score and await the verdict. While I waited, the press placed a call to Ray's business manager, Gabe Reynolds, to see if what I'd told them was true: that we were prepared to buy back the rights. Reynolds refused to play along with my bluff and told them my offer was absolutely absurd. Then he turned around and called Ray to apprise him of the nature of my business dealings, the negligence of my behavior, and the fact that I seemed bent on bankrupting him and had come very close to ruining his recording future.

Ray, naturally, immediately called me.

"I'm supposed to tell you to be more diplomatic," he said, none too ruffled by his accountant's hysterics.

"I'm not a politician. This isn't politics," I told him. "This is rock 'n' roll! I didn't choose this line of work to be diplomatic. I chose it so I wouldn't have to be. Did Reynolds happen to mention whether Mercury has decided yet to promote the record?"

"No, he didn't happen to say anything about that."

"That fat fuck blew it! How am I supposed to do my job if he goes and contradicts me? Now I have to call them back and straighten everything out if that's possible. But I can't be effective if they know all they have to do is go around me and call your business manager. I'm willing to work with him, but he refuses to work with me. . . . One of us has to go."

It was a pretty bold statement to make, and I knew it; but I was fairly certain of my standing. Ray had known Gabe since the very earliest Doors days, true, and for years the Doors had been Gabe's largest and most successful client. Because of the Doors, he'd gone on to attract accounts like Chicago, Lou Adler, Cheech and Chong, and the film director Hal Ashby. But I also knew as of late he'd been devoting less and less time to Ray and more and more attention to Lou Adler's new house getting built in Malibu. When he did comment on Ray's career, it was usually to criticize what I had been doing to it.

Years before, I'd scored Morrison a lid of grass and at his instruction added the sum into the fan mail bill, which he initialed before it was sent off to Reynolds to be paid. Reynolds immediately noticed the discrepancy between the total number of letters and the total dollar sum and accused me of trying to rip off the Doors. Ever since then he'd been trying to convince anyone who would listen that I was a dishonest thief only interested in cheating the Doors out of money.

More recently he'd been trying to convince Ray I was a direct threat to his career. Ever since Iggy had mentioned to me his desire to make music with Ray (a proposal I regarded as nothing less than inspired), I'd been working on Ray in an attempt to get him interested in working with the Ig as well. The first time I brought up the possibility, Ray reacted with something akin to revulsion. But I persisted until Ray finally relented and agreed to some trial rehearsals when he was finished with his own solo tour to promote the upcoming album. In the meantime, since Iggy had no income whatsoever, I proposed to Ray he be put on a monthly retainer. Ray had readily agreed.

But Reynolds flipped out when he heard about it. "Oh, that's just wonderful! Now he's got you supporting his friends, too! He'll have you reduced to being Iggy Stooge's backup piano player before he's finished with you! He's ruining your career," he told Ray. "If you were smart, you'd get a real manager who would have you associating with people worthy of your stature as a musician, people like Billy Preston or Richard Carpenter, people, professionals who are your equal! I won't stand idly by and let this maniac destroy your life. . . ."

There was nothing he could do. I, however, could begin looking for a new accountant.

Within a week the record company execs had made up their collective minds and announced a respectable, if not exactly confident, first-print run and a tentative release date for the new LP. They even committed to a budget to advertise and promote it—not a huge amount, but decent, especially considering we had next to nothing to start with. In return, all I had to do was deliver the masters (which I did) and guarantee a tour (which I did). I was promised confirmation in writing within a few days from the L.A. office. We also hired a new business manager. He was young, long-haired, smart, hip, and, best of all, in all the years I would know him for, he never once asked me to be more diplomatic. And then I fired Gabe Reynolds. It felt good.

A week later I still hadn't received the letter I'd been expecting from Mercury, confirming what the execs had verbally promised me over the phone. Even more frustrating, I couldn't get the head of the L.A. office on the phone to find out what was holding it up. Whenever I called, I was told he was out to lunch or in a meeting or had already left for the day. Each time I was told he'd call me back. When almost two weeks had passed and we still hadn't spoken and he hadn't returned one of my calls, I told his secretary if he didn't call me back within the hour, I'd be down there in person to confront him. I waited half an hour, took a black beauty to get the adrenaline flowing, and then left to find him.

I walked past the receptionist, past two painters and some workmen, and straight into his office, and when he wasn't there, I terrified half the staff, demanding I be told where he was hiding. No one answered me. After opening every door on the floor, I finally came to the record library, which was closed and locked. I knocked on the door. *"I know you're in there! I've looked everywhere else, you gotta be in there, because I didn't see you walk past me!"* No answer. The whole office staff was jammed around and behind me waiting to see what happened next.

I banged the door. Still no answer. I took off one of my clogs and banged the heel on the door as hard as I could. "WHY DON'T YOU ANSWER MY CALLS, YOU CHICKENSHIT?" I pounded some more. "IS THAT ANY WAY TO DO BUSINESS? YOU CALL ME *UNPROFESSIONAL*? YOU PATHETIC LITTLE SHIT! I SUPPOSE THIS IS WHAT YOU CALL REAL MATURE, *DIPLOMATIC* BEHAVIOR, ISN'T IT?"

He didn't say anything, but I could hear him breathing through the locked door. I went back into his office and looked for something destructive to do. I pulled his stereo down from the shelf and smashed it onto the floor and threw a few records out of their covers. When I couldn't find anything else, I went back down the hall to where I'd passed the workmen on the way in and asked them if I could borrow hammer and nails, then I went back into the office where I nailed my clogs to his desktop, along with a gold Bachman-Turner LP and a little note which read: "I KNOW WHERE YOU LIVE. CALL ME."

By the next afternoon, registered mail, I received, in writing, the promise to promote I'd been waiting for. Everything was contingent on the "artist" touring in support of the "product." Now all I had to do was find a tour.

* * *

We'd all been getting high and staying high for weeks on end. Hanging on to the nod, chins on chests, eyes pinned at half-mast . . . I'd found a booking agency to handle the tour-booking chores and other than call every few days to make sure it was on top of things, my time was my own to do as I pleased.

What pleased Tiffany was trying to get as fucked up as humanly possible and then see which personality might emerge. Trouble and fun were pretty synonymous in her head.

Iggy didn't even have to bother trying. Trouble followed him naturally.

Me? I was up for *anything*. I'd been developing what might be called a method to this madness, or maybe it was more of a goal. Whereas before, I was content to keep getting higher and higher until I passed out, I had recently discovered a strategically placed point en route to oblivion: Big Blue, a visceral experience, not merely hallucinogenic, though it was that, too, an expanse of openness of azure, warm and liquid, within and without, a sort of celestial womb, a veritable trance garden spot. I could float within it for what seemed hours but was probably more like a couple of minutes, pass contentment and nod and into the sphere of gratitude, grace itself.

I discovered it by accident at first, just a quick flash of silvery blue that filled my head, and passed it by much too quickly on my way to unconsciousness. But with practice I was getting better at catching it for longer and longer periods of time.

Of course, intentionally bombing yourself out on the strongest narcotic known to man and approaching death in order to jump off just before the final station had its drawbacks—like dying, for instance. Still, I thought the payoff was worth it, and I approached it with a confident recklessness whenever I got the chance.

I was lying on the bed doing dope and trying to catch the train that would take me to Big Blue. After an hour of trying, my eyes finally fluttered shut, and I entered the Land of Nod. Inky shadows hung among great gnarled and knotted leafy trees. All at once the tree trunk convulsed, the leaves jettisoned; the sky turned from the blue I was seeking to jet black, covered with a million crazed bird wings flying, flapping hysterically against me, into my face, talons clawing my cheeks. Drawing my hands before my face in protection, I frightened myself awake.

I snorted some more.

I went off again, this time drifting calmly down a shallow, crystal-clear stream. Smooth, small, round rocks covered the floor as I flowed down through the silvery current; minnows floated and dashed by me. The current quickened, the minnows' fins turned sharp, armor hard. The gully of the riverbed took a quick, steep turn downward. I looked up through the water and saw the sky, the Blue, but I couldn't get out of the current. The gully twisted again, turned at an absurdly illogical angle. I was tossed with it, going down, the once-smooth rocks now rough and uneven, rushing past; ugly, contorted fish with bulging eyes kept slapping against me. All at once everything was tossed into a huge V-shaped gutter, chrome, bright and hard. I couldn't reach the sides to stop myself or pull out. The sides were growing higher and harder and razor-sharp at the edges. I was going down, down . . . enveloped, tossed about. I couldn't breathe, and the water was changing from clear to a muddy brown. Now I had trouble seeing what was brushing beside me, and I was really getting frightened. The water was turning into blood red, warm and thick, pouring down. I felt something at my feet, brushing up my body until it rolled past my face—a baby's head, with eyes alive and pleading, tongue bloated and pale, touching me, faster . . . intestines wrapped about my arms, my legs, darting down my throat . . . strong hands clutching, pulling. I was falling and I couldn't move, I couldn't breathe . . . faster and faster and faster . . . until I shuddered violently awake.

"Jesus, you scared the shit out of me," Tiffany said, sitting on the bed beside me.

"I scared you?" I asked. "What's going on?"

Jesse's face leaned over next to hers, and he patted my shoulder. "You're gonna be all right, man." Then to Tiffany he said, "Maybe I better give him some more just to make sure he doesn't nod out again." He stuck a needle into my arm, and . . . it sure wasn't heroin. . . . Cocaine . . . I felt the roar building deep inside my brain and the mule kick to my heart.

Five minutes later I was gritting my teeth and pacing the room, making phone calls, trying to find a drug to bring me down.

"We don't have any more money," Tiffany said.

"What do you mean? What happened to all the money on the bureau?"

"I gave it to Jesse for the coke."

"What? For how much?"

"About a whole gram before you woke up."

Well, I thought, that explains why everything started getting so

309

fast during the nod. He probably hit me with it just as I was hitting the turn where things got violent.

"Thanks a lot," I said. "You scared the shit out of me," I told her. "I won't get to sleep until dawn now."

"I shoulda just let you OD, huh? You'd rather be dead, I suppose."

"At least I'd be asleep."

"You'd be *dead*."

"At least I wouldn't be *wired*. I feel like I'm ready to go climb Mount Rushmore."

"Enjoy it," Jesse said. "It's pure flake."

"I *hate* it," I told him.

He shrugged. "Well, I really should be going," he said.

"Not with my money, you shouldn't be!"

"Now wait a second, I sold you a gram."

"So you say. How do I know that?"

"Because *you* did it!" he said.

"So you say," I pointed out.

"Ask Tiffany," he told me.

"How do I know the two of you aren't in on this thing together? I wouldn't put it past either of you."

"She told me to bring it over," he whined.

"Well, then, let her pay for it," I told him.

"No way," Tiffany said.

"C'mon, man, lighten up, she was worried about you. She was afraid you were dying."

"Aw, fuck, come on, Jess, give me the money back. I'll pay you tomorrow, but let me get something else to bring me down. I feel like someone shoved a box of fizzies up my ass. I swear to God, I feel like I'm gonna explode if I don't get something down in me quick."

"That's not my problem," he said, backing up to the bedroom door. "That's the breaks."

"Okay," I said in a reasonable voice, moving toward him, "I tried being reasonable, tried being adult about this," and as I was going to pull open the door and let him out, he said, "I'm really sorry . . ."

"*Sorry, my ass!*" I yelled, grabbing his neck. "Now I try brute force!" and knocked his forehead into the door. "Give me back my fucking money, or I'll turn your skull into mush!"

"Tiffany, stop him!" he cried.

"No way, José, I'm staying out of this. . . ."

"Oh, great, *now* you stay out," he moaned.

"Come on, Danny, stop it, that really hurts," he said as I continued thumping his head into the door.

"Not until you give me my money back, you little dick . . . selling me cocaine when I'm not even conscious to close the deal, you little sleaze, it would serve you right if I gave you a face fulla splinters. . . ." I knocked his forehead against the door one more time.

"I was just trying to help," he said between thumps. "I don't know what you're so pissed off about."

"If I want your help, I'll ask for your help. . . . I was asleep, and *you* woke me up!"

"I saved your life! You should thank me!" he said.

"Shut the fuck up! I should kill you! First you sell it to me when I don't even know about it, and then you wake me up! What kind of business maneuver do you call that, huh?" I yelled, pushing my knee into the small of his back. I hit his hair, I was so wound up.

"What kind of shit sleaze piece of dreck lowlife hustler con artist pulls a move like that? What do you take me for? Give me my goddamn money back. . . ."

"Okay, okay, let me go, and I'll give you your money. . . ."

"No, you give me the money, and *then* I'll let you go."

"All right, all right." He reached into his back pocket and threw the money to the floor. "Gawd, what an asshole," he moaned.

I picked up my money. He rubbed his neck.

"Anything else?" he asked. "Can I leave now?"

"Sure, unless you happen to have any sleepers you want to sell me?"

He shook his head and walked out of the house.

Zola didn't want people coming over to his pad to score anymore because it had been getting too hot with the heat, so he'd begun making deliveries instead. That was nice because it saved me a drive to his house, and I hated driving when I was holding heroin. It wasn't smart. And jail, as I'd discovered already, was an experience I could do without.

The only problem was lately we'd been calling him so much and so consistently at such inconvenient hours and he'd been making so many deliveries to Wonderland, one night we all kind of mutually agreed it would be much better and easier if he just stayed with us for a while. So what I had then was, basically, a very nice house full of a lot of very nice but very stoned, very sloppy, and often very sick junkies.

311

It didn't take more than a week for the arrangement to deteriorate into total absurdity. Even Pamela, who was there less than anybody else and who loved dope as much as the next guy, said, "This is getting to be *real* excessive," and this from a gal who'd known excess firsthand for years. I agreed with her. Enough was enough.

I not only wanted to cool my dope intake but wanted my house back and in shape. Everyone who lived there was a slob, and just to complicate matters, Tiffany had adopted a stray dog. Since I'd cut out the maid so I could have more money for drugs, the house had become quite messy. I couldn't summon the energy to clean it up. For a while I'd stayed on top of it. But keeping house was a full-time job with these guys. Plus being a drug addict was a full-time job. So I needed to conserve energy wherever I could. I figured if I didn't clean up after them, sooner or later they'd have to start cleaning up after themselves. But of course, no one else did anything, so Wonderland just got worse.

It was really a wonder we hadn't had a fire yet. You tend to smoke a lot of cigarettes on heroin. Well, you light a lot of cigarettes; you don't actually get the chance to inhale because you're always drifting off to nod land. You spend more time dropping and picking them up than you do smoking, and each time you drop one, you burn a little round hole wherever it falls. As a result, there were about a thousand little holes on every couch, sheet, and carpet in the house.

A firm date had been set for the album's release, and it was my job to let the world know all about it. It was time to throw a party: a combination promotional bash and a last-chance blowout for the Wonderland Bums. Then I'd throw everybody out, lock up the house, go away with Tiffany to the desert or somewhere for a few days, and dry out.

I *had* to clean up. Ray was going to be leaving on tour soon, and the way I understood it, as the manager/publicist I was expected to accompany him. He'd also let me know in no uncertain terms he wouldn't have a junkie managing him, and he didn't know the half of it. Once in a while was one thing, he said, but this snorting-smack-every-day crap had got to go. I told him not to worry, everything was under control.

The party officially started early Wednesday night. We had two bars, one indoors, one outdoors. The invitation we'd printed up read "From 9 P.M. until?" Naturally I assumed everybody would assume I meant sometime that same night, but no such understanding was forthcoming. We sent out over 150 invitations to every rock critic, DJ, musician, editor, publicist, and program director in Hollywood. To show success hadn't gone to my head, I even invited my father. I figured there was even the off chance he might show and be impressed with what I'd thus far accomplished. By 10:00 P.M. Wednesday somebody counted around 500 people in and around Wonderland.

Around 11:00 Zola and Jesse got the vials of China White and cocaine mixed up, and nobody could tell which was what anymore. Shaun Cassidy hurried home to his mother's house. Alice Cooper held tightly to his can of Bud. Pat from Epic got so wasted he backed his Mercedes through the neighbor's wall and into their pool. MacKenzie Phillips curled up and passed out in the unlit fireplace. Paul from *Rock* magazine never even made it home. Someone found him OD'd in his car, just sitting at the wheel, key in the ignition, engine idling. No one wanted the party busted, so unbeknownst to me, a few people took it upon themselves to release the parking brake and give Paul a push off down Wonderland, making it look like an accident when the car crashed at the bottom of the hill. His girlfriend Gwen wasn't real pleased about it when she went out and saw the car gone and thought he'd left without her. She came back inside and eventually passed out before she learned the truth. John Carpenter, an old friend of Morrison's and currently the editor of the *L.A. Free Press*, was asleep on his feet, bottle of tequila in hand.

Dozens of people stood staring into space, many dazed and sick. Both bathrooms, upstairs and down, were full and locked with lines waiting. People were puking in practically every corner of the house. Actually that helped empty the place out a bit.

Around midnight my father surprised me by showing up with Joe. Within sixty seconds of their arrival Tiffany came over to meet them and, by way of a greeting, puked in the vicinity of Dad's left loafer. And then here comes Iggy, stumbling in our direction, with his big blue eyes gurgling in their sockets, pupils pinned like piss holes in the snow. His balls were falling out of his faded blue jeans, which were ripped from ankle to groin, and he had to keep pushing them back. Despite an inclination to do otherwise, I introduced my father to my friend.

So there's Iggy, holding his nuts back with his left hand, pumping my father's outstretched hand with his other one and telling my dad, "You've got a fine son, Mr. Sugerman, a fine fine son."

Dad just looked at me, right past Iggy, and with a voice filled more with regret than shock said, "So this is what you dropped out of college for?" Then he turned on his heel and, without so much as a good-bye, left Wonderland. My brother just shrugged as if to say, "I'm sorry, but this is no longer reconcilable," and followed him out.

Ray showed up next and started to leave less than a half hour later. He stayed just long enough to make an appearance and to have some photos taken before he headed to the front door. I tried to stop him.

"Where are you going?" I asked. "You just got here."

"Home," he said. "Now."

"Oh, come on, Ray, don't go, stay, it's just starting, it's *your* party, why are you leaving?"

He looked me in the eye and said, "I don't want to be here when the cops come."

That appealed to my newly acquired professional sense of managerial responsibility. "Good idea," I said, patting his back. "You better go."

When I finally went to sleep around 4:00 P.M. Thursday, there were still about thirty people in the house. When I woke up twelve hours later, the first thing I did was kick out the fifteen or so people who remained and, it appeared, liked my house just fine and wouldn't mind moving in. Second thing I did was take a few wake-up snorts to get rid of the cramps and sweats. Lastly, I called the cleaning crew to get rid of the worst mess I'd ever seen, indoors and out.

For the rest of the day Tiffany and I watched the cleaners carry out the broken barstools, bottles, cans, dozens of trash bags full of garbage. Then another crew came in and washed down the backyard, repaired the windows, got rid of the vomit, shampooed the carpets, got the stains off the walls, patched up a few holes, pulled the champagne corks out of the ceiling, and took care of the various other necessary repairs. After they left, the painters came in and made everything the right color again. Abbey Rents Furniture came by to pick up its bar equipment and all the chairs it'd rented us. A maid was the last one to come over to fine-tune everything, dust, clean the windows, and take care of whatever had been missed.

I didn't know where either Iggy or Zola were, and I wasn't about to wait around to find out.

Tiffany and I grabbed some jackets and swimsuits, mixed up what I sincerely believed was the last of the heroin and cocaine and had a speedball for the road, hopped in the Cobra, and, before anything else could go wrong, headed east to Palm Springs to recover and dry out.

* * *

We stayed in the Springs just over a day and a half. Tiffany had snuck up a half gram of smack, for which I was equally grateful and pissed. We snorted it the first morning when we woke up sick at the hotel.

"Guess what I have?" she said, hand out, foil packages in palm.

By the time the effects had worn off, we were on our way home, speeding back to Laurel Canyon to get high. We stopped midway and called Zola to make sure he was home and it was cool to drop by. After we scored, we hurried to Wonderland. That's where we found Iggy.

Actually we saw the mess first. We couldn't have missed it if our eyes had been closed; we would have smelled it, would have stepped in it. It began at the front door and continued down the hall: chicken bones, eggshells, and crayons. The volume of garbage increased as we neared the kitchen. Crusts of whole wheat bread, Saran wrap out of the box, unrolled across the floor, coming to rest at a broken mayonnaise jar, more broken eggs. The refrigerator was facedown against the bar counter, contents spilling and dripping out. The toaster was flipped over and open, and there were three slices of burned toast, cold, inside. The oven door was open, and on top all four pilot lights were out. Nothing was lit. The house reeked of gas. Had we decided at that moment we wanted a cigarette and lit a match, we would have created a crater on Wonderland Avenue. And there on the floor, not more than six inches away from a broken jar of the Skippy crunchy peanut butter for which he was so well known, facedown and bare-ass naked, lay my hero and friend. Iggy had pulled similar *Cat in the Hat* stunts at my house before, but never this severe.

People have asked me, "Well, what did you expect, inviting Iggy Pop to come and live in your guest room?" I didn't expect the volume and the consistency of the destruction he created. It was never malicious. I half expected maliciousness. But it never was. It was a definite lack of self-control, which I sympathized with, and it happened only when he was too stoned to know what he was doing (and consequently seldom remembered doing, come the next day). Lately he'd been taking excessive amounts of downers and was becoming increasingly spotty in terms of physical coordination. But I was used to excessive behavior. The only way to deal with it was to ignore it. If you didn't, and you made the mistake of letting people know they were getting to you, it only made things worse. They'd feel guilty and go get stoned and go do something even worse, or they'd get mad at you for telling them how to run their life and go out and do something twice as bad, or sometimes worst of all, they'd try to make it up to you and really destroy your sense of justice. Either way, acknowledgment of the deed only brought more of it. I had learned these truths from watching Morrison test everybody within yelling distance. I'd gotten pretty good at keeping my mouth shut, loving the person while silently abhorring the behavior and cleaning up the mess.

But when I saw Iggy lying in the middle of a garbage dump, that used to be my kitchen floor, something inside me snapped. I stomped over to the sink and pulled out a canister of Ajax from underneath it. I slammed it down on the cutting board and sliced off the top and proceeded to dump Ajax over Iggy and the neighboring area. I turned on the sink. Nothing. I turned the other faucet. It was broken. He'd managed, I don't know how, to break the plumbing in the sink.

I raced outside, grabbed the hose, ran back into the kitchen, and yelled to Tiffany to turn it on, aiming the nozzle at his platinum blond-with-mayonnaise-and-peanut-butter head.

"Turn it on!" I yelled again. She was giggling. "It's not funny!" I screamed.

"C'mon, Danny, you're not gonna do that to him. Cut it out. I'll help you clean it up. . . ."

"No! Not this time. Not anymore. Look at this! He bitches when we don't have any food, then he spends the money I give him for food on drugs, which he doesn't even share with us, so I go shopping, I pay for our drugs *and* I share them with him, I get the house cleaned, I mop the goddamn floor myself, and *look what he does! Just look at him*! I don't even see a plate anywhere. Do you see a plate? I don't think he got anything in his mouth. . . ."

Tiffany quietly stepped over a puddle of milk and a half loaf of bread, kicked over a collage of sandwich meats and some three-week-old coleslaw. There was the plate. Or, to be exact, half a plate. God knew where the other half was.

"That does it! Turn on the hose!"

"You're really an asshole sometimes, you know that? Some way to treat a friend."

I was indignant. "I'm an asshole? I'm surrounded by fucking morons. Between you, him, and the dog, I feel like I'm running a goddamn pet shop. All I do is clean up around here. There's food on the floor, shit in the hallway, and you call me an asshole for reacting like a goddamn human being."

"He'll kill you. . . ." She giggled.

"No. No, he won't. He won't touch me. He won't be here. Besides, I think he's already dead."

He hadn't moved since we'd come home.

"Don't say that," Tiffany warned me. "He could be, you know."

"No such wild luck. He's just passed out," I reassured her. "Can you imagine how much time and energy it takes to make a mess like this? Hours! It must have taken a half hour alone just to empty the refrigerator; turning it over must have taken a real burst of energy. He's gotta be exhausted. Now, turn that hose on," I said, aiming it back at his head.

She didn't. She wouldn't. So I did. I sprayed as much of the garbage up and around Iggy as I could. Then using him as a sort of rotating stop block and mop, I got the shovel out of the service pantry and piled everything into the sink where the garbage disposal was. I hosed him down and poured the rest of the Ajax out and wiped up the floor, holding him by the ankles. I can still see those blue specks dissolving in that platinum hair of his. I was almost done mopping up when he began to come to.

By this time Tiffany was in the hallway, stupid with laughter. It was probably her laughing which woke him up. He wasn't immediately aware of what was happening.

"Call me a cab, think you can do that?" I asked Tiffany.

"You're a cab." She laughed.

"Very funny. Now would you call a fucking cab and tell it to hurry up?"

"What for?"

"Just call the cab company, Tiffany, and get one over here as fast as possible."

We got Iggy into a bathrobe, stuck a pack of Camels filterless in the breast pocket, and, when the cab pulled up, carried him outside. He still wasn't coherent enough to disagree.

After we had dumped him in the back seat, the driver asked us, "What's wrong with him?"

"Omnipotent, self-destructive, narcissistic disorder, I think," I said.

"What do you want me to do about it?"

"Just drive," I told him. "All you have to do is drive him."

"Where to?"

"Anywhere," I said. "North." I handed him a hundred-dollar bill. "Go as far north as this will take you, stop fifteen, twenty bucks short, and then shove him out wherever you are." I stuck another fifty in with Iggy's cigarettes. Enough to help him, but not enough to allow him to return too soon.

The driver gave me an odd look, but he took the money and started off in the general direction of the San Fernando mountains.

Two days later, at 5:00 A.M., we were awakened by a furious banging on the front door. "Oh, who the fuck can that be?" I wondered.

Tiffany contributed a typical positive thought: "One of your asshole friends, no doubt."

"Sssshhh, listen," I said to her. We both began giggling.

Someone was outside, screaming, "I don't think it's funny; I'm not laughing, let me in, goddammit! Open this goddamn door!" Iggy had come home.

"See," Tiffany announced "I was right."

With the tour scheduled to begin in less than thirty days there wasn't much left for me to do more important than getting straight. But what I hadn't thought would be much of a problem was turning out to be a major obstacle. I had the desire to stop, but I lacked the willpower. I must have started to kick four or five times, but after two or three hours of withdrawal symptoms, I ran off to get high again. I was always finding excuses to put it off. Here's a partial list:

1. I don't have time to be sick. I need to be clear when I answer and work on the phones.
2. It's too cold.
3. It's too hot.
4. It's too nice a day to kick and be sick. I'll wait till it rains.
5. The rain depresses me, I'll stop just as soon as the sun comes out.
6. Just one more time won't hurt. I'll stop right after that.
7. Friday's coming up, and I have a lot of work to do Friday. I should wait for the weekend and kick then.
8. I can't sleep without it.
9. I can't stay awake without it. I get too drowsy and can't work.
10. I should stop slowly, a little at a time. It won't be so hard that way, and I won't get so sick.
11. It's better to do the drug and get it over with rather than think about it all the time.
12. Tiffany doesn't want to stop, and I can't have it around

without doing it. I don't want to kick without Tiffany here, so I can't quit now.

13. Ray wants me to stop, but he can't make me. I'll offer him some next time he brings it up, and we'll have a nice long conversation about it.

14. Heroin has removed all desire for booze. I shouldn't drink anyway, and heroin isn't as bad for me as alcohol is. I've never crashed a car just on heroin but gotten in several accidents because of booze.

15. William Burroughs took it for years, and it doesn't seem to have harmed him any.

16. I need it. I used to need Ritalin, and now I need heroin. I have a faulty body chemistry that is correctable only by heroin.

17. I'll quit tomorrow.

So you can see the difficulty I had whenever I set some time aside to kick the stuff.

I wasn't feeling real good about leaving my house in the hands of a nigger-fag-junkie, a high school B-movie actress, and a punk rock superstar, so I called my black athlete buddy from high school, Todd, and asked him to house-sit for me. I figured as a gymnast he might be able to ride herd for me while I was on tour. As a fledgling photographer, he could use the money I'd pay him and the rent he wouldn't have to pay.

I arranged with Ray to meet the band in San Francisco right after they played their warm-up dates, where my presence wasn't really required. It made sense professionally, and it made sense personally —I still had my habit to deal with. I planned things so the time to kick would be the week Ray was breaking the band in on the first week of his tour. In other words, I waited until the very last minute, and then I had to get off.

As it happened, things didn't work out as planned. The record company broke almost every single promise it'd made. When confronted, the executives merely shrugged their suited shoulders and said, "We lied," as if that explained everything. It came down to me to make sure the records were in the stores and writers had their copies and were on the guest lists at the gigs; that the radio stations had records and the promoters advertised the shows and the agency was booking the tour in a reasonable routing (like not scheduling

Dallas, Boston, New Orleans, Philadelphia, Oregon, Atlanta one right after the other), and so forth and so on, ad infinitum. So there was not a lot of time to kick heroin after all.

What was surprising was the degree to which I became effective in the work that needed to be done. It was almost as if to compensate for my lack of ability to do anything about my primary problem— i.e., drugs—I concentrated my attention on things I could do something about. Meanwhile, my habit just became proportionally worse.

I did make it to the opening in San Francisco, with a pocket full of smack and only for the night. I promised Ray, the road manager, and the rest of the crew I'd hook up with them in Dallas, a week and a half down the road. Back in L.A., a reporter friend of mine knew someone who was an acupuncturist who claimed he could alleviate the body's withdrawal symptoms by activating the endorphin hormone—that is, the body's own painkilling ingredient, an opiate a thousand times stronger than morphine that's secreted by the pituitary gland. When I asked the guy if he was qualified to be sticking needles into my ear and knee, he asked me if I was qualified to be sticking them in my arm. I told him I didn't do that. "You will be," he said. And then he told me an amazing story.

Seems he'd been in jail, convicted for something or other, when he began to meditate. ("There was nothing else to do," he told me.) Apparently he got pretty good at it, and it wasn't long before he started having out-of-body experiences and remembering past lives. He kept his spiritual activities up until one day he came across a past life he'd lived as an ancient Chinese acupuncturist. When he came down from his journey, he remembered not only the life but all the knowledge he had accumulated during it. He also discovered his brown hair had turned white. He showed me his driver's license picture where it was still brown. Anyway, he said he was working on his acupuncturist license, that he'd already taken the test and passed without any homework preparation, just what he'd remembered via meditation and yoga.

He not only looked spiritual with his flowing white beard and hair, but resonated serenity. I'm a sucker to begin with—Dad always told me I trusted people too easily—so I trusted him completely. The only drag was I actually had to start getting sick before he could treat me. Tiffany and I went out for one last blowout, and when I woke up sick, rather than roll over and reach for the mirror, I picked up the phone and called him, which I thought was ultraresponsible and committed of me.

He came right over with his little black cigar box-like contraption with two black knobs on top and lots of thin black and red (black for left, red for right) wires running out of it, hooking up to long, hin needles at the end. He stuck about fifteen needles into each ear and down in my knees and even two on the sides of each elbow. Talk about wired. Then, with the box sitting on my lap, he had me turn the knobs very slowly. This created a vibrating sensation not altogether painful, unless you turned them too far too fast (in which case you got vibed to death), but not altogether pleasant either. Theoretically the vibrations cleaned out my energy "meridians" and got my body producing endorphins that had been depleted. What happened, he told me, is that when you start taking heroin, your body stops making its own opiate, or endorphin. The more heroin you take, the less your body makes—that was why I was getting a resistance—until finally one day your body isn't making hardly any endorphin and you're just taking heroin to feel normal. After you stop taking heroin, it takes your body awhile to realize what has happened and start making the juice again. That's what he was helping it do. Sort of a pituitary-gland jump start.

Within five minutes of the first treatment I was already feeling better. At the end of twenty, at which time he pulled the needles out, I was feeling not only fine but great. The whole shebang really worked. For about eight hours. Then I felt like I'd walked off the edge of a cliff. My energy level dropped, my gut felt like I'd been punched out, and I had to run to the bathroom I got diarrhea so bad. Before I could even get to the phone to call him, he was at the front door.

"How did you know . . ." I started to ask him.

"I knew about this time you'd be ready for another treatment." We repeated the procedure, and magically all the symptoms disappeared again.

Next morning I was sick all over again, and again, instead of calling Zola, I called him. This time he brought over a protein drink he'd made specially for me, which almost made me sick all by itself it tasted so bad. He took me for walks through the canyon, and we talked about lots of different things.

At the end of the fourth day he told me he had to go to Aspen to give some movie star a "tune-up." After he finished what had to be my last treatment, he said he was worried about me.

"We should continue for at least another three or four days," he told me. "Are you sure you're gonna be okay?"

I told him I was sure, even though I wasn't, but I wasn't worried about it either. I felt fine at the time. And when you're feeling fine, you don't realize how horrible it is to be sick.

When I tried to pay him, he refused my offer.

"I can't take your money," he told me. "Let's just say we're even, karmicly speaking. You don't owe me anything."

I was confused. "But you didn't owe me anything," I pointed out.

"I feel better not taking anything from you. My reward is seeing you well again."

I'd never met anybody like this, someone who wouldn't take money when it was offered to him.

That evening I boarded the plane to meet Ray and the band in Dallas. I was feeling wonderful through the flight and celebrated by tying on my first drunk in over two months. At the gig, still feeling no pain, I drank some more—much more. Come the next morning, this boy had a hangover the likes of which you can't even begin to imagine. I tried to convince myself that's all it was, just a hangover, as I dragged myself down to the bar to cure it, but inside, I knew: This was postwithdrawal *compounded* by a vicious hangover.

For the next two weeks I stayed loaded, taking every pill and powder I could lay my hands on. And on the road the diversions, chemical as well as sexual, were plentiful. I was perpetually weak and exhausted and began doing enormous quantities of cocaine to keep up with the pace of the tour. When Ray wasn't doing interviews, he insisted on going out and dragging me along to every museum and art gallery within a thirty-mile radius.

In Atlanta, during one of the shows, I walked onstage and actually asked the audience if they had any drugs for a dope-sick manager. I was bombarded with joints, vials, and pills. A five-gallon pickle jar full of amyl nitrate was rolled onstage against my feet. I picked it up, along with everything else, and put it over my shoulder, and walked back into the wings as the band went into the next song.

In New Orleans I scored a bundle of bootleg Quaaludes and proceeded to drool and foam. Every fifteen minutes Ray would remind me, "Wipe your mouth; every five minutes just remember to wipe your mouth," and he handed me a handkerchief.

By Philadelphia I was so fucked up they were having me met by a wheelchair at the airplane and wheeled through the terminal to the limousine.

"Lookit," I tried to explain to Ray during the ride to the hotel, "I'm afraid this isn't working out. . . ."

"Wipe your mouth," Ray said.

"You don't need me, I'm just a burden. There's nothing that needs to be done that I can't do from home."

"Well, see if you can hang in until we get to New York. Then you can leave."

"Then I can go home and we can save some money," I pointed out. Ray looked doubtful. He knew what I was going home for. As far as saving was concerned, I'd been functioning with as much discipline as I could muster under the circumstances, trying to keep the expenses down among the band and crew. Then one day in New Orleans Ray suddenly rented a helicopter to fly him out to some art gallery auction, where he bought a picture of a fucking *bird* for a small fortune.

"But, Ray"—I had tried to reason with him when it was already too late—"this tour is already losing close to five grand a week."

"Don't worry about it. It's a good investment; it's an Audubon."

"I don't care if you bought a whole interstate, Ray! How am I supposed to tell the bass player not to call his girlfriend in L.A. and charge it to the room when you go and whisk yourself off and spend a fortune on a fucking bird picture?"

"An *Audubon*"—he corrected me—"for a few grand."

"Whatever . . . I'm trying to get Buck and Chub to excess baggage the equipment to save money." Buck and Chub were our two roadies, Chuck and Bub out of Detroit, two of the meanest, strongest motherfuckers you'd want to meet. Also two of the loyalest employees a guy could have. There was nothing they would not do for either me or Ray, and so far on this tour they had already carried me out of at least four clubs and two or three airports. Totally selfless, hardworking guys. "They're pinching pennies driving whenever they can—how is this going to look?"

"So you want to fly home and save us money, is that what you're saying? To make up for the personal investment I made?"

"Something like that . . ."

"After New York . . ."

"Right, after New York . . ."

"Wipe your mouth."

From Philadelphia we went on to Boston. I was going nuts I wanted heroin so badly. I could not get the stuff out of my mind for two consecutive minutes. I hung around a local methadone program center I'd looked up in the phone book, but it was closed for the day. I found the closest NA (Narcotics Anonymous) meeting and had the limousine pull up and wait outside while I checked out what was going on inside. I really felt like some sort of spy walking in there, looking for a connection. But I found what I was looking for. In the back row was a guy nodding out. To make sure he wasn't just sleeping, I nudged him. His eyes were constricted to a pinhead.

"When you got some time, I want to talk to you," I whispered to him. "I'll be outside." Then I went out and waited in the limousine.

A few minutes later the meeting ended, and when I saw him walk out, I put down the car window. "Over here," I called.

I was in luck. Not only was he involved in the music business, but he'd been dealing to Steve Tyler and Joe Perry of Aerosmith, and he knew where to get some dope, right away. I began salivating. By the time the car pulled up at his connect's apartment I was breaking out into a cold sweat, having miniwithdrawals at just the thought. I could taste the stuff dripping down my throat. . . .

I gave him six hundred bucks, all the money I had.

I stayed in the hotel room for the next three days and nights and snorted myself into a twenty-four-hour-a-day nod. I was in smack heaven. I didn't know it at the time, but my honeymoon with heroin had just about come to an end. By the time we left Boston for New York my resistance was up all the way to where it had been when I had quit two and a half weeks before. What had taken me six months to accomplish six months ago took me just three days this time. In other words, my habit picked up right where I'd left off.

As did my craving. By the time we arrived in New York I was more than ready to score again. I'd read about the heroin supermarket in Harlem around Lexington and 125th Street, and before I even unpacked, I was in the lobby of the hotel trying to get a cabbie who would take me all the way uptown. After two "No way," one "Get outta here," and one "Not this Jew, Jack," I found a driver who agreed to take me into Harlem, and back for fifty bucks. I knew we were getting close when I saw a sign in a coffee shop window that read NO JUNKIES ALLOWED.

It could have said, WELCOME. I asked the cabbie to slow down. As he did so, a dozen or so black guys began jamming around the cab, knocking on the window. I rolled it down and asked, "What's up?" The driver stopped, and more people came running up. "Don't stop!" I yelled at him, panicking and getting the window up as quickly as possible.

He unlocked the back doors. "Get out!" he yelled at me. "You want to get yourself killed, get out of my cab."

"No, no, *go!*" I told him; but he wouldn't move, and the door was yanked open. I had no choice. I got out.

A cute little black kid with red high-top tennies grabbed my hand and pulled me out of the crowd. A few of the guys protested, "Don't go with no kid, man. Come with a man." But the kid seemed the most harmless, so I let him lead.

On the sidewalk he laid it out for me. "You looking for some coke, man, got some fine cocaine, m'man. How about some reefer? Want some weed?"

I shook my head at each offer. "Know about any downtown?"

"My man, you come to the right boy. You want some her-on, I take care you, come on wid me."

He led, I followed, feeling distinctly self-conscious, the only white face in the crowd. I followed him up the street and around the corner. He stopped before a dark doorway. There was one concrete step up and then nothing but darkness. I peered inside, but I couldn't see anything. He went in in front of me. I started to follow. "No, wait," he told me. I still couldn't see anything, including him, but from where he was, facing me and the sidewalk and the street behind me, he could see everything just fine.

I felt something blunt jabbing me in the vicinity of my groin.

"Gimme wotcha got," I heard him say. I thought he meant the money to score. I peeled off a fifty, just to be safe. If it was good, I could always get some more. *You can't be too careful copping on the street*, I thought.

"*Alla it,*" he said, poking me again. I looked down and saw the reflection of something silver, this time directly on my nuts.

"Gimme yer gold or I blow yer fuggin' balls outta yer asshole, white boy." I felt him poke again, and this time I saw the muzzle of a gun, a big gun, almost as big as he was tall.

I gave him all my money. Sixteen hundred bucks. He was so happy he was dropping it on the street as he ran away, laughing like a fuggin' hyena.

At the hotel there was a message from Todd. When I got him on the phone back at Wonderland, he sounded on the verge of a nervous breakdown.

"I've got to get out of here," he cried. "I can't take this anymore. Please tell me I can go."

325

Poor stable Todd, I thought, *succumbing to the Laurel Canyon curse*.

"It can't be that bad," I said.

"Iggy is a total slob," he complained. "You know he hasn't used the bathroom once to piss? He just hangs it out an open window and goes. He's already rotted all the paint around the kitchen window. Plus, he leaves his dishes and his buggers everywhere, and I have to clean up because you left me in charge, and Tiffany," he sputtered, "Tiffany is almost as bad. She took me out and got me drunk at Palms last night and we were supposed to go to the Whisky, where your name was on the list, and she ditched me at Palms and went to the Whisky and used your name, so by the time I got there I couldn't get in."

"Where is she now?" I asked. "Is she there?"

"No, thank God. She went to New Mexico with some holy man and she took that damn dog with her, too. . . . Do me a favor, please, come home. I can't take it here much longer. I'm either going to have a breakdown or become an alcoholic." I guess my acupuncturist decided he wanted some form of payment after all.

"Is Jim there?"

I got Iggy on the phone and told him to behave. "If you can't find it in you to use the toilet, at least piss out a back window. And just because Todd is black is no reason to expect him to clean up after you, you know."

Iggy told me that Todd had thrown Zola out for dealing. I got Todd back on the line.

"But, Todd, that's what he does for a living; it's his gig."

"Danny, it's *illegal!*"

"That's right. I keep forgetting. . . ."

"Besides that, you shoulda seen all the weirdos that were coming around here, casing the place."

"Hmmm, you were probably right."

"And you know that guy in the bathrobe?" He was talking about the composer who always complained whenever we made music at the house or played the stereo too loud. He said he couldn't "compose." He wasn't real popular with the Wonderland crew.

"Yeah, what about him?"

"He threatened to call the cops."

I had been hoping Zola would be the first person I'd see when I returned. Now I'd have to track him down.

After my little misadventure in Harlem I stuck close to the hotel, listening in while Ray did his interviews in the suite at the St. Moritz.

We rented a large stereo from Studio Instrument Rentals and blasted his LP for the guests, set up a bar, scored some outtasight cocaine, and had a party.

At the gig was a little cutie from L.A. named Suzanne whom I'd always had the hots for but had always been with Tiffany whenever she'd been around. Another female Bowie clone, like Suzette. After the show we went to Max's Kansas City, stayed in the back room drinking and snorting coke till dawn, and then I brought her back to the hotel room, where I passed out on top of her.

Later in the day, when I awoke, she was gone. "Where's Suzanne?" I asked Ray, whom I was sharing the suite with.

"Who?" he asked.

"Suzanne," I said. "She was with me last night."

"Oh," he said, "I thought that was Suzette. I gave her five hundred bucks to get back to L.A. She said she had no way home."

"Ray, Suzette has blond hair. Suzanne's is brown. She doesn't look anything like Suzette. . . ."

"Sure she does . . . I can't keep all your girlfriends straight—they all look alike to me."

"Well, you can kiss that five hundred bucks good-bye."

"It wasn't mine," he pointed out. "It was yours."

As the band prepared to begin the trek across country, working its way back for the homecoming shows in Los Angeles, I climbed aboard Pan Am Flight 533 bound for L.A. and home. I was hung over, sore, and weak and craved heroin with an intensity I hadn't thought possible. The craving was not the result of any emotional sort of trauma or even prompted by any reason I could discern. Indeed, the want was totally *un*reasonable—pure, unyielding yen and consuming desire. I didn't want to get just high; I wanted to get fucked up. And the cost, the consequences, didn't matter one single solitary bit. I was going to dive into Big Blue headfirst, and that was that.

It didn't matter that within a matter of hours after doing it, I'd want to do it again and again. It didn't matter that I was fully aware of this and that within a matter of days I would be well on my way to becoming readdicted again and feeling its effects hardly at all. To put it simply, with the exception of getting high ASAP, *nothing* else mattered. The only thing that bothered me in the least was the sheer power with which I wanted the stuff. Would it ever go away? Or was the only way to quell this obsession to give in to it?

CHAPTER TWELVE

· · · · · · · · · ·

I ain't done nothing wrong
And I'm wasted and
I can't find my way home
—BLIND FAITH

BACK in L.A. I did not walk; I ran as fast as I could through the airline terminal. Not to the baggage claim, but straight to the front of the airport, where I dived into the first phone booth I saw to try to locate Zola and my first drug of choice. His boyfriend Lance answered and said the cops had finally made their move and Zola was in jail. Before he could hit me up for bail, I hit him up for dope.

"You can't talk like that on the phone anymore," he warned.

Then he hit me up for the bail money, and I told him I needed my money for dope, not a dope dealer.

"That's not cool," he told me.

"Fuck cool," I snapped, and hung up.

I dialed Wonderland, but there was nobody home, which seemed strange. Then, after the seventh or eighth ring, Tiffany's sleepy voice drawled over the line: "Ullo?" It was three-thirty in the afternoon.

"Does Dallas have any downtown?"

"No 'hi, hello, how are you, I missed you'?" she asked.

"Yeah, sure, why not, hihellohowareyoumissedyou, does Dallas have anything? I gotta score . . . I feel fucked. You gotta help me, Tif . . . I'm desperate."

"You must be if you want to score from Dallas. Well, you're in luck. I hear it's pretty good, too."

"How would you know?"

"I heard. I haven't done any since you left."

That was pretty hard to swallow. I couldn't believe anyone could know where to get smack and then not get it.

"Jesse almost OD'd on it. . . ."

"Couldn't have happened to a nicer guy. Listen, call Dallas and tell him to hold three hundred. Think he'll sell it to me?"

"Is your money green?"

"I'm on my way. . . ."

By the time the limousine pulled up to Wonderland, I was so excited I was almost hyperventilating. I called out for Tiffany, but she wasn't around. Before I entered a total apeshit panic state, I found a little note that read: "Gone to mother's, the goods are great and there w/me. Come on over, love, Tiffany."

I ran back down the stairs so fast I slipped into the ivy and continued running into the garage. The Cobra wasn't where I'd left it, which was nothing new except this time I was damn sure I'd left it there and had not driven it since. On the next thought it occurred to me I wasn't sure of anything anymore, and you know something? I didn't care a bit. I saw the limousine driver having a tough time trying to negotiate a turnaround on the narrow street and ran over and jumped into the back seat, leaving my bags at the front door.

"There's been a change of plans," I told him, and gave him directions to get to Dallas and Marilyn's Hollywood bungalow. Tiffany was at the top of the stairs leading to her mom's apartment, grinning from ear to ear; she hopped over and jumped into my arms. I gave her a quick hug and then practically dropped her on her ass before I grabbed her hand and dragged her up the stairs. Her mom was nodding at the kitchen table. Dallas was sitting on the couch with his scale and drugs on the coffee table.

"How much you got?" I asked him.

"How much *you* got?" he asked me.

"Here," I said, dropping 300 bucks on the table, "all yours." He took the gray powder that was in some paper and pushed it toward me. It wasn't 300 bucks' worth, but I wasn't up for arguing. I was up for getting down.

I took out another hundred just to piss him off 'cause he would have given me the same amount for $400, and I knew it, and I wanted him to know I knew it. I rolled up the bill, and instead of making lines as had been my custom, I stuck one end of the rolled bill into the smack and the other in my nose.

"Whoa, boy, watch it. This stuff is so good it's dangerous," he told me. I figured it was just his hustler's rap, ignored him, and took a deep breath, fully anticipating momentary relief.

I gave it my best snort, but nothing moved. After two and a half weeks snorting about two grams of blow a day, plus the smack in Boston, my nose was like a concrete block inside. I tried again, but the stuff wouldn't move so much as a millimeter. I started sweating, and before I knew it, I was in the bathroom, heaving *before* I even had the stuff in me. I tried blowing my nose, and out came an ugly mixture of blood, snot and little rocks of cocaine. I went at the smack again, and this time I got a little inside. I finally ended up taking the dope by rolling it up inside the bill, sticking the bill in my nose, and having Tiffany blow the shit up my nosehole. Ten minutes later I didn't feel a thing. I went back to the bathroom to check my eyes. Nothing.

I started complaining, calling Dallas a hustler, a thief, that the stuff was bunk, I should have known better, and so on.

"You really want to get high?" Dallas asked me, an evil little glint lighting his eyes.

"What the fuck do you think? Hell, yes, I want to get high, but no one could get off on this shit."

"I can," he said. "She can." He pointed to Tiffany's mom.

"Great. That does me one fuck of a lot of good, Dallas. I'm genuinely glad you guys got high and I didn't."

"Listen, asshole, it's not my fault you got the Great Wall of China up your nose. How do you expect to get high? It's got to get through your nostrils first. It has to get into the blood system somehow, ya know."

"You got anymore?"

"Just this," he said, reaching under the couch cushion and pulling out a loaded syringe.

"What's in there?"

"Pigeon piss. What do you think is in here? Smack, man."

"Well," I said, "I guess that's one way of making sure it gets into my blood system."

"You can say that again."

"How much for what's in there?"

"I don't know, man, a lot. . . . It was gonna be my wake-up."

"Come on, Dallas, how much?"

"That hundred should cover it. I'll even toss the needle for free."

"You gotta hit me," I told him. Tiffany, who had been quietly listening, got up and walked out of the room.

"Sure, no problem, man."

"Deal." I smoothed out the hundred and gave it to him.

He had me hold my arm out, took off his belt and wrapped it around my upper arm, had me make a fist, and then I turned my head because needles give me the heebie-jeebies, no shit. I felt the prick and thought, *This isn't nearly as painful as I imagined.* The belt loosened.

First I saw God.

Then I died.

I collapsed, facedown, onto the coffee table. At first Dallas thought I was faking it. He pulled me up by the hair, saw my lips were turning blue, and called Tiffany back into the living room.

"Hey, kiddo, I think your boyfriend here just died."

She jumped into action, walking me around as my feet dragged, trying to get me to the shower.

"*Unh-unh*, oh, no, you don't . . . get him out of here," Dallas yelled at her. "I ain't having no bodies in this house, fucking up my probation." Tiffany tried to lift me up.

"*Help me!*" she screamed as I slumped onto the floor. "For God's sake, *help me!*" She wasn't strong enough to get me up on my feet. "He's dying!" she cried.

"Not here, he ain't!" Dallas yelled back. Again she tried to lift me, taking one arm and pulling it around her neck and tugging, but my body slipped back down as she tried to stand. "I said *get him out!*" Dallas yelled.

"I'm trying!" she cried back, pulling me by the feet, crying pretty good now. "You could at least help me!"

"No problem," he said. He came over, threw me over his shoulder like a bag of potatoes, walked out the front door, and dumped me over the stair railing butt first into a trash can. Tiffany got frantic pretty quickly, but try as she might, she couldn't get me out of the trash can. I was stuck. She roused her loving mother, but when the two of them couldn't unsnag me, they each took a handle on either side of the can and hoisted me and the garbage can, ankles over windshield, into the passenger seat of the Cobra, which Tiffany had swiped from Wonderland. The problem was, Tiffany wasn't a swift gearshifter. Not only didn't she have a driver's license, but she really didn't know how to drive too well.

She got the car started and moving okay, but she swung a little wildly onto Santa Monica Boulevard, running an approaching car into oncoming traffic, attracting the attention of an LAPD, who put on his lights and siren. But Tiffany wasn't stopping for nobody. Instead of slowing down, she went faster, caught a late sight of the hospital, pulled a wide right turn into the driveway in third gear, bouncing her foot off the clutch, and proceeded to fly through the parking lot, careening straight up the steps and through the plate glass windows, where the car finally stalled.

Tiffany leaped out of the car. "My boyfriend is dying!" she hollered at the stunned medic who was sitting behind the counter not eight feet from where the car sat halfway into his lobby. "Don't just sit there, you asshole. He could be dead."

That's when the action started getting intense. The medic recovered and got help, so I was being helped. They lifted me out of the trash can and carried me back into the emergency room, where they laid me out on the table. They went to work, trying to resuscitate me with mouth-to-mouth and slugs to the chest, but my breath wasn't returning. One of the med guys ran out and asked Tiffany, who'd been joined by the cop, if I'd taken anything. She must have thought this guy was nuts. Tiffany had a great look when she got incredulous, and I like to think she gave this genius her number one best.

Of course, God bless her, she thought fast, and she wasn't going to tell this nerd anything. If I wasn't going to die, why get me in any unnecessary trouble? And if I did die, why get herself into a fine mess? So the guy ran back in and said, "The girlfriend isn't talking."

I'd been dead about ten minutes, and they couldn't treat me unless they knew what was wrong with me. My arms were clean, no tracks, just the one dinky little prick on the side of the arm, easily mistaken for a mosquito bite. They had no idea what was wrong with me; they didn't know if it was downers, suicide, poison, choking, OD, or heart attack.

Another doctor went out to try his luck with Tiffany. "If you don't tell us what he took, he *will* die," he told her. But Tiffany, with a backlog of loyalty and concern in her heart, wouldn't budge. That I was dying didn't seem to be sufficient cause to tell them what was wrong with me. She just wasn't about to fink and get me, and maybe her, too, thrown in jail.

"Give me a minute alone with her," the doc told the cop. To her he said, "Brain damage sets in after twelve minutes. No oxygen is going to the brain, and when the brain cells don't get oxygen, they die and don't return. If you don't tell us what's wrong now, there's no telling what shape he'll be in."

Tiffany wasn't biting. "How am I supposed to know? When I found him, he was already like he is now." Then she pulled a real smart move. She started crying, which sent the doctors back in to work on me. They went to work hooking those heart paddles up to my chest with wires, flicked a switch, and sent my body flopping like a beached eel. I was still dead.

But something moved. A smooth vapor lifted up through my skin. I thought I was levitating off the table. After momentarily hovering about three feet over my body, my vision came from the corner of the room, where I could see and hear everything. There was a nurse working a knob connected to the machine powering the paddles. Each time she cranked it, my body jumped off the table.

That looks really painful, I thought. Another nurse was unwinding a wheel of tube down my throat, feeding the line in and then taping my mouth shut. I tried to speak, to tell them to leave me the fuck alone, and then I realized I couldn't speak, and then I realized if that was me down there, who the fuck was it up here wanting to speak?

Everyone got farther away, and one of the walls beyond them cracked open, revealing two caves. An inviting golden white light was emanating from one side, while the other was dark at the front, jaw-like, and a horrible dirty dark blue inside. I was being drawn toward them, both sides pulling me. I aimed for the gold side, but just as I was about to slip inside, I felt as if a riptide had caught me and siphoned me off into the darker side.

The pressure, the tension, was too much. Fluttering in a spastic, topsy-turvy roll was something looking like a cross between a stingray and a waffle. Spirits in horrible shapes, no eyes or limbs, fish shapes, distorted grotesquely, with cancerous mouths. The whole thing was like a round tube, a cylindrical aquarium that had been in the dark too long, but the texture of the environment wasn't liquid, only its weight and gravity . . . dusty, and terrifyingly dark blue. Swamp blue. I tried to drag my feet along the floor, thinking it velvet, to slow myself down. But it just peeled off in clumps of mucky algae. I had a bad feeling about where I was headed.

Dozens of these hovering waffle-rays darted out of the murky bottom, sideways, spinning, taunting me and ignoring me at the same time. All at once the tide slowed, and whatever I was came face first against the biggest, darkest bars of pumicelike rock I'd ever seen. As soon as I touched it, the bars became a gate and were flung open, and very scared and very tired, I tumbled through them. All along both sides of the hallway before me were cells, hundreds of ominous caverns holding these really very vile spongelike beings, screaming, mouths stretched to breaking, making not a sound. The energy they were trying to express themselves with was, instead of becoming sound, sending them careening around the weightless cell. This was no dream. I was in hell and I knew it.

My intelligence wanted to escape, but my strength said "sleep." Just as I was about to lay myself down onto that netherworld floor which I was certain I would never wake from, I heard voices, yelling at me, not yelling mean or angry, yelling concerned, full of love: "Don't go to sleep. You have to fight it; you have to wake up." The voices belonged to my family.

Without speaking I told them, "I have to, I can't help it. . . ." They heard me.

"You'll never wake up," my sister said.

"It's too late," I whispered, falling away.

"Danny," my sister begged, "you've got to turn around and go back *now*."

She reached out to take my hand, and with my last ounce of energy, by the fingers, I took hers.

In a time-warp flash I was sprung from the joint, back in the emergency room, back against the ceiling, staring down at my body.

They'd brought Tiffany into the room, put her into a gown, and were explaining, "He's been dead, no pulse, no heartbeat, for seventeen minutes. He's probably already paralyzed," the doctor informed her, "and if we have to wait any longer, he will be dead *forever*, and you killed him." Tiffany maybe realized being named as an accomplice to murder, plus my being dead, was considerably worse than being busted for dope.

"Well, I know he used to like to snort heroin," she said, refusing to totally implicate me or her.

It was enough. That emergency room turned into a real bustle of activity quick. Before I knew what happened, I awoke, frantically trying to catch my breath. I couldn't breathe. My tongue was depressed, my mouth taped, a tube down my throat and my nose pinched. I couldn't move; the doctors had strapped all my limbs down. There must have been a half dozen people around me, masks and eyes.

These people are trying to kill me, I thought. But no, it was something else. I stared into their eyes, searching for an answer, and I saw reassurance in those eyes. *Please let me breathe!* I implored with mine. My eyes bulged. *Let me go!*

A nurse put her hand in mine and patted it. "You're okay, baby."

"It's okay, it's okay, he's out of it, he's out, we did it. . . ."

But the doctor jabbed me with a needle anyway.

"Now," the doctor's voice said to his assistant, "don't be surprised if he can't walk."

"He can see," a nurse said, "I'm sure he can still see."

"Can you feel this?" someone asked, pinching my left hand. I nodded. Another person tore the tape off my mouth and pulled out the tubing. I gulped the cool air.

"Let me up, please, let me up," I begged.

"Are you all right?" the doctor asked.

"I don't know," I said. "Let me up, and I'll tell you." They all gave each other puzzled glances. The nurse who'd taken my hand started untying the restraints. I sat up. I felt a jab of pain down my spine to my asshole.

"*Fucking youch!*" I yelled, grabbing my bottom, still sitting on the table.

"Are you all right? What's wrong? What hurts? Don't try to stand. . . ."

I stayed still and took a few deep breaths.

"How did I get here?" I asked, trying to get my bearings.

"Your girlfriend brought you."

Tiffany walked through the wall of medical personnel around the table, grinning like a champ from ear to ear.

"How's it going, bunky?" She smiled.

I just shook my head.

"She saved your life," the doctor told me.

"No shit?" I asked, hopping off the table onto the ground. As soon as my feet hit, I collapsed. They helped me up. Tiffany was with them and looked worried. Everyone looked worried. They started to lift me back onto the table.

"Put me down," I said. "Let go of my feet."

"Are you sure?

"Of course I'm sure. Why's my back hurt?" I had no idea dying hurt so much.

Tiffany answered for all of them, with bravery, honesty, and not a little bit of disgust. "Dallas threw you in the trash can, and I couldn't get you out."

The staff sent us on our way with a prescription for Somacompound—a neat mixture of codeine and effective muscle relaxant to help with my aching back—and handed over a bill. No cops, no reports, no hassles. I had to pay for the resuscitation and two pints of the narcotic antagonist Narcan plus two plate-glass sliding doors.

When we walked out and got into the car and were ready to back it down the steps, Tiffany remarked, "Jesus, I'm never gonna hear the end of this."

"I'll make you a deal," I told her, "I won't bring up what happened today if you don't."

"Deal." She smirked, pulling down the visor and fixing her hair.

That very same night I was at the Rainbow, getting back in form. Me, Tiffany and Ig, Nigel, Suzette and Ig's girl, Sabel Star, and her buddy Queenie having a homecoming: Everybody was getting drunk. One of the waitresses came over and, after getting Iggy's autograph, announced she had Quaaludes for sale, which was sort of like telling a room full of brats at a birthday party it was caketime. At five bucks a quack we tapped her out. I got three and three for Tiffany. Everyone else bought as many as their money allowed—about seven for the four of them, excepting Ig. He bought *ten*.

I ate one of mine but didn't pay attention to anyone else 'cause I was too busy watching Iggy as he took all of his, one right after the other, very methodically.

Tiffany told the table she was excusing herself to the ladies' room and took her double White Russian with her. I didn't believe her.

She'd pulled this stunt on me at least half a dozen times before, telling me she was going to the bathroom and not coming back. I'd have to go find her when I wanted to leave. Each time she'd been upstairs in the private club Over the Rainbow, either dancing with or conning a drink from some guy neither of us knew. She insisted on letting these complete strangers buy her drinks. She just couldn't get over the novelty—the completely beautiful simplicity of sitting down alone at a bar and within a few minutes having complete strangers come up and spend money on her.

As she got up to leave the table, I made her swear she'd be back within ten minutes. She promised.

Forty-five minutes later everybody around me was falling over. Iggy just stood up in the booth and, stepping over the back, walked away. I ordered six kamikazes and knocked them down, watched the insanity build and run around before I was hit with an enlightening thought: *Screw this sitting-around-the-table-drinking bullshit. I know what drug I want.*

Before I went and dug that drug, I thought it might be nice if I found my girlfriend first. It wasn't like I didn't know where to look.

No sooner did I find her at the bar and grab her arm than Tony, the maître d' of the restaurant downstairs, grabbed my arm, spun me around, and shouted in my face: *"Your singer. Downstairs. Out of here! Now!"* I yanked Tiffany off the barstool without bothering to wait for any exchange with her pickup.

Back downstairs, standing with his legs spread, pants to his knees, flat little ass facing us, was Iggy atop two adjoining booths, pissing into one of the potted palms. I walked up to him from behind, slapped his ass, and said, "Come on, we gotta go."

He spun around, and I ducked just as he sent a spray of piss sailing past my right ear into a booth full of diners.

"I'm not going anywhere. I piss on this hole." I caught him around the back of his legs and carried him out over my shoulder, his head down my back, a spray of urine continuing its arc on our way out of the club. Near the front door there was Tony, arms crossed, frowning. Just as we passed, he started yelling again. *"You're all 86'ed! Get out of my establishment!"*

I turned around to apologize and straighten everything out, maybe give him a fifty to forget the whole thing, but as I turned, so did Iggy and Iggy's relief—splashing Tony right across the chest. It was an aim worthy of Zorro.

Zola was out of jail and dealing from a bad motel on the sleazy eastern end of Sunset Boulevard. We asked him to front us the dope, something we'd never asked him before and believed he'd feel okay doing. We were wrong. He needed all the cash he could get to pay his lawyer and wasn't going to front any dope to anybody, including us. I'd been scoring from him every day for the past few weeks and in the process gotten my old habit back, plus some. It wasn't like he didn't have plenty of dope; I personally had just eyed at least a couple of grams of his good, rocky brown Mexican tar. So he had the goods. I just didn't have any money, and I couldn't believe that without money, I couldn't get some of that delicious dope. I couldn't budge him.

"Come on, Zola. You can hold my driver's license, I'll let you hold on to my credit card, for chrissakes," which I couldn't believe I was offering to anyone for anything. "What do you want? You can have anything I got . . . I'll bring over my stereo. Here take my watch. . . ."

"I don't want your watch."

I couldn't even write him a check because once upon a time I'd stopped a check to him for three hundred bucks because I thought the dope was bunk. "If you're not pleased with the quality of the merchandise, you have the prerogative of stopping the check," my father once told me. Only problem was, Zola thought the dope was fine, and not only that, he'd paid good money for it. Before he sold to me again, I first had to make good on the bad check.

I got what I thought was a pretty good idea: to buy him something on the credit card in exchange for dope.

"Come on, I'll take you and Lance out to dinner. Right now we'll all go wherever you want, my treat. What say we go get something to eat?"

"You know what I want to eat?" Zola asked me.

"Whatever you feel like, you got," I said, feeling good my suggestion was being taken so well.

"What you got," Zola said.

"Pardon me?" I said, puzzled. I thought he might be referring to my leather jacket.

"What you got is what I want."

"I don't *got* nothing," I corrected him. "But," I reassured him, "we can go *get* anything. We can make a trade—you know, the bartering with goods. I was thinking about food for junk."

"I'm not interested in food," he said.

I took off my jacket, ready to hand it to him.

"I'm saying I want what you got in your pants."

"Oh, Jesus." Tiffany half groaned, half laughed.

I folded the jacket next to me. For maybe the second time in my life I was totally speechless.

Zola took advantage of my lapse in consciousness to go on. "You let me do you, and I'll front you the dope you need. I promise you, Danny, you'll be turned on in more ways than one."

I remembered Crazy Nancy and Evan—about a mouth's being a mouth. . . . What he'd said about being turned on in more ways than one gave me an idea. I was surprised I thought of it, and I was even more surprised when I said it aloud.

"All right, I'll make you a deal. You can blow me, but I get the dope first." I wanted to make sure I wasn't going to make a fool of myself for nothing.

"No way." Zola shook his beret-covered head.

"How about at the same time?" I suggested.

This time Tiffany shook her head.

"What are you talking about? I can't do what I want and shoot you up at the same time."

"No, but with Lance's help you can."

"That's a great idea!" Zola clapped. "I've always wanted to do that!"

"You're both sick," Tiffany said.

"I'm doing this for you, too. You'll get high for nothing, soon, tonight, not tomorrow," I told her.

"Don't mind her, she's just jealous."

"Let's do it," I said, heading toward the couch and unzipping my pants.

Zola got down on his hands and knees, reached down and extracted my cock out of my jeans and put his big purple lips over it while Lance slipped the point of the insulin syringe into my arm. He registered the blood so it curled up like a little rose into the hot brown thick liquid, and then he pushed the plunger down and I went straight to heaven. Zola, who had been working to get me hard, nearly choked I got so hard so quick. Then he got excited. Then I got excited. Actually it wasn't so bad. Zola gave head better than Tiffany, but not as good as the Butter Queen in Dallas. After about five minutes he started getting a little aggressive, and I told him to cool it and tried to get up; he pushed me back down onto the couch, holding my legs down with his hands. When it became obvious I couldn't come, I pushed him off me. "I'm not done," he mumbled between mouthfuls.

"Fuck you," I told him. "I am."

"Want to make it a gram?" he asked, standing up, rubbing a hard-on beneath his tight white cords.

This time I knew exactly what he meant. I had my fix, and Tiffany had a couple of lines. I was okay, and so was she. I had no intention of sacrificing my virgin ass without a fight or at least a damn whole lot more dope than a measly gram.

"I wouldn't."

On the way home Tiffany turned to look at me.

"You're getting quite pathetic, you know that?"

I really loved her when she worried about me like that.

The homecoming shows at the Whisky, eight performances, four nights, were sold out weeks in advance. Because everyone lived in town, we'd be able to make up all the tour losses and then some with the L.A. engagement. The record company even did some work to sell some LPs. So business was okay.

Ray's new CPA Marty Fox called up to tell me some Doors' money had come in for me. "What do you want me to do with it?" he asked over the phone.

"Give it to me."

"Don't you think you should hold on to some?"

"For *what*?" I asked him, thinking I'd leave out the next words I was about to say, which were "Funeral costs?"

"For taxes," Marty said, "you have taxes coming up in a few months."

"That's not for a while. There's plenty of time."

"I don't know. You're going through cash faster than you get it. You're making good money now; you should be saving some."

"Marty, do me a favor, just tell me how much the check's for."

"Sixteen thousand dollars."

"I'll send a messenger right over to pick it up."

I wasn't unaware that what once were immovable moral certitudes were rapidly peeling away, each transgression more horrible than the one before. It was as if I were so shocked at what I'd been doing I felt compelled to do something even worse by comparison to erase, or at least to ease, the memory—a weird triangle comprised of morbid curiosity, reward, and punishment, propelled by the habit itself.

It was a nightmare with commercials of brief, intense pleasure. But the commercials were getting shorter and further apart, and the nightmare was getting more real. Even as I pinched myself, in the depths of my conscience, I already knew I just didn't know or care deeply enough. I had to continue pinching. *Wake up, wake up.* It's the conscience again. It simply cannot believe what is going on.

The way I looked at it was: If I didn't learn how to inject myself, it couldn't ever get out of control. (As if I were already in such good control.) I didn't trust my life in my hands, so I put it in someone else's, anyone else's. Not real confidence-building behavior on my part.

As God searched Adam out of the trees and leaves, I searched myself out among the guilt and shame. And just as Adam blamed the girl Eve, I evaded responsibility for what I'd been doing. Adam said, "Don't blame me, God, *you* made the girl, I didn't. It's not my fault."

Eve didn't sound off much better with her response. *She* blamed the serpent.

I blamed birth. I blamed my parents. I blamed my brain and all its circuitry. I blamed everything. And while I didn't love the concept of shooting up, I had to admit it wasn't nearly as painful or awful as I'd thought, and it was less painful than not doing it. I'll say this, boy, it sure *worked* better than snorting. Quickly. Instant pleasure. Immediate relief. For somebody with as little impulse control and as much impatience as me, you might say it was the ultimate solution. Stronger, faster than snorting. Better than sex. The rush kicked me in the back of the head and warmed my heart; it held me with tenderness and strength. It hugged me. It loved me and I loved it right back.

I don't want to give you the impression I necessarily liked what I was doing (or the how and why), I just loved how it made me feel. I did what I had to do. I wasn't *un*proud of it, though. A big part of me thought it might just be the bravest, most outrageous thing I had ever done. But just as big a part of me thought it was the most chickenshit, most vile thing I'd ever done. So I wasn't what you'd call real content with the way things were going. There was some conflict going on. But heroin cures conflict, too.

I'd gone to this doctor, not to get drugs but because I had a hard-on that wouldn't go away. Tiffany wasn't helping things get any better. She thought it was funny. She saw it as a joke and didn't appear anxious to eliminate the source of her entertainment.

I didn't think it was funny. I was aching for relief. I tried to reassure myself it would go away, but when it was still standing tall three days later *and* I'd begun urinating blood, I began to get a little concerned. I mean, if you had to go to the shower stall, turn on the water, and piss blood toward the ceiling, you'd worry, too. What I thought had maybe gone wrong was I'd sprung a leak, crossed some plumbing somewhere down there, and I'd better get it straightened out.

The urologist poked around, took some tests and X rays, and then told me there were a couple of different, unrelated problems here. First, the reason I had an erection that functioned more like a flagpole than a soft organ was that I'd been, in his words, "fucking too much." For somebody who had been a complete virgin for nineteen years, I took his words as nothing less than a Medal of Honor. He prescribed me some blood-pressure medication to help lower the fucker.

The pissing-blood part was neither so simply explained nor treated. It wasn't a leak, as I'd thought. The tests and bladder X ray indicated I had something inside, cutting away. He wanted to schedule surgery right away before more damage was done.

I got up to leave, to think about everything.

"I'll call you to schedule it," I said, putting on my jacket.

"Wouldn't you like to know what else is wrong with you?"

I was afraid to ask.

"You mean, there's *more*? If my dick's going to fall off, too, I don't want to hear about it."

He gave me a professional chuckle and told me I had gonorrhea.

And you know something? The news didn't upset me. I knew all I'd have to do was take a handful of pills or get an antibiotic shot, and it would be gone. Then he asked if I'd been sleeping with anybody lately. I asked him what he meant by "lately," and he told me within the past few months, and then I knew I wouldn't just have to take a handful of pills: I'd also have to tell Tiffany. And Zola. First time around with the clap, and I zap it to a girl and a guy, a fact I was not particularly proud of.

I could have caught the clap from any one of a dozen girls, but I fed Tiffany Suzanne's name when she asked for one mainly because it was the only name I could remember. Before I went and told her, I snuck off to see Dallas, who was now selling to me directly, *mano a mano*. He was back in form, but the dope looked more like a combination of crushed vitamin B¹² and coffee grounds than heroin. It must have had an opiate somewhere because after he hit me up, I did feel it a little bit. Still, I wasn't feeling nearly as numb as I'd have liked.

The main reason I went to Dallas was that I really didn't want to have to see Zola and tell him I'd given him VD. The whole notion didn't set real right in my head. Instead, I called him from Tiffany's mom's, none too delighted with making the call in front of someone like Dallas, whose ears, by the way, did perk up when I got Zola on the phone and told him I'd just been told I had VD and chances were he had it now.

"I'm real sorry, Zola, but it's not like I did it on purpose. It's not like I knew I had it." Then before he could say anything I didn't want to hear (like it was okay and I was forgiven), I said "And to try and make it up to you I want you and Lance to be my personal guests at Ray's opening night at the Whisky next Wednesday."

What I was really thinking about saying was "Serves you right, you dumb junkie faggot nigger. I hope your lips rot." I really resented the fuck out of him for the barrel he had me over on a daily basis. I wanted to kick the shit out of him on a number of occasions but couldn't because I always needed what he had. Now that I'd given him what I had, I wasn't too remorseful about it.

I was beginning to regret giving it to Tiffany, though. The minute I told her about Suzanne, she started packing her bags to leave. I really hated it whenever she did that. I felt like she was abandoning me.

"You can't leave me now!" I told her.

"Oh, I can't, can I?"

"Oh, I mean, you can, you could, but I need you."

That gave her pause. She stopped packing for the moment. "*Why?*" she asked me.

I almost told her, "Give me a few minutes and I'll think of a few reasons," just to slow her down but instead, I told her the truth, which isn't always the same thing as smart.

"I'm sick," I told her.

"I *knew* that," she said, resuming throwing her boots in her bag.

"I mean it," I told her, saving the best for last. "I have to go in for surgery."

"You're crazy."

"That may well be true, but I'm also serious."

"Too late," she said.

Seeing as how I wasn't going to get my way, I sort of got angry and said, "Let me help you then," took her bag, walked down the hallway into the guest room, opened the window, and yelled, "You want crazy, I'll show you crazy, you lazy, insensitive twat!"

Then I threw the bag into the middle of Wonderland Avenue.

The line of people in front of the Whisky stretched all the way down Sunset Boulevard, around the corner, and up the block. I pulled the Cobra up in front, let the car boy from Sneaky Pete's next door park it, tipped him, and walked past everybody to the front of the line. The doorman, one I didn't know, put out his hand and stopped me.

"End of the line," he said, pointing.

"I manage the band," I angrily informed him.

"Don't get me mad," he warned.

"Get mad, asshole, try it."

I ducked his arm and walked inside, handed the guest list to the girl in the box office, whom I did know, and locked the door behind me to keep the goon out.

She handed me the night's balance of seventy-five hundred dollars.

I said thanks and pocketed the roll.

Then I went to find Zola and, that done, led him to the upstairs bathroom, the same one I had first snorted heroin in. This time I sat on the toilet while Zola knelt in front of me and poked around for a vein. He went right through the vein and hit a nerve, and before I could stop myself, my right foot, which had been crossed over my left leg, automatically shot up and kicked him right in the chin, sending him tumbling against the wall.

"Sorry." I shrugged.

He got up and tried again. This time he hit the mainline. I put my head back against the bathroom tile and moaned

While everybody waited for Ray and his group to take the stage for the first show of the night, I was doing my best not to nod out in public, without much success. I noticed my guests, Iggy, Mac-Kenzie, Sabel, and Suzette, had no such moral qualms as they itched and nodded away, oblivious of all.

I forced myself up to the box office to check the guest list. I'd sent my father an invitation via the record company, and I was surprised how much I wanted and expected him to be there. I went over the list and almost every single name but his was checked off as already being inside. I told the girl if he showed up to let him right into the VIP area before Moose at the door could jerk him around.

Back at the booth I snorted more smack. I saw people in the business watching the booth. Through my fluttering eyelids, I saw Betty Lou, the cocktail waitress, looking at me, tray on hip. She didn't look happy to see me.

I opened my eyes as far as I could, which wasn't very wide.

"You're fucking up," she said.

In a very soft, sad voice all I could say was: "I know it."

Between sets Mario busted Zola and Lance for passing counterfeit twenties. Outside the cops frisked him and found Zola's dope and needle.

Tiffany materialized backstage and came over to the couch and sat with me. Ray came over, too, and sat down on my other side. "All right, man?" he asked me.

"I'm okay," I feebly reassured him.

"You don't look okay. Why don't you take a break, go on vacation or something? Get some rest, dry out . . ."

Suzette bounded over and gave me a kiss, said hi to Tiffany, and congratulated Ray on the great show.

"This," I said to Ray, "is Suzette."

"I know Suzette," Ray said. And then right on cue Suzanne came over and stood before us as if expecting a standing ovation.

"And this," I said without thinking, "is Suzanne."

Ray said, "I remember." Then I remembered.

Tiffany didn't blink.

She simply stood up, whispered something in Suzanne's ear, and led her into the backstage bathroom. Then Tiffany decked her, belted her right in the jaw. Knocked her out cold.

She returned to the room pridefully wiping her hands against each other with that shit-eating grin so indigenous to her mug when she was feeling particularly successful.

I grinned, too, shaking my head.

"Want to go home now?" she asked, putting her hand out to me.

"Let's do it," I said, taking her hand and pulling myself up.

"Nice shot, Tif." Ray smiled.

The band had played well, getting repeated standing ovations, but I didn't care. I couldn't feel the music. I couldn't feel anything but a wall between me and myself. I was glad for Ray. I had done a good job and for now my job was done.

* * *

All that was left to do was meet with the accountant, the road manager, and the lawyer. Up in Wonderland at 1:30 P.M., that's what I was doing. The four of us were closing the books on what had turned out to be a successful tour after all. I hadn't had any dope all day and was feeling far from fit.

The last time I had spoken to Zola, we'd agreed he'd be over by 2:00 P.M. to give me a shot. I didn't know if he was in jail or out, and I was getting real antsy. I didn't know if I wanted him to be on time (and walk in on the meeting) or his usual hour or two late.

The meeting was still going on when the doorbell rang. Suzette was standing there (barely), a total wreck, wasted out of her skinny blond skull on God knows what. I didn't want any part of it. I already had more than I could deal with.

"I need a place to crash," she begged. "I have to get some sleep, something to eat, please, Danny."

It wasn't like I liked doing what I was about to do. It was just that, to put it simply, I'd become a totally insensitive jerk, even to those I cared about.

"No. Not today. I'm sorry, Suzette, but I'm having a business meeting. Wait outside. I'll call you a taxi." I handed her fifty bucks by way of an apology. "Here, get yourself something to eat."

With eyes that melted my heart she said, "Danny, please, let me inside. I don't have anyplace else to go."

"Suzette, no, I can't. I'm sorry." Instead of letting her in, I gave her some more money. "Go home. Go to your mother's house. Get some help." Then I closed the door and finished the meeting.

When all the tour business was done, Marty announced he had something to tell me. "I've got some good news and some bad news."

"As long as they balance each other out," I said, "I can handle it." To myself I added, *I hope.*

"Ray's signed over his share of the house to you. It's all yours. That's the up side. The down side is you have to make your share of the payments. Ray'll continue to pay his half, but if you miss any payments, you have to deal with the consequences. Remember, it's all in your name now."

Because of the needles. Ever since the needles had come into the picture, Ray had begun to phase himself out. I could definitely sympathize with him. I wished I could phase myself out. Hell, I *was* phasing myself out, as far out as possible.

"I accept," I said. It wasn't a hard thing to do. The more I fucked up, the more goodies I got. It might've been perverse, but unacceptable it was not.

"And," Marty said, "he wants you to get help. He said you'd know what he meant." That was harder to swallow. So I chewed on it instead.

The next morning I woke up sick. Dope-sick, with no dope and fear sitting in my stomach like a chunk of cement. Zola had never shown. I wasn't strong enough even to think about what to do. Then the phone rang.

"Hi, my name's Penny, Zola gave me your number."

"Where is Zola?"

"In county jail. He'll never raise bail this time. They got that nigger for good."

"Christ," I said, "I hope he took care of the clap; otherwise half the prison population of greater Los Angeles County is going to go blind within the next few years."

"He told me to call you this morning. I guess he thought you might be needing something."

"Well, I sure like your timing." I sighed with relief.

As I was on my way out of the door, instructions to Penny's apartment in hand, the telephone rang again. The only reason I answered it was that I thought it might be Penny with a change in the scoring arrangements.

You can imagine my surprise when it turned out to be the police on the phone.

"We found your card on someone you might know." I thought they were talking about Zola, and I wasn't going to be caught off guard.

"Yeah, so? A lot of people I don't know probably have my business card."

"Do you know a girl named Suzette?"

That caught me a little off guard.

"Sure, I know her. . . ."

"Would you mind coming downtown and identifying her body?"

That one caught me completely off guard.

"Her what?"

"Your friend's dead. She OD'd and got raped, repeatedly. Her parents refuse to cooperate. When we asked them if they knew of you, they said you should take care of it." Here he paused, making me very nervous. "We need a positive ID."

I was already feeling guilty because maybe if I'd let her crash, this wouldn't have happened. It sounded as if her parents thought I was guilty anyway. I had no idea what the cops thought, and I didn't want to find out.

"Can't I just describe her to you?" I asked.

No, I couldn't. I had to go down there. In person. Soon.

Which meant I needed to make myself well first, but not get so high I'd get busted as I walked into the heart of the enemy camp. Well was what I may have needed, but loaded was what I wanted and what I got.

Penny didn't fit my standard image of a heroin dealer, or any sort of dealer, or any sort of addict at all, except maybe one hooked on porterhouse steak and Hostess Twinkies. She shared her funky, sprawling West Hollywood apartment with her roommate and best friend, an extraordinarily large Southern gal who was built like a quarterback. Jo (as in Namath) answered the door and led me into Penny's bedroom. This is exactly what I saw:

Where Jo was large and heavy, Penny was small and round. With her pale moon-shaped face and no neck to speak of, she looked like a white polliwog with its tail snipped and tucked. Both of them were easily three hundred pounds *apiece*. Penny was sitting on her canopied bed in an earth mother muumuu the size of a tent, having a tea party complete with teakettle, cups, saucers, little miniature sterling silver spoons, and about eight loaded syringes on the nightstand. There she sat, holding court, having conversation, and pouring tea for four or five people who were *not* there.

"Excuse me," I said.

"Can't you see I'm busy?" she chirped. She had a pleasant high-pitched melodic voice. "Would you mind turning off the TV?" she asked me.

I looked at the TV in front of her bed. It was off.

"She's been shootin' coke," Jo explained. "She gets a little out of it sometimes. What do you want to buy?"

Jo sold me the dope and jabbed around my arm for a vein. Good dope—jackpot.

"I'll be back. You'll definitely be seeing me again."

"Just remember to bring money. Money talks. Bullshit walks."

If you think hospitals are depressing, check out your local county morgue sometime. And then try to look your dead buddy in the eye. And her eyes were open. You can't do it. I couldn't. All I could do was say, "It's her," sign a paper, and get the fuck out of the place. I was so bummed out I went straight back to Penny's and stayed with her, and heroin, for the next two days. . . .

And on the second night I checked myself into the hospital to get my bladder checked out, and more drugs, these legal, potent, and next to free.

Early the next morning the staff shot me up with morphine and wheeled me into surgery, where they had to give me another shot on account of I hadn't gone under the way I was supposed to. The second one put me under. For a while. I woke up in the middle of the surgery, lifted my head, and said, "I think I need another shot." I got one.

When I came to back in the room, the doctor told me two interesting things. In my bladder he'd found and removed a large diamond-shaped chunk of crystallized alcohol and methaqualone, aka Quaalude.

First he'd chipped, and then he'd siphoned out the remnants. I lifted my pj's top and looked for the scar. When I didn't find one, I asked, "So where's the incision?"

"We didn't make one. A catheter cystoscope was inserted up your urinary tract, and we worked microscopically through that."

"And how did 'we' get into this urinary tract?"

"Access was gained through your urethra."

"My what?"

"Your penis," he clarified.

". . . Ouch." The thought of *anything* going up my pecker, instead of out, was painful. "I think I need another pain shot."

"That brings me to something else I want to talk to you about. You know we could have stopped a stampede of elephants with the amount of morphine we used to put you under."

I refused to comment on the grounds it might incriminate me.

"Well?" he asked.

"You want to talk honestly?" I asked, actually contemplating copping out to this doctor.

"Yes, I do," he said.

Then I thought better of my lapse of judgment and told him, "Go ahead, you talk, I'll listen." He left. When I didn't get my other pain shot, I left, too, to get one, maybe even two, with the Quarterback and the albino Polliwog.

Every day I drove over to Penny's apartment to score and get shot up three, four, sometimes five times. Not only was I feeding a rapidly developing first-rate heroin habit, but I was trying to fill the void inside me. The habit was the less demanding of the two. If I wasn't loaded, the hole in my gut was sucking air. It was getting almost impossible to stay loaded *enough*. If Penny was too stoned to hit me up, then Jo did the honor. If neither one of them had the time or the ability to focus clearly, whoever was around shot me up with whatever was handy. It wasn't pretty, it wasn't fun, it was humiliating, and it was getting awful bloody. I was beginning to feel like a human practice target while my arms began looking like a pincushion. Worst of all, I had to wait my turn while everyone got off before me.

I put up with this punishment and outside dependency for over a month before I finally said, "Fuck it." One night after the twelfth puncture attempt on the part of three different junkies, I simply took the dull needle out of someone else's hand and placed it into my own. I knew how it was done. I'd watched the process enough. I wasn't sure I could do it to myself, though. I wasn't sure I had either the nerve or the aim.

But I was damn sure I couldn't do any worse than everyone else. What I had once perceived as a strength not to do, I now easily saw as strength to be able to do. It was as simple as this: Before, I had thought shooting up would hurt me too much, whereas the time had arrived when shooting up myself was the only way to stop the hurt.

With a bloody nylon stocking wrapped around my arm, held tight by my jaw, I made a fist, saw the vein I wanted, picked a spot, jacked up my courage, and, syringe in hand, did what I had to do.

I got it on the first try. And any worry I might have once harbored about learning to fix myself was washed away by the rush and the powerful, soothing winds that followed.

Pamela had stumbled upon a lawyer who accomplished for her what had become her life's goal—i.e., Pamela Courson Morrison was officially named the legal heir to the estate of James Douglas Morrison.

She immediately went out and bought a convertible yellow VW, a monogrammed mink stole from Saks, and an ounce of China White.

She called on Wednesday and proposed a celebration, her treat. Naturally I accepted. We discussed having dinner at Musso and Franks on Hollywood Boulevard, going to the movies, and stopping at Rodney's afterward. We set the date for tomorrow night, Thursday.

The next morning I received a call from Gibson and Stromberg. They had been getting calls inquiring about Pamela's death. There had been some reports; people wanted information.

"That's impossible," I told Gary Stromberg. "I have a date with her tonight. Last time I talked to her she was ecstatic. I'm sure she's okay." I promised him if I heard anything I'd call back.

Elektra Records called next. "What do you know?" the publicist asked me.

"What do you want to know?" I asked her.

"Is Pam all right?"

"Pam's fine," I reassured her, and hung up.

I dialed Pam's apartment. It was busy.

Judy Sims from *Rolling Stone* called before I got a chance to redial.

"I'm trying to get in touch with Pam right now," I told her.

"You don't know?"

"I'm pretty sure she's okay."

"I'm at the police station. The blotter report says an ambulance was dispatched for an overdose to her address at eight forty-five this morning."

I didn't say good-bye. I didn't hang up the phone. Terrified it might be true, knowing it could be true, I threw the receiver on the bed and ran out to the car, panic rising in my throat.

When I arrived at Pamela's, I wanted to floor the car and get the hell away. My heart groaned; my throat clenched; my eyes burned. The police and paramedics were wheeling a gurney down the path from her apartment. On it was a body covered by a sheet and I could see her red hair falling over the side. I gripped the steering wheel and cursed God.

"*Fuck you, God!* Fuck you!" I just sat in the car and stared away. I felt anger and I felt loss and I felt fear. I felt pain, and I hated it. "Take me, *goddammit.* Why don't you just get it over with? *Take me!*"

Ray played organ at Pam's funeral. After the service he took me aside and told me he didn't want to lead the band anymore, and he certainly did not want to be the lead singer.

"What about working with Iggy?" he asked me.

"You mean, you and Iggy?"

"Unless you've learned how to sing."

"I'm sure he'll want to. I'll work on it."

"You clean up your act first. I'm taking the family to Hawaii for a few weeks. I need you, man. Get your shit together, and then we'll talk to Jim."

Ray left me and went to talk to Morrison's old friends Tom Baker and John Carpenter, the friendly editor of the *Free Press.*

As Ray went to Hawaii and I went nuts, Iggy went to San Francisco for a checkup with his San Francisco buddies. Tiffany and I were alone in Wonderland. For the first time the house felt eerie, haunted. Long ago I'd stopped spending any money on house maintenance, and it sure wasn't going to food. The pool was filthy with pine needles and leaves; everything inside was in disarray. I finally had my hair really long, but it didn't matter. None of it mattered. Junk mattered.

When we'd been snorting dope, Tiffany had a sort of revolving drug program worked out so she wouldn't get strung out. What it basically consisted of was drinking three days a week, using dope three days a week, and taking downers on the last night. Ever since I'd started shooting myself up, she'd been ragging me to fix her. I'd held out and held out. Then came downer night. She was whacked out of her nut on Tuinal, and so was I on account of the two I took to try to nod. Tiffany wasn't about to let me nod. She wanted to be shot up, and I guess she hit me in a selfish mood because I said yes. There would be no nod for me until I did what she wanted.

Before I even opened my eyes in the morning, I knew what I'd done. I remembered. All I could do was groan, "Oh fuck," 'cause I fucking well knew it wasn't the last or only time. It was only the first time. If I'd learned anything so far, it was that this sort of thing didn't improve with time.

So far I'd been sharing my dope with Tiffany—it was my way of saying, "I love you," of taking care of her, since I wasn't really good at verbalizing it—but lately I'd been getting greedy. I didn't want to share it. I'd been lying about how much I'd bought and brought home. I'd been doing most of it at Penny's, bringing a little back for Tiffany and telling her it was all I could get. She accused me of lying, one late night when I was getting a gram with *her* money, not mine, and she said she wanted to come along. "Why, don't you trust me?" I protested.

"Hell, no," she said.

I went out and scored alone and brought her back less than two-tenths of a gram. She demanded the rest. I said that was all there was, that I owed Penny money from last week. She threatened to call Penny.

"You don't believe me?" I asked, reaching for the needle she was holding in her hand.

"I don't even *like* you anymore," she yelled, pulling the kit out of my reach.

"Give me the fucking point!" I yelled back.

"Fuck you!" she screamed, holding it farther away.

So I hit her.

Three weeks after Iggy had gone north, I got a call from the president of the San Francisco branch of his gay fan club. He told me the club was sending him home.

"Be ready," he warned.

I got a distinct feeling of apprehension.

"Be ready for *what*?" I queried.

"He's a little out of it," he said as if that explained it all.

"What do you mean, 'a little'? Define 'a little.' "

"Well, maybe a lot." He laughed and hung up. This from guys for whom far-out was only a starting point, the norm, people who possessed no dividing line between male and female. I had no idea what went on up there in their apartment, but I managed to conjure up images of hypnotism, brainwashing, orgies, and massive drug sessions. If he had gotten too weird for them, I wasn't sure I could ever be ready.

It took them three days to get him to the airport in San Francisco. It took him two days to get from the airport up there to the airport down here. I wasn't in a big rush to get him when he arrived. I was beginning to really resent this taxi service I was running, but I was afraid if I wasn't there, if I didn't show up . . . I remembered Suzette at the door . . . Pamela . . . I thought of all of them as I drove south on the San Diego Freeway to pick up my friend.

Whenever Iggy had gone to visit these guys before, the residual effects of his stay had worn off within a few hours. This time they didn't seem to be going away.

They'd gone and feminized him again. Not just in drag either. He'd really been transformed. His hair had been dyed black, and he actually became a woman, or thought he was one. He sure looked like one, behaved like one. His mannerisms, even his features, had changed.

He glided into Wonderland like Cinderella entering the ballroom, wearing a full-length white dress with a slit up the side, a burgundy belt, a cute little burgundy hat, burgundy pumps, and burgundy nail polish. He had his hair slicked back, and he really was acting, behaving like a chick. It was unnerving. I mean, how would you react if your best friend left town a man and came back a woman? I avoided him.

But what really bugged me was I did not find him/her particularly unattractive, with the unnerving exception of the big bulge pushed against the front of the tight dress. He was pulling this feminine transformation off, consciously or unconsciously, and all I could do was not look too closely and hope it didn't continue for much longer.

"What if he gets worse?" Tiffany asked.

"He can't get worse," I pointed out, hoping I was right.

"Wanna bet?" she said, hand extended.

He got worse. The private line rang. Iggy was in jail, calling collect. While I'd been locked in the bathroom, trying to nod out and forget the whole ordeal, he'd wandered out of the house, down Laurel Canyon over to Alice Cooper's house, where he'd borrowed some clothes from Alice's girlfriend, Cindy Laing, and onto Hollywood Boulevard, where he'd been picked up.

"What's the charge?" I asked him.

"*Impersonating* a female," he said, as if the police didn't know a real woman when they saw one. He sounded so convincing I agreed to come get him. I didn't have the heart to tell him there was the off chance they might be right.

At the front desk the desk sergeant said, "Ya really want that guy?"

"He's all right, sir. He's really a good guy."

"He's a real *lucky* guy."

Fifteen minutes later Iggy was launched from a side door. I stood up. Tiffany stayed seated, rolling her eyes. He'd changed into a silky bathrobe, slippers, and jewelry. He was carrying his heels, stumbling over to us, still pretty stoned. After giving Tiffany a girl-to-girl kiss, he tried to give me a smooch, but I got away.

We walked out to the car, Iggy in front wobbling, me in the middle with my head down, hoping no one saw any of us, Tiffany bringing up the rear, arms crossed on her chest, shaking her head.

I did not discuss the possibility of his collaborating with Ray on that particular afternoon.

The telephone got me off the bed. It was 9:00 A.M. and I was sick. I'd fallen asleep, waiting for Penny to deliver.

"Are you awake?" a voice asked.

"If I'm alive, I'm awake."

It was MacKenzie Phillips's brother, Jeff. Laura had locked herself in the bathroom shooting cocaine and wouldn't come out. This

in itself was not so unusual. The problem was the studio limousine
had been waiting out front for two hours for her to finish "getting
ready" to go to the studio where she was scheduled for a seven-thirty
call on the set of her new series, *One Day at a Time*.

"She needs some heroin, or she won't come out."

"I'll be there as soon as I can."

I knew even though she was relatively new on the show, she'd
already been placed on probation for falling out of her car, stoned on
Quaaludes. The story had made the papers. One more bit of excess,
or worse, a no-show, and she was gone.

After going to Penny's to score, I drove back up into the hills,
and pulled up in front of Laura's log cabin on a hilltop. L.A. sat in
a basin of brown smog. A limousine driver from the studio was leaning
against the stretch, reading a paper.

"I'll get her to work," I told him. He checked his watch, folded
his paper silently, got into the car, and drove away.

Jeffrey met me at the door. After about twenty minutes I spent
trying to reason with Laura through the bathroom door, reassuring
her I had heroin, she cracked the door open. She looked as if she
hadn't slept in a week, was skinnier than was even fashionable, and
shook like a live wire, her eyes afraid, then pleased. I didn't think it
would be possible to get her before the cameras in a week's time, let
alone an hour's.

Using the works spread out by the sink, I readied her fix.

"That's not enough," she said. "I need more than that."

"I need some too, Laura. Be thankful I'm letting you go first."

I handed her the loaded outfit. She was shaking too badly to
shoot herself up. The needle was jumping off her arm like a stylus
hopping on a warped record. She couldn't hold her hand, either hand,
still enough to hit the vein.

"Here," I said, after enough blood was dripping down her arm
and onto the floor to form a little lake, and shot her up. I quickly
rinsed out the outfit, drew up the rest of the dope, sat down in the
corner of the bathroom, and prepared to fix myself.

Just as I finished tying off, I asked her how she felt. When she
didn't answer, I looked over to see her with her head back, just sitting
there on the john, staring at the ceiling. "What's up there?" I asked.
I didn't see anything and asked her again, "What are you looking at?"
She still didn't answer. She wasn't shaking anymore, I noted, as she
began slipping off the john like a Slinky. OD'd. Shit.

I didn't know whether to take my shot or help her up. I quickly
took my shot.

I hollered out the bathroom door for Jeffrey to bring me something cold from the refrigerator as I tried to lug her into the shower.

"There is nothing cold," he yelled back.

"Anything—juice, water, beer."

"There's nothing. We need to go shopping."

"Oh, fuck," I said out loud, trying to lean Laura against the wall. When she started to slide again, I called Jeff to help. There's nothing like someone dying on you to mess up your high.

He held her while I checked the refrigerator. He was right. There was nothing there. I needed something to wake her up, quick. There was only an old, rather scuzzy milk carton. I grabbed it and pulled the top off. Back in the bathroom, Jeffrey was still holding her up. He hadn't even begun to get her into the shower. I tossed the milk onto her face, but the milk had become something resembling cottage cheese.

No time for the shower route. We rushed her out to the car as I tried to administer mouth-to-mouth over the cottage cheese and onto her blue lips.

Leaving Jeffrey behind, we headed to an emergency room. I wish I could say I knew exactly what to do, that I took a gander at the situation, made a decision, and took the right action, but I did not. I mean, I continued driving us to the hospital, but I wasn't real clear on if I'd actually take her inside when I got there. I knew what needed to be done, what I should do, but I wasn't what you'd call real confident about it.

"If I take her to the hospital and she's okay," I thought frantically out loud, "and it gets in the press, or the cops show up, she'll lose her gig on the show. That's a shitload of money, plus it means tons to her.

"And what if she's okay? And I get her in all that trouble for nothing? She'll never forgive me. If she's not okay and she dies, I'll never forgive myself, and neither will she, wherever she'll be."

I stopped at a light and pounded on her heart, listened, pounded again, listened and heard her breathe. I put the car back in first and drove on. She stopped breathing. She started. She stopped. Each light, each stop, I pounded on her heart, gave her mouth-to-mouth, and debated with myself, hoping against time she'd come to life.

If she isn't breathing, I told myself as we neared the hospital, *when I pull up there, I'll take her in. I'll take my fucking chances.*

Next light her heart murmured to life. During the next mile it started and stopped three times. It started again just as I came up on the hospital. I decided to drive around the corner. It stopped. It started. It stopped again. "Come on, Laura, come on, you gotta help me, you gotta try," I pleaded on the sixth trip around the block. She stirred. I held the wheel with one hand and banged on her chest with the other. I slapped her face.

"Stop hitting me," she mumbled. "What're ya hitting me for?"

I headed back to the canyon. Driving around with a near corpse bearing an uncanny resemblance to a TV star was not my idea of a cool thing to be doing. Jeff could drive his sister to the studio.

Twelve hours later, after her work at the studio was finished, Laura called me.

"Do you know the trouble you got me into? You made me two hours late. What the fuck did you do with me?"

So what do you think? Did I do the right thing? I didn't know anymore.

Ray had returned from Hawaii, Iggy to male-oriented sanity, and the two had been working together in Wonderland's Workshop. Iggy was enjoying a period of relative calm and seemed to be enjoying the process. Ray was happy to be a keyboardist working with a lyricist/ singer again. Even I felt a glimmer of hope and tried to rise to the occasion by getting my strung-out ass together. Unfortunately the feelings of renewal I experienced were neither permanent nor strong enough to change one fucking thing, let alone myself.

After Suzette and Pam and the ordeal with Laura dying on me, I put myself on the waiting list for a bed at Camarillo State Hospital's detox unit. I waited, and used, for a month before I received a call indicating a bed was open if I wanted it. I stayed there for just over twenty-four hours and then left the place feeling I still had a long way down to go before I needed a lock-down loony bin with pimps and cons (and more tattoos in one place than I'd ever seen) and the largest, darkest lines of track marks I'd ever seen, especially compared with my puny little scars.

A few weeks later John Carpenter and Tom Baker came over and at Ray's behest held me hostage for two days before I was able to sneak out the bedroom window and down the tree at dawn to get loaded. They were gone when I returned. I'd been on a run ever since.

I'd gotten myself good and strung out this time. I wasn't feeling good about it either. But I still thought if I really wanted to quit, I could. However, I was secretly beginning to wonder when, and if, that would ever be.

CHAPTER THIRTEEN

- - - - - - - - - - - -

Yes, I'm lonely/wanna die
If I ain't dead already. . . .

The eagle picks my eye
The worm he licks my soul
Feel so suicidal
Even hate my rock 'n' roll
—JOHN LENNON

AFTER a good five, six months of promising "I'll quit tomorrow" and breaking that very same promise hundreds of times within twenty-four hours of saying it, finally, since I couldn't stop doing it, I just stopped saying it. The whole procedure had become too embarrassing. When it got to the point where those around me started laughing when I said it or, worse, ignored me, I knew it was getting serious. Every time was the last time. I must have said, "This is the last time," two hundred, three hundred times before I wised up and realized it was easy to say, and even mean, just before I got high, and sometimes I could even carry that resolve into the high itself; but it was another matter entirely the next day when the yen and sickness returned.

It was as if on awakening in the A.M. rested and refreshed, I had resolved never to fall asleep again, both promises being of equal unlikeliness and equally doomed to be broken. This is not a process that greatly contributes to any feeling resembling self-confidence or pride. To the contrary, it is a self-perpetuating cycle of guilt and dread, extinguishable only by the same item that creates it.

The way I was looking at it, the easiest way to put a stop to this shooting-heroin business was to ditch it and then quickly find something else to take its place while not becoming dependent on that replacement. Nature abhors a vacuum and all that. There was a pill I'd heard of, Dilaudid, a synthetic painkiller, renowned for its wonderful rush. After an hour on the phone someone who knew somebody who had a prescription called me back, and I arranged to buy a hundred of the little yellow pills and to have them delivered. The cost was 10 bucks a dip on the street, but since I was buying in quantity, I got 'em all for 350 bucks. The original prescription probably cost less than $75, including the visit to the doctor.

It took almost all the cash I had, but if it got me away from smack, it would be worth it. I was motivated, or so I thought.

The little fuckers really worked. There were no withdrawal symptoms forthcoming; there was no craving for any heroin. The Dilaudid rush was not only powerful but also plentiful. I must have been shooting up ten, fifteen times a day, but—I smiled to myself—I was finally getting away from smack. Each day was a successful new hurdle and another giant step away from heroin. They worked so well I increased the dose.

Six days later I awoke with the Dilaudid all gone. My arms were a mess, but I felt fine, good even, certain I'd left my heroin addiction in the dust and rush of the past week. Within an hour my skin had begun to crawl and the uneasiness in my stomach and bowels told me something wasn't right. What was it? Did I have the flu? It couldn't be withdrawal, could it? Maybe it was some sort of delayed reaction. I called Penny to see what she knew about this sort of thing.

"I haven't heard from you in a long time," she cooed over the telephone. "We all were taking bets you were dead."

You know you're in trouble when junkies start making bets against your survival.

"I wish I was dead. Listen, I'm really sick," I told her.

"Well, you're in luck, come on over. We just reupped, and this batch is really good, uncut."

"I want to, but I can't, I mean, I really shouldn't. I just spent a whole week away from it."

"So what's the problem then?" she wanted to know. "You should be fine."

"I know," I moaned. "I'm not, though, I'm really sick."

"Dope-sick or sick-sick?"

"*I don't know!* I should be okay, I kicked with some Dilaudid and haven't done any smack at all."

"Oh no," she rather dramatically remarked.

"Why? What? What's wrong?"

"You idiot! Dilaudid is an opiate, too! They call it hospital heroin. The only difference between Dilaudid and heroin is Dilaudid is available by prescription."

"So you mean I'm addicted to Dilaudid now?"

"I mean, you're still addicted to heroin. There's no difference between the two."

"Whoops."

"How many of them were you taking?"

"About twenty a day," I told her.

"Not the strong ones, the four milligrams?"

"I don't know," I said, holding my head in my hand. "Which ones are those?"

"The yellow ones," she replied.

"Oh-oh."

"Did you shoot them or swallow them?"

"What do you think?"

"Oh, no. I hope you at least took them in decreasing increments."

"No. If anything, I took them in *in*creasing increments."

"Oh, no."

"Oh, no, what?" I asked by way of elaboration.

"Oh, no," she said again.

"I wish you'd stop saying that."

"Not only are you not detoxed, but your habit is higher now than when you started your so-called withdrawal."

To which all I could think of to say was "Oh, *fuck*, no."

"Oh, fuck, *yes*." Penny laughed. "I guess we'll be seeing you in a little bit, huh?"

"I really don't see that I have much choice in the matter."

"I suppose you'll be needing more than usual, huh?" She chuckled.

"I don't think the idea of my resistance going up any more is funny," I said and hung up the phone. It was after the first of the month, and the money situation had again, for the time being, improved.

For the next few weeks I gave up even trying to make a choice. Why should I have to decide? What reason did I possibly have? Clean up? For what? What else was I going to do? What was I supposed to want to clean up *for*?

I'll just put it off, I thought, *for as long as possible. Ride this one out and see where it leads.*

I didn't feel up to kicking. I was waiting to gather my strength, the resolve to put my foot down once and for all to this drug-taking business. But the longer I waited, the more any desire to do anything about it rotted.

I wasn't doing the drugs anymore. The drugs were doing me.

The fun had gone. Was it still interesting? Sure. Sometimes. Which would you prefer, the convulsions of distress or the lethargy of boredom? War can be terribly exciting in a morbid sort of way. Was it worth it? Hell, no, but that didn't even matter. I was paying a horrible price for something I no longer wanted but something I *needed*. How much would you pay for air? Or, if you were starving, for food? You'd pay anything, and you'd pay it gladly.

Each morning I'd walk into the kitchen and tell Tiffany, "If this is as bad as it gets, I can take it." That's one hell of a wonderful attitude to roll through life with. That's not my definition of a good life.

I just *may* have assured Tiffany I was handling it, but I failed to convince myself, especially when the only certainty I could elicit from all this insanity was whatever else did happen, things *would* almost certainly be getting worse.

The plain truth was I was beginning to scare myself pretty badly. Because I had no limits—like a runaway train, out of control and on the verge of destroying everything in its path, already having destroyed quite a bit—the fear was not without foundation. As for the reassurance I tried to provide myself and Tiffany, it was nothing more than a bluff issued from nothing less than a person reaching for anything to hold on to.

Every day I watched myself kill myself a little more, and I found it endlessly fascinating, and that terrified me even more. The most frightening thing of all was I knew in my gut that tomorrow I would get up and shoot up regardless of what I said or did, starting the same thing all over again, standing idly by and watching myself die a little more. How much longer could this go on? It was inconceivable it could continue much longer. Something had to happen, didn't it? Something had better happen, and it had better happen soon.

As my tolerance increased, so did the pain proportionately rise. Obnoxiously, teasingly, just a breath away, inching closer to consciousness, it was a spreading shadow I now had no way of stopping. Getting a tolerance means you do more drugs more often to less effect until finally the tolerance itself tops out and you're not getting high at all—you're just pissing into the wind. The truth was the drugs had stopped working. The lie was my not believing it.

I reacted to this unpleasant reality the same way I reacted to any other: I increased the dose. But it didn't have the desired effect. So I used other drugs. Anything that would dissolve in a spoon. Anything to dissolve the pain.

Tiffany and I began hiding, isolating. We were in no condition to go out anyway, but that had never stopped us before. It was more than that. We didn't want to go out. We didn't want to do anything except more drugs, and that was all we did.

Locked in the bedroom together, we started fighting on an hourly basis—over everything from who got how much to who was going to answer the telephone. We never left the house anymore except to get more drugs, and those we were having delivered whenever we could arrange it. Nobody was welcome at Wonderland, except Greenblatt's deli delivery service and dealers, and even them we kicked out as soon as business was completed. It went on for weeks. It was purgatory.

Wonderland became a prison. Our nights and days were spent trying to recapture some sort of high. The more this simple satisfaction eluded us, the more our frustration grew. The more the frustrations grew, the more we wanted, needed, to get loaded. The amount of drugs we were doing went past just maintaining a habit or trying to get well, beyond catching a rush and a nod. We were seeking nothing less than oblivion. And oblivion wasn't forthcoming.

We started mixing: downers and junk, ludes, and junk; a then-unheard-of drug called Ketalar which medics were using on third-degree-burn victims to peel off their skin without their knowledge . . . and junk. Always the junk. Anything and junk . . . And cocaine. Lots of cocaine.

If it was heroin that had brought us to our knees, then it was coke that delivered the KO punch. We went from the bedroom and into the bathroom, locked inside, shades drawn, blood all over the walls and ceiling, the result of pushing down on clogged syringes. We never bothered wiping up the blood. We concentrated on shooting more coke, hours on end, fix after fix. We'd line up syringes on the bathroom counter, fixing one after the other. It was like a feeding frenzy. Once we started, we couldn't stop. And we didn't. Days at a time, nights on end, the passage of time marked only by the goddamn birds chirping outside the bathroom window at dawn.

We were getting desperate and paranoid. It *was* getting worse, and it was getting worse fast.

One afternoon, my forearms freckled with dried blood, I lifted myself off the bed, went over to the bureau, and took out the remaining dope. There was almost a gram of smack and over a gram of cocaine left. We were out of money. It was supposed to last us until payday, still three days away. It was more than twice the amount I had ever done at once. I took out a syringe and brought the bundle into the bathroom with me. After the heroin cooked up, I poured in the coke, dropped in a piece of cotton, and drew the potion up, anticipating being taken away from all this. I couldn't fit the spoonful into one syringe. I filled another. I didn't want to die. I just couldn't take living like this anymore. All I wanted was some form of sustained relief, and if that meant approaching death or even death itself, then so be it.

I sat on the edge of the tub, and I took both shots, one right after the other. Then I undid the tourniquet. The rush was overwhelming. I staggered into the bedroom and lay down on the bed, expecting to drift off into oblivion. The rush came and went and set me back down exactly where I had been before. Dazed and afraid, I headed downstairs, breaking out in a cold sweat from the cocaine. My hands trembled. My heart pounded against my chest. I couldn't live like this anymore, I couldn't get high, and I couldn't die. Letting my body drop down into the corner of the office couch, I looked across the room at Tiffany, drinking her vodka gimlet out of a large pewter coffee mug, wasted and thin, her once light and graceful features now set and hard.

"I can't do this anymore," I said to her softly. She ignored me.

"I can't go on like this." I tried not to cry. She looked up. "I hate it. I hate everything about it! I hate it so fucking much. I can't do it anymore!"

She stared at me, startled by the outburst. "I just can't. I'm killing us. *I love you, and I'm killing you!*" I told her. "Look at me," I implored, naked scarred arms held out, palms up, "I just want to die, I swear to God, I want to die, I can't take this. . . ."

She spoke to me in a scared little voice. "Then we'll just stop."

Looking at her, shaking, incredulous, I shouted, "*Don't you see? Don't you understand? I can't stop!* I've tried, *God*, how many times? I tried to stop." I paused, then wailed, "*I don't know how!* I don't know how anymore. . . ."

She came over and sat down next to me, put her arms around my neck, and I choked, "I'm so sorry, I'm so sorry," over and over again.

Not only had the drugs stopped working, but they had actually turned against us. Your best friend has betrayed you, and there is nothing you can do about it. Every effect you originally used the drugs for is now reversed. They don't make you cool; they make you uptight. They don't improve sex; they kill it. They don't help you sleep; they keep you up. They don't make you loving; they make you mean. And so it goes. You can't even stand the sound of your precious music anymore. You're sick two, three, sometimes four times a day. You need it; you hate it. You have to have it. You have to keep those feelings and that pain away. You can't stand it. But the moment it wears off, you still think you love it. The more you hurt, the more you need it. You have to get off. You simply cannot take it anymore.

"There's a limit, for chrissakes, every man has a limit, doesn't he?" you ask. And you pray to God you've reached yours.

But someone keeps raising the limit. The ceiling gets higher, your bottom gets lower, and the hole gets bigger as you dig yourself deeper and deeper.

I made up my mind to fight the son of a bitch. For real. That day on that couch. The only problem was how. How do you fight it? You have to try. But you can't because it's so pervasive, it's invisible. And even if you could see it, where would you begin? It's like an octopus with its tentacles alternately strangling and giving life to every aspect of your existence. How do you fight something that's within you and outside you at the same time? Where do you find it? Every time you strike out at it, you just end up hitting yourself.

You attack everywhere and every place at once all the time with everything you got, but it doesn't work. You hold strategy talks with God, and you hold peace talks with your soul; but all fails in the face of an enemy that neither sees nor cares.

You try getting into bed with it, beg it to be a friend, promise loyalty, and it warms you by its gentle fire and feeds you with its strength, and then it turns around and demands everything you have, your life itself. You run away, you flee, but you can't run far enough fast enough to escape; it's always right at your heels.

Do you know why they call it a monkey on your back? Because when you try to throw it off, it just jumps back. You try to ignore it, and it keeps chattering away until you finally feed it just to shut it up.

You throw it away, but it just scampers back to its perch on your back. It begins whacking you on the head, shoulders, and neck all over again, chattering its madness in a voice that speaks to your deepest fears and most secret thoughts. No matter how hard or how far you throw that monkey, it's just gonna scamper back and run up your leg and start humping your neck and jumping up and down and swatting your ears until you finally relent and give up and say, "Okay, okay already, stay here, you little fucker, and I'll take care of you, I'll feed you. Just . . . *leave me the fuck alone.*" And you *feed* that monkey. And you *take care* of that monkey because nothing is worse than that monkey's horrendous wrath. And you keep taking care of the monkey. Until one day you awaken and you discover *you've* become the *monkey's* pet.

One evening you think maybe the monkey is asleep, maybe you can ditch him. But the moment you reach up and try to get rid of it, it screams and bites and kicks and pisses poison in your eye. It's at this point I imagine most people simply give up and learn to live with the monkey. Because it's simply easier to live with the monkey than to try to get rid of it anymore.

But I couldn't. It was war, and one of us was going to have to win. I could not give up. I might never begin to forget the pleasure of drugs, but I couldn't live with the pain, the humiliation, the lack of living anymore.

And then one day I remembered. This is not what the whole of life is supposed to be. It can't be. It can't be one long fight. There had to be more to life than this; for this I wasn't born. And then it hit me. . . .

It hit me in the face like a goddamn mountain. One day, a day like any other, on my way to war, it became clear, and finally, at last, I could see. I met the enemy, and the enemy was me. And I laid down my arms, my ammunition, and my reasons. . . .

And I called a truce.

There was only one more thing I could do. Since I could not stop, the only way I could continue living with myself was to accept. Accept what I'd been denying—the unacceptable. I had to say it to myself, and I had to believe it because it was the truth: *I am a dope addict*.

It's said the truth will set you free. It was the only hope I had. I was powerless. I'd tried my very best and just gotten worse. No act of self-will could save me anymore. What I needed now was an act of God.

Rumors had gotten out about Iggy Pop and Ray Manzarek's "top secret" project being developed behind closed doors, and record companies began calling with inquiries and contract offers. Ray responded to this encouraging news by bearing down at work while Iggy responded by bailing out, slowly.

Basically he was Iggying out—out of his mind, out of his clothes at inopportune times, out of rehearsal whenever he felt like. And naturally, very, very stoned all the time.

Ray was frustrated. "It was one thing with Morrison. I *had* to put up with him. But it was worth it. The guy always delivered, no matter how loaded he was. Iggy can't even keep his pants on and sing at the same time anymore."

I was frustrated, too, although by now the only thing I really felt was more like a high-grade consistent depression. That my dream project was falling apart on the verge of success just pushed me further down. The weird thing is I wasn't totally surprised. Iggy had been on the verge of success a number of times. He was renowned for snatching defeat from the jaws of victory. I didn't even bother reasoning with him; there wasn't anything I could say or do. I couldn't help myself, I felt, how the fuck was I going to help someone else?

Maybe because he was appreciative of Ray's faith and financial aid, maybe because he knew the songs were good, maybe because he knew this was the last stop on his way down, he hung in there, albeit barely. I put off the record companies. But I did agree with a promoter who wanted to book the band to headline a show at the Hollywood Palladium October 11. My twenty-first birthday! Why not give myself a present? Besides, it might boost the morale of the guys if they had something concrete to work toward, and a live performance might get the juices going again. To my surprise, they agreed.

I think Iggy was thinking along the same lines I was. If there was something certain down the road, there was a reason to live, there was hope. I don't think either of us expected to be around for much longer, or particularly cared. Iggy had been on the "Most Likely to Die" list for years. He was overdue. I was ahead of time.

I'd gotten the number of an old croaker who agreed to help me. I did not tell him over the phone what my intentions were, only what my problem was. If I could get some pills, ones that would take me away from heroin rather than become substitutes for it, I could try to kick on my own. I'd just go to sleep for a week. I had to try something. One more time.

Sitting in the doctor's office, I listened to a sermon. "I've never met an old junkie and I've never met a happy junkie," the doctor lectured. "Have you ever talked to someone who's been on heroin for a few years?" he asked dramatically. "It's like this." He knocked a hollow sound on the wall, thunk-thunk. "Nobody's home."

When he finished with the lecture, he agreed to give me some pills to help me kick. But to be sure I didn't think he was some kind of old quack, he insisted on giving me a complete physical, X rays, blood tests, the whole bit. Then he wrote out a prescription for the good stuff—eighty ten-milligram Valium and a hundred Darvon. The idea was the Valium would take care of the impending muscle aches, sleeplessness, and cramping while the Darvon would take care of the cravings, crawling skin, and miscellaneous other symptoms.

I wrote a bad check for the visit and ran downstairs to the pharmacy, wrote another bad check, and as soon as possible swallowed about six Valium and ten Darvon.

On the way home I slammed into a parked Jeep and hit the curb at least three times. By the time I pulled up to Wonderland, I was seriously staggering. Tiffany helped me to bed and, helping herself to a palmful of pills, climbed in with me.

And we waited for the worst.

It's called kicking because of the involuntary reactions your muscles, especially in the calf and thigh, go through, a weird combination of cramps and spasms compelling you to kick your feet out to stretch the offending muscles. What also happens is your body decides it wants to turn inside out and kick you out. Whatever is inside that can come out does. Sperm, mucus, whatever you've drunk or eaten for the past three days, jettisons out of cock, asshole, throat, eyes, and nose in no particular order and with no attention whatsoever paid to readiness.

Tiffany and I barely spoke, preferring the silence of our separate suffering worlds. We may have shared the same bed and the same experience, but more moans than words were exchanged.

I spent most of my time on the bathroom floor, half in the toilet, face staring into the bowl, ready to puke. Half the time I didn't know what to expect, and the rest of the time I guessed wrong. I'd be expecting to throw up when there'd be a caldron of cramps and gas in my lower intestine and I'd have to drag myself, loaded on Valium and weak from withdrawal, onto the shitter in time to let it flow. The shit comes out like water from a cannon 'cause your stomach's digestive acids are so out of whack. When there is nothing left to throw up, you retch—green bile.

Around sunrise on the third morning I climbed back into bed with Tiffany, clammy gooseflesh rising off my legs and arms, scabs clinging to the crook of my arm, bones poking out all over. Cold, weak, and nauseated, I snuggled up to Tiffany under the covers, against her warm, smooth ass, and ejaculated onto her without so much as the slightest degree of an erection. Just like that. Touch. Spurt.

She was too out of it on pills to notice.

The moment the thought threaded its way through my consciousness, I knew I was in trouble. The monkey was waking up and whispering. "You can get high again!" it tempted. "You can *feel* it now."

"Forget it!" I ordered myself, but the impulse redoubled and came again.

The louder I told myself to knock it off, the more insistent the voice became, the more persuasive and logical its reasoning. "Your resistance is down. Not only can you feel it, but you'll even be able to catch a nod again, and you know how long it's been since you've done that. You've been away from the stuff long enough; it's been over seventy-two hours, it's all out of your system. You're clean, man, you did it! You won't get strung out again. You know better than that by now; you've learned your lesson. It's not like you need it; you don't have to have it. It would be a treat, like an after-dinner drink. And it won't cost hardly anything. You can afford it; you can get high on just a little. Besides, what good is it making money if you can't spend it on the one thing you really want? The *only* thing you want. Go ahead, you deserve it."

"*No!*" I shouted out loud.

It's easy to just say no when it's stopped working and it hasn't been working for a long time. It's easy to say no to it when it's more trouble than it's worth.

But it's a whole other thing to say no to the impulse to use when you're sick and in pain and there's only one thing in the world that will make you better. *If* you're lucky enough to make it through that stage, you've still just begun. It's a whole different story when you're well and bored and scared because the climb back into daily living is so steep and the end is so far away it's not even in sight, and you have money in your pocket and your tolerance has dropped back down from absurd to reasonable. It's hard to say no when you can feel the goodness again and you are in a position to reassure yourself you don't *need* it, you just *want* it.

It's hard to say no to the best feeling in the world when it's right around the corner.

It's damn hard to just say no when it will work again, and all the reasons not to use don't amount to a futile prayer in the wind. They're just thoughts, words, while the desire to use is an all-consuming, never-ending, maddening obsession, a passion that will not let up until it is fulfilled.

In the end it was not a question of why, but of why not. Everything else paled by comparison. It was all we wanted to do, and anything, even the hell from which we had just returned, was worth it. It was the only way to shut up all the voices ringing inside our heads. The monkey was fully awake and furious. Getting high was the only way to stop the arguments in our minds. Being straight was supposed to be good; instead, it was boring, and all we thought about, all we wanted were to get high. There was nothing else *to* do. Being straight had become as unbearable, in three short days, as being strung out had become after one long year.

The monkey's head was raised and he was paying very close attention.

There was no sense fighting it. There was only one choice to make and we made it.

"Maybe if we just do it today, it'll get rid of the aching bones, at least, and we won't want it as bad tomorrow, we won't want it anymore," Tiffany said during the ride over to Penny's apartment.

"Yeah. Sure," I said, disgusted with both of us but also too excited at the prospect of getting high to say anything to contradict her.

To take my mind off the situation, I flicked on the radio. KMET was playing a back-to-back doubleheader. Two songs in a row by the same band. The Stones' "Brown Sugar" had just faded out, and "The Last Time" had begun.

The chorus sang out of the speakers: "This may be the last time, may be the last time; Oh, but I don't know . . . Oh no!"

How appropriate. I chuckled under my breath and turned up the radio.

"What's so funny?" she asked.

"Nothing," I said, "nothing at all."

Neither one of us spoke until we were almost there.

"I'm scared," she said in a little voice.

"Be scared," I told her, "be *very* scared."

The monkey began rattling his bars in frustration and wild anticipation of having his freedom and power again.

Within twenty-four hours he was fully alert, back in control, and raising hell all over again.

Business was at an impasse. Rehearsals had been suspended. Ray had bailed out, and Iggy was on the street, sleeping in friends' garages, with groupies, in cars, anywhere he fell down. . . . We'd all agreed to the Palladium show thirty days away. In the meantime, there wasn't much to do. I put in a request to Marty to hire a secretary to take care of the phone calls, which never stopped and which I never returned anymore, update the filing, and handle the backlog of mail. That way I'd have even more free time with nothing to do except get loaded. Time off was one value I still clung to, even though it was usually boring and unpleasant. I figured no matter how bad off I was, it was still better than school or a nine-to-five.

"You keep this up, and you're gonna be dead, you know that, don't you?" Ray asked me. "What are you trying to do? Die younger than Jim did? Don't you have anything you want to live for? Is life really that bad? Or are you having that much fun? I look at you, and I see death. You're dying, man."

I felt like saying, "Yeah, so what do you expect me to do about it?" Or maybe, "If you only knew how bad." But what I *really* wanted to do was cry out, *"Help me! Stop me!"*

I didn't say any of those things. All I said was: "I'm aware of that."

"Doesn't it at least frighten you a little bit?"

"Yeah, sometimes it does. Sometimes it scares me a lot. Other times it excites me. Sometimes I'm frightened of something else I'm not entirely sure of. I think maybe that's when I look forward to getting high the most."

"Well," he asked, with an edge of helplessness creeping into his voice, "is there *anything* I could be doing for you?"

"Yeah, you could hire me a secretary."

"You got it. Anything else?"

"Yeah," I told him, "you might want to take out a life insurance policy."

"What do I need to get a life insurance policy on me for?" he asked.

"Not on you," I said, "on me."

Ray gave me the additional money I needed, and I hired Penny, putting her on a weekly salary, effectively making my drug habit a subsidized tax write-off, which I thought was pretty slick. The only way trouble could arise was if my drug intake were to rise much more than it already had. And if there was one thing I had learned, it was not likely my drug habits would mysteriously stabilize.

Within two weeks, in addition to the salary she was taking home (or wherever she was taking it), I was simply signing my salary check over to her and hoping the Doors' records were selling well enough around the world to bring in a substantial royalty commission so I could pay her the debt I was building. The monkey was so happy he was speaking in tongues.

Penny had taken the day off to go check out a new connection in San Bernardino. She was supposed to be back with the dope by noon. I'd made her promise me she'd stop by before she went home to bag it. She'd promised—no later than noon.

By 6:00 P.M. I was going out of my mind and wished I could take leave of my body as well. When 7:00 had come and gone, I pulled myself off the bed and announced to Tiffany, "I'm going to the street." I'd heard about a place on the street where heroin could be bought in the open, at Third and Main in downtown L.A. I knew the area. It was right around the corner from the Hard Rock Café, side two of the Doors' fifth LP, *Morrison Hotel*, which was also in the neighborhood. It was also said to be rife with cops, a rip-off *and* dangerous, but if you did manage to connect, it was well worth the effort.

I'd already made up my mind to take the risk. "Fuck it," I told Tiffany. "Tonight I either get burnt, busted, beat up, ripped off, or I score. The chances are five to one."

"Five to one," she chanted, "one in five . . . no one here"—I left the room before she finished—"gets out alive."

After I left the car, I hooked up with a street hype I knew from Zola's. After doing my best to make sure the guy not only would get the dope with the money I gave him, but would return with the dope within half an hour, I handed over the 150.

And I waited. I was so sick I couldn't stand sitting in the car. I went to walk, but that was unacceptable, too; I was too weak. I tried standing on the sidewalk, leaning against a wall, but I had to lie down. I gave in to the urge and lay down on the sidewalk, just for a few seconds, I thought. I started shivering, breaking out in a sweat, as the night turned cold. I let my eyes close. There was something immensely gratifying about lying there. I'd never been so tired.

You've got to get up, I told myself, but I couldn't obey the command. I saw a cop car pull up out of the corner of my eye, and I rolled myself over, pushed myself against the wall, and slid my back up the side of the building until I was standing upright. I lit a cigarette. I couldn't bear the thought of waiting any longer.

What if the guy had just ripped me off? I had no more money. Should I wait longer? He'd already been gone over an hour. Where did he go to get it? I should have asked. What if he'd already done it? What if the guy he went to see didn't have it? Would he try somewhere else, go on his way, or bring the money back? What if he had taken off? And there I was waiting. . . .

What could have gone wrong? Anything. I crouched and waited and hoped he'd hurry back soon. I tried to walk a few steps, stumbled, and fell down on the sidewalk. This time I gave up and stayed there, lying down, trying to sleep, huddled against a wall as the last of the rush-hour traffic and pedestrian shuffle whirled on around me. I felt naked, unprotected, totally unburdened and relieved. Soon I was out.

"Come on, man, that's not cool. I'm sorry I took so long." He'd come back. I looked at my watch. It was nine forty-five. I was filthy, bathed in sweat, and cold.

"Hey, I got your dope, man. You got to give me some, okay?"

We went to the car, and he directed me to a gas station. "I have plenty of gas," I told him.

"No, so we can use the bathroom. It's cool here, man. It's okay, I know the man."

In the dirtiest, sleaziest place I'd ever been, under a steamy yellow light, I dipped his big grungy syringe into the toilet water (the sink plumbing was broken), told myself since I was going to boil it, it was all right, put down the top, sat down, and cooked up the dope. Without waiting, I balled up a piece of toilet paper for cotton, suctioned the boiling brown heavy liquid into the syringe and shot myself up, there on that toilet seat in the worst environment I'd ever been in. The dope was much too hot. My arm felt like the blood itself was boiling. Big heat rashes broke out up and down the inside of my arm. My veins turned white and throbbed. There was a loud knock on the door. The guy grabbed the works. I gave him his balloon, and brushing past a wino pissing on the step, I got the fuck out of there.

I looked at the watch again. It was ten-thirty. I noticed the date. October 10. Tomorrow morning, God willing, I'd turn another year older.

"We've been trying to find you. You're a very difficult person to track down," someone, a lady, was telling me over the phone. The only reason I'd even answered it was that I was still expecting to hear from Penny.

"Who is this?" I asked.

"Oh, I'm sorry. This is the doctor's office."

Oh, shit. The bounced check. They had me.

"We've gotten the blood tests back from the lab," she went on. "The doctor wants you to return for some more tests." She didn't say a word about the bounced check.

"Why?" I asked. "Is there anything wrong?"

"It appears there might be," she said.

"But I feel fine." Which wasn't true at all. I felt sick most of the time; but I just did more heroin, and then I didn't feel anything. I felt okay when I was junked; otherwise I didn't feel one bit well.

When the smack wore off, I never knew for certain what was wrong. I always just assumed I was dope-sick.

"According to these tests, there might be something wrong with your liver. The doctor just wants to make sure."

"Can I let you know tomorrow?"

"On the twelfth, yes, that'll be fine. I'll speak to you then."

Penny had come through with the smack and cocaine, and once I started fixing, I couldn't get out of the bathroom. Tiffany had been dressed and waiting for almost two hours. If it weren't for her wanting to go, I probably wouldn't have gone . . . to my own birthday party.

The Palladium was sold out. The news of Ray and Iggy's making their first and only public appearance had brought out not only the curious but the rabid Doors and Iggy fans. Together they filled the house.

I missed the opening acts, the GTO's and Michael Des Barres (whom I didn't mind missing), but I wanted to see Flo & Eddie (Mark and Howard from the Turtles, whom I would bump into at the bank and who would cheerfully inquire, "Are we depositing today or are we *withdrawing?*").

It was as if I were walking through a dream, my dream, my last dream. I felt detached and transparent. There they were. Ray and Iggy. Onstage, live. Standing in the wings, I could see the colors. I could even see they were good. I saw the audience surging forward, pulling back, a tide of human beings sweaty and ecstatic, rocking . . . but I was numb to it. A girl leaped onstage to embrace Iggy, stopped, bent over to tie her shoelace with her back facing Iggy, who danced up and kicked her firmly in the ass, sending her flying head over feet in the air and back into the audience. The crowd roared. Ray grinned, shaking his shaggy head from side to side.

Keith Moon came up to me, birthday cake filling his hand, and shoved it into my face, crooning, "Happy bubble day to you," pouring champagne into my mouth. We hugged, he handed me a Quaalude, asked if I had anything for him, and I just shook my head.

Iggy and Ray were called back for an encore and did "Route 66." In rehearsal I'd loved the way they pumped up that song. I'd loved watching Iggy dance to it; even without sound his movements personified rock and roll. You could be deaf, but just by watching Iggy dance, you could feel it, you could *know* rock 'n' roll just by seeing him move. Tonight, standing onstage, just behind Ray sitting at the keyboard, I didn't feel or know anything anymore.

I didn't stick around to see if there would be another encore. My last dream had come true, and I didn't know whether to wake up or go to sleep forever.

When the telephone rang the next morning, I thought it would be the doctor's office calling to set an appointment.

"Hello?"

"Hello?" It was a man's voice. "Who is this?"

"Who's this?" I asked.

"This is Dr. Zucker."

"I don't think I know any Dr. Zucker."

"I know. I'm sorry. I work at the UCLA Neuropsychiatric Hospital. You gotta understand, I've been up on call for the past fifty-two hours, and since I've been on, I've admitted two Jesus Christs, a Napoleon Bonaparte, an albino who thinks he's Santa Claus, and now I have this guy the cops just brought in who claims he's an Iggy Pop and you're his manager."

The cops had picked up Iggy, I learned, and, seeing his condition, had given him a choice of jail or the mental hospital. He'd passed out at their feet before he could give them an answer. They'd taken him to the hospital.

I dropped off toiletries and a few bucks for Iggy, then went to the doctor's in Beverly Hills to get some more tests. I'd planned to spend some time with Iggy, but it was too hard. Not because he was so fucked up. Even at his absolute worst, he was still rescuable. It was part of his innate charm. You could hate his behavior, but you could not dislike him. I couldn't. And it didn't even hurt to see him there, in a wacko ward. It was a relief. He was relieved. I was happy for him.

But there was something else. I had to get the hell out of there, and I didn't know why. I wanted to let him know I was his friend and he could depend on me and I was there for him. But I couldn't get it out. I got out, instead. A part of me was really scared. I was afraid they'd lock the doors on me. I belonged in the room right next door to him.

And the other part of me was envious because it was over for him. No more hell. It would only get better from now on. Meanwhile, I sat in Beverly Hills at the doctor's office waiting for it to get worse for me.

"How are you feeling?" the doctor asked me, smiling.

"What are you smiling about?"

"I feel wonderful."

"That's wonderful. I feel fucked."

"You're going to feel worse before you feel better."

"I had a funny feeling you'd be saying something like that."

"We think you have hepatitis. We are going to draw more blood and find out what type and to what extent."

"Is there anything I should be doing?"

"You should stop shooting up drugs, but don't worry, I don't expect you to. Try to cut down. Get plenty of rest, eat well—"

"You want I should start swimming laps, too?"

"What's that?" he asked.

"Nothing. When will you know what type I have?"

"Hard to say, the tests aren't too accurate yet. Maybe after this round we'll be able to tell."

Before the week was up, his office called to tell me I needed to go see a liver specialist.

"I take it you got the test results back from the lab."

"Yes, we have. You do have hepatitis, and it is serious. Very serious."

They gave me the number of a Dr. Davin at the UCLA Medical Center, a short walk, which I never made, to the psychiatric ward. I made an appointment. The other doctor had sent him the lab tests, physical results, and all my records, so when I arrived to see him he knew what was going on.

"You should be in a hospital," he told me. "You are a very sick boy."

"Does anyone know yet what type of hepatitis I have?"

"Why? Is it important what type?"

I told him why. I was out of money and had no insurance. If it was the infectious type, there was a chance I could go to my family for help. If it was the serum type, that meant I'd been shooting up, and I figured I'd rather die by my own hand than my father's.

"They don't know? Your family?"

"They don't know jackshit."

"Are you by any chance related to Dr. Joe Sugerman?" he asked, checking out his clipboard.

I squinted at him, trying to see if I should confide in him. I sat there in silence for a while before I made up my mind. I told him the truth. I guess I was just tired. Tired of being sick. Sick of being tired.

"I want you to call him."

"No way . . ."

"Why won't you call him?"

" 'Cause he'd call my father and I already told you what my dad would do."

"Do you mind if I call him?"

I told him the truth again. "Yes, I mind. I'd consider it a breach of patient confidentiality."

"Okay," he said, "let's do some more tests."

For the next four weeks, I was supposed to go in for blood tests every third day. I made it in about once every other week. So I'd been there two more times. Two times too many as far as I was concerned.

It was a major test of my will to get out of bed. Getting outside and into the car seemed impossible. Driving and staying awake tired me out. I was puking every time I shot up. I was shitting where I ate. I was too sick to score and too sick not to. The amount of weight I'd been losing was frightening. But you know what bothered me the most? My life—*hell*—had become boring. It wasn't tragic; it wasn't interesting; it was unendingly, achingly dull.

When I hadn't come in for a week and still hadn't kept my appointments after I promised over the phone I would, and made more appointments and then missed those, the doctor's office called me just one more time and dropped the final verdict.

"Hold for the doctor," a nurse said.

"Hello, Danny? This is Dr. Davin from UCLA Hospital. . . . You must listen to me . . . you cannot continue injecting heroin. I cannot help you and you cannot kick this on your own. . . . You must get yourself into a hospital . . . immediately . . . you have less than a week to live . . . you are dying. . . . If you don't call your brother, I'm going to—"

"Right. Thanks," I mumbled, and hung up the phone.

"What was that all about?" Tiffany asked.

"It was the doctor," I said, not totally surprised by the news.

"What did he have to say?"

"That I've got to stop shooting dope. That if I don't get myself into a hospital, I'm dead."

She sat up on the bed. "What are you going to do?"

I was trying to figure out my next move as I spoke. "I guess I'm going to have to call in the cavalry."

"You mean, your father?"

"Fuck, no. I may be sick, I'm not suicidal. The whole idea here is to prolong my life, not end it. I'll call my brother."

"Won't he tell your father?"

"Probably. But what other choice do I have?" I asked both of us. "If I don't call him, the doctor will anyway." I picked up the phone and called the County Hospital, where my brother was doing his medical residency. They put me through.

"Hello, Joey? This is your little brother. I'm afraid I have some rather bad news." I apprised him of the situation, as it was, with as little sugarcoating as possible. He told me he was on his way over to pick me up. I didn't ask him where we were going. I simply put down the phone and went into a genuine, 100 percent apeshit panic attack.

And then, to calm myself down, I shot up the last of my dope for what I truly believed to be the very last time.

E P I L O G U E

· · · · · · · · · · ·

The end of laughter and soft lies
The end of nights we tried to die. . . .
—THE DOORS

EVEN a cat will jump into water if it gets hot enough on shore.

It had just gotten too goddamn hot where I was, and anyplace had to be better. It's not like I planned where I'd land; otherwise I certainly would not have chosen my current environment for recuperation. I just closed my eyes and jumped.

Now here I was, in an insane asylum, albeit a very nice one. It still wasn't the type of hospital I'd envisioned for myself, hooked up to a kidney dialysis machine, which was being used to wash my blood. The doctors had whipped up some kind of magic potion combining antibiotics and vitamin-enriched blood, spiked it with some phenobarbital and Valium, and hooked one IV up to my left arm which dripped the juice in and another IV to my right arm which fed it all back into the machine to be rinsed and mixed.

Even if I wanted to leave, I couldn't. Besides being tied up to this contraption, I was feeling so crappy I didn't even think about leaving. I felt like they'd taken all my blood and returned none. It's kind of hard to run when you can't even sit up and the mere thought of walking makes you tired. Mainly, thanks to the Valium, I was sleeping a lot.

Modern medical test techniques had finally revealed I had managed to get *both* types of hepatitis—type A and type B. All the medical personnel who continued dropping by and checking in on me kept telling me how lucky I was to be alive. I wasn't too sure about that yet.

Voices were talking in my room. My eyes opened and saw my father, sister, and brother.

"He's awake," my sister said.

Dad, who was sitting in the chair farthest from the bed, asked me how I was feeling.

"Not too good," I told him.

"Good," he said. "You think the party's over now?"

"If that was a party I was having, then it's over."

"You've had enough fun?"

"It wasn't fun, Dad. Maybe at first, for a while. But if you think the last year was a party or fun, forget it."

"Don't bullshit me, Danny. Don't start. No one heard from you because you didn't want anyone stopping you."

"I didn't want anyone *seeing* me."

"Because you knew we'd stop you—"

I didn't know how to explain to him no one could have stopped me, and even if I thought someone could have, that wasn't the reason either.

"I didn't want to lose you." I tried to explain, "If you think I was running around, shooting drugs and dancing in the streets, laughing behind your backs, you're wrong. It was purgatory."

"Then why didn't you stop yourself?"

"I don't know. I couldn't. I tried."

"You didn't try hard enough."

"I tried as hard as I could."

"But you're ready now?"

"Yeah, now I'm ready." I leaned my head back on the pillow.

"As long as you're willing to give up that crap you've been living, we're all here to help you."

I didn't ask him to define "crap." I didn't want to know. I was just relieved we were talking. I was glad he was here and not handing me my head. I guess he figured not much sense in killing someone who was already on the verge of dying anyway. I had his sympathy this time around, and I liked how that felt.

Otherwise I wasn't feeling too hot. So far I'd been in the hospital five days. The worst was supposed to be over.

For a trial run I'd been disconnected from the tubes and needles and was walked over to the cafeteria to join the rest of the gang for lunch. They wanted to get me started on solid food. I was down to 120 pounds and finding it very difficult to walk. The male nurses Dad had hired were supporting me while I begged to rest every ten steps.

Physically I felt like a little kitten. Mentally I felt like someone ripped off my space helmet just as I was entering hyperspace. I could barely hold up the silverware. I felt disoriented, awkward; just working the food into my mouth was a real exercise. After two bites I pushed away the plate. It was too much work, and I was already full. The sight of fifty space cadets at chowtime wasn't real appetizing either.

That night I was lying in my bed when the welcome wagon arrived through the bedroom window.

"Hi, I'm Judy from the adolescent unit."

She pulled off her little *Creem* magazine T-shirt and climbed under the covers with me. "What are you in for?" she asked, throwing one leg over my waist.

"Hepatitis," I told her, "and some bacteria on my heart."

"I heard you were a doper."

"Yeah," I said, "that, too."

"Boy, you're really fucked up."

"That depends, I guess. How about you?" I asked her as she slipped her hand under the covers and over my crotch.

"The judge sent me here," she said as she began a hand job.

I let out a little groan, put my head back on the pillow, and asked, "What for?"

"For stabbing my boyfriend with a steak knife."

My head came up in a hurry, just as she was getting ready to go down on me. I pulled her back up.

"Wait a second. Maybe it would be better if we talked for a while first."

She looked confused.

"I mean, it's not like I don't appreciate the gesture. I'd just like to get to know you first."

"What do you want to know about?"

"What did your boyfriend do that made you stab him?"

"He pissed me off."

"Right."

"He called me a slut." She gave me a challenging look.

"That punk," I said. "Serves him right."

"I thought so." She harrumphed.

She filled me in on what went on around the Brentwood, who the inmates were, and what therapists were the coolest.

"Stay away from Dr. Pullman," she warned me. "He's a real ass."

Then she slid under the covers and went to work. Not bad for a thirteen-year-old homicidal maniac, I thought, not bad at all, all the while staying very mindful of her teeth.

I couldn't sleep that night, or the next. The night after that I lay on the bed, utterly exhausted. The sleeplessness was the worst. It was like I'd forgotten how it was done. First the mind was tired but the body wasn't. Then when the body grew tired, the mind was wide awake. My body was so sore I couldn't stay in the same position for five consecutive minutes, but I was too tired and weak to move.

Even though they weren't making me go into activities like group therapy and individual counseling, it was impossible for me to get any sleep during the day. It seemed as if the patients of this place had banded together and agreed to make me feel welcome by stopping in and saying hello as often as possible. I wasn't absolutely sure whether it was a bad dream or a misdirected joke.

"You're not making much of an effort to fit in," a nurse lectured me.

"Good," I said.

"You could at least try to be nice," she said.

"No," I said, "I don't think so."

"Is there anything you want me to tell the rest of the patients?"

"Yeah. Leave me alone."

I wasn't feeling jovial about the situation, and having thirty mental retards poking their heads into my room thirty times a day, disturbing the little rest I was getting, wasn't helping improve my mood.

One afternoon I did manage to drift off into what felt like sleep. No sooner had I done so than a Spanish maid came into the room and plugged in a vacuum. *"Turn it off, get the hell out,"* I yelled over the din. She ignored me. "Leave! *Vamoose,*" I said, sitting up and waving my hand. She continued vacuuming. I leaped out of bed, wobbled a bit, unplugged the vacuum cleaner, and chased her out of the room into the hallway, where people stopped whatever they were doing and stared at me. I didn't have anything on.

"Five hundred bucks a day and you can't afford a fucking maid who speaks English?" I yelled, and walked back into my room and fell onto the bed so tired I thought I might die.

Next time I came out of my room was to take my first phone call. Tiffany was calling on the pay phone in the "Patients Lobby."

"Hi, sweetmeat!" she chirped. "When you getting out?"

"I don't even know when I came in."

"Guess what?"

"I don't know, Tiffany."

"I'm pregnant."

I had nothing to say to that.

"Aren't you going to say anything?"

"Congratulations?"

"We need to talk about what we're going to do."

"What we're going to do? What's there to talk about?"

"When are you getting out?"

"I don't know yet. What's there to talk about?"

"All the gynecologists are booked through March."

I lost my patience with her. "So what do you want me to do about it? Call a plumber? Go to an emergency room. Call Joe for help."

"You could help me."

"I'm in a fucking mental hospital!" I yelled at her. "I can't help me, how the fuck am I supposed to help you?"

"What are you so pissed off about? It's your baby, too. Geez, I thought you'd be happy about it."

"Listen, Tiffany, find a doctor and get rid of it. Just get an abortion." God, Tiffany and I having a baby. What a nightmare. With us for parents the poor kid wouldn't have a chance. Maybe if we sent it back now, he'd get a return ticket with some parents who could take care of him.

She was crying.

"I can't deal with this now," I told her, and hung up the phone.

On my tenth day in the hospital the staff forced me out of bed to get my "strength back." I still felt like I was lost in space. The linebackers, as I'd taken to referring to them, walked me into the group therapy room.

I took one look at the circle of dog-faced crazies and just groaned, "Oh, Jesus," and turned around to leave. Having them drop in on me one at a time was one thing. Seeing them all together like a fucking circus tribunal was another. And joining them was not even within my realm of considerations.

"Where are you going? Come in and join us," the therapist called out.

"To my room. That's okay. Thanks anyway."

That afternoon the psychiatrist I'd met on admission, Dr. Pullman, a balding Israeli munchkin, came into my room to "have a talk."

"What are you still doing in bed? I want you up. I wrote an order for you to start going to therapy today."

"So that was *your* idea."

"It was an order."

"Well, excuse me. I'm sorry to disobey your orders, Doctor, but no fucking way."

"If you're going to stay in this hospital, you're going to follow directions."

"Fine. I'll leave."

"I'm afraid it's not as simple as that."

"Why not? If you think I'm well enough to get up and sit through that shit, then I must be well enough to leave."

"Maybe so, but the only way you leave this hospital is when I discharge you."

"So discharge me."

"When it's time, I will be happy to."

"Why not now?"

"You're still too much a danger to yourself. We've just healed your body, now we have to take care of the rest of you. That's why I want you in those groups."

"Those people are sick!"

"So are you."

"I don't have anything in common with them. I have nothing to talk about with them."

"How do you know?"

"Because they're nuts! It's obvious! Just look at them!"

"And what makes you so different?"

"They're *crazy*! *I* have a drug problem!"

"*They* don't take drugs!"

"Maybe they *should*!"

"They can't help how they are. You can."

"What's that supposed to mean?"

"They have organic chemical imbalances and serious psychological disorders that cause them to act as they do. You choose to behave the way you do. I think you're crazier than they are."

I didn't like the whole direction this conversation was taking. In the past I'd always prided myself on being a bit nuts. Now here I was arguing against that stand.

"Look. It's simple. Painkillers are my problem."

"No pain, no gain." He threw me one of his professional slogans, so I threw him back one of mine.

"No dope, no hope."

"Life without painkillers can be very painful."

"No shit."

"You cannot use drugs ever again."

That was an absolutely, primordially unacceptable statement. There was no way around it. I did not like one word this guy had to say.

I looked out into the hallway and saw Edie, a sixty-year-old lady dressed up with clown makeup, twirling in circles, thinking she was dancing with her husband, who'd been dead for twenty years. Leaning against the wall was Eugene, a Vietnam vet who'd been shell-shocked for ten years and whose face looked like a little baby's, toothless and all. There were others, too. Beth, who was so in love with Charles Bronson she spent *all* her time writing, "I love Charles Bronson," over and over again. The nurses kept stealing the paper and pencil from her, but she kept trying to steal them back. Once I even gave her a pen and paper. It wasn't out of generosity. If she didn't write the slogan, she said it, chanted it, over and over again. I gave her the stuff to shut her up. Little Ben was in for shoving sharp objects up his asshole, and was particularly fond of Beth's writing material. The only other drug case was James, the twenty-eight-year-old heir to a dairy fortune who hadn't spoken to anyone but his ex-shrink (who was also his connection) for the past ten years. A beautiful-looking guy, but he literally couldn't look anyone in the eye.

Was I that fucked up?

The whole situation was so absurd and terrifying I couldn't stand it anymore. I went to the closet to put on my street clothes.

"Where are you going?"

"Home."

"I'm afraid I can't allow that."

I was sick of talking to this toad. "Fuck you and your Loony Toon brigade."

"You cannot leave. I have the authority to place you on a seventy-two-hour hold."

"Try it," I said, zipping up my jacket and walking out the room.

I wasn't planning on getting loaded, just free. The walls were closing in.

I made it out the back door and into the parking lot before the linebackers came running out with two hospital techs right behind them. I took off, hobbling through the cars, hopped over a couple of hoods, and then just went across the cars. They captured me when I slipped and fell.

Seventy-two hours was the maximum amount of time allowed by law that the hospital could hold me against my will. I'd asked for, and received, a copy of the patients' rights handbook and researched my position and theirs. From what I read I was as good as committed for the next three days. After that, if they still deemed me a danger to myself or others, they could hold me *again*.

* * *

Word had gotten out about my rock 'n' roll connections, and it turned out the Doors were real heroes on the ward. "The End," ironically enough, was the most popular song and played nonstop. Despite myself, I began to feel right at home. I even started participating in group therapy, even going up against the therapist on behalf of Mary, a little teenager who habitually ran away from home and, from what I'd heard, for damned good reasons.

Inside Dr. Pullman's office during individual counseling I had the distinct feeling someone was taking a large ladle, sticking it into the caldron of my emotions, and turning it around, very slowly at first, yet firmly, then faster.

Pullman was sitting in his chair with his back to the window, facing me, sun streaming past him. I was sitting in a chair in front of his desk.

"This friend of yours Jim Morrison? Why do you idealize him so? He was just an ordinary man, you know."

"How would you know? You didn't know him. You don't know anything about it." Just the thought of trying to explain Morrison to this guy made me tired.

"I don't need to know about it. I know he was just a man. He was a scared man at that."

"What the fuck are you talking about?"

"He was a father figure for you, too, no?"

"Where are you getting this shit? I prefer to think of him more as an older-brother figure."

"You prefer. . . . What you prefer doesn't count. The truth is he was a surrogate father to you."

Now I was intrigued. "Yeah? How so?"

"He protected you. Or at least you believed he did."

"He did. Just knowing him was sort of protection for me."

"You wanted to be just like him. You have strived to become like him."

"You don't know what you're talking about. I'm nothing like him. There are some qualities of his I might—"

He waved his hands away, dismissing my words and, "If he was a father figure," he continued, leaning back in his chair, "what do you think that makes his wife? And if it makes her that, then what were you doing sleeping with her? Who does that make you?"

I thought a moment. "That's sick!"

"That's right!" he exclaimed, leaning forward. "It's also true! You wanted to be just like him."

I was reeling. "Wait a second . . ."

He waved his hand away. "How did your father feel about him?"

"He hated him." Boy, was I dizzy.

"And you liked that?"

"I never thought about it like that."

"Good. Think about it now. Time's up for today."

The following day Pullman got the ladle going a little quicker.

"How did you react to Jim Morrison's death?"

"I never thought he'd die."

"You thought he was omnipotent?" he asked, surprised.

"What's that mean?"

"Indestructible, all-powerful."

"Yeah, I mean, in a way."

"And you think you are, too!" he said, delighted.

"No, I don't. I don't think I'm him," I told him, lest he be trying to build a case of schizophrenia against me. Just to be certain he got the point, I said, "I told you I'm nothing like him."

"I don't believe it."

"I don't care. It's true. You'll just have to take my word for it because you didn't know him."

"But I know your actions. You do not think you can die. You behave in a way that defies death, just like your friend."

I grinned at the comparison, I couldn't help myself.

"See," he said, "you are smiling. It shows it is so. You like being like him."

"I guess so."

"But he is dead."

"That's what they say."

"You say you loved him, yet you do not seem sad."

"He's not dead to me." In other words, my Jim Morrison is not dead, sorry about yours.

"Now we're getting someplace good."

"Where's that?"

"He is not dead to you, exactly. You carry him around with you. You keep him alive by behaving like him. You never let him die. Since you have never let him die, you have never grieved his loss, your loss. You have lost nothing. You won't let go. You have learned nothing."

"I don't think I want to let go," I said.

"That is natural. But you must if you want to get better."

"I'll have to think about that one."

"Think. You have plenty of time to think. Our time is up for today."

While I was fully dressed and reading in my room, waiting to be called for lunch, Dad came in to see me.

I was happy to see him. "Hi, Dad!" I jumped up, full of energy, shaking his hand.

"Sit down," he said, not very happy at all.

"What's wrong? What's the matter?" I thought for a moment there maybe he'd heard about my weak-kneed attempt to run away.

"Your girlfriend is dead."

"What?" I thought he might have been speaking metaphysically or emotionally, like "dead" as in the "past."

But Dad wasn't too cosmic in that way. He lived in reality, and the facts didn't scare him—I was the one who had trouble with the facts—and what he meant was that Tiffany was dead as in overdosed, found dead, stiff, and white, alone on the Wonderland bed, two and a half months pregnant. Some loan officer from the bank found her when he came to repossess the house.

No! Not Tiffany! As ignorant as she might have been, the girl knew drugs, she knew her tolerance, she knew how much to do and how much to leave in the spoon for later. She'd never do too much. Hell, it was Tiffany who used to warn me, "Two in the arm are better than one in the ground," meaning, it's better to shoot up a little bit twice than a lot once.

Unless—unless she did it on purpose. Boy, I might have been clean, but I was still an insensitive asshole. She wanted the baby or at least some help in getting rid of it, and all I could think about was myself. I thought she was being the insensitive one, bothering me when I was already being bothered way more than enough.

I could hear her say, "Serves you right, asshole." And I kicked the shit out of myself some more.

"Talk to me," my father said.

"I miss her already," I said, then told him, "She was pregnant and wanted my help."

"What could you have done? It's just as well, Danny. Forget her, it's over. You've got to help yourself now. You're lucky it wasn't you. This is it. You wanted help; you got it. You're here. Now you better make the best of it because there's not going to be any second chance this time. This *is* the second chance. This is your *last* chance."

For the first time in recent memory I decided to take my father's advice and try to forget the whole thing. It was either forget about it or do something unusually satisfying (i.e., self-destructive), and I recognized that urge for what it was. Another choice was to run, but wasn't that the same thing as getting loaded? And even if I succeeded in getting away this time, where was I running to and with whom? Everything was gone. It was down to either pain now, pain later, or deny the whole fucking thing. I opted for a concentrated attempt at denial. I tried to forget about it

Pullman wasn't going to let me deny anything. He wanted my eyes open, and I'm certain he wanted to break down my defenses and see me squirm in order to learn new coping devices so I wouldn't need drugs. And I wasn't about to give him the news on Tiffany. He had more than enough ammo to attack my id with already.

"I think you like being crazy," he started the session.

"Yeah," I decided, "maybe I do. It keeps nosy assholes off my back."

"You must enjoy it. You pick a crazy hero. You act crazy."

"So what? What the fuck does that mean? Three weeks, and all you can tell me is something I knew six years before I ever saw you. You're a real Sigmund Freud, aren't you? Why don't you tell me something I don't know?"

I wanted a confrontation. I was ready.

He ignored my taunting. "You like being crazy, yet you are here in a mental hospital to get well. Don't you see that as strange?"

"You seem to be forgetting I didn't put myself here," I told him. "My family thinks I'm crazy, too. Talk to them, get them to accept it. I can handle it fine."

"You can't handle it fine. It is against your nature."

What the fuck was he babbling about now?

"I think you want to be here. I think you were waiting to be saved."

"Bullshit. I was waiting to die."

"Nonsense. You may have tried to convince yourself this was so, but actions speak louder than words and certainly louder than thoughts. You were sending out messages. You were screaming for help. Do you know what the message of the person who keeps falling is?"

"Get out of my way?"

"*No!* Pick me up. Save me."

I thought of lying on the sidewalk downtown, not wanting to get back up. I remembered wanting to tell Ray, "Help me. Stop me."

The bald little fucker was right.

"You listen to me, and you listen to me good." He went on. "You are not crazy, however much you want to believe you are. You act insane only because it's easy. You knew what you were doing was wrong, you knew you were hurting yourself, but you did it anyway. There must be a reason."

"I thought I could get away with it."

"That's a child's way of thinking. You are not a child."

"I knew that."

"I think you were aware of how much it would hurt your parents if they knew what you were doing. I think a part of you wanted to punish them."

"Oh, yeah? Then why didn't I tell them sooner?"

"You already know the answer to that. You were too afraid to."

"But I was only hurting myself!"

"That's right. Somewhere along the line in your life you became convinced you did something very wrong." And then with a voice that made my throat clench he said, "Don't you think it's time you quit punishing yourself for something you never did? When are you going to be able to forgive yourself?"

I looked at him, and I did not know what to say. About half his words hit home while the rest were still circling the room, threatening to strike.

"Do you want to get well?" he asked.

I knew any answer, affirmative or negative, confirmed the presumption that I knew I was sick.

"I want to think about it," I said.

He went into his drawer and filled his pipe. I got up to leave.

"Time's not up," he told me.

"It is for today," I said, and left the room with a headful of reasons and questions that refused to lie down and shut up.

For the next dozen sessions Pullman kept harping on me about some decision I was supposed to be making while he refused to give me any clue to what that decision was supposed to be.

"How am I supposed to make it if I don't know what it is?"

"You will figure it out."

"Why won't you tell me?"

"That's too easy."

It went on like that session after session.

"Have you made your decision yet?"

"What decision?"

I'd been racking my head. What was he talking about? What did he mean, decision about what? To use drugs or not? "No," he said, "that's too obvious."

"My hair? Whether to get a haircut or not?"

"I thought you were smarter than that," he said, waving his hand away.

"Maybe you thought wrong."

That's when he finally told me. "I want you to decide what you are going to do when you get out of here."

My eyes brightened. "When am I getting out?"

"That depends on when you make your decision."

"If you'd told me two weeks ago what I was supposed to be making a decision about, maybe I'd know by now."

We'd spent so much time talking about the past I really hadn't thought much about the future, until now, that is, and now it came on like a fucking blizzard. I'd assumed I'd simply go back to the music business; it wasn't like I'd been fired or anything irredeemable like that. It was all I knew, all I wanted to do. It seemed simple enough to me.

"You cannot do that," Pullman warned me. "You cannot go back to the music business."

Boy, that pulled me up in my chair. "Why not?"

"Our time's up for today."

"No fucking way, hold on here, no you don't, not this time . . . you can't just—"

He got up and was headed toward the door. "Think about it," he said over his shoulder.

"I'm not finished!" I yelled.

He kept walking. I ran after him. "I said I'm not finished! You can't just drop something like that on me and walk away, you chicken-shit."

He turned the corner and disappeared from sight.

Next session.

I got the jump on him this round. "What's this bullshit about not being able to go back to the music business?"

"We don't know very much about drug addiction, but one thing we do know from the research is that statistically those who return to the same environment, the same social structure in which they used drugs stand much less of a chance of abstaining than those who make a change."

"That doesn't affect me. I'm not one of those statistics. I haven't been counted yet. I don't care what the odds are. What is it? One in a hundred who make it anyway? Regardless of what they do? So, what's that make it? One in three hundred who go back to the same job and make it?"

"Your chances are better if you find something else to do. For once in your life don't buck the odds."

"Oh great, now you not only know what's wrong with my past, but can predict what's going to be wrong with my future. In one month you've gone from thinking you're Sigmund Freud to playing God. Suppose I don't want to do anything else? What if I want to go back to rock 'n' roll?"

"I won't discharge you."

"What? You're gonna put me on another hold? You can't keep me on seventy-two-hour holds forever, you know."

"I'm afraid it's a little more complicated than that. Without a discharge indicating you successfully completed your recovery program, insurance won't cover your stay here."

"So it seems to me it behooves you to discharge me if you want to get paid."

"Your father assumed financial liability for all your medical costs in the event insurance fails to cover. Correct me if I'm wrong, but from what I understand, your father doesn't want you returning to the music business either."

"What about what I want to do? Doesn't that mean anything to anybody? Why doesn't anybody ask me what I want to do?"

"Ask you? Who could stop you? What you want isn't good for you."

"What did you two do, get together and come up with a plan on how best to fuck me into doing whatever you want? What did my father do? Bribe you? Offer to build a new hospital wing with your name over the entrance if you get the kid to give up drugs and his rock and roll?"

"There was no plan. We want what's best for you. It would be nice if you could see that for yourself."

"What if I refuse to go along with your little detour? What if I go ahead and do what I want to? It's my goddamn life, isn't it? How the fuck am I ever supposed to find contentedness or happiness or any of that sort of stuff if I run around doing what everybody else wants me to do? Isn't one of the goals of all this to find out who I am and what I want? To stop doing what other people want? Jesus, half my life I've been trying to please people who were impossible to please, and the other half of my life I spent reacting and rebelling against what they expected of me. What about what *I* want for me? Without any outside interference? Why doesn't everybody just leave me the fuck alone!"

There were three distinct possibilities here, and I saw them even as I spoke. The most obvious was to take their advice, agree with them, and do whatever they wanted. Agreement is always a good way to shut someone up. That led me to the next alternative, which I felt a little more comfortable with: Agree with them by lying to them. Tell them what they wanted to hear, get the discharge, and then do whatever I wanted. But you want to know something? I was sick and tired of taking the easy way out. And that realization brought me to my third choice: Tell the truth and do it, do what you want to do.

I liked the last choice the least. That's the way I knew it was the one I had to make. But why was I so scared to say it? Was it, maybe, that I didn't know anymore what was the truth and what was the lie? Or did I just not trust myself anymore, period?

Or maybe it was the right answer, but the wrong question?

That had to be it. The question was not what I was going to do when I got out. That had nothing to do with the real issue here. They had it all wrong. The real issue, the big topic for discussion and conclusion wasn't Rock 'n' Roll versus Something Else.

Christ knows they have bathrooms in law firms and baseball coliseums and locker rooms to shoot up in, too. There's dope on every street corner in every city. If you want it, it's there. It's everywhere. It doesn't matter if you're a rock manager, a fireman, or the President of the United States. Hiding from it is an illusion. The way I saw it, unless I resolved the real issue first, I'd be dead wherever I went, whatever I did. And if I did resolve it, I could make it anywhere.

So the question wasn't: What are you going to do with the rest of your life? I knew the answer to that. That was the easy part.

The real question was: Do you want to live or do you want to die? But no one was asking me that question, and no one could answer it but me. And that was the hard part. I wanted to run and keep on running and never stop. I left his office in a rage, stormed down the hallways toward my room, patients and staff hurrying out of my path. Those who didn't, I either pushed or yelled aside.

"*Get the fuck outta my way!*" I thundered, rounding a bend. Then I slammed the door to my bedroom and proceeded to punch in the wall, kick the bureau, and beat up the bed.

For the rest of the night I fought with myself.

Jesus. The first thing I wanted to do was find the jerk who first said, "If it feels good, do it," and then go after the bozo who started the rumor that drugs enhance creativity, tie them both to the nearest tree, and blow their fuggin' brains out, or better yet, OD the troublemakers.

Yeah, okay, fine, now what? What about all your buddies? What about Arthur Rimbaud? What about Baudelaire? And Artaud? What about Coleridge and Cocteau? And Byron? What about James Dean? And Jimi Hendrix? What about all of them? What about all the others you love so much?

Only the good die young, remember? Whether in word or deed, that's what they stood for. "Hope I die before I get old," right?

What about the life-style? What about the best feelings in the world? What about the path? The drama and the excitement? *What about everything you know and believe and hold precious?*

What about Morrison?

These men. My heroes. Our revered artists. The noble dead. Better to go out in a blaze of passion and youth than an old, shattered body. Live fast, die young . . . remember? The path of excess. They walked it the way they talked it. They died of addiction and disease and madness, and they died long before their primes.

These great men, these geniuses, what would they have to say? Could they speak, what would they tell us? "I died for writers and artists everywhere, and my life is a fine example of how to live."

Or, "I'm glad I'm dead because I died young."

No, I don't think so.

I think the best feeling they knew was the feeling of relief! *That's* what these once-glorious men were reduced to. Pain didn't inspire them anymore. It overwhelmed them, engulfed them, and ate them up alive. They were not strong enough or smart enough to fight it, to deal with it, or beat it. It obsessed them shamefully, pitifully, and completely.

Would any of them say, "Look at me, hold me up as an example to the young and impressionable of the world because I led a good and courageous life. I drank and drugged myself to death and I'm glad I did it and I'm glad my life is over"?

Not real fucking likely.

Jim Morrison never found what he was looking for. That intensely dramatic, charismatic search? It was all for naught. He got nothing. *We* got Morrison's life. But he lost it. He got zip. He got *dead*.

Would he do it over again given the chance?

Would any single one of these guys say, "I like death better than living"?

You're goddamn right they wouldn't. And were they to speak to us today, if they were really so goddamn brave and true and honest, they'd admit it. They'd tell us what it was really like. They died crying in their minds like little babies, lonely and afraid, yearning for the face of a friend. They died depressed and sick, wanting another look at the sun or the seashore; they wanted again to hear the voice of a mother, a father, a lover or a child. They died moaning and sighing for life. Because in the end they knew what was really important. They knew. Goddamn right they did. They died with one thought and one thought only in their mind, and that thought was: *I want to live I want to live I want to live.*

But nobody knows for sure what the dead would say except the dead. And the dead can't speak. And they can't write. And they can't sing or play for us anymore.

Should I run after them? Is *that* what Morrison would tell me to do? Stay on that path? Suicide? However fast or slow, isn't that what it comes down to? Is that courageous? Is that cool? Is that what the man whom I loved so much and who believed in me so much, is that what he'd want for me? To jump into the grave with both feet, lie down alongside next to him, and die?

Not on your fucking life.

Remember the words? Nobility and pride. Liberation. Suffering. Ecstasy. Freedom.

Death. If someone says to you, you've got to kill yourself a little to really feel alive, or you have to risk death to truly live, he is either a fool or a liar because he doesn't know what death is. He isn't able to tell you; he's simply in no position to judge. He knows only about living. And if he believes that garbage, let *him* go and die. But you, you turn around and you run as fast as you can in the other direction because life is all you've got. And it's harder and braver to live than it is to die. Dying is easy. It's living that takes real courage.

The path of excess leads to the palace of wisdom, huh? Well, maybe, but what kind of excess, and who said it has to be chemical? And what sort of wisdom? At what price? And will somebody please tell me what's so excessive about being a drug addict anyway? It's the most limiting existence I can think of.

What the fuck was I looking for anyway? What was so goddamn all important?

Freedom? From what? For what? Did I get it? Was I right, and did I win? And what good is freedom if you use it to kill yourself?

I'm sorry, but there's nothing noble about dying. There is nothing glamorous about being an addict. There's nothing noble about a rotting liver, nothing heroic about a rotting corpse. A heart attack at twenty-seven years old? Like Morrison? Or dead at twenty-one? Is *that* winning? Come on, it's not hip, and it's not romantic. It's *over*. When you're dead, that's it, you're just dead. You're less than a maggot or an ant. You're just like a rock or a dirt clod or a piece of dung. *Dead.* You're dead, boy, and you died for nothing but a false ideal and some bad advice.

Me? I want to live.

You know what *I* think Morrison would have said?

"*Experience*, feel the pain. Without pain there is no change. . . . Without change there is no growth, and if you don't grow, you die. Don't make the same mistakes I made. Make different ones. Don't be stupid. Grow. *Live.*"

It was, if not Jim's voice directly, the truth nonetheless.

Morrison always was a better teacher than role model.

Finally, and at last, I cried. Softly at first, then harder. I cried for Jim and I cried for Pamela and I cried for Tiffany. I cried for Suzette. I cried for the dead and I cried for the living and I cried for the sadness and the tragedy and the waste of it all.

I cried for myself. Like a baby in agony, I cried. In pain I cried. Isn't that okay? To cry? I didn't even care anymore. So what if it wasn't cool? Cool almost killed me. Cool will freeze you to death.

I couldn't keep it locked inside anymore. It was coming out at last, and I couldn't have stopped it even if I'd wanted to or tried. And through the tears I could finally see that what I was looking for I was looking *from*.

I cried harder. *I was going to make it.* In relief I cried.

I was really going to live. In gratitude I cried. In joy I cried. I cried and I cried and I cried, grinning my idiot head off.

That's one of the damnable yet wonderful things about being human: We feel—the good and the bad. You chop off one, the other dies, too. It's an all-or-nothing deal.

And I was learning. That's one of the riotously objectionable things about being a human being: Sometimes you really do know right from wrong, and you have the damned liberty of making the wrong choice. Or the difficult privilege of making the right choice. Sure, it can be a hell of a task, one enormous risk, but at least it's *yours*. That makes it valuable and, depending on how you feel about yourself, worth it.

* * *

"So where do we go from here?" I asked Pullman. God, I really felt good, calm, centered, confident, healthy.

He turned his big swivel chair around to face me. "Well"—he clasped his fingers steeplelike—"that all depends."

And just like the Caterpillar said to Alice after she turned up lost in Wonderland, trying to find her way back home, he said to me, "Where do you want to go from here?"

I didn't even have to think about it. I'd already thought about it. The time had come for some action.

"I want to go home. I want to go back to work. I want my family back. I want my music back. I don't want drugs. Screw the drugs. They killed my love for everything that ever meant anything to me, including myself."

"I would really like to believe you."

"I don't give a fuck whether you believe me or not!" I laughed. "I believe me. I believe *in* me. Do you know how long it's been since I felt that? I miss my music; I feel like I betrayed it. I miss my family. I don't miss dope. Drugs took everything I loved away from me. I know what I want. For the first time in my life I want something that's good for me. I want to feel love. I want to be trusted and I want to learn how to trust someone else. For the first time in my life I want to be *good*." I don't know what I was closer to, tears or glee. "And," I added with a special relish, "I want to rock and roll. If *that's* fucked up, if *that's* crazy, then I don't care. I can live with *that*. *That* won't kill me."

There I was in Pullman's office, prepared for this gigantic confrontation, reasons at the ready, argument hot and ready to flame.

And there was Dad, the target, the mind I had to change, the same one I'd been unable to change for the past twenty years. What would be different this time? This time around I had to make him understand while at the same time I knew it didn't matter. This time *was* different. I wasn't simply reacting or rebelling. I'd thought about it. I understood. I was certain about how I felt. Now all I had to do was convince him. And if I couldn't . . . then I couldn't.

"I've been thinking a lot," I started to tell him.

"I've been thinking," he told me at almost the same time. "Go ahead," he said.

"No," I told him, wanting a chance to pick my momentum back up, "you go ahead."

"I've been thinking," he began, "and I don't care anymore what you want to do for a living—what *I* care about is you having a life to live. I want to see you healthy and happy. You can hump garbage cans for all I care. You want to go back to school, I'll put you through. You want to start your own business, I'll back you. Whatever you want to do, I'm with you. You're still young—the whole world is in front of you, for godsakes, enjoy it. You're my son and I love you no matter what . . . I just won't, I *can't* stand by and watch you blow yourself up with dope. If you think you can go back to the music business without succumbing to it, I'm behind you all the way."

Then to Pullman, Dad said, "If you won't discharge him, send me the bill. It doesn't matter to me one way or another . . ."

I wish you could have heard it exactly as he said it, 'cause it was so beautiful. It was totally Dad yet totally un-Dad. In the whole time I'd known him, my father had never changed his mind so dramatically.

There was nothing for me to say. My argument was totally useless and unnecessary now and I hadn't prepared anything else. What else did I want to say? What did I really want to tell him? What did I want him to know?

I went over to where he was sitting and knelt in front of him and put my head on his chest and my arms around his neck. "I love you," I said.

He looked questioningly over at Dr. Pullman for a moment and then put his arms around me and patted my back, hugging me. "I love you, son. I love you, too."

I guess it all makes sense, in the end. When I was living, and living was unbearable, I wanted to die. Then, when I was dying, I finally realized I wanted to live. It's just more of the same old shit— the same human insanity as always—wanting what we don't have right up to the moment we get it.

The difference this time was I felt satisfied, even content, with where I was ending up. And I wasn't about to start questioning or rejecting the process. I guess when you surrender, you surrender completely. But what I was beginning to see was you lose the battle to win the war and that makes it more acceptable.

That's another one of the wonderful things about human beings. We can, and often do, change. Not always gracefully and not often willingly, but occasionally just like that, in a *SNAP*! We change. Sometimes fast, sometimes slowly; sometimes for no reason at all or maybe a hundred and fifty.

A F T E R W O R D

· · · · · · · · · · ·

SOMETIMES, these days, I feel so
alive I almost can't stand it. But then, wasn't that always part of the
problem? The difference is today I not only stand, I withstand it, and
even find myself, usually, incredibly, enjoying it. Today I know what
the phrase "natural high" means, whereas not only didn't I relate to
it before, I didn't even want to. Natural highs, along with meditation,
granola, and behaving, were not my goals—my idea of a good time.
And come to think of it, they still aren't. All I'm trying to say is I've
learned how to feel good without chemicals. It took a while, longer
than I would have liked. It hasn't been easy, and it's not always fun,
but the good news is *it's not that bad.*

Overall, nothing is good, nothing is bad. It just *is.* I always sensed
that; now I believe it, too. The good I enjoy and the bad I grow from,
and how can something that has such a positive result possibly be
perceived as bad? I wish I could claim some conscious, responsible
source of will-power here, but the truth is that if it hurts enough, and
you don't use drugs to chase the pain away, then you almost have to
grow. You can't help it, or at least, I can't. Like the man said, "That
which does not kill me makes me stronger." Ain't it true.

Hurting other people, now that's not good. And, when you hurt
yourself you are hurting the people who love you. I can see that now.
I don't know where I was looking before. I still don't like hurting,
myself, and I don't hurt myself anymore, either. At least I try not
to. But I can still feel the pain of Jim and Pamela's loss and my father's
death now, too, and I know it's real and I'll probably carry it with
me forever but I kinda like that. It's a constant reminder of my love
for them and their love for me. It's just pain and I can take it because

I know now you don't get one without inviting the other, too. And I know, little by little, time will heal it all. And I also know I have another chance where so many others don't.

I feel very fortunate. Others weren't so lucky.

Tiffany is dead.

Mark Ladd is dead.

Suzette is dead.

Zola is dead. Lance is dead.

Penny is dead.

Blake is dead.

John Carpenter is dead.

Tim Hardin is dead.

Tom Baker is dead.

Gabor Szabo is dead.

Keith Moon is dead.

Jesse is dead.

Sammy's whereabouts are unknown.

Marilyn is living in a wheelchair, blind and unable to speak, her left side paralyzed by an overdose.

Jo is in jail.

Shane is living in a residential addict-recovery facility. It's a two-year program. This is his third trip.

Dallas is in jail.

Even Dr. Pullman is dead—shot by a presumed embittered ex-patient. The FBI came by to speak with me when they were investigating the death, apparently believing I had some kind of motive. I agreed with them, I did. But I didn't kill him. I was far too busy trying to keep myself alive, at the time.

Pamela Morrison is dead.

Jim Morrison, as far as I know, is still dead.

Ray Manzarek, John Densmore, and Robby Krieger remain on good terms and together keep a watchful, loving eye on the Doors' continuing legacy. I feel very privileged to have been able to work with them as closely and for as long as I have.

Gabe Reynolds confessed to the Doors a "misappropriation of funds." In other words, he did to the Doors exactly what he was always so afraid I'd do—he ripped them off.

The acupuncturist now owns a pizzeria.

Mackenzie Phillips recently gave birth to a healthy baby boy.

Iggy Pop and Jim Osterberg have reconciled their differences and, at last report, are functioning these days as a happy team.

My mother and Clarence are still married. Some things, alas, never change.

My father passed away, in peace and of natural causes.

My brother and sister are still my brother and sister and these days are even somewhat inclined to admit to it. Joe is a successful doctor practicing in Beverly Hills and Nan Dee is married and residing in Europe where she had her first child, my nephew, Alexander Charles.

Your author is pleased to report he recently turned thirty-four years old.

Who woulda thunk, huh?

And last of all, a belated dedication is hereby made to all of us who, by not wanting to grow up at all, have had to grow up too fast. You know who you are. Shine on, you crazy diamonds . . .